THE JOSSEY-BASS READER ON
EDUCATIONAL LEADERSHIP

JB JOSSEY-BASS

THE
JOSSEY-BASS READER
ON
EDUCATIONAL
LEADERSHIP

Second Edition

o

Introduction by
Michael Fullan

John Wiley & Sons, Inc.

Published by Jossey-Bass
A Wiley Imprint
989 Market Street, San Francisco, CA 94103-1741   www.josseybass.com

Jossey-Bass books and products are available through most bookstores. To contact Jossey-Bass directly call our Customer Care Department within the U.S. at 800-956-7739, outside the U.S. at 317-572-3986, or fax 317-572-4002.

Jossey-Bass also publishes its books in a variety of electronic formats. Some content that appears in print may not be available in electronic books.

Library of Congress Cataloging-in-Publication Data

The Jossey-Bass reader on educational leadership.—2nd ed.
        p. cm.—(Jossey-Bass teacher series)
  Includes bibliographical references.
  ISBN-13: 978-0-7879-8400-7 (pbk.)
  ISBN-10: 0-7879-8400-0 (pbk.)
 1. Educational leadership—United States. 2. School management and organization—United States. I. Jossey-Bass Inc.
  LB2806.J597 2007
  371.2—dc22

                                                        2006026759

Printed in the United States of America
SECOND EDITION
PB Printing   10 9 8 7 6 5 4

CONTENTS

PART SIX
The Future of Leadership

SOURCES

CHAPTER ONE
Peter M. Senge. *The Fifth Discipline*. New York: Doubleday, 1990.

CHAPTER TWO
John W. Gardner. *On Leadership*. New York: Free Press, 1990.

CHAPTER THREE
Jim Collins. *Good to Great: Why Some Companies Make the Leap . . . and Others Don't*. New York: HarperBusiness, 2001.

CHAPTER FOUR
Phi Delta Kappan, May 1968, pp. 654–659.

CHAPTER FIVE
James M. Kouzes and Barry Z. Posner. *The Leadership Challenge* (3rd ed.). San Francisco: Jossey-Bass, 2002.

CHAPTER SIX
Thomas J. Sergiovanni. *Moral Leadership*. San Francisco: Jossey-Bass, 1992.

CHAPTER SEVEN
David E. Purpel. *Reflections on Moral and Spiritual Crisis in Education*. New York: Peter Lang, 2004.

CHAPTER EIGHT
Megan Tschannen-Moran. *Trust Matters*. San Francisco: Jossey-Bass, 2004.

CHAPTER NINE
Lee G. Bolman and Terrence E. Deal. *Reframing Organizations*. (3rd ed.) San Francisco: Jossey-Bass, 2003.

CHAPTER TEN
Robert Evans. *The Human Side of School Change.*
San Francisco: Jossey-Bass, 1996.

CHAPTER ELEVEN
Roland S. Barth. *Learning by Heart.* Hoboken, N.J.: Wiley, 2004.

CHAPTER TWELVE
Michael Fullan. *Leading in a Culture of Change.*
San Francisco: Jossey-Bass, 2001.

CHAPTER THIRTEEN
Kenneth A. Leithwood. [This piece is not previously published.]

CHAPTER FOURTEEN
Terrence E. Deal and Kent D. Peterson. *Shaping School Culture.*
San Francisco: Jossey-Bass, 1999.

CHAPTER FIFTEEN
Roland S. Barth. *Learning by Heart.*
San Francisco: Jossey-Bass, 2001.

CHAPTER SIXTEEN
Phillip C. Schlechty. *Creating Great Schools: Six Critical Systems at the
Heart of Educational Innovation.* San Francisco: Jossey-Bass, 2005.

CHAPTER SEVENTEEN
Douglas B. Reeves. *The Leader's Guide to Standards.*
San Francisco: Jossey-Bass, 2002.

CHAPTER EIGHTEEN
Interstate School Leaders Licensure Consortium.
Standards for School Leaders. Washington, D.C.:
Council of Chief State School Officers, 1996.

CHAPTER NINETEEN
Harvard Business Review, Sept./Oct. 1996, pp. 79–90.

CHAPTER TWENTY
Educational Leadership, 61(2), Oct. 2003.

CHAPTER TWENTY-ONE
James A. Banks and Cherry A. McGee Banks, eds.
Handbook of Research on Multicultural Education, 2nd ed.
San Francisco: Jossey-Bass, 2003.

CHAPTER TWENTY-TWO
Theory Into Practice, 1991, 30(2), 134–139.

CHAPTER TWENTY-THREE
Marc S. Tucker and Judy B. Codding, eds. *The Principal Challenge.*
San Francisco: Jossey-Bass, 2002.

CHAPTER TWENTY-FOUR
Ann Lieberman, ed. *Building a Professional Culture in Schools.*
New York: Teachers College Press, 1988.

CHAPTER TWENTY-FIVE
The Educational Forum, Spring 2006, 70(3).

CHAPTER TWENTY-SIX
Andy Hargreaves and Dean Fink. *Sustainable Leadership.*
San Francisco: Jossey-Bass, 2006.

ABOUT THE AUTHORS

CHERRY A. MCGEE BANKS is associate professor of education at the University of Washington, Bothell. She also serves as a faculty associate at the Center for Multi-Cultural Education at the University of Washington-Seattle.

ROLAND S. BARTH is an education consultant in the United States and abroad. A former public school teacher and principal, he was a member of the faculty of Harvard University for thirteen years, where he founded the Harvard Principals' Center and the International Network of Principals' Centers. In 1976 Barth received a Guggenheim Fellowship.

LEE G. BOLMAN is the Marion Bloch/Missouri Chair in Leadership at the University of Missouri, Kansas City. An author, teacher, consultant, and speaker, he has written numerous books on leadership and organizations with coauthor Terry Deal, including *Leading With Soul: An Uncommon Journey of Spirit* and *Reframing Organizations: Artistry, Choice, and Leadership*.

JIM COLLINS is a student of enduring great companies—how they grow, how they attain superior performance, and how good companies can become great companies. Having invested more than a decade of research into the topic, he has authored or coauthored four books, including the classic *Built to Last* and *Good to Great: Why Some Companies Make the Leap . . . and Others Don't.*

TERRENCE E. DEAL is the Irving R. Melbo Professor at University of Southern California's Rossier School. He is an internationally famous lecturer and author and has written numerous books on leadership and organizations.

ROBIN J. ELY is associate professor of organizational behavior at Harvard Business School. She investigates how organizations can better manage their race and gender relations while at the same time increasing their effectiveness. Her research in this area focuses on organizational change, group dynamics, learning, conflict, power, and social identity.

ROBERT EVANS is an internationally renowned author and presenter. Evans is a clinical and organizational psychologist and the executive director of the Human Relations Service in Wellesley, Massachusetts.

DEAN FINK is an independent consultant with experience in more than twenty countries. A former teacher, principal, and superintendent, he is the author or coauthor of five books.

MICHAEL FULLAN is the former dean of the Ontario Institute for Studies in Education of the University of Toronto. Recognized as an international authority on educational reform, Fullan is engaged in training, consulting, and evaluating change projects around the world. In April 2004 he was appointed special advisor to the premier and minister of education in Ontario.

JOHN W. GARDNER was a distinguished leader in America's educational, philanthropic, and political arenas before his death in 2002. He served as president of the Carnegie Foundation for the Advancement of Teaching, was the founding chairman of Common Cause, and led many other organizations. He was the architect of the Great Society programs, as Lyndon Johnson's secretary of health, education, and welfare, and counseled five other presidents.

ANDY HARGREAVES is the Thomas More Brennan Chair in Education at the Lynch School of Education in Boston College. He has authored and edited more than twenty-five books in education, which have been published in many languages.

CAROLYN KELLEY is a member of the faculty at the University of Wisconsin, Madison.

JAMES M. KOUZES is chairman emeritus of the Tom Peters Company and an executive fellow at the Center for Innovation and Entrepreneurship at the Leavey School of Business, Santa Clara University.

LINDA LAMBERT is founder of the Center of Educational Leadership at California State University, Hayward, where she is professor emeritus.

MEL LEVINE is professor of pediatrics at the University of North Carolina Medical School in Chapel Hill, North Carolina, and director of the University's Clinical Center for the Study of Development and Learning. Over the past thirty years he has pioneered programs for the evaluation of children and young adults with learning, development, and behavioral problems. He is also the cofounder of All Kinds of Minds, a nonprofit institute for the study of differences in learning, with financier Charles R. Schwab.

KENNETH A. LEITHWOOD is professor and associate dean of the Ontario Institute for Studies in Education of the University of Toronto, as well as director of the Centre for Leadership Development. Also, he is cofounding editor of the *Leadership and Policy in Schools* journal and a member of four additional journal editorial boards.

ANN LIEBERMAN is professor emeritus at Teachers College, Columbia University, and a senior scholar at the Carnegie Foundation for the Advancement of Teaching. She is widely known for her work in the areas of teacher leadership and development, networks, and school improvement. She has written and edited numerous books and articles on the professional development of teachers and the conditions of school reform.

MATTHEW B. MILES was a senior research associate at the Center for Policy Research at Columbia University Teachers College before his death in 1996.

JEROME T. MURPHY is a specialist in the management and politics of education. For almost twenty years, Murphy was a full-time administrator at the Harvard Graduate School of Education, first as associate dean from 1982 to 1991 and then as dean from 1992 to 2001. He helped develop domestic legislation in the former U.S. Department of Health, Education, and Welfare, acted as associate director of the White House Fellows Program, and founded and directed the Massachusetts Internships in Education.

IRENE NOWELL is superintendent of the Remsenburg-Speonk Union Free School District in Remsenburg, New York.

ANDY PERRY is principal of the Wilson School in Westfield, New Jersey.

KENT D. PETERSON is professor in the Department of Educational Administration at the University of Wisconsin, Madison, and the founding director of the Vanderbilt Principals' Institute. His research focuses on the impact of culture on school achievement, change and reform, and student learning.

BARRY Z. POSNER is dean of the Leavey School of Business and professor of leadership at Santa Clara University. Posner has published more than eighty research and practitioner-oriented articles.

DAVID E. PURPEL is professor emeritus at the University of North Carolina, Greensboro. Purpel is recognized as one of the founders and leaders of moral theory in education and received a Lifetime Achievement Award from the American Educational Research Association (AERA) in 2001. He is the author of several books, including *Moral Outrage in Education*.

DOUGLAS B. REEVES is chairman and founder of the Center for Performance Assessment and one of the nation's leading experts on educational standards. He is the author of many books, including *The Leader's Guides to Standards*. Reeves was named to the Distinguished Authors Series by the Harvard University Graduate School of Education in 2002.

ELLEN R. SAXL is president of Educational Agenda Company, a research and consulting firm.

PHILLIP C. SCHLECHTY is founder and CEO of the Schlechty Center for Leadership in School Reform. The creator of some of the nation's most innovative professional development programs for educators, he has been the recipient of the American Federation of Teachers Quest Citation and the American Educational Research Association's Professional Service Award.

THOMAS J. SERGIOVANNI is the Lillian Radford Professor of Education and Administration at Trinity University in San Antonio, Texas. He is also a senior fellow at the Center for Educational Leadership and founding director of the Trinity Principals' Center.

CHAROL SHAKESHAFT is professor in foundations, leadership, and policy studies at Hofstra University. She has been studying equity in schools for more than twenty-five years and is an internationally recognized researcher in the area of gender patterns in educational delivery and classroom interactions.

PETER M. SENGE is senior lecturer at the Massachusetts Institute of Technology and chairman of the Society for Organizational Learning, a global community of corporations, researchers, and consultants dedicated to personal and institutional development. He is the author of the widely acclaimed *The Fifth Discipline*.

DAVID A. THOMAS is senior associate dean, director of faculty recruiting, and H. Naylor Fitzhugh Professor of Business Administration at Harvard Graduate School of Business Administration. His research addresses issues related to executive development, cultural diversity in organizations, leadership, and organizational change.

MEGAN TSCHANNEN-MORAN is a member of the faculty at the College of William and Mary in Williamsburg, Virginia. She has examined the relationships between trust and collaboration, organizational citizenship, leadership, conflict, and school climate.

INTRODUCTION

NEVER BEFORE has leadership been more critical for society and its organizations, both public and private. Concern about performance has mounted, while at the same time we are beginning to appreciate the complexities of bringing about improvement. When systems are complex and when the tendencies of such systems are toward overload and fragmentation, the need for leadership to forge synergy and coherence is paramount.

We are beginning to realize that the answer does not lie in locating ad hoc charismatic leaders-as-saviors—they are too few in number, their contributions do not have lasting effects, nor do they always do good. Compounding this problem is demographics: high turnover of leaders combined with lack of attention to cultivating the next generation of leaders. The result is a shortage of qualified leaders at all levels in the system.

A number of key themes are emerging in the field. First is the realization that quality leadership in business and in education have a lot in common. Second, moral purpose—again for both public and private enterprises—has risen to the fore. Third, sustainability has become a major focus (Hargreaves and Fink, 2006; Fullan, 2005). Fourth, distributive leadership is increasing in importance—not the delegation of leadership, but the coalescing of leaders with a common purpose and reflective theories of action. Distributive leadership also helps to address a fifth and related theme; namely, how to build in succession practices that create and enhance a pipeline of leaders over time and will aid continuous improvement. Sixth, leadership has now become a key component for addressing large-scale transformation of systems—what we call in education trilevel reform at the school or community, district, and state levels (Fullan, 2006). Seventh, standards and performance levels have become a core feature, not just for accountability but also as part and parcel of forming strategies.

These seven themes represent a tall order. The good news—and this reader is an example of it—is that strong theoretical and practical work has been underway over the past decade that has laid the groundwork for the resurgence of leadership. Thus, as we enter a crucial period in public education we recognize the centrality of educational leadership for the success of school systems on a large scale. This period is critical because schools are now expected to educate to a high level—close to 100 percent of the population, when they have been used to serving the needs of 50 or 60 percent. Moreover, closing the gap between high and low performance has become of central concern because of its many individual and societal consequences.

We have mapped out much of the territory, including broadening the concept of leadership, and we have put in place higher standards of leadership and have begun to establish programs and leadership academies designed to prepare and sustain leaders. The burgeoning attention to leadership has produced countless articles over the past decade that are scattered throughout the literature. This second edition of *The Jossey-Bass Reader on Educational Leadership* provides a much-needed anthology that organizes in one place the best of this literature.

Part One contains five groundbreaking articles from leading thinkers in organizational leadership. These are deliberately selected to demonstrate that leadership has a strong conceptual base that is basic in all human situations. Peter M. Senge's classic article "Give Me a Lever Long Enough" introduces the section, followed by several featured pieces on theories of quality leadership. This section does indeed establish the core principles of leadership.

Part Two is no less theoretical but is equally concerned with principles. In this case, the five chapters each take up one of the strongest new themes in recent literature on the moral imperative of leadership.

Part Three tackles one of the most enduring dilemmas in the history of leadership and change; namely, how does one change organizational cultures? Five chapters take the reader through understanding change and the complex issues involved in transformational leadership.

Part Four, with three chapters, moves us into the realm of standards—not simply establishing a set of high standards, but using standards as strategies for improving leadership across the system.

Society has become more complex and more diverse. Leading amidst diversity has become essential. The four chapters in Part Five add this dimension to the repertoire of leadership perspectives developed across this reader.

Finally, Part Six focuses on the future of leadership. Four chapters examine in turn how to prepare school principals, foster teacher leadership, build leadership capacity, and understand the ins and outs of renewal.

The phenomenon of leadership has interested humankind for millennia. The scientific study of leadership has never been greater, and one reason is that more writing is focusing on "leaders in action." Thus we are getting the best of theory and practice. There is now an acknowledgment that broad-based leadership is the only way forward. Broad-based leadership will require "leaders of leaders"—those who can help create the conditions for leadership to flourish. *The Jossey-Bass Reader on Educational Leadership, Second Edition,* will be of interest to those scores of people who not only want to understand leadership, but also want to participate as part of the shared leadership process. This book, in one anthology, marks what we know about educational leadership: where the field is now and where it should be heading. Its value lies in its broad perspective, focusing on the field of education but also going beyond it. It is a highly significant compendium that will be of widespread interest to all those concerned about the performance of the educational system.

University of Toronto   MICHAEL FULLAN
July 2006

REFERENCES

Fullan, M. *Leadership and Sustainability.* Thousand Oaks, Calif.: Corwin Press, 2005.
Fullan, M. *Turnaround Leadership.* San Francisco: Jossey-Bass, 2006.
Hargreaves, A., and Fink, D. *Sustainable Leadership.* San Francisco: Jossey-Bass, 2006.

ACKNOWLEDGMENTS

THE JOSSEY-BASS EDUCATION TEAM would like to thank Kent Peterson, Don Larsen, Roma Bowen Angel, Sharon Cramer, and Kenneth Jenkins for their invaluable comments and feedback on this Reader. We are also indebted to Kenneth Leithwood for allowing us to use a previously unpublished piece, and to Michael Fullan for providing us with the all important "big picture."

In addition, we'd like to thank Rayme Adzema for her leadership in developing the first edition, and Sheri Gilbert for handling permissions with calm efficiency. Finally, we are grateful for the leadership and tenacity of our second edition project manager, Kate Gagnon, who deftly brought all pieces and people together for the next generation of readers.

WELCOME to *The Jossey-Bass Reader on Educational Leadership, Second Edition*. With the Jossey-Bass education readers we hope to provide a clear, concise overview of important topics in education and to give our audience a useful knowledge of the theory and practice of key educational issues. Each volume in this series is designed to be informative, comprehensive, and portable.

*In the interest of readability, the editors
have slightly adapted the following selections
for this volume. For the complete text,
please refer to the original source.*

PART ONE

THE PRINCIPLES
OF LEADERSHIP

THE NOTION OF LEADERSHIP is universal and pervades all forms of society: business, government, and—of course—education. In Part One, we've included works by experts from the business world because, as Peter M. Senge notes in his work, "Business is the locus of innovation in an open society . . . [it] has a freedom to experiment."

"Give Me a Lever Long Enough," written by Senge, opens with an excellent discussion of the concept of systems. It's a simple idea that is intuitively known by all and is best described by the adage "the whole is greater than the sum of its parts."

In "The Nature of Leadership," John W. Gardner describes the key challenges of leadership: long-term, big-picture thinking with an expansive reach. It's the leader's responsibility to articulate and highlight intangibles like vision, values, and motivation.

These complex ideas from the stellar thinkers of our time provide a comprehensive road map of leadership. As discussed further in Jim Collins's chapter from the business book *Good to Great,* exemplary leaders are individuals who invest their ambition in the institution, not in themselves. This notion resonates even more forcefully in the field of education, where the stakes are higher and the constituents more sensitive than in the private business realm.

Jerome T. Murphy debunks myths about leaders in his aptly named piece, "The Unheroic Side of Leadership: Notes from the Swamp." He warns against setting unrealistic standards and "lionizing" leadership. Murphy believes that leaders must cultivate local, situational, and people knowledge.

James M. Kouzes and Barry Z. Posner, as with the other four authors in Part One, discuss the need for leaders to inspire and build a shared vision. They also show that leaders must challenge the process, enable others to act, and encourage the heart. If new and veteran leaders ingrain these works and strive to manifest these theories within their own systems, then all will be better for the effort.

1

"GIVE ME A LEVER LONG ENOUGH . . . AND SINGLE-HANDED I CAN MOVE THE WORLD"

Peter M. Senge

FROM A VERY EARLY AGE, we are taught to break apart problems, to fragment the world. This apparently makes complex tasks and subjects more manageable, but we pay a hidden, enormous price. We can no longer see the consequences of our actions; we lose our intrinsic sense of connection to a larger whole. When we then try to "see the big picture," we try to reassemble the fragments in our minds, to list and organize all the pieces. But, as physicist David Bohm says, the task is futile—similar to trying to reassemble the fragments of a broken mirror to see a true reflection. Thus, after a while we give up trying to see the whole altogether.

The tools and ideas presented here are for destroying the illusion that the world is created of separate, unrelated forces. When we give up this illusion—we can then build "learning organizations," organizations where people continually expand their capacity to create the results they truly desire, where new and expansive patterns of thinking are nurtured, where collective aspiration is set free, and where people are continually learning how to learn together.

As *Fortune* magazine recently said, "Forget your tired old ideas about leadership. The most successful corporation of the 1990s will be something called a learning organization." "The ability to learn faster than

3

your competitors," said Arie de Geus, head of planning for Royal Dutch/ Shell, "may be the only sustainable competitive advantage." As the world becomes more interconnected and business becomes more complex and dynamic, work must become more "learningful." It is no longer sufficient to have one person learning for the organization, a Ford or a Sloan or a Watson. It's just not possible any longer to "figure it out" from the top, and have everyone else following the orders of the "grand strategist." The organizations that will truly excel in the future will be the organizations that discover how to tap people's commitment and capacity to learn at *all* levels in an organization.

Learning organizations are possible because, deep down, we are all learners. No one has to teach an infant to learn. In fact, no one has to teach infants anything. They are intrinsically inquisitive, masterful learners who learn to walk, speak, and pretty much run their households all on their own. Learning organizations are possible because not only is it our nature to learn but we love to learn. Most of us at one time or another have been part of a great "team," a group of people who functioned together in an extraordinary way—who trusted one another, who complemented each others' strengths and compensated for each others' limitations, who had common goals that were larger than individual goals, and who produced extraordinary results. I have met many people who have experienced this sort of profound teamwork—in sports, or in the performing arts, or in business. Many say that they have spent much of their life looking for that experience again. What they experienced was a learning organization. The team that became great didn't start off great— it learned how to produce extraordinary results.

One could argue that the entire global business community is learning to learn together, becoming a learning community. Whereas once many industries were dominated by a single, undisputed leader—one IBM, one Kodak, one Procter & Gamble, one Xerox—today industries, especially in manufacturing, have dozens of excellent companies. American and European corporations are pulled forward by the example of the Japanese; the Japanese, in turn, are pulled by the Koreans and Europeans. Dramatic improvements take place in corporations in Italy, Australia, Singapore—and quickly become influential around the world.

There is also another, in some ways deeper, movement toward learning organizations, part of the evolution of industrial society. Material affluence for the majority has gradually shifted people's orientation toward work—from what Daniel Yankelovich called an "instrumental" view of work, where work was a means to an end, to a more "sacred" view, where people seek the "intrinsic" benefits of work. "Our grandfathers worked six days a week to earn what most of us now earn by Tuesday afternoon," says Bill O'Brien, CEO of Hanover Insurance. "The ferment in management will continue until we build organizations that are more consistent with man's higher aspirations beyond food, shelter and belonging" (Yankelovich, 1981).

Moreover, many who share these values are now in leadership positions. I find a growing number of organizational leaders who, while still a minority, feel they are part of a profound evolution in the nature of work as a social institution. "Why can't we do good works at work?" asked Edward Simon, president of Herman Miller, recently. "Business is the only institution that has a chance, as far as I can see, to fundamentally improve the injustice that exists in the world. But first, we will have to move through the barriers that are keeping us from being truly vision-led and capable of learning."

Perhaps the most salient reason for building learning organizations is that we are only now starting to understand the capabilities such organizations must possess. For a long time, efforts to build learning organizations were like groping in the dark until the skills, areas of knowledge, and paths for development of such organizations became known. What fundamentally will distinguish learning organizations from traditional authoritarian "controlling organizations" will be the mastery of certain basic disciplines. That is why the "disciplines of the learning organization" are vital.

Disciplines of the Learning Organization

On a cold, clear morning in December 1903, at Kitty Hawk, North Carolina, the fragile aircraft of Wilbur and Orville Wright proved that powered flight was possible. Thus was the airplane invented; but it would take more than thirty years before commercial aviation could serve the general public.

Engineers say that a new idea has been "invented" when it is proven to work in the laboratory. The idea becomes an "innovation" only when it can be replicated reliably on a meaningful scale at practical costs. If the idea is sufficiently important, such as the telephone, the digital computer, or commercial aircraft, it is called a "basic innovation," and it creates a new industry or transforms an existing industry. In these terms, learning organizations have been invented, but they have not yet been innovated.

In engineering, when an idea moves from an invention to an innovation, diverse "component technologies" come together. Emerging from isolated developments in separate fields of research, these components gradually form an "ensemble of technologies that are critical to each others' success. Until this ensemble forms, the idea, though possible in the laboratory, does not achieve its potential in practice" (Graham, 1982; Graham and Senge, 1980. I am indebted to my MIT colleague Alan Graham for the insight that basic innovation occurs through the integration of diverse technologies into a new ensemble.)

The Wright Brothers proved that powered flight was possible, but the McDonnell Douglas DC-3, introduced in 1935, ushered in the era of commercial air travel. The DC-3 was the first plane that supported itself economically as well as aerodynamically. During those intervening thirty years (a typical time period for incubating basic innovations), myriad experiments with commercial flight had failed. Like early experiments with learning organizations, the early planes were not reliable and cost effective on an appropriate scale.

The DC-3, for the first time, brought together five critical component technologies that formed a successful ensemble. They were: the variable-pitch propeller, retractable landing gear, a type of lightweight molded body construction called "monocque," radial air-cooled engine, and wing flaps. To succeed, the DC-3 needed all five; four were not enough. One year earlier, the Boeing 247 was introduced with all of them except wing flaps. Lacking wing flaps, Boeing's engineers found that the plane was unstable on take-off and landing and had to downsize the engine.

Today, I believe, five new "component technologies" are gradually converging to innovate learning organizations. Though developed separately, each will, I believe, prove critical to the others' success, just as occurs with any ensemble. Each provides a vital dimension in building organizations that can truly "learn," that can continually enhance their capacity to realize their highest aspirations:

Systems Thinking. A cloud masses, the sky darkens, leaves twist upward, and we know that it will rain. We also know that after the storm, the runoff will feed into groundwater miles away, and the sky will grow clear by tomorrow. All these events are distant in time and space, and yet they are all connected within the same pattern. Each has an influence on the rest, an influence that is usually hidden from view. You can only understand the system of a rainstorm by contemplating the whole, not any individual part of the pattern.

Business and other human endeavors are also systems. They, too, are bound by invisible fabrics of interrelated actions, which often take years to fully play out their effects on each other. Since we are part of that lacework ourselves, it's doubly hard to see the whole pattern of change. Instead, we tend to focus on snapshots of isolated parts of the system, and wonder why our deepest problems never seem to get solved. Systems thinking is a conceptual framework, a body of knowledge and tools that has been developed over the past fifty years, to make the full patterns clearer, and to help us see how to change them effectively.

Though the tools are new, the underlying worldview is extremely intuitive; experiments with young children show that they learn systems thinking very quickly.

Personal Mastery. Mastery might suggest gaining dominance over people or things. But mastery can also mean a special level of proficiency. A master craftsman doesn't dominate pottery or weaving. People with a high level of personal mastery are able to consistently realize the results that matter most deeply to them—in effect, they approach their life as an artist would approach a work of art. They do that by becoming committed to their own lifelong learning.

Personal mastery is the discipline of continually clarifying and deepening our personal vision, of focusing our energies, of developing patience, and of seeing reality objectively. As such, it is an essential cornerstone of the learning organization—the learning organization's spiritual foundation. An organization's commitment to and capacity for learning can be no greater than that of its members. The roots of this discipline lie in both Eastern and Western spiritual traditions, and in secular traditions as well.

But surprisingly few organizations encourage the growth of their people in this manner. This results in vast untapped resources: "People enter business as bright, well-educated, high-energy people, full of energy and desire to make a difference," says Hanover's O'Brien. "By the time they are 30, a few are on the 'fast track' and the rest 'put in their time' to do what matters to them on the weekend. They lose the commitment, the sense of mission, and the excitement with which they started their careers. We get damn little of their energy and almost none of their spirit."

And surprisingly few adults work to rigorously develop their own personal mastery. When you ask most adults what they want from their lives, they often talk first about what they'd like to get rid of: "I'd like my mother-in-law to move out," they say, or "I'd like my back problems to clear up." The discipline of personal mastery, by contrast, starts with clarifying the things that really matter to us, of living our lives in the service of our highest aspirations.

Here, I am most interested in the connections between personal learning and organizational learning, in the reciprocal commitments between individual and organization, and in the special spirit of an enterprise made up of learners.

Mental Models. "Mental models" are deeply ingrained assumptions, generalizations, or even pictures or images that influence how we understand the world and how we take action. Very often, we are not consciously aware of our mental models or the effects they have on our behavior. For example, we may notice that a coworker dresses elegantly, and say to ourselves, "She's a country club person." About someone who dresses shabbily, we may feel, "He doesn't care about what others think." Mental models of what can or cannot be done in different management settings are no less deeply entrenched. Many insights into new markets or outmoded organizational practices fail to get put into practice because they conflict with powerful, tacit mental models.

Royal Dutch/Shell, one of the first large organizations to understand the advantages of accelerating organizational learning, came to this realization when they discovered how pervasive was the influence of hidden mental models, especially those that become widely shared. Shell's extraordinary success in managing through the dramatic changes and unpredictability of the world oil business in the 1970s and 1980s came in large measure from learning how to surface and challenge managers' mental models. (In the early 1970s Shell was the weakest of the big seven oil companies; by the late 1980s it was the strongest.) Arie de Geus, Shell's recently retired Coordinator of Group Planning, says that continuous adaptation and growth in a changing business environment depend on "institutional learning, which is the process whereby management teams change their shared mental models of the company, their markets, and their competitors. For this reason, we think of planning as learning and of corporate planning as institutional learning" (de Geus, 1988).

The discipline of working with mental models starts with turning the mirror inward; learning to unearth our internal pictures of the world, to bring them to the surface and hold them rigorously to scrutiny. It also includes the ability to carry on "learningful" conversations that balance inquiry and advocacy, where people expose their own thinking effectively and make that thinking open to the influence of others.

Building Shared Vision. If any one idea about leadership has inspired organizations for thousands of years, it's the capacity to hold a shared picture of the future we seek to create. One is hard pressed to think of any organization that has sustained some measure of greatness in the absence of goals, values, and missions that become deeply shared throughout the organization. IBM had "service"; Polaroid had instant photography; Ford had public transportation for the masses and Apple had computing power for the masses. Though radically different in content and kind, all these organizations managed to bind people together around a common identity and sense of destiny.

When there is a genuine vision (as opposed to the all-too-familiar "vision statement"), people excel and learn, not because they are told to, but because they want to. But many leaders have personal visions that never get translated into shared visions that galvanize an organization. All too often, a company's shared vision has revolved around the charisma of a leader, or around a crisis that galvanizes everyone temporarily. But, given a choice, most people opt for pursuing a lofty goal, not only in times of crisis but at all times. What has been lacking is a discipline for translating individual vision into shared vision—not a "cookbook" but a set of principles and guiding practices.

The practice of shared vision involves the skills of unearthing shared "pictures of the future" that foster genuine commitment and enrollment rather than compliance. In mastering this discipline, leaders learn the counterproductiveness of trying to dictate a vision, no matter how heartfelt.

Team Learning. How can a team of committed managers with individual IQs above 120 have a collective IQ of 63? The discipline of team learning confronts this paradox. We know that teams can learn; in sports, in the performing arts, in science, and even, occasionally, in business, there are striking examples where the intelligence of the team exceeds the intelligence of the individuals in the team, and where teams develop extraordinary capacities for coordinated action. When teams are truly learning, not only are they producing extraordinary results but the individual members are growing more rapidly than could have occurred otherwise.

The discipline of team learning starts with "dialogue," the capacity of members of a team to suspend assumptions and enter into a genuine "thinking together." To the Greeks *dia-logos* meant a free-flowing of meaning through a group, allowing the group to discover insights not attainable individually. Interestingly, the practice of dialogue has been preserved in many "primitive" cultures, such as that of the American Indian, but it has been almost completely lost to modern society. Today, the principles and practices of dialogue are being rediscovered and put into a contemporary context. (Dialogue differs from the more common "discussion," which has its roots with "percussion" and "concussion," literally a heaving of ideas back and forth in a winner-takes-all competition.)

The discipline of dialogue also involves learning how to recognize the patterns of interaction in teams that undermine learning. The patterns of defensiveness are often deeply engrained in how a team operates. If unrecognized, they undermine learning. If recognized and surfaced creatively, they can actually accelerate learning.

Team learning is vital because teams, not individuals, are the fundamental learning unit in modern organizations. This is where "the rubber meets the road"; unless teams can learn, the organization cannot learn.

If a learning organization were an engineering innovation, such as the airplane or the personal computer, the components would be called "technologies." For an innovation in human behavior, the components need to be seen as *disciplines*. By "discipline," I do not mean an "enforced order" or "means of punishment," but a body of theory and technique that must be studied and mastered to be put into practice. A discipline is a developmental path for acquiring certain skills or competencies. As with any discipline, from playing the piano to electrical engineering, some people have an innate "gift," but anyone can develop proficiency through practice.

To practice a discipline is to be a lifelong learner. You never "arrive"; you spend your life mastering disciplines. You can never say, "We are a learning organization," any more than you can say, "I am an enlightened person." The more you learn, the more acutely aware you become of your ignorance. Thus, a corporation cannot be "excellent" in the sense of having arrived at a permanent excellence; it is always in the state of practicing the disciplines of learning, of becoming better or worse.

That organizations can benefit from disciplines is not a totally new idea. After all, management disciplines such as accounting have been around for a long time. But the five learning disciplines differ from more familiar management disciplines in that they are "personal" disciplines. Each has to do with how we think, what we truly want, and how we interact and learn with one another. In this sense, they are more like artistic disciplines than traditional management disciplines. Moreover, while accounting is good for "keeping score," we have never approached the subtler tasks of building organizations, of enhancing their capabilities for innovation and creativity, of crafting strategy and designing policy and structure through assimilating new disciplines. Perhaps this is why, all too often, great organizations are fleeting, enjoying their moment in the sun, then passing quietly back to the ranks of the mediocre.

Practicing a discipline is different from emulating "a model." All too often, new management innovations are described in terms of the "best practices" of so-called leading firms. While interesting, I believe such descriptions can often do more harm than good, leading to piecemeal copying and playing catch-up. I do not believe great organizations have ever been built by trying to emulate another, any more than individual greatness is achieved by trying to copy another "great person."

When the five component technologies converged to create the DC-3 the commercial airline industry began. But the DC-3 was not the end of the process. Rather, it was the precursor of a new industry. Similarly, as the five component learning disciplines converge they will not create *the* learning organization but rather a new wave of experimentation and advancement.

The Fifth Discipline

It is vital that the five disciplines develop as an ensemble. This is challenging because it is much harder to integrate new tools than simply apply them separately. But the payoffs are immense.

This is why systems thinking is the fifth discipline. It is the discipline that integrates the disciplines, fusing them into a coherent body of theory and practice. It keeps them from being separate gimmicks or the latest organization change fads. Without a systemic orientation, there is no motivation to look at how the disciplines interrelate. By enhancing each of the other disciplines, it continually reminds us that the whole can exceed the sum of its parts.

For example, vision without systems thinking ends up painting lovely pictures of the future with no deep understanding of the forces that must be mastered to move from here to there. This is one of the reasons why many firms that have jumped on the "vision bandwagon" in recent years have found that lofty vision alone fails to turn around a firm's fortunes. Without systems thinking, the seed of vision falls on harsh soil. If nonsystemic thinking predominates, the first condition for nurturing vision is not met: a genuine belief that we can make our vision real in the future. We may say, "We can achieve our vision" (most American managers are conditioned to this belief), but our tacit view of current reality as a set of conditions created by somebody else betrays us.

But systems thinking also needs the disciplines of building shared vision, mental models, team learning, and personal mastery to realize its potential. Building shared vision fosters a commitment to the long term. Mental models focus on the openness needed to unearth shortcomings in our present ways of seeing the world. Team learning develops the skills of groups of people to look for the larger picture that lies beyond individual perspectives. And personal mastery fosters the personal motivation to continually learn how our actions affect our world. Without personal mastery, people are so steeped in the reactive mindset ("someone/something else is creating my problems") that they are deeply threatened by the systems perspective.

Lastly, systems thinking makes understandable the subtlest aspect of the learning organization—the new way individuals perceive themselves and their world. At the heart of a learning organization is a shift of mind—from seeing ourselves as separate from the world to connected to the world, from seeing problems as caused by someone or something "out there" to seeing how our own actions create the problems we experience. A learning organization is a place where people are continually discovering how they create their reality. And how they can change it. As Archimedes has said, "Give me a lever long enough . . . and single-handed I can move the world."

Metanoia—A Shift of Mind

When you ask people about what it is like being part of a great team, what is most striking is the meaningfulness of the experience. People talk about being part of something larger than themselves, of being connected, of being generative. It becomes quite clear that, for many, their experiences as part of truly great teams stand out as singular periods of life lived to the fullest. Some spend the rest of their lives looking for ways to recapture that spirit.

The most accurate word in Western culture to describe what happens in a learning organization is one that hasn't had much currency for the past several hundred years. It is a word we have used in our work with organizations for some ten years, but we always caution them, and ourselves, to use it sparingly in public. The word is "metanoia" and it means a shift of mind. The word has a rich history. For the Greeks, it meant a fundamental shift or change, or more literally transcendence (*"meta"*— above or beyond, as in "metaphysics") of mind ("noia," from the root *"nous,"* of mind). In the early (Gnostic) Christian tradition, it took on a special meaning of awakening shared intuition and direct knowing of the highest, of God. "Metanoia" was probably the key term of such early Christians as John the Baptist. In the Catholic corpus the word metanoia was eventually translated as "repent."

To grasp the meaning of "metanoia" is to grasp the deeper meaning of "learning," for learning also involves a fundamental shift or movement of mind. The problem with talking about "learning organizations" is that the "learning" has lost its central meaning in contemporary usage. Most people's eyes glaze over if you talk to them about "learning" or "learning organizations." Little wonder—for, in everyday use, learning has come to be synonymous with "taking in information." "Yes, I learned all about that at the course yesterday." Yet, taking in information is only distantly related to real learning. It would be nonsensical to say, "I just read a great book about bicycle riding—I've now learned that."

Real learning gets to the heart of what it means to be human. Through learning we re-create ourselves. Through learning we become able to do something we never were able to do. Through learning we reperceive the world and our relationship to it. Through learning we extend our capacity to create, to be part of the generative process of life. There is within each of us a deep hunger for this type of learning. It is, as Bill O'Brien of Hanover Insurance says, "as fundamental to human beings as the sex drive."

This, then, is the basic meaning of a "learning organization"—an organization that is continually expanding its capacity to create its future. For such an organization, it is not enough merely to survive. "Survival learning," or what is more often termed "adaptive learning," is important—indeed it is necessary. But for a learning organization, "adaptive learning" must be joined by "generative learning," learning that enhances our capacity to create.

A few brave organizational pioneers are pointing the way, but the territory of building learning organizations is still largely unexplored. It is my fondest hope that this book can accelerate that exploration.

Putting the Ideas into Practice

I take no credit for inventing the five major disciplines of this book. The five disciplines described below represent the experimentation, research, writing, and invention of hundreds of people. But I have worked with all of the disciplines for years, refining ideas about them, collaborating on research, and introducing them to organizations throughout the world.

When I entered graduate school at the Massachusetts Institute of Technology in 1970, I was already convinced that most of the problems faced by humankind concerned our inability to grasp and manage the increasingly complex systems of our world. Little has happened since to change my view. Today, the arms race, the environmental crisis, the international drug trade, the stagnation in the Third World, and the persisting U.S. budget and trade deficits all attest to a world where problems are becoming increasingly complex and interconnected. From the start at MIT I was drawn to the work of Jay Forrester, a computer pioneer who had shifted fields to develop what he called "system dynamics." Jay maintained that the causes of many pressing public issues, from urban decay to global ecological threat, lay in the very well-intentioned policies designed to alleviate them. These problems were actually "systems" that lured policymakers into interventions that focused on obvious symptoms, not underlying causes, which produced short-term benefit but long-term malaise, and fostered the need for still more symptomatic interventions.

As I began my doctoral work, I had little interest in business management. I felt that the solutions to the Big Issues lay in the public sector. But I began to meet business leaders who came to visit our MIT group to learn about systems thinking. These were thoughtful people, deeply aware of the inadequacies of prevailing ways of managing. They were engaged in building new types of organizations—decentralized, nonhierarchical organizations dedicated to the well-being and growth of employees as well as to success. Some had crafted radical corporate philosophies based on core values of freedom and responsibility. Others had developed innovative organization designs. All shared a commitment and a capacity to innovate that was lacking in the public sector. Gradually, I came to realize why business is the locus of innovation in an open society. Despite whatever hold past thinking may have on the business mind, business has a freedom to experiment missing in the public sector and, often, in nonprofit organizations. It also has a clear "bottom line," so that experiments can be evaluated, at least in principle, by objective criteria.

But why were they interested in systems thinking? Too often, the most daring organizational experiments were foundering. Local autonomy produced business decisions that were disastrous for the organization as a whole. "Team building" exercises sent colleagues white-water rafting together, but when they returned home they still disagreed fundamentally about business problems. Companies pulled together during crises, and then lost all their inspiration when business improved. Organizations which started out as booming successes, with the best possible intentions toward customers and employees, found themselves trapped in downward spirals that got worse the harder they tried to fix them.

Then, we all believed that the tools of systems thinking could make a difference in these companies. As I worked with different companies, I came to see why systems thinking was not enough by itself. It needed a new type of management practitioner to really make the most of it. At that time, in the mid-1970s, there was a nascent sense of what such a management practitioner could be. But it had not yet crystallized. It is crystallizing now with leaders of our MIT group: William O'Brien of Hanover Insurance, Edward Simon from Herman Miller, and Ray Stata, CEO of Analog Devices. All three of these men are involved in innovative, influential companies. All three have been involved in our research program for several years, along with leaders from Apple, Ford, Polaroid, Royal Dutch/Shell, and Trammell Crow.

For eleven years I have also been involved in developing and conducting Innovation Associates' Leadership and Mastery workshops, which have introduced people from all walks of life to the fifth discipline ideas that have grown out of our work at MIT, combined with IA's path-breaking work on building shared vision and personal mastery. Over four thousand managers have attended. We started out with a particular focus on corporate senior executives, but soon found that the basic disciplines such as systems thinking, personal mastery, and shared vision were relevant for teachers, public administrators and elected officials, students, and parents. All were in leadership positions of importance. All were in "organizations" that had still untapped potential for creating their future. All felt that to tap that potential required developing their own capacities, that is, learning. . . .

REFERENCES

de Geus, A. "Planning as Learning." *Harvard Business Review,* Mar./Apr. 1988, pp. 70–74.

Graham, A. K. "Software Design: Breaking the Bottleneck." *IEEE Spectrum,* Mar. 1982, pp. 43–50.

Graham, A. K., and Senge, P. "A Long-Wave Hypothesis of Innovation." *Technological Forecasting and Social Change,* Aug. 1980, pp. 283–311.

Yankelovich, D. *New Rules: Searching for Self-Fulfillment in a World Turned Upside Down.* New York: Random House, 1981.

2

THE NATURE
OF LEADERSHIP

John W. Gardner

LEADERSHIP IS A WORD that has risen above normal workaday usage as a conveyor of meaning. There seems to be a feeling that if we invoke it often enough with sufficient ardor we can ease our sense of having lost our way, our sense of things unaccomplished, of duties unfulfilled.

All of that simply clouds our thinking. The aura with which we tend to surround the words *leader* and *leadership* makes it hard to think clearly. Good sense calls for demystification.

Leadership is the process of persuasion or example by which an individual (or leadership team) induces a group to pursue objectives held by the leader or shared by the leader and his or her followers.

In any established group, individuals fill different roles, and one of the roles is that of leader. Leaders cannot be thought of apart from the historic context in which they arise, the setting in which they function (e.g., elective political office), and the system over which they preside (e.g., a particular city or state). They are integral parts of the system, subject to the forces that affect the system. They perform (or cause to be performed) certain tasks or functions that are essential if the group is to accomplish its purposes.

All that we know about the interaction between leaders and constituents or followers tells us that communication and influence flow in both directions; and in that two-way communication, nonrational, nonverbal, and unconscious elements play their part. In the process leaders shape and are shaped. This is true even in systems that appear to be led in quite autocratic fashion. In a state governed by coercion, followers can-not prevent the leader from violating their customs and beliefs, but they have many ways of making it more costly to violate than to honor their norms, and leaders usually make substantial accommodations. If Julius Caesar had been willing to live more flexibly with the give-and-take he might not have been slain in the Senate House. Machiavelli (1952), the ultimate realist, advised the prince, "You will always need the favor of the inhabitants. . . . It is necessary for a prince to possess the friendship of the people."

The connotations of the word *follower* suggest too much passivity and dependence to make it a fit term for all who are at the other end of the dialogue with leaders. I don't intend to discard it, but I also make frequent use of the word *constituent*. It is awkward in some contexts, but often it does fuller justice to the two-way interchange.

Elements of physical coercion are involved in some kinds of leadership; and of course there is psychological coercion, however mild and subtle, including peer pressure, in all social action. But in our culture, popular understanding of the leadership process distinguishes it from coercion—and places those forms involving the least coercion higher on the scale of leadership.

The focus of this book is leadership in this country today. Examples are drawn from other cultures and many of the generalizations are relevant for all times and places; but the focus is here and now. The points empha-sized might be different were I writing fifty years ago or fifty years hence, or writing of Bulgaria or Tibet.

Distinctions

We must not confuse leadership with status. Even in large corporations and government agencies, the top-ranking person may simply be bureau-crat number 1. We have all occasionally encountered top persons who couldn't lead a squad of seven-year-olds to the ice cream counter.

It does not follow that status is irrelevant to leadership. Most positions of high status carry with them symbolic values and traditions that enhance the possibility of leadership. People expect governors and corporation pres-idents to lead, which heightens the possibility that they will. But the selec-tion process for positions of high status does not make that a sure outcome.

Similarly, we must not confuse leadership with power. Leaders always have some measure of power, rooted in their capacity to persuade, but many people with power are without leadership gifts. Their power derives from money, or from the capacity to inflict harm, or from control of some piece of institutional machinery, or from access to the media. A military dictator has power. The thug who sticks a gun in your ribs has power. Leadership is something else.

Finally, we must not confuse leadership with official authority, which is simply legitimized power. Meter maids have it; the person who audits your tax returns has it.

Leadership requires major expenditures of effort and energy—more than most people care to make. When I outlined to a teenager of my acquaintance the preceding distinctions and then described the hard tasks of leadership, he said, "I'll leave the leadership to you, Mr. Gardner. Give me some of that power and status."

Confusion between leadership and official authority has a deadly effect on large organizations. Corporations and government agencies everywhere have executives who imagine that their place on the organization chart has given them a body of followers. And of course it has not. They have been given subordinates. Whether the subordinates become followers depends on whether the executives act like leaders.

Is it appropriate to apply to leaders the word *elite?* The word was once applied to families of exalted social status. Then sociologists adopted the word to describe any group of high status, whether hereditary or earned; thus, in addition to the elites of old families and old money, there are elites of performance and profession.

Some social critics today use the word with consistent negative overtones. They believe that elite status is incompatible with an equalitarian philosophy. But in any society—no matter how democratic, no matter how equalitarian—there are elites in the sociologist's sense: intellectual, athletic, artistic, political, and so on. The marks of an open society are that elite status is generally earned, and that those who have earned it do not use their status to violate democratic norms. In our society, leaders are among the many "performance elites."

Leaders and Managers

The word *manager* usually indicates that the individual so labeled holds a directive post in an organization, presiding over the processes by which the organization functions, allocating resources prudently, and making the best possible use of people.

Many writers on leadership take considerable pains to distinguish between leaders and managers. In the process leaders generally end up looking like a cross between Napoleon and the Pied Piper, and managers like unimaginative clods. This troubles me. I once heard it said of a man, "He's an utterly first-class manager but there isn't a trace of the leader in him." I am still looking for that man, and I am beginning to believe that he does not exist. Every time I encounter utterly first-class managers they turn out to have quite a lot of the leader in them.

Even the most visionary leader is faced on occasion with decisions that every manager faces: when to take a short-term loss to achieve a long-term gain, how to allocate scarce resources, whom to trust with a delicate assignment. So even though it has become conventional to contrast leaders and managers, I am inclined to use slightly different categories, lumping leaders and leader/managers into one category and placing in the other category those numerous managers whom one would not normally describe as leaders. Leaders and leader/managers distinguish themselves from the general run of managers in at least six respects:

1. They think longer term—beyond the day's crises, beyond the quarterly report, beyond the horizon.

2. In thinking about the unit they are heading, they grasp its relationship to larger realities—the larger organization of which they are a part, conditions external to the organization, global trends.

3. They reach and influence constituents beyond their jurisdictions, beyond boundaries. Thomas Jefferson influenced people all over Europe. Gandhi influenced people all over the world. In an organization, leaders extend their reach across bureaucratic boundaries—often a distinct advantage in a world too complex and tumultuous to be handled "through channels." Leaders' capacity to rise above jurisdictions may enable them to bind together the fragmented constituencies that must work together to solve a problem.

4. They put heavy emphasis on the intangibles of vision, values, and motivation and understand intuitively the nonrational and unconscious elements in leader–constituent interaction.

5. They have the political skill to cope with the conflicting requirements of multiple constituencies.

6. They think in terms of renewal. The routine manager tends to accept organizational structure and process as it exists. The leader or leader/manager seeks the revisions of process and structure required by ever-changing reality.

The manager is more tightly linked to an organization than is the leader. Indeed, the leader may have no organization at all. Florence Nightingale, after leaving the Crimea, exercised extraordinary leadership in health care for decades with no organization under her command. Gandhi was a leader before he had an organization. Some of our most memorable leaders have headed movements so amorphous that management would be an inappropriate word.

The Many Kinds of Leaders

One hears and reads a surprising number of sentences that describe leaders in general as having such and such attributes and behaving in such and such a fashion—as though one could distill out of the spectacular diversity of leaders an idealized picture of The Leader.

Leaders come in many forms, with many styles and diverse qualities. There are quiet leaders and leaders one can hear in the next county. Some find their strength in eloquence, some in judgment, some in courage. I had a friend who was a superior leader in outdoor activities and sports but quite incapable of leading in a bureaucratic setting.

The diversity is almost without limit: Churchill, the splendidly eloquent old warrior; Gandhi, the visionary and the shrewd mobilizer of his people; Lenin, the coldly purposeful revolutionary. Consider just the limited category of military leadership. George Marshall was a self-effacing, low-keyed man with superb judgment and a limitless capacity to inspire trust. MacArthur was a brilliant strategist, a farsighted administrator, and flamboyant to his fingertips. (Eisenhower, who had served under MacArthur, once said, "I studied dramatics under a master.") Eisenhower in his wartime assignment was an outstanding leader/administrator and coalition builder. General Patton was a slashing, intense combat commander. Field Marshal Montgomery was a gifted, temperamental leader of whom Churchill said, "In defeat, indomitable; in victory, insufferable." All were great leaders—but extraordinarily diverse in personal attributes.

The fact that there are many kinds of leaders has implications for leadership education. Most of those seeking to develop young potential leaders have in mind one ideal model that is inevitably constricting. We should give young people a sense of the many kinds of leaders and styles of leadership, and encourage them to move toward those models that are right for them.

Leaders and History

All too often when we think of our historic leaders, we eliminate all the contradictions that make individuals distinctive. And we further violate reality by lifting them out of their historical contexts. No wonder we are left with pasteboard portraits. As first steps toward a mature view of leaders we must accept complexity and context.

Thomas Jefferson was first of all a gifted and many-sided human, an enigmatic man who loved—among other things—abstract ideas, agriculture, architecture and statecraft. He was a man of natural aloofness who lived most of his life in public; a man of action with a gift for words and a bent for research; an idealist who proved himself a shrewd, even wily, operator on the political scene. Different sides of his nature came into play in different situations.

Place him now in the context of the exhilarating events and themes of his time: a new nation coming into being, with a new consciousness; the brilliant rays of the Enlightenment reaching into every phase of life; the inner contradictions of American society (e.g., slavery) already rumbling beneath the surface.

Finally, add the overpowering impulse of succeeding generations to serve their own needs by mythologizing, idolizing or debunking him. It turns out to be an intricately textured story—and not one that diminishes Jefferson.

It was once believed that if leadership traits were truly present in an individual, they would manifest themselves almost without regard to the situation in which the person was functioning. No one believes that any more. Acts of leadership take place in an unimaginable variety of settings, and the setting does much to determine the kinds of leaders that emerge and how they play their roles.

We cannot avoid the bewhiskered question, "Does the leader make history or does the historical moment make the leader?" It sounds like a seminar question but it is of interest to most leaders sooner or later. Corporate chief executive officers fighting a deteriorating trend in an industry feel like people trying to run up the down escalator. Looking across town at less able leaders riding an upward trend in another industry, they are ripe for the theory that history makes the leader.

Thomas Carlyle placed excessive emphasis on the great person, as did Sidney Hook (1955): "all factors in history, save great men, are inconsequential." Karl Marx, Georg Hegel, and Herbert Spencer placed excessive emphasis on historical forces. For Marx, economic forces shaped history; for Spencer, societies had their evolutionary course just as species did, and the leader was a product of the process; for Hegel, leaders were a part of the dialectic of history and could not help what they did.

The balanced view, of course, is that historical forces create the circumstances in which leaders emerge, but the characteristics of the particular leader in turn have their impact on history.

It is not possible to understand Queen Isabella without understanding fifteenth-century Europe (when she was born, Spain as we know it did not exist), or without understanding the impact of the Reformation on the

Catholic world and the gnawing fear stirred by the Muslim conquests. But many monarchs flourished on the Iberian Peninsula in that historical context; only Isabella left an indelible mark. Similarly, by the time Martin Luther emerged, the seeds of the Reformation had already sprouted in many places, but no one would argue that the passionate, charismatic priest who nailed his ninety-five theses to the church door was a puppet of history. Historical forces set the stage for him, but once there, he was himself a historical force.

Churchill is an even more interesting case because he tried out for leadership many times before history was ready for him. After Dunkirk, England needed a leader who could rally the British people to heroic exertions in an uncompromising war, and the eloquent, combative Churchill delivered one of the great performances of the century. Subsequently the clock of history ticked on and—with the war over—the voters dropped him unceremoniously. When a friend told him it was a blessing in disguise, he growled "If it is, the disguise is perfect."

Forces of history determined his rise and fall, but in his time on the world stage he left a uniquely Churchillian mark on the course of events.

Settings

The historical moment is the broadest context affecting the emergence and functioning of leaders, but immensely diverse settings of a more modest nature clearly affect leadership.

The makeup of the group to be led is, of course, a crucial feature of the context. According to research findings, the approach to leadership or style of leadership that will be effective depends on, among other things, the age level of the individuals to be led; their educational background and competence; the size, homogeneity and cohesiveness of the group; its motivation and morale; its rate of turnover; and so on.

Other relevant contextual features are too numerous and diverse to list. Leading a corporation is one thing, leading a street gang is something else. Thomas Cronin (1989) has pointed out that it may take one kind of leadership to start a new enterprise and quite another kind to keep it going through its various phases. Religious bodies, political parties, government agencies, the academic world—all offer distinctive contexts for leadership.

Judgments of Leaders

In curious ways, people tend to aggrandize the role of leaders. They tend to exaggerate the capacity of leaders to influence events. Jeffrey Pfeffer (1978) says that people want to achieve a feeling of control over their environment, and that this inclines them to attribute the outcomes of group performance to leaders rather than to context. If we were to face the fact—so the argument goes—that outcomes are the result of a complex set of interactions among group members plus environmental and historical forces, we would feel helpless. By attributing outcomes to an identifiable leader we feel, rightly or not, more in control. There is at least a chance that one can fire the leader; one cannot "fire" historical forces.

Leaders act in the stream of history. As they labor to bring about a result, multiple forces beyond their control, even beyond their knowledge, are moving to hasten or hinder the result. So there is rarely a demonstrable causal link between a leader's specific decisions and consequent events. Consequences are not a reliable measure of leadership. Franklin Roosevelt's efforts to bolster the economy in the middle-to-late 1930s were powerfully aided by a force that did not originate with his economic brain trust—the winds of war. Leaders of a farm workers' union fighting for better wages may find their efforts set at naught by a crop failure.

Frank Lloyd Wright said, "A doctor can bury his mistakes. An architect can only advise his client to plant vines." Unlike either doctor or architect, leaders suffer from the mistakes of predecessors and leave some of their own misjudgments as time bombs for successors.

Many of the changes sought by leaders take time: lots of years, long public debate, slow shifts in attitude. In their lifetimes, leaders may see little result from heroic efforts, yet may be setting the stage for victories that will come after them. Reflect on the long, slow unfolding of the battles for racial equality or for women's rights. Leaders who did vitally important early work died without knowing what they had wrought.

Leaders may appear to have succeeded (or failed) only to have historians a generation later reverse the verdict. The "verdict of history" has a wonderfully magisterial sound, but in reality it is subject to endless appeals to later generations of historians—with no court of last resort to render a final judgment.

In the real world, the judgments one makes of a leader must be multidimensional, taking into consideration great strengths, streaks of mediocrity, and perhaps great flaws. If the great strengths correspond to the needs of a crucial moment in history, the flaws are forgiven and simply provide texture to the biographies. Each leader has his or her own unique pattern of attributes, sometimes conflicting in curious ways. Ronald Reagan was notably passive with respect to many important issues, but vigorously tenacious on other issues.

Leaders change over the course of their active careers as do other human beings. In looking back, it is natural for us to freeze them in that moment when they served history's needs most spectacularly, but leaders evolve. The passionately antislavery Lincoln of the Douglas debates was not the see-both-sides Lincoln of fifteen years earlier. The "national unity" Churchill of 1942 was not the fiercely partisan, adversarial Churchill of the 1930s.

Devolving Initiative and Responsibility

I have already commented on our dispersed leadership and on its importance to the vitality of a large, intricately organized system. Our most forward-looking business concerns are working in quite imaginative ways to devolve initiative downward and outward through their organizations to develop their lower levels of leadership.

There is no comparable movement in government agencies. But in the nation as a whole, dispersed leadership is a reality. In Santa Barbara County, California, Superintendent of Schools William Cirone is a leader in every sense of the word. A healthy school system requires a vital and involved citizenry. How does one achieve that? Given the aging population, fewer and fewer citizens have children in the schools. How do we keep them interested? Education is a lifelong process. How do we provide for that? These are questions to which Cirone has addressed himself with uncommon energy and imagination (Cirone and Margerum, 1987).

The leaders of the Soviet Union did not launch the reforms of 1987 because they had developed a sudden taste for grass-roots democracy. They launched them because their system was grinding to a halt. Leader/ managers at the lower levels and at the periphery of the system had neither the motivation nor the authority to solve problems that they understood better than the Moscow bureaucrats.

We have only half learned the lesson ourselves. In many of our large corporate, governmental, and nonprofit organizations we still make it all too difficult for potential leaders down the line to exercise initiative. We are still in the process of discovering how much vitality and motivation are buried at those levels awaiting release.

To emphasize the need for dispersed leadership does not deny the need for highly qualified top leadership. But our high-level leaders will be more effective in every way if the systems over which they preside are made vital by dispersed leadership. As I argued in *Excellence,* we must demand high performance at every level of society (Gardner, 1984).

Friends of mine have argued that in view of my convictions concerning the importance of middle- and lower-level leaders, I lean too heavily on examples of high-level leaders. My response is that we know a great deal about the more famous figures, statements about them can be documented, and they are comfortably familiar to readers. No one who reads this book with care could believe that I consider such exalted figures the only ones worth considering.

Institutionalizing Leadership

To exercise leadership today, leaders must institutionalize their leadership. The issues are too technical and the pace of change too swift to expect that a leader, no matter how gifted, will be able to solve personally the major problems facing the system over which he or she presides. So we design an institutional system—a government agency, a corporation—to solve the problems, and then we select a leader who has the capacity to preside over and strengthen the system. Some leaders may be quite gifted in solving problems personally, but if they fail to institutionalize the process, their departure leaves the system crippled. They must create or strengthen systems that will survive them.

The institutional arrangements generally include a leadership team. Often throughout this book when I use the word *leader,* I am in fact referring to the leadership team. No individual has all the skills—and certainly not the time—to carry out all the complex tasks of contemporary leadership. And the team must be chosen for excellence in performance. Loyalty and being on the boss's wavelength are necessary but not sufficient qualifications. I emphasize the point because more than one recent president of the United States has had aides who possessed no other qualifications.

REFERENCES

Cirone, W. J., and Margerum, B. "Models of Citizen Involvement and Community Education." *National Civic Review,* May–June 1987, 76(3).

Cronin, T. E. *Chronicle of Higher Education,* Feb. 1, 1989, pp. B1–B2.

Gardner, J. W. *Excellence.* (rev. ed.) New York: Norton, 1984.

Hook, S. *The Hero in History.* Boston: Beacon, 1955.

Machiavelli, N. *The Prince.* New York: New American Library, 1952.

Pfeffer, J. "The Ambiguity of Leadership." In M. W. McCall Jr. and M. Lombardo (eds.), *Leadership: Where Else Can We Go?* Durham, N.C.: Duke University Press, 1978.

3

LEVEL 5 LEADERSHIP

Jim Collins

You can accomplish anything in life,
provided that you do not mind who gets the credit.

—Harry S. Truman
(McCullough, 1992, p. 564)

IN 1971, a seemingly ordinary man named Darwin E. Smith became chief executive of Kimberly-Clark, a stodgy old paper company whose stock had fallen 36 percent behind the general market over the previous twenty years.

Smith, the company's mild-mannered in-house lawyer, wasn't so sure the board had made the right choice—a feeling further reinforced when a director pulled Smith aside and reminded him that he lacked some of the qualifications for the position (R. Spector, based on Wicks, 1997). But CEO he was, and CEO he remained for twenty years.

What a twenty years it was. In that period, Smith created a stunning transformation, turning Kimberly-Clark into the leading paper-based consumer products company in the world. Under his stewardship, Kimberly-Clark generated cumulative stock returns 4.1 times the general market, handily beating its direct rivals Scott Paper and Procter & Gamble and outperforming such venerable companies as Coca-Cola, Hewlett-Packard, 3M, and General Electric. See Figures 3.1 and 3.2.

It was an impressive performance, one of the best examples in the twentieth century of taking a good company and making it great. Yet few people—even ardent students of management and corporate history—know anything about Darwin Smith. He probably would have liked it that way. A man who carried no airs of self-importance, Smith found his favorite companionship among plumbers and electricians and spent his vacations rumbling around his Wisconsin farm in the cab of a backhoe, digging holes and moving rocks ("Former CEO of K-C Dies," 1995; Kelly, 1988; "Rae Takes on the Paper Industry," 1991). He never cultivated hero status or executive celebrity status (research interview #5-E). When a journalist asked him to describe his management style, Smith, dressed unfashionably like a farm boy wearing his first suit bought at JC Penney, just stared back from the other side of his nerdy-looking black-rimmed glasses. After a long, uncomfortable silence, he said simply: "Eccentric" (research interview #5-E, p. 26). The *Wall Street Journal* did not write a splashy feature on Darwin Smith.

But if you were to think of Darwin Smith as somehow meek or soft, you would be terribly mistaken. His awkward shyness and lack of pre-

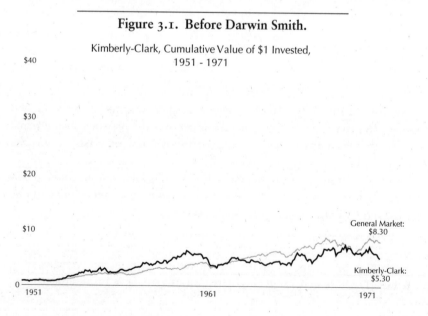

Figure 3.1. Before Darwin Smith.

Kimberly-Clark, Cumulative Value of $1 Invested, 1951 - 1971

Figure 3.2. Darwin Smith Tenure.

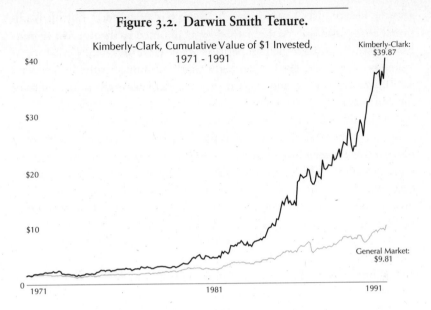

Kimberly-Clark, Cumulative Value of $1 Invested, 1971 - 1991

tense was coupled with a fierce, even stoic, resolve toward life. Smith grew up as a poor Indiana farm-town boy, putting himself through college by working the day shift at International Harvester and attending Indiana University at night. One day, he lost part of a finger on the job. The story goes that he went to class that evening and returned to work the next day. While that might be a bit of an exaggeration, he clearly did not let a lost finger slow clown his progress toward graduation. He kept working full-time, he kept going to class at night, and he earned admission to Harvard Law School (Kelly, 1988). Later in life, two months after becoming CEO, doctors diagnosed Smith with nose and throat cancer, predicting he had less than a year to live. He informed the board but made it clear that he was not dead yet and had no plans to die anytime soon. Smith held fully to his demanding work schedule while commuting weekly from Wisconsin to Houston for radiation therapy and lived twenty-five more years, most of them as CEO ("Kimberly-Clark Bets, Wins on Innovation," 1991; "Darwin E. Smith, 69," 1995; R. Spector, based on Wicks, 1997).

Smith brought that same ferocious resolve to rebuilding Kimberly-Clark, especially when he made the most dramatic decision in the company's history: Sell the mills (R. Spector, based on Wicks, 1997). Shortly after he became CEO, Smith and his team had concluded that the traditional core business—coated paper—was doomed to mediocrity. Its economics were had and the competition weak (*International Directory of Company Histories*, 1991; "Kimberly-Clark—Aiming for the Consumer," 1970). But, they reasoned, if Kimberly-Clark thrust itself into the fire of the *consumer* paper-products industry, world-class competition like Procter & Gamble would force it to achieve greatness or perish.

So, like the general who burned the boats upon landing, leaving only one option (succeed or die), Smith announced the decision to sell the mills, in what one board member called the gutsiest move he'd ever seen a CEO make. Sell even the mill in Kimberly, Wisconsin, and throw all the proceeds into the consumer business, investing in brands like Huggies and Kleenex (R. Spector, based on Wicks, 1997; "Darwin E. Smith, 69," 1995; "Former CEO of K-C Dies," 1995; research interview #5-E; "Paper Tiger," 1987).

The business media called the move stupid and Wall Street analysts downgraded the stock ("The Battle of the Bottoms," 1997). Smith never wavered. Twenty-five years later, Kimberly-Clark owned Scott Paper outright and beat Procter & Gamble in six of eight product categories ("The Battle of the Bottoms," 1997). In retirement, Smith reflected on his exceptional performance, saying simply, "I never stopped trying to become qualified for the job" (R. Spector, based on Wicks, 1997, p. 10).

Darwin Smith stands as a classic example of what we came to call a Level 5 leader—an individual who blends extreme personal humility with intense professional will. We found leaders of this type at the helm of every good-to-great company during the transition era. Like Smith, they were self-effacing individuals who displayed the fierce resolve to do whatever needed to be done to make the company great.

Level 5 leaders channel their ego needs away from themselves and into the larger goal of building a great company. It's not that Level 5 leaders have no ego or self-interest. Indeed, they are incredibly ambitious—but *their ambition is first and foremost for the institution, not themselves.*

The term Level 5 refers to the highest level in a hierarchy of executive capabilities that we identified in our research (see Figure 3.3). While you don't need to move in sequence from Level 1 to Level 5—it might be possible to fill in some of the lower levels later—fully developed Level 5 leaders embody all five layers of the pyramid. I am not going to belabor all five levels here, as Levels 1 through 4 are somewhat self-explanatory and are discussed extensively by other authors. This chapter will focus instead

Figure 3.3. The Five Levels of Leadership.

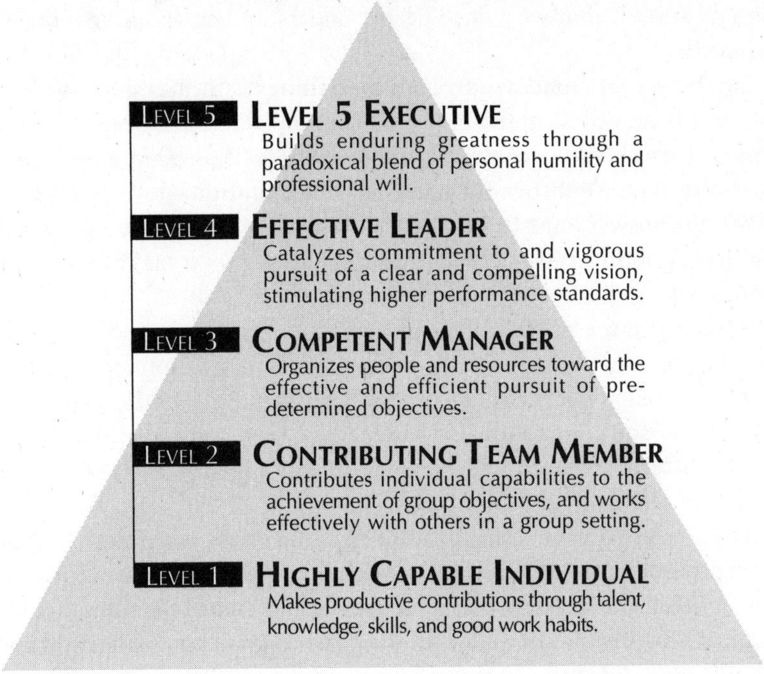

LEVEL 5 **LEVEL 5 EXECUTIVE**
Builds enduring greatness through a paradoxical blend of personal humility and professional will.

LEVEL 4 **EFFECTIVE LEADER**
Catalyzes commitment to and vigorous pursuit of a clear and compelling vision, stimulating higher performance standards.

LEVEL 3 **COMPETENT MANAGER**
Organizes people and resources toward the effective and efficient pursuit of pre-determined objectives.

LEVEL 2 **CONTRIBUTING TEAM MEMBER**
Contributes individual capabilities to the achievement of group objectives, and works effectively with others in a group setting.

LEVEL 1 **HIGHLY CAPABLE INDIVIDUAL**
Makes productive contributions through talent, knowledge, skills, and good work habits.

on the distinguishing traits of the good-to-great leaders—namely Level 5 traits—in contrast to the comparison leaders in our study.

But first, please permit a brief digression to set an important context. We were not looking for Level 5 leadership or anything like it. In fact, I gave the research team explicit instructions to *downplay* the role of top executives so that we could avoid the simplistic "credit the leader" or "blame the leader" thinking common today.

To use an analogy, the "Leadership is the answer to everything" perspective is the modern equivalent of the "God is the answer to everything" perspective that held back our scientific understanding of the physical world in the Dark Ages. In the 1500s, people ascribed all events they didn't understand to God. Why did the crops fail? God did it. Why did we have an earthquake? God did it. What holds the planets in place? God.

But with the Enlightenment, we began the search for a more scientific understanding—physics, chemistry, biology, and so forth. Not that we became atheists, but we gained deeper understanding about how the universe ticks.

Similarly, every time we attribute everything to "Leadership," we're no different from people in the 1500s. We're simply admitting our ignorance. Not that we should become leadership atheists (leadership does matter), but every time we throw our hands up in frustration—reverting back to "Well, the answer must be Leadership!"—we prevent ourselves from gaining deeper, more scientific understanding about what makes great companies tick.

So, early in the project, I kept insisting, "Ignore the executives." But the research team kept pushing back, "No! There is something consistently unusual about them. We can't ignore them." And I'd respond, "But the comparison companies also had leaders, even some great leaders. So, what's different?" Back and forth the debate raged. Finally—as should always be the case—the data won.

The good-to-great executives were all cut from the same cloth. It didn't matter whether the company was consumer or industrial, in crisis or steady state, offered services or products. It didn't matter when the transition took place or how big the company. All the good-to-great companies had Level 5 leadership at the time of transition. Furthermore, the absence of Level 5 leadership showed up as a consistent pattern in the comparison companies. Given that Level 5 leadership cuts against the grain of conventional wisdom, especially the belief that we need larger-than-life saviors with big personalities to transform companies, it is important to note that Level 5 is an empirical finding, not an ideological one.

HUMILITY + WILL = LEVEL 5

Level 5 leaders are a study in duality: modest and willful, humble and fearless. To quickly grasp this concept, think of United States President Abraham Lincoln (one of the few Level 5 presidents in United States history), who never let his ego get in the way of his primary ambition for the larger cause of an enduring great nation. Yet those who mistook Mr. Lincoln's personal modesty, shy nature, and awkward manner as signs of weakness found themselves terribly mistaken, to the scale of 250,000 Confederate and 360,000 Union lives, including Lincoln's own (Foote, 1975; McPherson, 1989).

While it might be a bit of a stretch to compare the good-to-great CEOs to Abraham Lincoln, they did display the same duality. Consider the case of Colman Mockler, CEO of Gillette from 1975 to 1991. During Mockler's tenure, Gillette faced three attacks that threatened to destroy the company's opportunity for greatness. Two attacks came as hostile takeover bids from Revlon, led by Ronald Perelman, a cigar-chomping raider with a reputation for breaking apart companies to pay down junk bonds and finance more hostile raids (McKibben, 1998). The third attack came from Coniston Partners, an investment group that bought 5.9 percent of Gillette stock and initiated a proxy battle to seize control of the board, hoping to sell the company to the highest bidder and pocket a quick gain on their shares (Company "Chronology," 1995; McKibben, 1998; Ricardo-Campbell, 1997). Had Gillette been flipped to Perelman at the price he offered, shareowners would have reaped an instantaneous 44 percent gain on their stock (McKibben, 1998). Looking at a $2.3 billion short-term stock profit across 116 million shares, most executives would have capitulated, pocketing millions from flipping their own stock and cashing in on generous golden parachutes (Ricardo-Campbell, 1997).

Colman Mockler did not capitulate, choosing instead to fight for the future greatness of Gillette, even though he himself would have pocketed a substantial sum on his own shares. A quiet and reserved man, always courteous, Mockler had the reputation of a gracious, almost patrician gentleman. Yet those who mistook Mockler's reserved nature for weakness found themselves beaten in the end. In the proxy fight, senior Gillette executives reached out to thousands of individual investors—person by person, phone call by phone call—and won the battle.

Now, you might be thinking, "But that just sounds like self-serving entrenched management fighting for their interests at the expense of shareholder interests." On the surface, it might look that way, but consider two key facts.

First, Mockler and his team staked the company's future on huge investments in radically new and technologically advanced systems (later known as Sensor and Mach3). Had the takeover been successful, these projects would almost certainly have been curtailed or eliminated, and none of us would be shaving with Sensor, Sensor for Women, or the Mach3—leaving hundreds of millions of people to a more painful daily battle with stubble. "We invested almost $1.5 billion in Sensor and Mach3. We believed that these projects would have been scrapped had the takeover happened" (personal conversation with Gillette CEO, summer 2000).

Second, at the time of the takeover battle, Sensor promised significant future profits that were not reflected in the stock price because it was in secret development. With Sensor in mind, the board and Mockler believed that the future value of the shares far exceeded the current price, even with the price premium offered by the raiders. To sell out would have made short-term shareflippers happy but would have been utterly irresponsible to long-term shareholders (see Figure 3.4).

In the end, Mockler and the board were proved right, stunningly so. If a shareflipper had accepted the 44 percent price premium offered by Ronald Perelman on October 31, 1986, and then invested the full amount in the general market for ten years, through the end of 1996, he would have come out three times worse off than a shareholder who had stayed with Mockler and Gillette (McKibben, 1998; calculations run using CRSP data). Indeed, the company, its customers, *and* the shareholders would have been ill served had Mockler capitulated to the raiders, pocketed his millions, and retired to a life of leisure.

Sadly, Mockler was never able to enjoy the full fruits of his effort. On January 25, 1991, the Gillette team received an advance copy of the cover of *Forbes* magazine, which featured an artist's rendition of Mockler standing atop a mountain holding a giant razor above his head in a triumphal pose, while the vanquished languish on the hillsides below. The other executives razzed the publicity-shy Mockler, who had likely declined re-

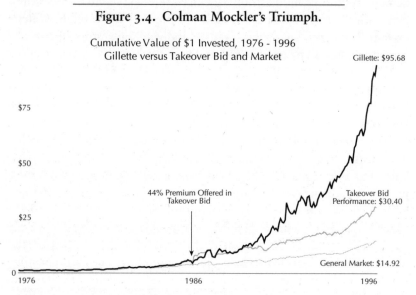

Figure 3.4. Colman Mockler's Triumph.

Cumulative Value of $1 Invested, 1976 - 1996
Gillette versus Takeover Bid and Market

Gillette: $95.68

$75

$50

44% Premium Offered in
Takeover Bid

Takeover Bid
Performance: $30.40

$25

General Market: $14.92

0

1976   1986   1996

This chart shows how an investor would have fared under the following scenarios:
1. $1 invested in Gillette, held from December 31, 1976 through December 31, 1996.
2. $1 invested in Gillette, held from December 31, 1976 *BUT THEN SOLD* to Ronald Perelman for a 44.44% premium on October 31, 1986, the proceeds then invested in the general stock market.
3. $1 invested in General Market held from December 31, 1976 through December 31, 1996.

quests to be photographed for the cover in the first place, amused at seeing him portrayed as a corporate version of Conan the Triumphant. Walking back to his office, minutes after seeing this public acknowledgment of his sixteen years of struggle, Mockler crumpled to the floor, struck dead by a massive heart attack (McKibben, 1998).

I do not know whether Mockler would have chosen to die in harness, but I am quite confident that he would not have changed his approach as chief executive. His placid persona hid an inner intensity, a dedication to making anything he touched the best it could possibly be—not just because of what he would get, but because he simply couldn't imagine doing it any other way. It wouldn't have been an option within Colman Mockler's value system to take the easy path and turn the company over to those who would milk it like a cow, destroying its potential to become great, any more than it would have been an option for Lincoln to sue for peace and lose forever the chance of an enduring great nation.

Ambition for the Company: Setting Up Successors for Success

When David Maxwell became CEO of Fannie Mae in 1981, the company was losing $1 million every single business day. Over the next nine years, Maxwell transformed Fannie Mae into a high-performance culture that rivaled the best Wall Street firms, earning $4 million every business day and beating the general stock market 3.8 to 1. Maxwell retired while still at the top of his game, feeling that the company would be ill served if he stayed on too long, and turned the company over to an equally capable successor, Jim Johnson. Shortly thereafter, Maxwell's retirement package, which had grown to be worth $20 million based on Fannie Mae's spectacular performance, became a point of controversy in Congress (Fannie Mae operates under a government charter). Maxwell responded by writing a letter to his successor, in which he expressed concern that the controversy would trigger an adverse reaction in Washington that could jeopardize the future of the company. He then instructed Johnson not to pay him the remaining balance—$5.5 million—and asked that the entire amount be contributed to the Fannie Mae foundation for low-income housing ("Maxwell Relinquishes Rights," 1992; "$5.5 Million Declined by Ex-Official," 1992).

David Maxwell, like Darwin Smith and Colman Mockler, exemplified a key trait of Level 5 leaders: ambition first and foremost for the company and concern for its success rather than for one's own riches and personal renown. Level 5 leaders want to see the company even more successful in the next generation, comfortable with the idea that most people won't even know that the roots of that success trace back to their efforts. As one Level 5 leader said, "I want to look out from my porch at one of the great companies in the world someday and be able to say, 'I used to work there.'"

In contrast, the comparison leaders, concerned more with their own reputation for personal greatness, often failed to set the company up for success in the next generation. After all, what better testament to your own personal greatness than that the place falls apart after you leave? In over three quarters of the comparison companies, we found executives who set their successors up for failure or chose weak successors, or both.

Some had the "biggest dog" syndrome—they didn't mind other dogs in the kennel, as long as they remained the biggest one. One comparison CEO was said to have treated successor candidates "the way Henry the VIII treated wives" ("Iacocca's Last Stand," 1992, p. 63).

Consider the case of Rubbermaid, an unsustained comparison company that grew from obscurity to number one on *Fortune*'s annual list of America's Most Admired Companies and then, just as quickly, disintegrated into such sorry shape that it had to be acquired by Newell to save itself. The architect of this remarkable story, a charismatic and brilliant leader named Stanley Gault, became synonymous in the late 1980s with the success of the company. In 312 articles collected on Rubbermaid, Gault comes through as a hard-driving, egocentric executive. In one article, he responds to the accusation of being a tyrant with the statement, "Yes, but I'm a sincere tyrant" ("Sincere Tyranny," 1985, p. 54). In another, drawn directly from his own comments on leading change, the word *I* appears forty-four times ("I could lead the charge"; "I wrote the twelve objectives"; "I presented and explained the objectives"), whereas the word *we* appears just sixteen times ("Managing," 1992). Gault had every reason to be proud of his executive success. Rubbermaid generated forty consecutive quarters of earnings growth under his leadership—an impressive performance, and one that deserves respect.

But—and this is the key point—Gault did not leave behind a company that would be great without *him*. His chosen successor lasted only one year on the job and the next in line faced a management team so shallow that he had to temporarily shoulder four jobs while scrambling to identify a new number-two executive ("Chairman Quits Post," 1992; "Rubbermaid's Sad Succession Tale," 1987). Gault's successors found themselves struggling not only with a management void, but also with strategic voids that would eventually bring the company to its knees ("Is Rubbermaid Reacting Too Late?" 1996).

Of course, you might say, "Yes, Rubbermaid fell apart after Gault, but that just proves his personal greatness as a leader." Exactly! Gault was indeed a tremendous Level 4 leader, perhaps one of the best in the last fifty years. But he was not a Level 5 leader, and that is one key reason why Rubbermaid went from good to great for a brief shining moment and then, just as quickly, went from great to irrelevant.

A Compelling Modesty

In contrast to the very I-centric style of the comparison leaders, we were struck by how the good-to-great leaders *didn't* talk about themselves. During interviews with the good-to-great leaders, they'd talk about the company and the contributions of other executives as long as we'd like but would deflect discussion about their own contributions. When pressed to talk about themselves, they'd say things like, "I hope I'm not sounding like a big shot." Or, "If the board hadn't picked such great successors, you probably wouldn't be talking with me today." Or, "Did I have a lot to do with it? Oh, that sounds so self-serving. I don't think I can take much credit. We were blessed with marvelous people." Or, "There are plenty of people in this company who could do my job better than I do."

It wasn't just false modesty. Those who worked with or wrote about the good-to-great leaders continually used words like *quiet, humble, modest, reserved, shy, gracious, mild-mannered, self-effacing, understated, did not believe his own clippings;* and so forth. Board member Jim Hlavacek described Ken Iverson, the CEO who oversaw Nucor's transformation from near bankruptcy to one of the most successful steel companies in the world:

> Ken is a very modest and humble man. I've never known a person as successful in doing what he's done that's as modest. And I work for a lot of CEOs of large companies. And that's true in his private life as well. The simplicity of him—I mean little things like he always gets his dogs at the local pound. He has a simple house that's he's lived in for ages. He only has a carport and he complained to me one day about how he had to use his credit card to scrape the frost off his windows and he broke the credit card. "You know, Ken, there's a solution for it; enclose your carport." And he said, "Ah, heck, it isn't that big of a deal." He's that humble and simple. [research interview #7-D, p. 17]

The eleven good-to-great CEOs are some of the most remarkable CEOs of the century, given that only eleven companies from the Fortune 500 met the exacting standards for entry into this study. Yet, despite their remarkable results, almost no one ever remarked about them! George Cain, Alan Wurtzel, David Maxwell, Colman Mockler, Darwin Smith, Jim Herring, Lyle Everingham, Joe Cullman, Fred Allen, Cork Walgreen, Carl Reichardt—how many of these extraordinary executives had you heard of?

When we systematically tabulated all 5,979 articles in the study, we found fewer articles surrounding the transition date for the good-to-great companies than for the comparisons, by a factor of two (Jones and Duffy, 1998, 1999). Furthermore, we rarely found articles that focused on the good-to-great CEOs.

The good-to-great leaders never wanted to become larger-than-life heroes. They never aspired to be put on a pedestal or become unreachable icons. They were seemingly ordinary people quietly producing extraordinary results.

Some of the comparison leaders provide a striking contrast. Scott Paper, the comparison company to Kimberly-Clark, hired a CEO named Al Dunlap, a man cut from a very different cloth than Darwin Smith. Dunlap loudly beat on his own chest, telling anyone who would listen (and many who would prefer not to) about what he had accomplished. Quoted in *Business Week* about his nineteen months atop Scott Paper, he boasted, "The Scott story will go down in the annals of American business history as one of the most successful, quickest turnarounds ever, [making] other turnarounds pale by comparison" ("Did CEO Dunlap Save Scott Paper?" 1996).

According to *Business Week,* Dunlap personally accrued $100 million for 603 days of work at Scott Paper (that's $165,000 *per day*), largely by slashing the workforce, cutting the R&D budget in half, and putting the company on growth steroids in preparation for sale ("Did CEO Dunlap Save Scott Paper?" 1996; "Chain Saw Al to the Rescue?" 1996; "After the Fall," 1996; "Only the Paranoid Survive," 1996; Dunlap and Andelman, 1997). After selling off the company and pocketing his quick millions, Dunlap wrote a book about himself, in which he trumpeted his nickname, Rambo in Pinstripes. "I love the Rambo movies," he wrote. "Here's a guy who has zero chance of success and always wins. Rambo goes into situations against all odds, expecting to get his brains blown out. But he doesn't. At the end of the day he succeeds, he gets rid of the bad guys. He creates peace out of war. That's what I do, too" (Dunlap and Andelman, 1997). Darwin Smith may have enjoyed the mindless Rambo movies as well, but I suspect he never walked out of a theater and said to his wife, "You know, I really relate to this Rambo character; he reminds me of me."

Granted, the Scott Paper story is one of the more dramatic in our study, but it's not an isolated case. In over two-thirds of the comparison cases, we noted the presence of a gargantuan personal ego that contributed to the demise or continued mediocrity of the company. (The cases where a charismatic CEO eventually became a liability for the company were Great Western, Warner-Lambert, Scott Paper, Bethlehem Steel, R. J. Reynolds, Addressograph-Multigraph, Eckerd, Bank of America, Burroughs, Chrysler, Rubbermaid, and Teledyne.)

We found this pattern particularly strong in the unsustained comparisons—cases where the company would show a leap in performance under a talented yet egocentric leader, only to decline in later years. Lee Iacocca, for example, saved Chrysler from the brink of catastrophe, performing one of the most celebrated (and deservedly so) turnarounds in American business history. Chrysler rose to a height of 2.9 times the market at a point about halfway through his tenure. Then, however, he diverted his attention to making himself one of the most celebrated CEOs in American business history. *Investor's Business Daily* and the *Wall Street Journal* chronicled how Iacocca appeared regularly on talk shows like the *Today* show and *Larry King Live,* personally starred in over eighty commercials, entertained the idea of running for president of the United States (quoted at one point, "Running Chrysler has been a bigger job than running the country. . . . I could handle the national economy in six months."), and widely promoted his autobiography. The book, *Iacocca,* sold seven million copies and elevated him to rock star status, leading him to be mobbed by thousands of cheering fans upon his arrival in Japan ("President Iacocca," 1982; "Iacocca Hands Over the Keys," 1993). Iacocca's personal stock soared, but in the second half of his tenure, Chrysler's stock fell 31 percent behind the general market.

Sadly, Iacocca had trouble leaving center stage and letting go of the perks of executive kingship. He postponed his retirement so many times that insiders at Chrysler began to joke that Iacocca stood for "I Am Chairman of Chrysler Corporation Always" ("Iacocca Hands Over the Keys," 1993). And when he did finally retire, he demanded that the board continue to provide a private jet and stock options ("How Chrysler Filled Detroit's Biggest Shoes," 1994). Later, he joined forces with noted takeover artist Kirk Kerkorian to launch a hostile takeover bid for Chrysler ("Why Certain Stocks," 1995; "Chrysler's New Plan," 1995).

Chrysler experienced a brief return to glory in the five years after Iacocca's retirement, but the company's underlying weaknesses eventually led to a buyout by German carmaker Daimler-Benz ("Will Success Spoil Chrysler?" 1994; "Company of the Year," 1997; "Daimler-Benz Will

Acquire Chrysler," 1998). Certainly, the demise of Chrysler as a stand-alone company does not rest entirely on Iacocca's shoulders (the next generation of management made the fateful decision to sell the company to the Germans), but the fact remains: Iacocca's brilliant turnaround in the early 1980s did not prove to be sustained and Chrysler failed to become an enduring great company.

Unwavering Resolve . . . to Do What Must Be Done

It is very important to grasp that Level 5 leadership is not just about humility and modesty. It is equally about ferocious resolve, an almost stoic determination to do whatever needs to be done to make the company great.

Indeed, we debated for a long time on the research team about how to describe the good-to-great leaders. Initially, we penciled in terms like "selfless executive" and "servant leader." But members of the team violently objected to these characterizations.

"Those labels don't ring true," said Anthony Chirikos. "It makes them sound weak or meek, but that's not at all the way I think of Darwin Smith or Colman Mockler. They would do almost anything to make the company great."

Then Eve Li suggested, "Why don't we just call them Level 5 leaders? If we put a label like 'selfless' or 'servant' on them, people will get entirely the wrong idea. We need to get people to engage with the whole concept, to see *both* sides of the coin. If you only get the humility side, you miss the whole idea."

Level 5 leaders are fanatically driven, infected with an incurable need to produce *results*. They will sell the mills or fire their brother, if that's what it takes to make the company great.

When George Cain became CEO of Abbott Laboratories, it sat in the bottom quartile of the pharmaceutical industry, a drowsy enterprise that had lived for years off its cash cow, erythromycin. Cain didn't have an inspiring personality to galvanize the company, but he had something much more powerful: inspired standards. He could not stand mediocrity in any form and was utterly intolerant of anyone who would accept the idea that good is good enough. Cain then set out to destroy one of the key causes of Abbott's mediocrity: nepotism. Systematically rebuilding both the board and the executive team with the best people he could find, Cain made it clear that neither family ties nor length of tenure would have anything to do with whether you held a key position in the company. If you didn't have the capacity to become the best executive in the industry in your span of responsibility, then you would lose your paycheck ("A Drug-maker's Return to Health," 1976; Kogan, 1963; research interview #1-A; research interview #1-G).

Such rigorous rebuilding might be expected from an outsider brought in to turn the company around, but Cain was an eighteen-year veteran insider *and* a family member, the son of a previous Abbott president. Hol-iday gatherings were probably tense for a few years in the Cain clan. ("Sorry I had to fire you. Want another slice of turkey?") In the end, though, family members were quite pleased with the performance of their stock, for Cain set in motion a profitable growth machine that, from its transition date in 1974 to 2000, created shareholder returns that beat the market 4.5 to 1, handily outperforming industry superstars Merck and Pfizer.

Upjohn, the direct comparison company to Abbott, also had family leadership during the same era as George Cain. Unlike George Cain, Upjohn's CEO never showed the same resolve to break the mediocrity of nepotism. By the time Abbott had filled all key seats with the best people, regardless of family background, Upjohn still had B-level family members holding key positions (*International Directory of Company Histories,* 1991; "The Medicine Men of Kalamazoo," 1959). Virtually identical companies with identical stock charts up to the point of transition, Upjohn then fell 89 percent behind Abbott over the next twenty-one years before capitulating in a merger to Pharmacia in 1995.

As an interesting aside, Darwin Smith, Colman Mockler, and George Cain came from inside the company. Stanley Gault, Al Dunlap, and Lee Iacocca rode in as saviors from the outside, trumpets blaring. This reflects a more systematic finding from our study. The evidence does not support the idea that you need an outside leader to come in and shake up the place to go from good to great. In fact, going for a high-profile outside change agent is *negatively correlated* with a sustained transformation from good to great.

Ten out of eleven good-to-great CEOs came from *inside* the company, three of them by family inheritance. The comparison companies turned to outsiders with *six times* greater frequency—yet they failed to produce sustained great results (Wilbanks, 1998).

A superb example of insider-driven change comes from Charles R. "Cork" Walgreen III, who transformed dowdy Walgreens into a company that outperformed the stock market by over fifteen times from the end of 1975 to January 1, 2000 (University of Chicago Center for Research in Securities Prices data; all dividends reinvested and adjusted for stock splits). After years of dialogue and debate within his executive team about

Walgreens' food-service operations, Cork sensed that the team had finally reached a watershed point of clarity and understanding: Walgreens' brightest future lay in convenient drugstores, not food service. Dan Jorndt, who succeeded Walgreen as CEO in 1998, described what happened next:

> Cork said at one of our planning committee meetings, "Okay, now I am going to draw the line in the sand. We are going to be out of the restaurant business completely in five years." At the time, we had over five hundred restaurants. You could have heard a pin drop. He said, "I want to let everybody know the clock is ticking." Six months later, we were at our next planning committee meeting and someone mentioned just in passing that we only had five years to be out of the restaurant business. Cork was not a real vociferous fellow. He sort of tapped on the table and said, "Listen, you have four and a half years. I said you had five years six months ago. Now you've got four and a half years." Well, that next day, things really clicked into gear to winding down our restaurant business. He never wavered. He never doubted; he never second-guessed. [research interview #10-D, pp. 9–10]

Like Darwin Smith selling the mills at Kimberly-Clark, Cork Walgreen's decision required stoic resolve. Not that food service was the largest part of the business (although it did add substantial profits to the bottom line). The real problem was more emotional. Walgreens had, after all, invented the malted milkshake and food service was a long-standing family tradition dating back to his grandfather. Some food-service outlets were even named after the CEO himself—a restaurant chain named Corky's. But no matter, if Walgreens had to fly in the face of long-standing family tradition in order to focus its resources where it could be the best in the world (convenient drugstores), Cork would do it. Quietly, doggedly, simply (Kogan and Kogan, 1989; research interview #10-F).

The quiet, dogged nature of Level 5 leaders showed up not only in big decisions, like selling off the food-service operations or fighting corporate raiders, but also in a personal style of sheer workmanlike diligence. Alan Wurtzel, a second-generation family member who took over his family's small company and turned it into Circuit City, perfectly captured the gestalt of this trait. When asked about differences between himself and his counterpart CEO at Circuit City's comparison company, Wurtzel summed up: "The show horse and the plow horse—he was more of a show horse, whereas I was more of a plow horse" (research interview #2-G, p. 10).

The Window and the Mirror

Alan Wurtzel's plow horse comment is fascinating in light of two other facts. First, he holds a doctor of jurisprudence degree from Yale—clearly, his plow horse nature had nothing to do with a lack of intelligence. Second, his plow horse approach set the stage for truly *best in show* results. Let me put it this way: If you had to choose between $1 invested in Circuit City or $1 invested in General Electric on the day that the legendary Jack Welch took over GE in 1981 and held to January 1, 2000, you would have been better off with Circuit City—by six times (University of Chicago Center for Research in Securities Prices data; all dividends reinvested and adjusted for stock splits). Not a bad performance, for a plow horse.

You might expect that extraordinary results like these would lead Alan Wurtzel to discuss the brilliant decisions he made. But when we asked him to list the top five factors in his company's transformation, ranked by importance, Wurtzel gave a surprising answer: The number-one factor was *luck*. "We were in a great industry, with the wind at our backs."

We pushed back, pointing out that we selected the good-to-great companies based on performance that surpassed their industry's average. Furthermore, the comparison company (Silo) was in the same industry, with the same wind and probably bigger sails! We debated the point for a few minutes, with Wurtzel continuing his preference for attributing much of his success to just being in the right place at the right time. Later, when asked to discuss the factors behind the enduring nature of the transformation, he said, "The first thing that comes to mind is luck. I was lucky to find the right successor" (research interview #2-G, p. 16).

Luck. What an odd factor to talk about. Yet the good-to-great executives talked a lot about luck in our interviews. In one interview with a Nucor executive, we asked why the company had such a remarkable track record of good decisions; he responded, "I guess we were just lucky" (research interview #7-H, p. 12). Joseph F. Cullman III, the Level 5 transition CEO of Philip Morris, flat-out refused to take credit for his company's success, attributing his good fortune to having great colleagues, successors, and predecessors (research interview #8-A). Even the book he wrote—a book he undertook at the urging of his colleagues, which he never intended to distribute widely outside the company—had the unusual title *I'm a Lucky Guy*. The opening paragraph reads: "I was a very lucky guy from the very beginning of my life: marvelous parents, good genes, lucky in love, lucky in business, and lucky when a Yale classmate had my orders changed to report to Washington, D.C., in early 1941, instead of to a ship that was sunk with all hands lost in the North Atlantic, lucky to be in the Navy, and lucky to be alive at eighty-five" (Cullman, 1998).

We were at first puzzled by this emphasis on good luck. After all, we found no evidence that the good-to-great companies were blessed with more good luck (or more bad luck, for that matter) than the comparison companies. Then we began to notice a contrasting pattern in the comparison executives: They credited substantial blame to bad luck, frequently bemoaning the difficulties of the environment they faced.

Compare Bethlehem Steel to Nucor. Both companies operated in the steel industry and produced hard-to-differentiate products. Both companies faced the competitive challenge of cheap imported steel. Yet executives at the two companies had completely different views of the same environment. Bethlehem Steel's CEO summed up the company's problems in 1983 by blaming imports: "Our first, second, and third problems are imports" ("Searching for Profits," 1983, p. C1). Ken Iverson and his crew at Nucor considered the same challenge from imports *a blessing,* a stroke of good fortune ("Aren't we lucky; steel is heavy, and they have to ship it all the way across the ocean, giving us a huge advantage!"). Iverson saw the first, second, and third problems facing the American steel industry not to be imports, but *management* ("Steel Man Ken Iverson," 1986). He even went so far as to speak out publicly against government protection against imports, telling a stunned gathering of fellow steel executives in 1977 that the real problems facing the American steel industry lay in the fact that management had failed to keep pace with innovation (Rodengen, 1997).

The emphasis on luck turns out to be part of a pattern that we came to call the *window and the mirror.* Level 5 leaders look out the window to apportion credit to factors outside themselves when things go well (and if they cannot find a specific person or event to give credit to, they credit good luck). At the same time, they look in the mirror to apportion responsibility, never blaming bad luck when things go poorly.

The comparison leaders did just the opposite. They'd look out the window for something or someone outside themselves to blame for poor results, but would preen in front of the mirror and credit themselves when things went well. Strangely, the window and the mirror do not reflect objective reality. Everyone outside the window points inside, directly at the Level 5 leader, saying, "He was the key; without his guidance and leadership, we would not have become a great company." And the Level 5 leader points right back out the window and says, "Look at all the great people and good fortune that made this possible; I'm a lucky guy." They're both right, of course. But the Level 5s would never admit that fact.

Cultivating Level 5 Leadership

Not long ago, I shared the Level 5 finding with a gathering of senior executives. A woman who had recently become chief executive of her company raised her hand and said, "I believe what you say about the good-to-great leaders. But I'm disturbed because when I look in the mirror, I know that I'm not Level 5, not yet anyway. Part of the reason I got this job is because of my ego drives. Are you telling me that I can't make this a great company if I'm not Level 5?"

"I don't know for certain that you absolutely must be a Level 5 leader to make your company great," I replied. "I will simply point back to the data: Of 1,435 companies that appeared on the Fortune 500 in our initial candidate list, only eleven made the very tough cut into our study. In those eleven, all of them had Level 5 leadership in key positions, including the CEO, at the pivotal time of transition."

She sat there, quiet for moment, and you could tell everyone in the room was mentally urging her to ask *the question*. Finally, she said, "Can you learn to become Level 5?"

Summary: The Two Sides of Level 5 Leadership

PROFESSIONAL WILL	PERSONAL HUMILITY
Creates superb results, a clear catalyst in the transition from good to great	Demonstrates a compelling modesty, shunning public adulation; never boastful
Demonstrates an unwavering resolve to do whatever must be done to produce the best long-term results, no matter how difficult	Acts with quiet, calm determination; relies principally on inspired standards, not inspiring charisma, to motivate
Sets the standard of building an enduring great company; will settle for nothing less	Channels ambition into the company, not the self; sets up successors for even greater success in the next generation
Looks in the mirror, not out the window, to apportion responsibility for poor results, never blaming other people, external factors, or bad luck	Looks out the window, not in the mirror, to apportion credit for the success of the company—to other people, external factors, and good luck

My hypothesis is that there are two categories of people: those who do not have the seed of Level 5 and those who do. The first category consists of people who could never in a million years bring themselves to subjugate their egoistic needs to the greater ambition of building something larger and more lasting than themselves. For these people, work will always be first and foremost about what they get—fame, fortune, adulation, power, whatever—not what they *build*, create, and contribute.

The great irony is that the animus and personal ambition that often drive people to positions of power stand at odds with the humility required for Level 5 leadership. When you combine that irony with the fact that boards of directors frequently operate under the false belief that they need to hire a larger-than-life, egocentric leader to make an organization great, you can quickly see why Level 5 leaders rarely appear at the top of our institutions.

The second category of people—and I suspect the larger group—consists of those who have the potential to evolve to Level 5; the capability resides within them, perhaps buried or ignored, but there nonetheless. And under the right circumstances—self-reflection, conscious personal development, a mentor, a great teacher, loving parents, a significant life experience, a Level 5 boss, or any number of other factors—they begin to develop.

In looking at the data, we noticed that some of the leaders in our study had significant life experiences that might have sparked or furthered their maturation. Darwin Smith fully blossomed after his experience with cancer. Joe Cullman was profoundly affected by his World War II experiences, particularly the last-minute change of orders that took him off a doomed ship on which he surely would have died (Cullman, 1998). A strong religious belief or conversion might also nurture development of Level 5 traits. Colman Mockler, for example, converted to evangelical Christianity while getting his MBA at Harvard, and later, according to the book *Cutting Edge,* became a prime mover in a group of Boston business executives who met frequently over breakfast to discuss the carryover of religious values to corporate life (McKibben, 1998). Other leaders in our study, however, had no obvious catalytic event; they just led normal lives and somehow ended up atop the Level 5 hierarchy.

I believe—although I cannot prove—that potential Level 5 leaders are highly prevalent in our society. The problem is not, in my estimation, a dearth of potential Level 5 leaders. They exist all around us, if we just know what to look for. And what is that? Look for situations where extraordinary results exist but where no individual steps forth to claim excess credit. You will likely find a potential Level 5 leader at work.

For your own development, I would love to be able to give you a list of steps for becoming Level 5, but we have no solid research data that would support a credible list. Our research exposed Level 5 as a key component inside the black box of what it takes to shift a company from good to great. Yet inside that black box is yet another black box—namely, the inner development of a *person* to Level 5. We could speculate on what might be inside that inner black box, but it would mostly be just that—speculation. So, in short, Level 5 is a very satisfying idea, a powerful idea, and, to produce the best transitions from good to great, perhaps an essential idea. A "Ten-Step List to Level 5" would trivialize the concept.

My best advice, based on the research, is to begin practicing the other good-to-great disciplines we discovered. We found a symbiotic relationship between Level 5 and the remaining findings. On the one hand, Level 5 traits enable you to implement the other findings; on the other hand, practicing the other findings helps you to become Level 5. Think of it this way: This chapter is about what Level 5s *are;* the rest of the book describes what they do. Leading with the other disciplines can help you move in the right direction. There is no guarantee that doing so will turn you into a full-fledged Level 5, but it gives you a tangible place to begin.

We cannot say for sure what percentage of people have the seed within, or how many of those can nurture it. Even those of us who discovered Level 5 on the research team do not know for ourselves whether we will succeed in fully evolving to Level 5. And yet, all of us who worked on the finding have been deeply affected and inspired by the idea. Darwin Smith, Colman Mockler, Alan Wurtzel, and all the other Level 5s we learned about have become models for us, something worthy to aspire toward. Whether or not we make it all the way to Level 5, it is worth the effort. For like all basic truths about what is best in human beings, when we catch a glimpse of that truth, we know that our own lives and all that we touch will be the better for the effort.

Level 5 Leadership: Key Points

• *Every good-to-great company had Level 5 leadership during the pivotal transition years.* "Level 5" refers to a five-level hierarchy of executive capabilities, with Level 5 at the top. Level 5 leaders embody a paradoxical mix of personal humility and professional will. They are ambitious, to be sure, but ambitious first and foremost for the company, not themselves.

Level 5 leaders set up their successors for even greater success in the next generation, whereas egocentric Level 4 leaders often set up their successors for failure.

Level 5 leaders display a compelling modesty, are self-effacing and understated. In contrast, two-thirds of the comparison companies had leaders with gargantuan personal egos that contributed to the demise or continued mediocrity of the company.

Level 5 leaders are fanatically driven, infected with an incurable need to produce sustained results. They are resolved to do whatever it takes to make the company great, no matter how big or hard the decisions.

• *Level 5 leaders display a workmanlike diligence—more plow horse than show horse.* Level 5 leaders look out the window to attribute success to factors other than themselves. When things go poorly, however, they look in the mirror and blame themselves, taking full responsibility. The comparison CEOs often did just the opposite—they looked in the mirror to take credit for success, but out the window to assign blame for disappointing results.

One of the most damaging trends in recent history is the tendency (especially by boards of directors) to select dazzling, celebrity leaders and to de-select potential Level 5 leaders. I believe that potential Level 5 leaders exist all around us, if we just know what to look for, and that many people have the potential to evolve into Level 5.

UNEXPECTED FINDINGS

• Larger-than-life, celebrity leaders who ride in from the outside are negatively correlated with going from good to great. Ten of eleven good-to-great CEOs came from *inside* the company, whereas the comparison companies tried outside CEOs six times more often.

• Level 5 leaders attribute much of their success to good luck, rather than personal greatness.

• We were not looking for Level 5 leadership in our research, or anything like it, but the data was overwhelming and convincing. It is an empirical, not an ideological, finding.

REFERENCES

"After the Fall." *Across the Board,* Apr. 1996, pp. 28–33.
"The Battle of the Bottoms." *Forbes,* Mar. 24, 1997, p. 98.
"Chain Saw Al to the Rescue?" *Forbes,* Aug. 26, 1996.
"Chairman Quits Post." *New York Times,* Nov. 17, 1992, p. D5.
"Chrysler's New Plan: Sell Cars." *Fortune,* June 26, 1995, p. 19.
Company "Chronology." Gillette corporate typescript, 1995.
"Company of the Year: Chrysler Has the Hot Cars. More Important, It Has a Smart, Disciplined Management Team." Jan. 13, 1997, p. 82.

Cullman, J. F., III. *I'm a Lucky Guy.* Richmond, Va.: Philip Morris, 1998.

"Daimler-Benz Will Acquire Chrysler in $36 Billion Deal That Will Reshape Industry." *New York Times,* May 7, 1998, p. A6.

"Darwin E. Smith, 69, Executive Who Remade a Paper Company," *New York Times,* Dec. 28, 1995, p. B9.

"Did CEO Dunlap Save Scott Paper—or Just Pretty It Up? The Shredder." *Business Week,* Jan. 15, 1996.

"A Drugmaker's Return to Health." *Business Week,* Apr. 26, 1976, p. 38.

Dunlap, A. J., with Andelman, B. *Mean Business: How I Save Bad Companies and Make Good Companies Great.* New York: Fireside, 1997.

"$5.5 Million Declined by Ex-Official." *Washington Post,* Jan. 22, 1992, p. F1.

Foote, S. *The Civil War: A Narrative. Red River to Appomattox.* New York: Random House, 1975.

"Former CEO of K-C Dies," *Dallas Morning News,* Dec. 27, 1995.

"How Chrysler Filled Detroit's Biggest Shoes." *Wall Street Journal,* Sept. 7, 1994, p. B1.

"Iacocca Hands Over the Keys to Chrysler." *Investor's Business Daily,* Jan. 4, 1993, p. 1.

"Iacocca's Last Stand." *Fortune,* Apr. 20, 1992, p. 63.

International Directory of Company Histories, vol. 3. Chicago: St. James Press, 1991.

"Is Rubbermaid Reacting Too Late?" *New York Times,* Dec. 22, 1996, p. A1.

Jones, C., and Duffy, D. "Media Hype Analysis." Unpublished *Good to Great* research project, 1998, 1999.

Kelly, K. "Darwin Smith May Have Done Too Good a Job," *Business Week,* Aug. 1, 1988, p. 57.

"Kimberly-Clark—Aiming for the Consumer." *Financial World,* Apr. 1, 1970, p. 15.

"Kimberly-Clark Bets, Wins on Innovation." *Wall Street Journal,* Nov. 22, 1991, p. A5.

Kogan, H. *The Long White Line: The Story of Abbott Laboratories.* New York: Random House, 1963.

Kogan, H., and Kogan, R. *Pharmacist to the Nation.* Deerfield, Ill.: Walgreens Co., 1989.

"Managing: Leaders of Corporate Change." *Fortune,* Dec. 14, 1992, p. 104.

"Maxwell Relinquishes Rights to $5.5 Million Final Retirement Payment." *PR Newswire,* Jan. 21, 1992.

McCullough, D. *Truman.* New York: Simon & Schuster, 1992.

McKibben, G. *Cutting Edge: Gillette's Journey to Global Leadership.* Boston: Harvard Business School Press, 1998.

McPherson, J. M. *Battle Cry of Freedom: The Civil War Era.* New York: Ballantine, 1989.

"The Medicine Men of Kalamazoo." *Fortune,* July 1959, p. 106.

"Only the Paranoid Survive." *Worth Online,* Oct. 1996.

"Paper Tiger: How Kimberly-Clark Wraps Its Bottom Line in Disposable Huggies." *Wall Street Journal,* July 23, 1987, p. 1.

"President Iacocca." *Wall Street Journal,* July 28, 1982, p. 1.

"Rae Takes on the Paper Industry's Tough Lone Wolf," *Globe and Mail,* July 20, 1991.

Ricardo-Campbell, R. *Resisting Hostile Takeovers: The Case of Gillette.* Westport, Conn.: Praeger, 1997.

Rodengen, J. L. *The Legend of the Nucor Corporation.* Fort Lauderdale, Fla.: Write Stuff, 1997.

"Rubbermaid's Sad Succession Tale." *New York Times,* July 5, 1987, p. C1.

"Searching for Profits at Bethlehem." *New York Times,* Dec. 25, 1983, p. C1.

"Sincere Tyranny," *Forbes,* Jan. 28, 1985, p. 54.

"Steel Man Ken Iverson." *Inc.,* Apr. 1, 1986, p. 40.

"Why Certain Stocks." *Wall Street Journal,* Apr. 13, 1995, p. A1.

Wicks, W. W. *Shared Values: A History of Kimberly-Clark.* Old Saybrook, Conn.: Greenwich Publishing Group, 1997.

Wilbanks, L. "CEO Analysis Unit." Unpublished *Good to Great* research project, 1998.

"Will Success Spoil Chrysler?" *Fortune,* Jan. 10, 1994.

4

THE UNHEROIC
SIDE OF LEADERSHIP

NOTES FROM THE SWAMP

Jerome T. Murphy

WHEN I ACCEPTED my current position as associate dean, I had grand ideas about helping to lead the Harvard Graduate School of Education in its dealings with such challenging issues as organizational mission and fiscal stability. Here was a chance to influence the direction of an important institution. Early on, however, I was abruptly brought down to earth by a fellow faculty member. In the midst of a dinner conversation about world affairs, he suddenly blinked and said, "By the way, what are you going to do about the odor strips?" Sensing my puzzlement, he pressed on, "I am allergic to the new odor strips in the fourth-floor bathroom, and something needs to be done!" I expressed concern and moved off to the bar to ponder the heroic aspects of decanal life at Harvard.

In my ponderings, I recalled a poster I had once seen tacked to the office wall of a seasoned administrator. It read:

> NOTICE
> The objective of all dedicated department employees should be to thoroughly analyze all situations, anticipate all problems prior to their occurrence, have answers for these problems, and move swiftly to solve these problems when called upon. . . .
> However . . .

> When you are up to your ass in alligators it is difficult to remind yourself that your initial objective was to drain the swamp.

What follows are some observations about educational leadership by a researcher-turned-administrator immersed in the everyday reality of the swamp. I am struck by how the popular view of the leader as hero fails to capture the character of leadership in a world of grand designs and daily problems. Leaders are quiet lambs as much as roaring lions, and leadership is not found only at the top of an organization. (Many of the ideas herein grew out of conversations with and out of the writings of Louis B. Barnes and Barry C. Jentz. See, for example, Barnes and Kriger, 1986; Jentz and Wofford, 1979.)

Today's Top Tune

Leadership is back in fashion in education,[1] and the conventional wisdom suggests a heroic boss who meets at least six expectations. First and most insistently, leaders are supposed to possess a clear personal vision. A sense of purpose is central to success, and center-stage leaders define it for their organizations. Second, leaders are extremely knowledgeable; they have the right answers to the most pressing problems. Third, leaders are expected to be strong: to display initiative, courage, and tenacity. Fourth, leaders communicate forcefully, using their knowledge to convey their vision aggressively and persuasively. Fifth, leaders amass power and use it for organizational improvement. Finally, leaders are take-charge individuals who solve knotty problems along the way as they move toward achieving their personal visions. (For a similar portrayal of the conventional wisdom on leadership, see Heifetz and Sinder, 1987.)

In a scathing review of the new literature on leadership, Robert Reich depicts the popular image of corporate heads thus:

> They are crusty, strong-willed characters who have no patience for fools or slackers. They buck the system. They take no crap. They win. . . . [They] are colorful and outspoken. They are the antithesis of the gray-flanneled professional of yore. . . . They believe in "hands-on" management. They want to confront people directly, touch them, challenge them, and motivate them through the sheer force of personality. . . . [They] are missionaries. Their stories take on an evangelical tone because these men have been inspired. They have found meaning and value in the services they provide. They manage their enterprises by ensuring that employees share those same meanings and values. . . . The evangelical message is that with enough guts, tenacity, and charisma

you too—gentle reader—can be a great manager, a captain of industry. [Reich, 1985, p. 26]

In a word, the leader is a lion. Those who lionize leadership miss important behind-the-scenes aspects of day-to-day leadership. They depict the grand designs without the niggling problems. They assume that leadership is the exclusive preserve of the heroic boss.

Those who lionize leadership set unrealistic standards for measuring administrative success. For example, only a relative handful of individuals possess extraordinary vision. Unrealistic standards make it easy to devalue ordinary competence and to view leadership as the only important ingredient in organizational success.

The image of the leader as hero can also undermine conscientious administrators who think that they should live up to these expectations. If leaders are supposed to have all the answers, for example, how do administrators respond when they are totally confused about what to do? If they have learned that leaders are consistently strong, what do administrators think of themselves when they are terrified about handling a difficult situation?

Finally, notions of heroism misconstrue the character of organizational leadership in many situations. Problems are typically so complex and so ambiguous that to define and resolve them requires the knowledge and participation of more than a visionary leader.

At best, the image of the leader as lion depicts only one side of the coin. Moreover, this heroic image ignores the invisible leadership of lower-level staff members throughout effective organizations.

In an attempt to restore balance, allow me to present the *unheroic* side of the six dimensions of leadership that I cited above: developing a shared vision (as well as defining a personal vision), asking questions (as well as having answers), coping with weakness (as well as displaying strength), listening and acknowledging (as well as talking and persuading), depending on others (as well as exercising power), and letting go (as well as taking charge). These unheroic—and seemingly obvious—activities capture the time, the attention, the intellect, and the emotions of administrative leaders who often work offstage to make educational organizations succeed.

Developing a Shared Vision

As a policy researcher, I am struck by the similarities between the current discussions of vision in organizations and earlier discussions of policy in government. Policy makers made policy, so the theory went, and implementers carried it out. Blueprints for action were carefully laid out by the best and the brightest—and then were installed by presumably less creative bureaucrats. Similarly today, many observers believe that organizational vision is articulated by the boss and then installed by the staff. Leaders lead; followers follow.

However, the research of the past twenty years on policy implementation demonstrates that this model seldom describes reality. Programs are typically characterized by shifting goals, changing activities, and wide variation across sites. Program priorities and content are determined as staff members learn from experience and as programs adapt to their environments. Purposes and policies are often "discovered" through an evolutionary process. In other words, policies are less often installed than negotiated to maturation over time, and true policy makers can be found both at the top and at the bottom of the system.

Likewise, in educational organizations it is rare to see a clearly defined vision articulated by a leader at the top of the hierarchy and then installed by followers. Top administrators tend to point out a general direction rather than a specific destination; they are more likely to provide a scaffolding for collaboration than a blueprint for action. They take the initiative, set the agenda, establish the pace, and contribute to the conversation—all the while involving other key actors and then clarifying and synthesizing their views. During this process, organizational vision is often discovered, since vision setters, like policy makers, are frequently dispersed throughout an organization.

A close look at the development of organizational vision shows the untidiness, plural parentage, and emergent nature of that process.[2] Leaders act as catalysts. In the words of Ronald Heifetz and Riley Sinder, "A leader becomes a guide, interpreter, and stimulus of engagement." A leader's vision is "the grain of sand in the oyster, not the pearl" (Heifetz and Sinder, 1987, pp. 194, 197).

Asking Questions

Striking similarities also exist between the work of researchers, particularly those who do fieldwork, and administrative leaders. Members of both groups spend a great deal of time formulating and asking good questions. Both groups are in the business of seeking knowledge. Both groups establish and nurture intelligence networks.

Gathering intelligence is crucial because administrative life is marked by great uncertainty, confusion, and distortion. Heroes and saints may be in a "state of grace," but administrators are regularly in a "state of ignorance."

Of course, effective administrators bring to their jobs a store of relevant knowledge, such as an understanding of schools and a firm grasp of theories of organizational change. But much of what happens—or *should* happen—in organizations is highly dependent on information that administrators frequently do not possess. This includes "local" knowledge (the histories, key actors, rituals, and contexts of various units within the organization); "situational" knowledge (the who, what, where, when, and how of a given issue); and "people" knowledge (staff members' thoughts and feelings, their perceptions of reality, and the meanings they attach to these perceptions).

These kinds of data are essential. But management information systems typically don't provide such data, because they are confidential, sensitive, verbal, or not generally available. Crucial information is often highly emotional in content, and such information is kept from top administrators. Yet a school administrator would be well served by knowing such things as the underlying feelings of the parents who oppose a new preschool initiative, the rumors on how an administrator landed his or her job, the level of morale in the English department, what issues currently concern students, the latest word from the grapevine regarding the superintendent's leadership, and the political obstacles to expanding the arts program.

Administrators need to recognize and acknowledge their ignorance and then take action. They need to develop an informal "system" of constantly gathering information—from meetings, chance encounters, and casual conversations (by phone or in person) with candid and knowledgeable colleagues. Administrators need to recognize that the ability and willingness to ask good questions is central; administrators, like researchers, should be judged by the quality of their questions. (For ideas that can be adapted to fit the information-gathering needs of administrators, see Murphy, 1980.)

There are limits, of course. Administrators need to ask questions freely, but they also need to know when to stop. Too much knowledge, or the endless pursuit of knowledge, stalls action. Not knowing all the complexities is sometimes a good thing. As Albert Hirschman has noted: "The only way we can bring our creative resources fully into play is by misjudging the nature of the task, by presenting it to ourselves as more routine, simple, undemanding of genuine creativity than it will turn out to be. Or, put differently: since we necessarily underestimate our creativity, it is desirable that we underestimate to a roughly similar extent the difficulties of the tasks we face" (quoted in Nakamura and Smallwood, 1980, p. 175).

Too much information, as well as too little, can be a problem.

Coping with Weakness

"Great man" theories of leadership—the leader as lion—are making a comeback. Deep in the swamp, however, exceptional leaders not only draw on their strengths but also accept their weaknesses and develop a capacity to cope.

To deal with personal deficiencies in skills, knowledge, attributes, or disposition, four coping strategies seem particularly useful. Those strategies are matching, compensation, candor, and acceptance.

Matching. Wise administrators recognize that administrative positions differ significantly in their requirements. Some positions require rhetorical artistry, for example, while others call for political skill, creative genius, or a flair for coordination. Administrators who succeed hold positions that match their talents and their personalities. As a corporate head once put it, "You can't grow lemons in Antarctica."

Compensation. Successful leaders have the capacity to recognize their own shortcomings, and they take steps to compensate for them. They surround themselves with staff members who have complementary skills and inclinations, and they rely on these individuals. They often hire staff members whose knowledge of particular areas exceeds their own—people who are able and willing to criticize the boss's pet ideas.

Candor. Administrators need to acknowledge to close associates their weaknesses and the feelings that those weaknesses engender. I am not advocating detailed confessions, but forthright and critical self-disclosure on significant job-related issues. A leader who is unwilling to treat subordinates as colleagues and to share self-assessments and feelings with them cannot expect shared confidences in return. Without candid exchanges, crucial intelligence will be withheld, jeopardizing decision making and implementation efforts.

Acceptance. Psychologists say that one must recognize, acknowledge, and accept one's weaknesses and the feelings associated with them before one can move beyond them. If an administrator is fearful of giving negative feedback to a subordinate, for example, the administrator is wiser to accept those feelings and act within that framework than to try to banish the feelings as signs of weakness. Though it is counterintuitive, "giving in seems to allow one to move forward and act successfully" (Jentz and Wofford, 1979). These coping strategies are far easier to advocate than to implement. Individuals who function superbly in one administrative position may be tempted to think that they can handle any administrative position, ample evidence to the contrary notwithstanding (see, for example, Doig and Hargrove, 1987). It can be threatening to be surrounded by smarter people. Because leaders tend to be lionized, they often find it difficult to acknowledge a need for help. Moreover, because they have learned that leaders are consistently strong, administrators often have trouble accepting the emotional upheavals of administrative life. Paradoxically, the more a leader acknowledges and accepts personal weaknesses and feelings, the more effective he or she becomes.

At the heart of all these coping strategies, of course, are self-knowledge and the capacity to act on it. These traits are rare, I suspect, among those who aspire to positions of leadership. John Gardner is on target when he says: "It is a curious fact that from infancy on we accumulate an extensive knowledge of the effect others have on us, but we are far into adulthood before we begin to comprehend the impact we have on others. It is a lesson young leaders must learn" (Gardner, 1987, p. 20). Young leaders must also learn the impact they have on themselves.

Listening and Acknowledging

That leaders should be good listeners seems obvious. Yet very little high-quality listening goes on in the swamp. Why is listening such a problem for leaders?

The heroic image of leadership is one source of the problem. When leaders believe that they possess—or should possess—all the important information and knowledge, they do not see listening to others as essential. Can-do administrators persuade others to adopt their visions, and they give short shrift to alternative perspectives. To such administrators, listening is passive, reactive, and thus unappealing. To listen is to appear uninformed, weak, and inactive. To be a lion, one cannot act like a lamb.

In addition, good listening fails to occur because administrators often make faulty assumptions about others. They assume, for example, that their colleagues share—or *should* share—their own worldview. They assume that confrontations signify ill will, rather than a misunderstanding or a differing perspective. Recognizing that people are different and giving others the benefit of the doubt are behaviors that facilitate listening.

Administrators also underestimate the skill and effort that are required to listen well (Jentz and Wofford, 1979). Good listening involves an active effort to understand the world from another's perspective. It requires both an instant analysis of what has been said (and of the accompanying tone and body posture) and a sense of what has been left unsaid. Good listening involves testing aloud what one has heard, to make certain that the speaker's meaning has been captured. Good listening requires the ability to act as if the speaker's topic is central—even when the listener is preoccupied with other matters. To listen well takes practice, patience, energy, and hard work.

Clearly, good listening is essential for gathering information about organizational activities. In my experience, however, listening is crucial for other reasons as well.

First, when an administrator fails to understand the varying perspectives of others, organizational problems do not get solved—and new ones are likely to be created. It is not enough to know just the facts; a leader also needs to understand the feelings, the meanings, and the perceptions that are tied to those facts. Such understanding requires careful listening to what is said and careful reading between the lines.

At a more emotional level (and administrative work is highly emotional), listening is frequently the best thing that an administrator can do. Colleagues often want only an opportunity to express their concerns. Many professionals are passionate about their work; not surprisingly, they get upset when things go wrong. Sometimes they get upset when nothing is wrong, simply because no one is listening to them. The very process of verbalizing frustrations and having them acknowledged often enables these individuals to move forward. Asked about his job change, a former therapist who is now a dean smiled and replied, "Now my patients have tenure."

Moreover, since demands on organizational resources typically outstrip the supply, and even reasonable demands cannot be met, listening is often the *only* thing an administrator can do. Under these circumstances, there is a big difference between a disappointed employee (who can deal with the limited resources) and an employee who feels unheard (and therefore angry).

Finally, one rule of thumb in administrative life invariably turns out to be correct: if you don't listen to others, they won't listen to you. A key to effective persuasion, then, is the capacity to listen to the perspectives of others. To be a lion, one must first be a lamb.

Depending on Others

The study of policy implementation has demonstrated that different levels of government are highly dependent on one another and on competing interests. In our federal system of shared power, hierarchical strategies based on assumptions of centralized authority are simply inadequate in promoting change. Softer strategies are required—strategies that mix authority, persuasion, and incentives; strategies that take other interests into account. Even for Presidents, orders don't work, as Richard Neustadt (1960) documented more than 25 years ago.

Likewise, top administrators in educational organizations are surprisingly dependent on others to bring about change. This dependence on others seems typical of even the most hierarchical organizations. In the army, for example, generals depend on the leadership of lower-ranking soldiers to carry out objectives (Barnes, 1987). In part, this is a matter of shared power and the current shift toward empowering teachers. But it is also a matter of skill: teachers and other staff members possess expertise and information that are crucial for defining problems and making progress. And it is a matter of will: if those at the bottom don't accept responsibility for resolving problems, change efforts will come unglued.

Thus educational organizations are increasingly marked by a high level of mutual dependence. The superintendent's success depends on the actions of the principals within the school system; the dean's success, on the actions of the tenured faculty; the principal's success, on the teachers—and vice versa.

While hierarchical strategies for promoting change are becoming outmoded, new strategies that are based on an assumption of mutual dependence need further development. Administrators need to find better ways to involve teachers and other staff members and to help them adjust to conflicting interests. Even when they are not required to do so, administrators need to depend on others for active leadership because, by sharing power and asking for help, they can tap latent resources in an organization. By relying on staff members, administrators give them a greater sense of efficacy, responsibility, and control. That leads, in turn, to organizational progress.

The capacity for dependency is rare among top administrators, however. Having been taught that top administrators exercise power, they don't want to appear weak. Paradoxically, when power within an organization is shared and leadership is shifted among various staff members, the administrator's position is often strengthened, reflecting what sociologists call the norm of reciprocity: if you share your power, I'll share my power in return. In other words, leaders can often achieve results by acting like followers and depending on followers to act like leaders.

Letting Go

An important dimension of organizational leadership is dealing with what John Dewey called problem situations. Such situations come in various forms: student test scores continue to decline; the boiler has broken down; a teacher is livid about his treatment by a parent; the history department is ignoring the new curriculum; faculty members are complaining about inadequate resources. Such situations are the everyday stuff of ordinary leadership—punctuated occasionally by loftier issues. How does an administrator respond, as he or she skips, in the words of Henry Rosovsky (1987, p. 37), "from the sublime to the ridiculous five times a day"?

One crucial step is deciding who should address a problem situation. Many times, of course, an issue is important enough to demand the intense involvement of a take-charge leader. Often, however, the lion needs to let go. The administrator's "problem" is not usually solving problems per se, but helping others define and resolve problems—doing what Russell Ackoff calls "managing messes" (quoted in Schön, 1983, p. 16).

Insuring that messes end up on the right desks is surprisingly complicated, however. Employees typically view the top administrator as the chief problem solver. I have dubbed the outcome the "goose theory of leadership." Honking and hissing like geese, faculty and staff members will cruise into the boss's office, ruffle their feathers, poop on the rug, and leave. It then becomes the boss's job to clean up the mess.

This happened to me one summer day when a program director phoned me at home at 7:30 A.M. to announce: "We've got some big dormitory problems. A student says his room is filthy, with ashes on the floor and two used condoms under his bed!" Indeed, this matter deserved prompt attention. But sensing that the problem was headed my way and believing that the program director should take responsibility instead, I raised some questions and then closed with the words, "I know you can handle it."

Some administrators unwittingly adopt the goose theory of leadership because they like to solve problems and therefore take them on. (Administrators often reach the top because of their problem-solving skills, and it is always rewarding to do what one knows how to do.) Many administrators also believe that their job is to be responsive to demands; therefore, they automatically assume responsibility for any problem dumped on their rug.

The challenge is to be responsive while simultaneously developing a sense of responsibility in others. This involves encouraging subordinates to take risks—and back them up when they fail. It means working hard to make other people successful—and giving them the credit.[3] In short, taking charge involves letting go.

In letting go, administrators must decide to ignore issues that they believe ought not to be ignored and to do some things superficially that ought to be done with careful attention. A conscientious leader always has more high priorities to address than time and organizational resources allow. In the face of competing demands, deciding to do some things badly, letting go before the time seems right, and coping with the consequences are all ingredients of leadership behavior.

Administrative leadership involves both grand designs and careful attention to the mundane. High-minded intentions are inextricably intertwined with such everyday problems as allergies to odor strips.

Perhaps it feels less than heroic to help develop a shared vision, to ask questions, to acknowledge weakness, to listen carefully, to depend on others, and to let go. Yet, where heroism is concerned, less can be more. To be a lamb is really to be a lion.

NOTES

1. Within the last year, for example, the National Commission on Excellence in Educational Administration issued its report *Leaders for America's Schools;* Arkansas Governor Bill Clinton, as chairman of the Educational Commission of the States, pointed to leadership as the most important yet least understood aspect of school reform; and the Office of Educational Research and Information announced plans for a $5 million research center to study educational leadership.

   If belief in leadership as the ticket to organizational success waxes and wanes, it is clearly ascendant at the moment.

2. If this view of organizational vision is accurate, a puzzle still remains: Why do so many accounts of effective schools mention visionary principals? I suspect that three factors are at work. First, in some schools (as in some corporations and government agencies), there are extraordinary visionaries who dominate their organizations. However, my guess is that such visionaries are in the minority, even among effective principals. Second, the accounts may in part reflect what researchers call "the treachery of recollection" or "the reconstruction of biography." In other words, gaps in stories are filled in with what *might* have happened, and confusing and uncertain plans are recalled as logical, coherent, and rational acts. Finally, respondents often say what the society expects them to say, and our society expects leaders to have a clear sense of purpose, both in their organizational lives and in their personal lives.

3. I am particularly indebted to Harold Howe II for this thought.

REFERENCES

Barnes, L. B. "Leadership from Strange Places." Paper presented at the Wingspread Invitational Seminar on Leadership Research, Racine, Wis., April 1987.

Barnes, L. B., and Kriger, M. P. "The Hidden Side of Organizational Leadership," *Sloan Management Review,* Fall 1986, pp. 15–25.

Doig, J. W., and Hargrove, E. C. (eds.). *Leadership and Innovation: A Biographical Perspective on Entrepreneurs in Government.* Baltimore: Johns Hopkins University Press, 1987.

Gardner, J. W. *Leadership Development* (Leadership Papers, no. 7). Washington, D.C.: INDEPENDENT SECTOR, 1987.

Heifetz, R. A., and Sinder, R. M. "Political Leadership: Managing the Public's Problem Solving." In R. B. Reich, (ed.), *The Power of Public Ideas.* Cambridge, Mass.: Ballinger, 1987.

Jentz, B. C., and Wofford, J. W. *Leadership and Learning: Personal Change in a Professional Setting.* New York: McGraw-Hill, 1979.

Murphy, J. T. *Getting the Facts: A Fieldwork Guide for Evaluators and Policy Analysts.* Santa Monica, Calif.: Goodyear, 1980.

Nakamura, R. T., and Smallwood, F. *The Politics of Policy Implementation.* New York: St. Martin's, 1980.

Neustadt, R. E. *Presidential Power: The Politics of Leadership.* New York: Wiley, 1960.

Reich, R. B. "The Executive's New Clothes." *New Republic,* May 13, 1985, p. 26.

Rosovsky, H. "Deaning." *Harvard Magazine,* Jan./Feb. 1987.

Schön, D. A. *The Reflective Practitioner: How Professionals Think in Action.* New York: Basic Books, 1983.

5

THE FIVE PRACTICES
OF EXEMPLARY
LEADERSHIP

James M. Kouzes
Barry Z. Posner

FACED WITH DIFFERENT CULTURES and difficult circumstances, Lindsay
Levin and Alan Keith each seized the opportunity to lead. They chose a
pioneering path and led their organizations to new summits of excellence.
And although their cultures and circumstances are distinct, we learned
some important lessons about leadership from Lindsay, Alan, and the
thousands of others who told us their personal-best experiences. From
them we learned what it takes to mobilize other people—by the force of
their own free will and despite hard work and potential risk—to want to
climb to the summit.

Through our studies of personal-best leadership experiences, we've discovered that ordinary people who guide others along pioneering journeys
follow rather similar paths. Though each case we looked at was unique
in expression, each path was also marked by some common patterns of
action. Leadership is not at all about personality; it's about practice. We've
forged these common practices into a model of leadership, and we offer
it here as guidance for leaders to follow as they attempt to keep their own
bearings and guide others toward peak achievements.

As we looked deeper into the dynamic process of leadership, through
case analyses and survey questionnaires, we uncovered five practices common to personal-best leadership experiences. When getting extraordinary

things done in organizations, leaders engage in these Five Practices of
Exemplary Leadership:

- Model the way
- Inspire a shared vision
- Challenge the process
- Enable others to act
- Encourage the heart

These practices—which we discuss briefly in this chapter and then in
depth in later chapters—aren't the private property of the people we studied or of a few select shining stars. They're available to anyone, in any organization or situation, who accepts the leadership challenge. And they're
not the accident of a special moment in history. They've stood the test of
time, and our most recent research confirms that they're just as relevant
today as they were when we first began our investigation over two
decades ago—if not more so.

Model the Way

Titles are granted, but it's your behavior that wins you respect. As Gayle
Hamilton, a director with Pacific Gas & Electric Company, told us, "I
would never ask anyone to do anything I was unwilling to do first."[1] This
sentiment was shared across all the cases that we collected. Exemplary
leaders know that if they want to gain commitment and achieve the highest standards, they must be models of the behavior they expect of others.
Leaders model the way.

To effectively model the behavior they expect of others, leaders must
first be clear about their guiding principles. Lindsay Levin says, "You have
to open up your heart and let people know what you really think and
believe. This means talking about your values." Alan Keith adds that one
of the most significant leadership lessons he would pass along is, "You
must lead from what you believe." Leaders must find their own voice, and
then they must clearly and distinctively give voice to their values. As the
personal-best stories illustrate, leaders are supposed to stand up for their
beliefs, so they'd better have some beliefs to stand up for.

Eloquent speeches about common values, however, aren't nearly enough.
Leaders' deeds are far more important than their words when determining
how serious they really are about what they say. Words and deeds must be
consistent. Exemplary leaders go first. They go first by setting the example

through daily actions that demonstrate they are deeply committed to their beliefs. Toni-Ann Lueddecke, for example, believes that there are no unimportant tasks in an organization's efforts at excellence. She demonstrates this to her associates in her eight Gymboree Play & Music centers in New Jersey by her actions. As just one example, she sometimes scrubs floors in addition to teaching classes.

The personal-best projects we heard about in our research were all distinguished by relentless effort, steadfastness, competence, and attention to detail. We were also struck by how the actions leaders took to set an example were often simple things. Sure, leaders had operational and strategic plans. But the examples they gave were not about elaborate designs. They were about the power of spending time with someone, of working side by side with colleagues, of telling stories that made values come alive, of being highly visible during times of uncertainty, and of asking questions to get people to think about values and priorities. Modeling the way is essentially about earning the right and the respect to lead through direct individual involvement and action. People first follow the person, then the plan.

Inspire a Shared Vision

When people described to us their personal-best leadership experiences, they told of times when they imagined an exciting, highly attractive future for their organization. They had visions and dreams of what could be. They had absolute and total personal belief in those dreams, and they were confident in their abilities to make extraordinary things happen. Every organization, every social movement, begins with a dream. The dream or vision is the force that invents the future. Lindsay Levin saw a new and even more responsive Whites Group; Alan Keith imagined people at Hanna-Barbera taking creativity seriously—and playfully—to rejuvenate and reenergize a decaying organizational culture.

Leaders inspire a shared vision. They gaze across the horizon of time, imagining the attractive opportunities that are in store when they and their constituents arrive at a distant destination. Leaders have a desire to make something happen, to change the way things are, to create something that no one else has ever created before. In some ways, leaders live their lives backward. They see pictures in their mind's eye of what the results will look like even before they've started their project, much as an architect draws a blueprint or an engineer builds a model. Their clear image of the future pulls them forward. Yet visions seen only by leaders are insufficient to create an organized movement or a significant change in a company. A person with no constituents is not a leader, and people will not follow until they accept a vision as their own. Leaders cannot command commitment, only inspire it.

To enlist people in a vision, leaders must know their constituents and speak their language. People must believe that leaders understand their needs and have their interests at heart. Leadership is a dialogue, not a monologue. To enlist support, leaders must have intimate knowledge of people's dreams, hopes, aspirations, visions, and values.

Leaders breathe life into the hopes and dreams of others and enable them to see the exciting possibilities that the future holds. Leaders forge a unity of purpose by showing constituents how the dream is for the common good. Leaders ignite the flame of passion in others by expressing enthusiasm for the compelling vision of their group. Leaders communicate their passion through vivid language and an expressive style.

And leaders are in all places. When he was named captain of the soccer team as a high school junior, Dave Praklet knew he would have to do something to inspire his teammates to always give 110 percent. As he explained to us: "I had to get personal with them and tell them how good it feels to win a league championship. Or how good it feels as you step on the field for a championship game—how the adrenaline sends a tingling feeling through your entire body. Recounting these memorable moments helped me inspire the team to want to work hard. They wanted to see what it feels like and play with your heart."

Whatever the venue, and without exception, the people in our study reported that they were incredibly enthusiastic about their personal-best projects. Their own enthusiasm was catching; it spread from leader to constituents. Their belief in and enthusiasm for the vision were the sparks that ignited the flame of inspiration.

Challenge the Process

Leaders venture out. None of the individuals in our study sat idly by waiting for fate to smile upon them. "Luck" or "being in the right place at the right time" may play a role in the specific opportunities leaders embrace, but those who lead others to greatness seek and accept challenge. Lindsay Levin, for instance, rose to the occasion when circumstances required her to take over the family business. In the process, she also found innovative ways to transform the business (Jones, 1997; Glozen, 1999). Alan Keith succeeded in confronting a traditional culture with some radical new ideas.

Every single personal-best leadership case we collected involved some kind of challenge. The challenge might have been an innovative new product, a cutting-edge service, a groundbreaking piece of legislation, an invigorating campaign to get adolescents to join an environmental program, a revolutionary turnaround of a bureaucratic military program, or the start-up of a new plant or business. Whatever the challenge, all the cases involved a change from the status quo. Not one person claimed to have achieved a personal best by keeping things the same. All leaders challenge the process.

Leaders are pioneers—people who are willing to step out into the unknown. They search for opportunities to innovate, grow, and improve. But leaders aren't the only creators or originators of new products, services, or processes. In fact, it's more likely that they're not: innovation comes more from listening than from telling. Product and service innovations tend to come from customers, clients, vendors, people in the labs, and people on the front lines; process innovations, from the people doing the work. Sometimes a dramatic external event thrusts an organization into a radically new condition.

The leader's primary contribution is in the recognition of good ideas, the support of those ideas, and the willingness to challenge the system to get new products, processes, services, and systems adopted. It might be more accurate, then, to say that leaders are early adopters of innovation.

Leaders know well that innovation and change all involve experimentation, risk, and failure. They proceed anyway. One way of dealing with the potential risks and failures of experimentation is to approach change through incremental steps and small wins. Little victories, when piled on top of each other, build confidence that even the biggest challenges can be met. In so doing, they strengthen commitment to the long-term future. Yet not everyone is equally comfortable with risk and uncertainty. Leaders also pay attention to the capacity of their constituents to take control of challenging situations and become fully committed to change. You can't exhort people to take risks if they don't also feel safe.

It would be ridiculous to assert that those who fail over and over again eventually succeed as leaders. Success in any endeavor isn't a process of simply buying enough lottery tickets. The key that unlocks the door to opportunity is learning. In his own study of exemplary leadership practices, Warren Bennis writes that "leaders learn by leading, and they learn best by leading in the face of obstacles. As weather shapes mountains, problems shape leaders. Difficult bosses, lack of vision and virtue in the executive suite, circumstances beyond their control, and their own mistakes have been the leaders' basic curriculum" (1998, p. 146). In other words, leaders are learners. They learn from their failures as well as their successes.

Enable Others to Act

Grand dreams don't become significant realities through the actions of a single person. Leadership is a team effort. After reviewing thousands of personal-best cases, we developed a simple test to detect whether someone is on the road to becoming a leader. That test is the frequency of the use of the word *we*. In our interview with Alan Keith, for instance, he used the word "we" nearly three times more often than the word "I" in explaining his personal-best leadership experience.

Exemplary leaders enable others to act. They foster collaboration and build trust. This sense of teamwork goes far beyond a few direct reports or close confidants. They engage all those who must make the project work—and in some way, all who must live with the results. In today's "virtual" organization, cooperation can't be restricted to a small group of loyalists; it must include peers, managers, customers and clients, suppliers, citizens—all those who have a stake in the vision.

Leaders make it possible for others to do good work. They know that those who are expected to produce the results must feel a sense of personal power and ownership. Leaders understand that the command-and-control techniques of the Industrial Revolution no longer apply. Instead, leaders work to make people feel strong, capable, and committed. Leaders enable others to act not by hoarding the power they have but by giving it away. Exemplary leaders strengthen everyone's capacity to deliver on the promises they make. As a budget analyst for Catholic Healthcare West, Cindy Giordano would ask "What do you think?" and use the ensuing discussion to build up the capabilities of others (as well as educate and update her own information and perspective). She discovered that when people are trusted and have more discretion, more authority, and more information, they're much more likely to use their energies to produce extraordinary results.

In the cases we analyzed, leaders proudly discussed teamwork, trust, and empowerment as essential elements of their efforts. A leader's ability to enable others to act is essential. Constituents neither perform at their best nor stick around for very long if their leader makes them feel weak, dependent, or alienated. But when a leader makes people feel strong and capable—as if they can do more than they ever thought possible—they'll give it their all and exceed their own expectations. When leadership is a relationship founded on trust and confidence, people take risks, make changes, keep organizations and movements alive. Through that relationship, leaders turn their constituents into leaders themselves.

Encourage the Heart

The climb to the top is arduous and long. People become exhausted, frustrated, and disenchanted. They're often tempted to give up. Leaders encourage the heart of their constituents to carry on. Genuine acts of caring uplift the spirits and draw people forward. Encouragement can come from dramatic gestures or simple actions. When Cary Turner was head of Pier 1 Imports' Stores division, he once showed up in a wedding gown to promote the bridal registry. On another occasion, he promised store employees he'd parasail over Puget Sound and the Seattle waterfront if they met their sales targets. They kept their commitment; he kept his. As mayor of New York City, Rudy Giuliani wore different hats (literally) to acknowledge various groups of rescue workers as he toured ground zero after the World Trade Center towers were destroyed on September 11, 2001. But it doesn't take events or media coverage to let people know you appreciate their contributions. Terri Sarhatt, customer services manager at Applied Biosystems, looked after her employees so well that at least one reported that the time she spent with them was more valuable than the tangible rewards she was able to give out.

It's part of the leader's job to show appreciation for people's contributions and to create a culture of celebration. In the cases we collected, we saw thousands of examples of individual recognition and group celebration. We've heard and seen everything from handwritten thank-yous to marching bands and "This Is Your Life" ceremonies.

Recognition and celebration aren't about fun and games, though there is a lot of fun and there are a lot of games when people encourage the hearts of their constituents. Neither are they about pretentious ceremonies designed to create some phony sense of camaraderie. When people see a charlatan making noisy affectations, they turn away in disgust. Encouragement is curiously serious business. It's how leaders visibly and behaviorally link rewards with performance. When striving to raise quality, recover from disaster, start up a new service, or make dramatic change of any kind, leaders make sure people see the benefit of behavior that's aligned with cherished values. And leaders also know that celebrations and rituals, when done with authenticity and from the heart, build a strong sense of collective identity and community spirit that can carry a group through extraordinarily tough times.

Leadership Is a Relationship

Leadership is an identifiable set of skills and practices that are available to all of us, not just a few charismatic men and women. The "great person"—woman or man—theory of leadership is just plain wrong. Or, we should say, the theory that there are only a few great men and women who can lead us to greatness is just plain wrong. We consider the women and men in our research to be great, and so do those with whom they worked. They are the everyday heroes of our world. It's because we have so many—not so few—leaders that we are able to get extraordinary things done on a regular basis, even in extraordinary times.

Our findings also challenge the myth that leadership is something that you find only at the highest levels of organizations and society. We found it everywhere. To us this is inspiring and should give everyone hope. Hope, because it means that no one needs to wait around to be saved by someone riding into town on a white horse. Hope, because there's a generation of leaders searching for the opportunities to make a difference. Hope, because right down the block or right down the hall there are people who will seize the opportunity to lead you to greatness. They're your neighbors, friends, and colleagues. And you are one of them, too.

There's still another crucial truth about leadership—more apparent to us this time around than it was before. It's something that we've known for a long time, but we've come to prize its value even more today. In talking to leaders and reading their cases, there was a very clear message that wove itself throughout every situation and every action: leadership is a relationship. Leadership is a relationship between those who aspire to lead and those who choose to follow.

Evidence abounds for this point of view. For instance, in examining the critical variables for success in the top three jobs in large organizations, Jodi Taylor and her colleagues at the Center for Creative Leadership found the number one success factor to be "relationships with subordinates" (Jodi Taylor, telephone interview, April 1998). We were intrigued to find that even in this nanosecond world of e-everything, opinion is consistent with the facts. In an on-line survey, respondents were asked to indicate, among other things, which would be more essential to business success in five years—social skills or skills in using the Internet. Seventy-two percent selected social skills; 28 percent, Internet skills ("FC Roper Starch Survey," 1999). Internet literati completing a poll on-line realize that it's not the web of technology that matters the most, it's the web of people.

Similar results were found in a study by Public Allies, an AmeriCorps organization dedicated to creating young leaders who can strengthen their communities. Public Allies sought the opinions of eighteen- to thirty-year-olds on the subject of leadership. Among the items was a question about the qualities that were important in a good leader. Topping the respondents' list is "Being able to see a situation from someone else's point of view." In second place, "Getting along well with other people" (Public Allies, 1998).

Success in leadership, success in business, and success in life has been, is now, and will continue to be a function of how well people work and play together. We're even more convinced of this today than we were twenty years ago. Success in leading will be wholly dependent upon the capacity to build and sustain those human relationships that enable people to get extraordinary things done on a regular basis.

The Ten Commitments of Leadership

Embedded in The Five Practices of Exemplary Leadership are behaviors that can serve as the basis for learning to lead. We call these The Ten Commitments of Leadership. These ten commitments serve as the guide for our discussion of how leaders get extraordinary things done in organizations and as the structure for what's to follow. Before delving into the practices and commitments further, however, let's consider leadership from the vantage point of the constituent. If leadership is a relationship, as we have discovered, then what do people expect from that relationship? What do people look for and admire in a leader? What do people want from someone whose direction they'd be willing to follow?

THE FIVE PRACTICES AND TEN COMMITMENTS OF LEADERSHIP

PRACTICE	COMMITMENT
Model the Way	1. Find your voice by clarifying your personal values.
	2. Set the example by aligning actions with shared values.
Inspire a Shared Vision	3. Envision the future by imagining exciting and ennobling possibilities.
	4. Enlist others in a common vision by appealing to shared aspirations.

Challenge the Process	5. Search for opportunities by seeking innovative ways to change, grow, and improve.
	6. Experiment and take risks by constantly generating small wins and learning from mistakes.
Enable Others to Act	7. Foster collaboration by promoting cooperative goals and building trust.
	8. Strengthen others by sharing power and discretion.
Encourage the Heart	9. Recognize contributions by showing appreciation for individual excellence.
	10. Celebrate the values and victories by creating a spirit of community.

NOTE

1. Unless otherwise noted, all quotations are taken from personal interviews or from personal-best leadership case studies written by the respondent leaders. The titles and affiliations of the leaders may be different today from what they were at the time of their case study or publication of this volume. We expect many have moved on to other leadership adventures while we were writing, or will do so by the time you read this.

REFERENCES

Bennis, W. *On Becoming a Leader.* Reading, Mass.: Addison-Wesley, 1998.
"FC Roper Starch Survey: The Web," *Fast Company,* Oct. 1999, p. 302.
Glozen, G. "Driving Force." *HR,* Mar. 1999, pp. 28–31.
Jones, D. T. "Changing Gear." Cardiff, South Wales: Lean Enterprise Research Centre, Cardiff Business School, Oct. 1997.
Public Allies. *New Leadership for a New Century.* Washington, D.C.: Public Allies, 1998.

PART TWO

MORAL
LEADERSHIP

MORALS, ETHICS, TRUST, values, integrity, respect, and commitment are words with lofty connotations. Thrust to the forefront of our collective consciousness during the corporate ethics scandals of recent history, the meanings of these societal cornerstones have become confused and trivialized in nearly every sphere of public life. If we genuinely want the next generation to become moral, ethical, and trustworthy beings, it is especially important for school leaders to model the way.

In this section, five authors shed light on this complex topic. Thomas J. Sergiovanni presents moral authority as a pillar of leadership practice and discusses why school leaders must use this authority to serve the larger mission of the school community.

David E. Purpel outlines the higher calling to which leaders must answer and offers an inspiring credo of social responsibility.

In "Becoming a Trustworthy Leader," Megan Tschannen-Moran proposes five facets of leadership and five facets of trust, and explores the current challenges of fostering trusting relationships in an age of higher standards and competing interests.

Lee G. Bolman and Terrence E. Deal pose the ultimate tough question: "Is it possible to be political and still do the right thing?" They introduce four values to guide ethical choice and also focus on four basic skills all managers as politicians must cultivate.

Finally, Robert Evans echoes the other authors of this section in his reflection on authentic leadership: "Authentic leaders translate their beliefs and values into concrete actions at a fundamental level." He contends that successful leaders uphold the belief that all people possess great potential. If this creed is embraced at the highest levels, the effects will permeate the school community, and the promise of each and every student will be recognized.

6

LEADERSHIP
AS STEWARDSHIP

"WHO'S SERVING WHO?"

Thomas J. Sergiovanni

MANY SCHOOL ADMINISTRATORS are practicing a form of leadership that is based on moral authority, but often this practice is not acknowledged as leadership. The reason for this problem is that moral authority is underplayed and that the management values undergirding this authority are largely unofficial. When I asked Larry Norwood, principal of Capital High School, Olympia, Washington, to participate in one of my studies on leadership, he responded, "I have wrestled with this—and finally decided to pass. First, because I am so late in responding and, second, I can think of nothing of literary significance that I have achieved (in the way of leadership) in the past twenty-two years. My style is to delegate and empower, and my successes have been through other people. If I have a strength it is as a facilitator—that doesn't make good copy. Sorry." Larry Norwood is a successful school administrator. Although he does not think of himself as a leader, he is one.

I suspect that one of the reasons for Norwood's success may be that he implicitly rejects leadership, as we now understand it. The official values of management lead us to believe that leaders are characters who single-handedly pull and push organizational members forward by the force of personality, bureaucratic clout, and political know-how. Leaders must be decisive. Leaders must be forceful. Leaders must have vision. Leaders must successfully manipulate events and people, so that vision becomes reality. Leaders, in other words, must lead.

From time to time, there may be a place for this kind of direct leadership. But it is only part of the story. The leadership that counts, in the end, is the kind that touches people differently. It taps their emotions, appeals to their values, and responds to their connections with other people. It is a morally based leadership—a form of stewardship. Greenfield (1991) found this to be the case in his study of an urban elementary school. The moral orientation of its teachers was central in fixing their relationship with the principal and with each other. Greenfield comments, "Their persistence in searching out strategies to increase their colleagues' or their personal effectiveness in serving the needs of the school's children was motivated not by bureaucratic mandate or directives from superiors, but by moral commitment to children, rooted in their awareness of the needs of these children and their beliefs about the significance of their roles, as teachers, in these children's lives. Much of the principal's efforts to foster leadership among the teachers . . . was directed to further developing and sustaining this moral orientation among teachers" (p. 3). To those teachers, shared ideals and beliefs became duties to which they willingly responded. These findings parallel those of Johnson (1990). Morally based leadership is important in its own right, but it is also important because it taps what is important to people and what motivates them.

Stewardship in Practice

Implicit in traditional conceptions of leadership is the idea that schools cannot be improved from within: school communities have neither the wit nor the will to lead themselves; instead, principals and teachers are considered pawns, awaiting the play of a master or the game plan of an expert to provide solutions for school problems. In his chronicle of Madeline Cartwright, principal of Blaine School, Philadelphia, Richard Louv (1990) points out that too many teachers and administrators doubt the power of determination and the ability of schools themselves to make a difference. "It just won't work," they maintain, or "The central office won't let us," or "We can't do that because. . . ." Madeline Cartwright is one principal who thinks differently. For her, being a school administrator is a form of stewardship, and the responsibilities of stewardship simply require that obligations and commitments be met, regardless of obstacles. "I tell my staff, Don't tell me what I can and can't do. I can do something if I want to. It can happen. It's like people say to me, 'You cannot wash this child's clothes, put 'em in the washing machine and give him some clean clothes to put on.' I can do that" (p. 75). And that she does.

Shortly after becoming principal at Blaine, Cartwright organized a raffle to buy a washer and dryer for the school. They are used every morning, to launder the clothes of many of the children. Cartwright often does the washing personally, believing that this is the only way many of the children know what it is like to have clean clothes. In her words, "This is one of the things you can do to bring about a change. My kids look good" (p. 63). When Cartwright arrived at Blaine, she found a school that was "black as soot." She told the parents, "This place is dirty! How can your kids go to school in a place like this? We're going to clean this building this summer. Raise your hands if I can depend on you. Keep your hands up! Somebody get their names!" Eighteen parents showed up and began the work. "We cleaned it, and cleaned it good. I made these parents know that you don't accept anything less than that which is right because you live in North Philadelphia!" (p. 66).

Parental involvement at Blaine is high. Parents help supervise the yard in the morning and the hallway during the day. They work in classrooms, help prepare food, and decorate the school. "Everybody is involved in the washing" (p. 67).

What kind of leader is Madeline Cartwright? She is one who will do whatever it takes to make Blaine work and work well: "If a child isn't coming to school, I'll go into a home and bring kids out" (p. 74). On one such venture, Cartwright and a friend walked into an apartment she describes as follows: "This place was cruddy. I mean, beyond anything I could ever imagine for little children to live in. The kitchen was a hotplate sitting on a drainboard. I saw no refrigerator. There was no running water and no electricity. There were dirty dishes, food caked in piles. The bathroom had a bedspread wrapped around the bottom of the toilet and the toilet was full to the brim with human waste. To the *brim*. And the little girl had one foot on one side of the toilet, and one foot on the other and she squatted over this toilet while she used it, and it was seeping over the sides." She sent one of the persons in the apartment off to get a snake. Then, using a plastic container and buckets from the school, "we dug this mess out. . . . While we were in the apartment, we scrubbed the floors, took all the dirty clothes out, all the sheets off the beds, brought them back to the school, washed them up. And we left food for dinner from our school lunch. The mother came home to a clean house and clean children. This lady had gotten so far behind the eight ball she didn't even know where to go to get out" (p. 74).

Some experts on the principalship might comment, "All well and good, but what about Cartwright's being an instructional leader? What about her paying attention to teaching and learning, to charting, facilitating, and monitoring the school's educational program?" Cartwright does that, all right, and with a flair. As Louv points out, Cartwright maintains that there are two types of principals, "office principals" and "classroom principals," and she is clearly the latter. She is in and out of classrooms regularly, often taking over the teaching of classes. She not only communicates high expectations but also demands performance from her staff. She is a no-nonsense disciplinarian, as well as a devoted and loving one. But all this "instructional leadership" just is not enough to make this school work. What makes Blaine work is that Cartwright practices leadership by washing clothes, scrubbing the building, and, yes, cleaning toilets (one of the chores that Mahatma Gandhi cheerfully claimed for himself as part of his leadership in the Indian independence movement). Both Cartwright and Gandhi were practicing something called *servant leadership*. In the end, it is servant leadership, based on a deep commitment to values and emerging from a groundswell of moral authority, that makes the critical difference in the lives of Blaine's students and their families. As Louv explains (p. 74), "Maybe Madeline Cartwright's dreams are naïve, maybe not. But they do make a kind of mathematical sense: one safe and clean school, one set of clean clothes, one clean toilet, one safe house—and then another safe school . . . and another . . . and another. 'I'm tellin' you, there's things you can do!'"

The Many Forms of Leadership

The practices of Madeline Cartwright and Larry Norwood demonstrate one of the themes of this book: leadership takes many forms. Further, as has been argued, today's crisis in leadership stems in part from the view that some of these forms are legitimate and others are not. For example, a vast literature expounds the importance of practicing command leadership and instructional leadership. Both kinds provide images of direct leadership, with the principal clearly in control—setting goals, organizing the work, outlining performance standards, assigning people to work, directing and monitoring the work, and evaluating. This kind of direct leadership is typically accompanied by a human relations style designed to motivate and keep morale up.

Command and instructional leadership have their place. Heavy doses of both may be necessary in schools where teachers are incompetent, indifferent, or just disabled by the circumstances they face. But if command and instructional leadership are practiced as dominant strategies, rather than supporting ones, they can breed dependency in teachers and cast them in roles as subordinates. Subordinates do what they are supposed to, but little else. They rely on others to manage them, rather than acting as self-managers. This is hardly a recipe for building good schools.

Command leaders and instructional leaders alike are being challenged by the view that school administrators should strive to become leaders of leaders. As leaders of leaders, they work hard to build up the capacities of teachers and others, so that direct leadership will no longer be needed. This is achieved through team building, leadership development, shared decision making, and striving to establish the value of collegiality. The leader of leaders represents a powerful conception of leadership, one that deserves more emphasis than it now receives in the literature on school administration, and more attention from policymakers who seek to reform schools. Successful leaders of leaders combine the most progressive elements of psychological authority with aspects of professional and moral authority.

Servant Leadership

Virtually missing from the mainstream conversation on leadership is the concept of servant leadership—the leadership so nobly practiced by Madeline Cartwright, Larry Norwood, and many other principals. Greenleaf (1977) believes that "a new moral principle is emerging which holds that the only authority deserving one's allegiance is that which is freely and knowingly granted by the led to the leader in response to, and in proportion to, the clearly evident servant stature of the leader" (p. 10). He developed the concept of servant leadership after reading Herman Hesse's *Journey to the East*. As Greenleaf explains (p. 7),

> In this story we see a band of men on a mythical journey. . . . The central figure of the story is Leo, who accompanies the party as the servant who does their menial chores, but who also sustains them with his spirit and his song. He is a person of extraordinary presence. All goes well until Leo disappears. Then the group falls into disarray and the journey is abandoned. They cannot make it without the servant Leo. The narrator, one of the party, after some years of wandering, finds Leo and is taken into the Order that had sponsored the journey. There he discovers that Leo, whom he had known first as servant, was in fact the titular head of the Order, its guiding spirit, a great and *noble* leader [p. 7].

For Greenleaf, the great leader is a servant first.

Servant leadership is the means by which leaders can get the necessary legitimacy to lead. Servant leadership provides legitimacy partly because one of the responsibilities of leadership is to give a sense of direction, to establish an overarching purpose. Doing so, Greenleaf explains, "gives certainty and purpose to others who may have difficulty in achieving it for themselves. But being successful in providing purpose requires the trust of others" (p. 15). For trust to be forthcoming, the led must have confidence in the leader's competence and values. Further, people's confidence is strengthened by their belief that the leader makes judgments on the basis of competence and values, rather than self-interest.

When practicing servant leadership, the leader is often tempted by personal enthusiasm and commitment to define the needs of those to be served. There is, of course, a place for this approach in schools; sometimes students, parents, and teachers are not ready or able to define their own needs. But, over the long haul, as Greenleaf maintains, it is best to let those who will be served define their own needs in their own way. Servant leadership is more easily provided if the leader understands that serving others is important but that the most important thing is to serve the values and ideas that help shape the school as a covenantal community. In this sense, all the members of a community share the burden of servant leadership.

Schools should not be viewed as ordinary communities but as communities of learners. Barth (1990) points out that, within such communities, it is assumed that schools have the capacity to improve themselves; that, under the right conditions, adults and students alike learn, and learning by one contributes to the learning of others; that a key leverage point in creating a learning community is improving the school's culture; and that school-improvement efforts that count, whether originating in the school or outside, seek to determine and provide the conditions that enable students and adults to promote and sustain learning for themselves. "Taking these assumptions seriously," Barth argues (pp. 45–46), "leads to fresh thinking about the culture of schools and about what people do in them. For instance, the principal need no longer be the 'headmaster' or 'instructional leader,' pretending to know all, one who consumes lists from above and transmits them to those below. The more crucial role of the principal is as head learner, engaging in the most important enterprise of the schoolhouse—experiencing, displaying, modeling, and celebrating what it is hoped and expected that teachers and pupils will do." The school as learning community provides an ideal setting for joining the practice of the "leader of leaders" to servant leadership.

Command and instructional leadership, "leader of leaders" leadership, and servant leadership can be viewed developmentally, as if each were built on the others. As the emphasis shifts from one level to the next, leadership increasingly becomes a form of virtue, and each of the preceding levels becomes less important to the operation of a successful school. For example, teachers become less dependent on administrators, are better able to manage themselves, and share the burdens of leadership more fully.

The developmental view is useful conceptually, but it may be too idealistic to account for what happens in practice. A more realistic perspective is to view the expressions of leadership as being practiced together. Initially (and because of the circumstances faced) the command and instructional features of the leadership pattern may be more prominent. In time, however (and with deliberate effort), they yield more and more to the "leader of leaders" style and to servant leadership, with the results just described.

The idea of servant leadership may seem weak. After all, since childhood, we have been conditioned to view leadership in a much tougher, more direct light. The media portray leaders as strong, mysterious, aloof, wise, and all-powerful. Lawrence Miller (1984) explains:

> Problems were always solved the same way. The Lone Ranger and his faithful Indian companion (read servant of a somewhat darker complexion and lesser intelligence) come riding into town. The Lone Ranger, with his mask and mysterious identity, background, and lifestyle, never becomes intimate with those whom he will help. His power is partly in his mystique. Within ten minutes the Lone Ranger has understood the problem, identified who the bad guys are, and has set out to catch them. He quickly outwits the bad guys, draws his gun, and has them behind bars. And then there was always that wonderful scene at the end. The helpless victims are standing in front of their ranch or in the town square marveling at how wonderful it is now that they have been saved, you hear hoofbeats, then the *William Tell* overture, and one person turns to another and asks, "But who was that masked man?" And the other replies, "Why, that was the Lone Ranger!" We see Silver rear up and with a hearty "Hi-yo Silver," the Lone Ranger and his companion ride away.
>
> It was wonderful. Truth, justice, and the American Way protected once again.
>
> What did we learn from this cultural hero? Among the lessons that are now acted out daily by managers are the following:

- There is always a problem down on the ranch [the school] and someone is responsible.

- Those who got themselves into the difficulty are incapable of getting themselves out of it. "I'll have to go down or send someone down to fix it."

- In order to have the mystical powers needed to solve problems, you must stay behind the mask. Don't let the ordinary folks get too close to you or your powers may be lost.

- Problems get solved within discrete periodic time units and we have every right to expect them to be solved decisively.

These myths are no laughing matter. Anyone who has lived within or close to our corporations [or schools] knows that these myths are powerful forces in daily life. Unfortunately, none of them bears much resemblance to the real world [pp. 54–55].

One way in which the servant leader serves others is by becoming an advocate on their behalf. Mary Helen Rodriguez, principal of San Antonio's De Zavala School, provides an example:

A teacher came to Mrs. Rodriguez to discuss problems she had been having in arranging a field trip for her grade level. The teacher, in reality, had begun planning too late to get the bus and sack lunch requests conveniently through the district bureaucracy for the planned day of the trip. Mrs. Rodriguez first asked the teacher how important the field trip was for the students. After a bit of discussion, Mrs. Rodriguez and the teacher decided that a trip to the zoo was indeed important, given what students were studying in class at the time. Mrs. Rodriguez then immediately set about making the necessary preparations. Although it took a bit of cajoling over the telephone, sack lunches and busses were secured, and the teacher was most appreciative.

The remarkable thing about this episode is the extra effort Mrs. Rodriguez put in, even though it would have been perfectly reasonable to say, "No, I'm sorry. It's just too late." In a situation where another principal might have saved her powder and not fought the system, Mrs. Rodriguez proved to be a successful advocate for the teacher and her students [Albritton, 1991, p. 8].

Such ideas as servant leadership bring with them a different kind of strength—one based on moral authority. When one places one's leadership practice in service to ideas, and to others who also seek to serve these ideas, issues of leadership role and of leadership style become far less important. It matters less who is providing the leadership, and it matters even less whether the style of leadership is directive or not, involves others or not, and so on. These are issues of process; what matter are issues of substance. What are we about? Why? Are students being served? Is the school as learning community being served? What are our obligations to this community? With these questions in mind, how can we best get the job done?

Practicing Servant Leadership

Summarized in the following sections are practices that, taken together, show how servant leadership works and how the burden of leadership can be shared with other members of the school community.

Purposing

Vaill (1984) defines *purposing* as "that continuous stream of actions by an organization's formal leadership which has the effect of inducing clarity, consensus and commitment regarding the organization's basic purposes" (p. 91). The purpose of purposing is to build within the school a center of shared values that transforms it from a mere organization into a covenantal community.

Empowerment

Empowerment derives its full strength from being linked to purposing: everyone is free to do what makes sense, as long as people's decisions embody the values shared by the school community. When empowerment is understood in this light, the emphasis shifts away from discretion needed to function and toward one's responsibility to the community. Empowerment cannot be practiced successfully apart from enablement (efforts by the school to provide support and remove obstacles).

Leadership by Outrage

It is the leader's responsibility to be outraged when empowerment is abused and when purposes are ignored. Moreover, all members of the school community are obliged to show outrage when the standard falls.

Leadership by outrage, and the practice of kindling outrage in others, challenge the conventional wisdom that leaders should be poker-faced, play their cards close to the chest, avoid emotion, and otherwise hide what they believe and feel. When the source of leadership authority is moral, and when covenants of shared values become the driving force for the school's norm system, it seems natural to react with outrage to short-comings in what we do and impediments to what we want to do.

Madeline Cartwright regularly practiced leadership by outrage. In one instance, she was having trouble with teachers' attendance. She learned of another principal who solved this problem by answering the phone per-sonally, and she decided to follow suit: "I started answering the phone. I say, 'Good morning, this is the Blaine School, this is Madeline Cart-wright.' They hang right up. Two, three minutes later, phone rings again. 'Good morning, this is Blaine School and still Madeline Cartwright.' Hang right up. Next time the phone rang I said: 'Good morning, this is Mrs. Cartwright. If you're going to take off today, you have to talk to me. You either talk to me or you come to school, simple as that'" (Louv, 1990, p. 64). The school is the only thing that the kids can depend on, Cart-wright maintains, and for this reason it is important to make sure that the teachers will show up. She tells the teachers, "As old as I am, you haven't had any disease I haven't had, so you come to school, no matter what."

Some administrators who practice the art of leadership by outrage do it by fighting off bureaucratic interference. Paperwork is often the villain. Other administrators capitulate and spend much of their time and effort handling this paperwork. As a result, little is left for dealing with other, more important matters. Jules Linden, a junior high school principal in New York City, and Linda Martinez, principal of San Juan Day School, San Juan Pueblo, New Mexico, belong in the first group.

In Linden's words, "The only thing the bureaucracy hasn't tried to solve by memo is cancer. . . . My rule of thumb is, when people can't see me because of the paperwork demands, I dump [the paperwork]—and most of it is not missed" (Mustain, 1990, p. 14). Martinez has devised a unique filing system to handle the onslaught of memos, rules, directives, and the like, which she receives from above: "I decided to 'bag it.' Every Friday I would clear my desk. Everything would be tossed in a garbage bag, dated and labeled weekly." Should Martinez be contacted about something filed (and that is not often the case), the proper bag is opened and dumped on the floor, and the item is retrieved for further consideration. Linda Mar-tinez remarks, "I had never really considered my 'filing system' of garbage bags to be associated with leadership. I've been told it borders on lunacy." In a redefined leadership, what first appears to be lunacy may not be, and vice versa.

Not all schools share the dire conditions of Blaine School, and not all are deluged with a mountain of paperwork. But every school stands for something, and this something can be the basis of practicing leadership by outrage. Many administrators and teachers believe that students do not have the right to fail—that, for example, it should not be up to students to decide whether to do assigned work. Unless this belief rests on the practice of leadership by outrage, however, it is likely to be an academic abstraction rather than a heartfelt value, a slogan rather than a solution.

How is failure to complete assigned work handled in most schools? Typically, by giving zeros—often cheerfully, and without emotion. It is almost as if we are saying to students, "Look, here is the deadline. This is what you have to do. If you don't meet the deadline, these are the consequences. It's up to you. You decide whether you want to do the assignments and pass, or not do the assignments and fail." Adopting a "no zero" policy and enforcing it to the limit is one expression of leadership by outrage. It can transform the belief that children have no right to fail from an abstraction to an operational value. When work is not done by Friday, for example, no zeros are recorded. Instead, the student is phoned Friday night, and perhaps the principal or the teacher visits the student at home after brunch on Sunday to collect the work or press the new Monday deadline. If the student complains that she or he does not have a place to do homework, homework centers are established in the school, in the neighborhood, and so on.

Just remember Madeline Cartwright, and follow her lead. Granted, not all students will respond, but I believe that most will, and those who finally do wind up with zeros will get them with teachers' reluctance. Even if the school does not "win them all," it demonstrates that it stands for something. The stakes are elevated when the problem is transformed from something technical to something moral.

As important as leadership by outrage is, its intent is to kindle outrage in others. When it is successful, every member of the school community is encouraged to display outrage whenever the standard falls. An empowered school community, bonded together by shared commitments and values, is a prerequisite for kindling outrage in others.

Power *Over* and Power *To*

It is true that many teachers and parents do not always respond to opportunities to be involved, to be self-managed, to accept responsibility, and to practice leadership by outrage. In most cases, however, this lack of interest is not inherent but learned. Many teachers, for example, have become jaded as a result of bad experiences with involvement. Louise E. Coleman, principal of Taft Elementary School, Joliet, Illinois, believes that trust and integrity have to be reestablished after such bad experiences. When she arrived at Taft as a new principal, the school was required to submit to the central office a three-year school-improvement plan, designed to increase student achievement:

> Teachers were disgruntled at first. They were not really interested in developing a school-improvement plan. They had been through similar exercises in shared decision making before, and that's exactly what they were—*exercises*. Taft had had three principals in three years. The staff assumed that I would go as others had in the past. After writing a three-year plan based on the staff's perceptions, influencing teachers by involving them in decision making, helping them to take ownership in school improvement, [we have] made some progress. Trust and integrity have been established. Most of the staff now has confidence in me. We have implemented new programs based on students' needs. The staff now volunteers to meet, to share ideas. Minority students are now considered students. Communication is ongoing. Minority parents are more involved. Positive rewards are given for student recognition. The overall school climate has changed to reflect a positive impact on learning.

Coleman was able to build trust and integrity by gently but firmly allowing others to assume leadership roles. She did not feel too threatened to relinquish some of her power and authority. Power can be understood in two ways—as power *over*, and as power *to*. Coleman knows the difference. Power *over* emphasizes controlling what people do, when they do it, and how they do it. Power *to* views power as a source of energy for achieving shared goals and purposes. Indeed, when empowerment is successfully practiced, administrators exchange power *over* for power *to*. Power *over* is rule-bound, but power *to* is goal-bound. Only those with hierarchically authorized authority can practice power *over*; anyone who is committed to shared goals and purposes can practice power *to*.

The empowerment rule (that everyone is free to do whatever makes sense, as long as decisions embody shared values), and an understanding of power as the power to, are liberating to administrators as well as teachers. Principals, too, are free to lead, without worrying about being viewed as autocratic. Further, principals can worry less about whether they are using the right style and less about other process-based concerns; their leadership rests on the substance of their ideas and values. Contrary to the laws of human relations, which remind us always to involve people and say that it is autocratic for designated leaders to propose ideas for implementation, we have here a game that resembles football: everyone gets a chance to be quarterback and is free to call the play; if it is a good call, then the team runs with it.

Wayne K. Myers, a principal in Madison, Georgia, welcomes teachers to the role of quarterback, but he is not afraid to call some plays himself. In the spring of 1989, he declared one week in August as International Week, having organized the major activities on his own. He contacted parents for volunteers, asked foreign students from the University of Georgia to come to the campus and make presentations, arranged an exhibit from UNICEF, and even asked the lunchroom to serve meals from the cuisines of different countries:

> In describing this week, I keep [saying] "I" because the major activities were completed by me, but the real success of the week came from the teachers. It was based on a general understanding I had gained from working with these teachers: that they felt the true spirit of schooling had been lost, and that we were committed to recovering it. I shared my idea with them only one month before the start-up date. But, within that month, each grade organized a fantastic array of activities for students. The media specialist located all the materials she had on foreign countries. The hallways were full of displays of items, made by the students, that represented other countries. Since each homeroom would have a visitor with information about another country, each teacher centered activities on that country. The real significance was that the general theme of the week may not have been [the teachers'] idea, but the response was unbelievable. They were, of course, free to take the idea and run with it. It became a learning experience for everyone—administrators, teachers, students, and the community. All were involved, and all enjoyed themselves. . . . I am not sure what type of leadership this is. All I know is that the results have been very positive. I do not believe in telling people what to do or how to do it, but I do believe that sometimes we all have ideas that need to be proposed, sometimes unilaterally.

Myers does not have to worry about leadership—that is, about who does what, or whether he is being too pushy or if he is passing the ball off to teachers. But he would have to worry if trust, integrity, and shared values were not already established in the school. Moreover, Myers understands the difference between charting a direction and giving people maps, between providing a theme and giving teachers a script. Finally, although human relations remain important, Myers is confident that if he acts from the standpoint of what is right and good for the school, human relationships will have a way of taking care of themselves.

The Female Style

It is difficult to talk about power *to* and servant leadership without also addressing the issue of gender. Power *to,* for example, is an idea close to the feminist tradition, as are such ideas as servant leadership and community. By contrast, the more traditional conceptions of leadership seem decidedly more male-oriented. Modern management, for example, is a male creation that replaced emphasis on family and community with emphasis on individual ambition and other personal considerations. As Debra R. Kaufman and Barbara L. Richardson (1982) explain, "Most contemporary social science models [of which modern school management is one]—the set of concepts that help social scientists select problems, organize information, and pursue inquiries—are based on the lives men lead." They go on to say, "In general, social science models of human behavior have focused on rather narrow and male-specific criteria regarding the relationships of ability, ambition, personality, achievement, and worldly success" (p. xiii).

Joyce Hampel (1988) argues that the concept of servant leadership is not likely to be valued in male-dominated institutions or professions. Relying on the research of Carol Gilligan (1982), Joyce Miller (1986), and Charol Shakeshaft (1987), as well as on her own experiences in schools, Hampel points out that men and women generally have different goals when it comes to psychological fulfillment. Men tend to emphasize individual relationships, individual achievement, power as a source for controlling events and people, independence, authority, and set procedures. Women, by contrast, tend to emphasize successful relationships, affiliation, power as the means to achieve shared goals, connectedness, authenticity, and personal creativity. For most men, achievement has to do with the accomplishment of goals; for most women, achievement has to do with the building of connections between and among people. Hampel quotes Miller as follows: "In our culture 'serving others' is for losers, it is low-level stuff. Yet serving others is a basic principle around which women's lives are organized; it is far from such for men" (p. 18).

Shakeshaft (1987), in her groundbreaking research on the topic, characterizes the female world of schooling as follows:

> 1. *Relationships with Others Are Central to All Actions of Women Administrators.* Women spend more time with people, communicate more, care more about individual differences, are concerned more with teachers and marginal students, and motivate more. Not surprisingly, staffs of women administrators rate women higher, are more produc-

tive, and have higher morale. Students in schools with women principals also have higher morale and are more involved with student
affairs. Further, parents are more favorable toward schools and districts run by women and thus are more involved in school life. This
focus on relationships and connections echoes Gilligan's (1982) ethic
of care.

2. *Teaching and Learning Are the Major Foci of Women Administrators.* Women administrators are more instrumental in instructional
learning than men and they exhibit greater knowledge of teaching
methods and techniques. Women administrators not only emphasize
achievement, they coordinate instructional programs and evaluate student progress. In these schools and districts, women administrators
know their teachers and they know the academic progress of their students. Women are more likely to help new teachers and to supervise
all teachers directly. Women also create a school climate more conducive to learning, one that is more orderly, safer, and quieter. Not surprisingly, academic achievement is higher in schools and districts in
which women are administrators.

3. *Building Community Is an Essential Part of a Woman Administrator's Style.* From speech patterns to decision-making styles,
women exhibit a more democratic, participatory style that encourages
inclusiveness rather than exclusiveness in schools. Women involve
themselves more with staff and students, ask for and get higher participation, and maintain more closely knit organizations. Staffs of
women principals have higher job satisfaction and are more engaged
in their work than those of male administrators. These staffs are also
more aware of and committed to the goals of learning, and the members of the staffs have more shared professional goals. These are
schools and districts in which teachers receive a great deal of support
from their female administrators. They are also districts and schools
where achievement is emphasized. Selma Greenberg (1985, p. 4)
describes this female school world: "Whatever its failures, it is more
cooperative than competitive, it is more experiential than abstract, it
takes a broad view of the curriculum and has always addressed 'the
whole child.'"

The female perspective on school leadership is important, for a number of reasons. The teaching force is predominantly female, and this raises
moral questions about giving full legitimacy to management conceptions
and leadership practice that take women's lived experience into account.
Female principals need to feel free to be themselves, rather than have to

follow the principles and practices of traditional management theory. The record of success for female principals is impressive. Women are under-represented in the principalship but overrepresented among principals of successful schools. Giving legitimacy to the female perspective would also give license to men who are inclined toward similar practice. The good news is that such ideas as value-based leadership, building covenantal communities, practicing empowerment and collegiality, adopting the stance of servant leaders, and practicing leadership by outrage are gaining in acceptance among male and female administrators alike.

Servant Leadership and Moral Authority

The link between servant leadership and moral authority is a tight one. Moral authority relies heavily on persuasion. At the root of persuasion are ideas, values, substance, and content, which together define group purposes and core values. Servant leadership is practiced by serving others, but its ultimate purpose is to place oneself, and others for whom one has responsibility, in the service of ideals.

Serving others and serving ideals is not an either-or proposition. Chula Boyle, assistant principal of Lee High School, San Antonio, Texas, for example, can often be seen walking the halls of the school with a young child in arm or tow. Student mothers at Lee depend on extended family to care for their children while they are in school. When care arrangements run into problems that might otherwise bar student mothers from attending class, Boyle urges them to bring the children to school. By babysitting, Boyle is serving students but, more important, she reflects an emerging set of ideals at Lee. Lee wants to be a community, and this transformation requires that a new ethic of caring take hold. Lee High School Principal Bill Fish believes that this type of caring is reciprocal. The more the school cares about students, the more students care about matters of schooling. When asked about the practice of babysitting at Lee, he modestly responds, "From time to time kids get in a bind. We are not officially doing it [babysitting] but unofficially we do what we can." His vision is to establish a day-care center in the school for children of students and teachers.

Administrators ought not to choose among psychological, bureaucratic, and moral authority; instead, the approach should be additive. To be additive, however, moral authority must be viewed as legitimate. Further, with servant leadership as the model, moral authority should become the cornerstone of one's overall leadership practice.

Stewardship

The "leader of leaders" and servant leadership styles bring stewardship responsibilities to the heart of the administrator's role. When this happens, the rights and prerogatives inherent in the administrator's position move to the periphery, and attention is focused on duties and responsibilities—to others as persons and, more important, to the school itself.

Stewardship represents primarily an act of trust, whereby people and institutions entrust a leader with certain obligations and duties to fulfill and perform on their behalf. For example, the public entrusts the schools to the school board. The school board entrusts each school to its principal. Parents entrust their children to teachers. Stewardship also involves the leader's personal responsibility to manage her or his life and affairs with proper regard for the rights of other people and for the common welfare. Finally, stewardship involves placing oneself in service to ideas and ideals and to others who are committed to their fulfillment.

The concept of stewardship furnishes an attractive image of leadership, for it embraces all the members of the school as community and all those who are served by the community. Parents, teachers, and administrators share stewardship responsibility for students. Students join the others in stewardship responsibility for the school as learning community. Mary Giella, assistant superintendent for instruction in the Pasco County (Florida) Schools, captures the spirit of stewardship as follows: "My role is one of facilitator. I listened to those who taught the children and those who were school leaders. I helped plan what they saw was a need. I coordinated the plan until those participating could independently conduct their own plans."

The organizational theorist Louis Pondy (1978, p. 94) has noted that leadership is invariably defined as behavioral: "The 'good' leader is one who can get his subordinates to do something. What happens if we force ourselves away from this marriage to behavioral concepts? What kind of insights can we get if we say that the effectiveness of a leader lies in his ability to make activity meaningful for those in his role set—not to change behavior but to give others a sense of understanding what they are doing, and especially to articulate it so that they can communicate about the meaning of their behavior?"

Shifting emphasis from behavior to meaning can help us recapture leadership as a powerful force for school improvement. Giving legitimacy to the moral dimension of leadership, and understanding leadership as the acceptance and embodiment of one's stewardship responsibilities, are important steps in this direction.

REFERENCES

Albritton, M. *De Zavala Elementary School: A Committed Community.* Case study, Department of Education, Trinity University, 1991.

Barth, R. *Improving Schools from Within.* San Francisco: Jossey-Bass, 1990.

Gilligan, C. *In a Different Voice.* Cambridge, Mass.: Harvard University Press, 1982.

Greenberg, S. "So You Want to Talk Theory?" Paper presented at the annual meeting of the American Educational Research Association, Boston, 1985.

Greenfield, W. "The Micropolitics of Leadership in an Urban Elementary School." Paper presented at the annual meeting of the American Educational Research Association, Chicago, 1991.

Greenleaf, R. K. *Servant Leadership.* New York: Paulist Press, 1977.

Hampel, J. "The Administrator as Servant: A Model for Leadership Development." Unpublished manuscript, Department of Education, San Diego State University, 1988.

Johnson, S. M. *Teachers at Work: Achieving Success in Our Schools.* New York: Basic Books, 1990.

Kaufman, D. R., and Richardson, B. L. *Achievement and Women: Challenging the Assumptions.* New York: Free Press, 1982.

Louv, R. "Hope in Hell's Classroom." *New York Times Magazine,* Nov. 25, 1990, pp. 30–33, 63–67, and 74–75.

Miller, J. B. *Toward a New Psychology of Women.* Boston: Beacon Press, 1986.

Miller, L. M. *American Spirit: Visions of a New Corporate Culture.* New York: Morrow, 1984.

Mustain, G. "Bottom-Drawer Bureau." *Washington Monthly,* Sept. 1990, p. 14.

Pondy, L. R. "Leadership Is a Language Game." In M. W. McCall, Jr., and M. M. Lombardo (eds.), *Leadership: Where Else Can We Go?* Durham, N.C.: Duke University Press, 1978.

Shakeshaft, C. *Women in Educational Administration.* Newbury Park, Calif.: Sage, 1987.

Vaill, P. "The Purposing of High-Performance Systems." In T. J. Sergiovanni and J. E. Corbally (eds.), *Leadership and Organizational Culture.* Urbana: University of Illinois Press, 1984.

7

AN EDUCATIONAL CREDO FOR A TIME OF CRISIS AND URGENCY

David E. Purpel

The Problematics of Our Religious and Moral Framework

We find on reflection that we are comfortable in reaffirming the discussion of how the commonalities of our political, moral, and intellectual heritage are valuable resources available to us in our search for a common set of transcendent values. One key element upon which we do need to expand is what we originally characterized as the eternal argument over the question of the reality or lack thereof behind religious belief, illustrated with quotations from Durkheim and Eliade. The revision we believe is needed here is the addition of a category. To move toward a new mythos for our time, we shall need to make a distinction between religion (if construed as requiring acceptance of a set of rigid doctrines) and spirituality (if construed as the initial inspiration for the construction of religions). We believe that this distinction is necessary because the capacity for self-deception has historically been nowhere more apparent than when humanity has ventured into this area. As a result, the concept that spiritual insight might offer some access to truth beyond our other capacities has often been tainted by the excesses of the adherents of derivative doctrines. We will elaborate on the implication of this distinction in the next chapters in an attempt to support our conviction that our first edition needed more emphasis on the spiritual aspect of the crisis.

We still hold to the first edition's appreciation for all the cautions and safeguards that our political, moral, and intellectual heritage provides against the dangers of "arrogance, self-righteousness, self-delusion and corruption that ensue when power and piety are integrated." At the same time, we concluded with a call not to allow these very appropriate concerns to drive us to a retreat into amorality and vulgar pragmatism. To that end there was an affirmation of the truly noble aspects of our common heritage and a condemnation of the evil and destructive forces in our culture, all of which pointed toward the fifth chapter and the Credo.

The Credo as an Exemplar of the Goal of Education

What we find now in looking back is that, despite the value and power of the noble aspects of our culture, they have historically failed and continue to fail the goal which we seek: an overarching moral and spiritual framework that provides a center of meaning for the culture. Our political, moral, and intellectual heritage is necessary but not sufficient—these resources alone have not, will not take us to where we want to go. They give us the capacity to describe the outcome we desire, but they have failed to find the path to get us there. Therefore in reflecting on that work today, we must affirm that the spiritual crisis which we face today will not abate until we find a way to wisdom that does not pass through arrogance, self-righteousness, self-delusion, and corruption.

The Credo is re-stated here in its entirety, so that it may be read as a whole (with revisions from Purpel and Shapiro, 1995, pp. 154–156). We consider the Credo to be an example of the sort of behavior to which we believe educators (and citizens) are called, the sort of behavior that would resolve many of the problems of education and of our society. The Credo is necessary; we cannot get to where we want to go without bringing to bear our political, moral and intellectual heritage, and we hold this Credo to be an exemplar of the application of that heritage to the present crisis. What we now add is the notion that the nature of human beings apparently requires something more than our political, moral, and intellectual heritage to enable us to change our behavior to comply with the Credo. The following chapters will provide our response to what we think is missing.

An Educational Credo for a Time of Crisis and Urgency

Educators are primarily moral, political, and cultural agents charged with the responsibility of grounding their specialized insights in a cultural, political, and moral vision. An educator without some kind of moral and cultural grounding is either tragically alienated, cynically deceptive, or naively shallow. John Dewey reminds us that education is about learning to create a world and that our most vital and demanding task as educators is to be mindful of the kind of world that we want to create. Absolutely essential, therefore, in the ethics of education are the twin pillars of freedom, namely, responsibility and choice. As educators, we are required to respond to the challenges of life and to choose among the many moral, political, and cultural possibilities open to us.

We Choose, Celebrate, and Affirm These Propositions

1. *We recognize the wonder, mystery, and awe that surrounds our life and that beckons us to contemplate, examine, and make meaning of it and of our part in it.* As educators, we must encourage and help students to separate mystery and awe from ignorance and superstition, but we must be careful to witness and be informed by what is beyond our present human capacity to comprehend. As educators, our responsibility is to present with respect varying interpretations of life's meaning. But our most compelling responsibility is to renew and reenergize the commitment to pursue lives of individual and communal meaning.

2. *We renew our faith in the capacity to celebrate diversity and difference while working to create a world of harmony, peace, and justice.* As educators, we must avoid the perils of pride and arrogance that emerge from a posture of cultural superiority. We recognize that meaning and fulfillment derive, in part, from cultural identity, and we must therefore strive to revere and respect, not patronize and romanticize, the ethos of particular cultural, racial, and ethnic groups. This consciousness requires basic trust in the recognition that harmony is not synonymous with homogeneity, that peace is not to be equated with control, and that justice is not to be blurred with freedom.

As educators, we must move from a consciousness of mastery, domination, submission, and docility in which some persons are subjects and others are objects. As educators, we must strive to see our students not as black boxes, not as clay to be molded or minds to be trained, but as sentient beings deserving of dignity, love, and fulfillment. As educators, we must not require people to earn their dignity, but we must strive to celebrate the sanctity, miracle, and preciousness of life. This consciousness does not bring us to punishment, tracking, grading, and honors programs, but to an education that reveres life as sacred and inviolate. Such a consciousness does not urge us to get ahead, but to stand with; does not idealize competition, but venerates dignity; does not legitimate privilege and advantage, but rather seeks to heal the deadly quarrels that divide the human family.

We renew our faith in the human impulse to seek to create a world of justice, compassion, love, and joy, and in the human capacity to create such a world. As educators, our responsibility is to nurture these impulses that have permeated human history not only by increasing awareness and understanding of them but by confronting the equally human impulses to oppress, dominate, and objectify. As educators, we can be guided and comforted by the immensity of human intellectual, creative, and intuitive potential to re-create our world; and at the same time, we should be sobered by the human capacity to be destructive, cruel, and callous. We speak to an education that is grounded in our strongest and deepest moral traditions, which urge us to love our neighbor, to seek justice, and to pledge ourselves to a nation committed to liberty and justice for all and a government of the people, by the people, and for the people. We speak to an education based on traditions that urge us to beat swords into ploughshares, not to develop more deadly swords; a vision in which lions lie down with lambs, not one in which we train lambs to be lions; and a universal dream of milk and honey for all, not the American Dream of champagne and caviar for a few.

3. *We reaffirm our commitment to the joys of community, the profundity of compassion, and to the power of interdependence.* As educators, we must become aware of the spiritual disease of alienation, loneliness, fragmentation, and isolation and must act to reduce the perilous effects of an education directed toward success, achievement, and personalism. As educators, we have the responsibility of nurturing the impulse for meaningful and cooperative relationships and for exposing the myths and dangers of individual achievement. Education must not act to convert the uncivilized, but neither should it serve to create a myriad of individual universes. Compassion serves neither to distance nor to blur or annihilate differences, but rather seeks to share the struggles, pain, and joys that are common to us all. If we are to compete, we as educators need to confront the significance of the race not only for the winners but also for the losers. If we are to be committed to individual excellence, then we must know if it is achieved at the expense of others. More important, we as educators must participate in the process of creating a society in which people are more united than divided, where differences are not translated into hierarchy, and where pain and anguish are occasions for neither pity nor exploitation, but for compassion and solidarity.

4. *We affirm the central importance of nourishing a consciousness of moral outrage and social responsibility.* As educators, we must go far beyond informing, describing, and analyzing and must free ourselves from the destructive force of moral numbness. We must help our students to

become aware of our failures to meet our moral and cultural imperatives and to help them inform their intellectual understanding with moral judgments. An education that engenders a posture of promiscuous tolerance, scholarly detachment, or cynical weariness toward unnecessary human suffering is an abomination! We must avoid the temptation to teach only what makes one feel good or to teach that social problems are only "interesting." Education is not about finding out things, but about finding ourselves. It is not enough to say further research is needed when what is needed is not more information but more justice. To know without a sense of outrage, compassion, or concern deadens our souls and significantly eases the struggle of demonic forces to capture our consciousness. We need an education that produces moral indignation and energy rather than one that excuses, mitigates, and temporizes human misery. Heschel reminds us that although only a few are guilty, all are responsible. Our task as educators is therefore to teach students to identify the guilty, to have compassion for the victims, and to exercise their responsibility to reduce, if not eliminate, injustices.

Self-Deception

If the Credo exemplifies the behavior that would grow out of an overarching moral and spiritual framework that provided a center of meaning for the culture, then what is the nature of the path that would provide us with the capacity to comply with it? At the beginning of this chapter, we asserted a belief that most of the bad choices that have led us to the present state of our culture have derived more from confusion than from a fundamentally evil nature. In that same spirit we suggest that the reason such appropriate and noble sentiments as those we just offered are so incredibly difficult for human beings to honor lies in our immense capacity for self-deception, a failure that creates confusion and that neglected will often lead us to evil acts. Our first edition quoted Fingalate as saying that in self-deception, there is, ". . . a genuine subversion of personal agency and, for this reason in turn, a subversion of moral capacity." Perhaps we might now say that the confusion to which we have attributed the perversity of human behavior in opposing human aims might be explained as the result of this subversion by means of self-deception.

As an example, among the most self-deceptive assumptions of the worldview that is American market culture (and its associated reductionist cousins) are the ones holding that there is a single rational agent that constitutes each human consciousness and that this single agent makes all the choices that a human life entails. Yet so often, we seem to confront the consequences of some behavior that is "unlike us." Rather than always acting in a unified and coherent manner, most of us have found ourselves, at least on a few occasions astonished at our own anger or our unexpected emotion. Surely each of us has at least had the experience of deeply wishing that we could un-say some hurtful word or undo some "unintended" action.

REFERENCES

Heschel, A. J. *Man Is Not Alone*. New York: Farrar, Straus and Giroux, 1951.
Heschel, A. J. *God in Search of Man: A Philosophy of Judaism*. New York: Farrar, Straus and Giroux, 1955.
Heschel, A. J. *The Prophets*. New York: Harper & Row, 1962.
Heschel, A. J. *Who Is Man?* Palo Alto, Calif.: Stanford University Press, 1965.
Purpel, D., and Shapiro, S. *Beyond Liberation and Excellence*. New York: Bergin & Garvey, 1995.

8

BECOMING A TRUSTWORTHY LEADER

Megan Tschannen-Moran

To be trusted is a greater compliment than to be loved.

—George MacDonald

THE FIVE FACETS OF TRUST—benevolence, honesty, openness, reliability, and competence—relate directly to the five constituencies of schools (administrators, teachers, students, parents, and the general public). These considerations demonstrate the importance of trust to building successful schools. It follows, then, that the absence of trust impedes effectiveness and progress. If trust breaks down among any constituency, it can spread like a cancer by eroding academic performance and ultimately undermining the tenure of the instructional leader. In this day and age, no leader can long survive the demise of trust.

School leaders need to build trust with teachers because although governance structures such as collaborative decision making and site-based management can bring the insights of more people to solving the complex problems of schooling, they depend upon trust (Hoy and Tarter, 2003; Smylie and Hart, 1999). Without trust, communication becomes constrained and distorted, thus making problems more difficult to resolve (Roberts and O'Reilly, 1974). A proliferation of rules stemming from a lack of trust causes resentment and alienation among teachers and students alike (Fox, 1974; Govier, 1992). Even when school leaders work to build a common vision and foster acceptance of group goals, without trust these leaders do not inspire their constituencies to go beyond minimum requirements (Podsakoff, MacKenzie, Moorman, and Fetter, 1990; Tschannen-Moran, 2003).

Teachers need trust to cope with the stress of changing expectations and the demands of accountability being asked of them. As teachers are asked to change their fundamental beliefs and instructional techniques, they need to build new professional communities anchored in trust and teamwork (Little, 1990; Putnam and Borko, 1997). Even within the classroom, relationships are shifting to forms that require greater trust. Cooperative learning and project-based learning create higher levels of interdependence, which demand higher levels of trust.

Students need trust to engage productively with the learning environment at school and to access the opportunities made available to them (Meier, 2002). Without trust, students' energies are diverted toward self-protection and away from the learning process. Learning to trust the people at school can be a transformative experience for students whose lives outside of school have not taught them to trust (Watson, 2003).

Schools need the trust of parents and the wider school community. Making parents more active partners in the educational process involves fostering trusting relationships. Including parents in school governance requires trust that they will be motivated to work for the common good, not just their own narrow interests. Garnering additional resources from the community through entrepreneurial efforts and partnerships requires trust that the school is making the most of the resources it already has. In short, school leaders need to foster trust within each of the constituencies of their schools.

At the same time that schools face a greater need for trust, they encounter many obstacles to fostering trust. The difficulties of achieving new and higher societal expectations for equity in schools have led to suspicion of schools and school personnel. Higher standards and greater accountability have fostered conditions of distrust and blame. Moreover, schools have to cope with greater diversity and transience. A multicultural society with diverse values and shifting populations makes the cultivation of trust a significant challenge. Adding to this formidable task is the tendency for distrust, once established, to be self-perpetuating. There is a propensity for news of broken trust to spread faster and further than news of intact or restored trust, and the media often feed off of and aggravate the spiral of distrust.

For schools to realize the kinds of positive transformation envisioned by school reform efforts, attention must be paid to issues of trust. Finding ways to overcome the breakdown of trust is essential if we want schools to reach the aspirations we hold for them. This challenge is one of the most important tasks facing school leaders at the start of the twenty-first century.

Trustworthy School Leadership

The principal sets the tone for a school. The principal's behavior has a significant influence on the culture of the school. If schools are to reap the rewards of a trusting work environment, it is the principal's responsibility to build and sustain trusting relationships (Whitener, Brodt, Korsgaard, and Werner, 1998). In order to understand how this works in practical terms, it is useful to consider the five facets of trust in relation not only to the five constituencies of schools but also in relation to the five functions of instructional leaders. These functions include visioning, modeling, coaching, managing, and mediating. It takes a multidimensional model to understand the matrix of trustworthy leadership (see Figure 8.1).

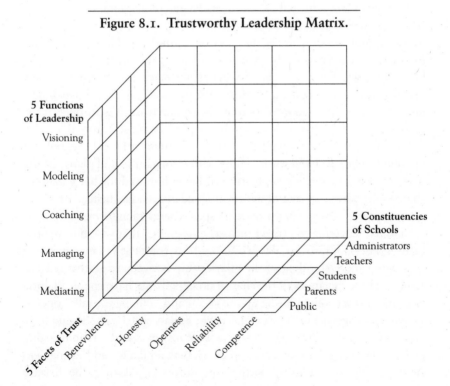

Figure 8.1. Trustworthy Leadership Matrix.

Visioning

If anyone is responsible for lifting up a vision of the school as a trustworthy environment for all constituencies, it is the person charged with
the responsibility for school leadership. This exploration of trust gives
school leaders a framework from which to speak of trust in dynamic and
proactive ways. Once they take stock of the importance of trust to successful schools, they can promote trust before it goes sour. Had Gloria,
Fred, and Brenda made use of this framework, it could have made their
jobs easier and their leadership more effective.

When Gloria arrived at Lincoln she took over a school in need of
change. The students were not being educated well enough to meet even
minimal accountability standards. She suspected that members of the faculty were not doing their best for the students of Lincoln. Her vision of
turning the school around was an admirable one. But her methods were
not. By failing to first establish a benevolent relationship with the people
she was charged to work with, her zeal for change came across as judg-
mental impatience. It damaged the trust with the teachers before it had
time to be established.

Even when the principal has taken leadership of a school in which he or
she feels that the teachers do not deserve to be trusted, such as in a truly
dysfunctional school with negative, cynical attitudes and low expectations
for student achievement, the principal is not relieved of the obligation to
be trustworthy. There are schools where some teachers actively try to sow
discord and distrust toward the administrator, and yet the principal must
not retaliate or respond in ways that undermine trust. It is through trustworthy leadership that such situations can best be turned around.

Gloria had a vision for improved student learning at Lincoln School, but
in failing to be open and forthcoming with information and plans, Gloria
was not seen as trustworthy. Instead of being honored for her vision for
change, she was suspected of harboring hidden agendas. Instead of working toward the same goal, the teachers spent energy monitoring her behavior and maneuvering to protect themselves—energy that would have been
better spent on improving the educational environment at Lincoln.

A better understanding of the relationship between trustworthy leadership and the dynamics of the change process would have enabled Gloria
to be more successful in lifting up the vision and "talking the talk" of constructive change at Lincoln (Evans, 1996; Fullan, 2001). She would have
structured a process whereby teachers were involved in the vision-casting
process, wrestling with the data and developing a plan for addressing deficiencies. This would have laid the foundation for Gloria to be directly

engaged with teachers without being disrespectful. She would have been better positioned to assist them to make needed changes.

Modeling

Effective school leaders not only know how to "talk the talk" of trust, they also know how to "walk the talk." If being a role model is ever necessary, it's when it comes to cultivating a culture of trust. Discontinuity between word and example will quickly erode a principal's ability to lead. Setting an example is not to be flaunted. Skillful principals often earn the trust of their faculty by leading quietly. They are soft on people and hard on projects. They combine personal humility—exercising restraint and modesty—with tenacity and the professional will to see that the task is accomplished and accomplished well (Collins, 2002; Fullan, 2003).

Fred failed to earn the trust of his faculty because his actions did not reflect his talk of high expectations and stern consequences. In wanting too much to be liked, and in his fear and avoidance of conflict, Fred failed to provide trustworthy leadership for the teachers and students at Fremont. Although Fred genuinely cared about the students and teachers in his school, his lack of leadership left them vulnerable to the mounting problems at the school.

Dealing with problems is where having a framework of trust can assist school leaders to monitor their own behavior and communicate in a straightforward manner. Part of the art of trustworthy leadership is the ability to speak hard truths in a way that communicates value and caring. This takes courage, but it is also more likely to produce constructive change. Trustworthy leaders model norms of conduct that promote the well-being of all members of the school community and explicitly invite others to abide by those norms as well. They defend those norms in ways that make clear that disrespect is not an option.

We see this approach modeled in Brenda's more trustworthy leadership. When Brenda arrived at Brookside, she had many innovative ideas for what she would like to see happening at the school. But Brenda understood wisely that these changes would require extra effort and risk taking on the part of her teachers. She knew she couldn't get there alone. She knew she would need the teachers to be on board, so she was patient and developed relationships. A strategy of small early wins on some key tasks can help build trust in the principal's competence as well as motivation. This builds momentum toward more successful schools.

To consistently serve as a model of trustworthy leadership, it is important for educational leaders to reflect regularly on their words and actions.

In the pressure-cooker of a school system, this is a particularly challenging task. Who has the time to STOP—step back, think, and organize their thoughts before proceeding (Gallwey, 2000)? Trustworthy leaders view reflection as a required part of their daily and weekly routines. Brenda arrived at school early, before everyone else, giving her a chance to collect herself at the start of the day. Others engage in regular reflective writing. And school breaks may provide a venue for taking a broader view.

> What makes the biggest difference is to have a principal who really listens. When you talk to our principal, he is not really paying attention. You can talk to him later about the same topic and he has no memory of the conversation.
>
> —*Erika, art teacher*
>
> I was a struggling new teacher at a school for students with emotional disturbances. I soon learned that if I approached my principal with concerns about a classroom management problem, I would read my own words back to me in my next teacher evaluation. I sought other avenues of support after that.
>
> —*Bud, special education teacher*

Coaching

Beyond lifting up the vision and modeling the behavior of trustworthy leadership, principals can also build or damage trust by how they engage around the instructional matters of the school. Applying either too much or too little pressure serves to undermine trust and makes principals' leadership of the instructional program less effective.

The school leader as coach is one way to frame and understand the role of instructional leadership that fosters a culture of trust. Coaches assist people to move forward toward their goals through conversation and their way of being with people. They know when to push and when to back off, based on the needs of the situation. They show genuine concern for both the task at hand and the welfare of those who have to accomplish that task. Great coaches epitomize the five facets of trust in their dealings with people.

There is a growing body of research and literature that summarizes the core coaching competencies. These include personal presence, active listening, powerful questioning, creation of awareness, planning and goal setting, design of actions, as well as management of progress and accountability (International Coach Federation, 1999). Mastering these competencies is important for the process of instructional leadership to generate the professional development, self-efficacy beliefs, and enthusiasm of teachers.

Such mastery is predicated on the establishment of trust. As principals issue the challenge to their teachers to find new ways to meet the diverse needs of high-achieving students and those with special needs without neglecting more typical students, those with the trust of their teachers will be more successful at motivating teachers for the extra effort required. Teachers will be more willing to take the risk to try new instructional strategies when a culture of trust pervades the school. In cultivating a professional learning community committed to professional inquiry, data-based decision making, and best practice, as well as helping teachers learn to adapt to new standards of accountability, trustworthy principals can move their schools to higher levels of productivity and success.

Supervision is one aspect of the principal's role as instructional leader in which the establishment of trust and the language of coaching are especially important. Not surprising, trust has been found to play a significant role in employee reactions to supervision. In a study of the perceptions of fairness of performance evaluations by supervisors, the level of trust in the supervisor was more important in regard to perceived fairness than any other characteristics of the performance evaluation process (Fulk, Brief, and Barr, 1985). The traditional norms of schools have allowed teachers a great deal of autonomy and little supervision. Teachers have enjoyed the trust, or at least the neglect, of their supervisors. In the age of accountability, however, this state of affairs is changing. New systems of teacher evaluation require greater inspection of teachers' classroom practice. Greater scrutiny may be perceived as a lessening of trust by both teachers and administrators and might in fact lead to less trust. However, if supervision is practiced in such a way that the greater attention is perceived as increased care with a focus on problem solving and coaching, principals will have an opportunity to demonstrate their competence and expertise. Trustworthy leadership is likely to lead to more active and constructive supervision that contributes to improved instruction in the school.

One of the greatest dilemmas faced by school leaders occurs when they don't trust the competence and motivation of their teachers. It is the responsibility of the principal as coach to create the circumstances that extend the sense of purpose and competence of these teachers. The trustworthy principal understands that teachers function within the culture of a school that influences their behavior. If they have worked within a culture that tolerated or even encouraged a slackening of effort, the principal's responses need to take into consideration these environmental factors that have contributed to poor performance.

Because a school culture emerges as a group of people who solve problems together, a principal who wants to change the culture of a school needs to unleash creativity as teachers and administrators alike find new solutions to old problems (Schein, 1992). When a faculty member fails to meet expectations, the principal as coach addresses the issues directly but discretely and in a way that preserves that person's dignity. In this way, teachers can modify their behavior and conform to expectations without compromising their standing or identity in the school community. This coach approach to instructional leadership both stems from and results in a culture of disciplined professional inquiry (Fullan, 2003).

> We had a problem of stealing. Things were missing—people's lunch from the refrigerator, money from sales would be missing here and there, small items would disappear from your classroom. After we complained to our principal about what was going on, there was an investigation. Then it was announced that a certain staff person would be taking a leave of absence. After that, the problems stopped. We were glad the situation was dealt with but also that it was handled discretely so as not to embarrass anyone.
>
> —Jodi, middle school teacher

Managing

In addition to their role as instructional leader and coach, principals are also charged with the responsibility for management and administration. Here, too, the effective understanding and implementation of the five facets of trust are important to a principal's effectiveness and success. In their managerial capacity, trusting and trustworthy principals will earn critical efficiencies in what is at times an overwhelming task. Principals willing to delegate control will find that they are not so bound by the need to do everything themselves. High-trust principals who have been successful in cultivating a high-trust culture in their schools will find that they need fewer rules and rigid procedures to ensure that teachers are doing what they are supposed to be doing. Greater organizational citizenship will lubricate the smooth functioning of the organization. And principals who have fostered a strong sense of trust with parents and their communities will find that they spend less time explaining their actions and engaging in investigations of the actions of others.

Trustworthy leaders cultivate "a culture of discipline" within their schools in which the norms and expectations support people in being productively engaged with the task so that each person contributes constructively (Collins, 2002). Here, too, principals need to strike a balance in how they handle the rules between how much and how little they push. Gloria pushed too hard. She adopted a manipulative and overly rigid approach to the enforcement of rules. Gloria tried to pressure her teachers through using the teaching contract against them, but this technique did not foster a productive school environment. Fred didn't push hard enough. Fred was not trustworthy because, in his attempts to be supportive and empowering of teachers, he did not confront bad behavior and take action to correct it. Fred lost the trust of his faculty by avoiding conflict and by lax enforcement of rules. Trustworthy principals find the right balance in their handling of policies, rules, and procedures. They do not abuse their power through manipulation or an overreliance on a strict interpretation of rules. But neither do they abdicate their responsibility for leadership. Trustworthy principals demonstrate flexibility by focusing more on generating possibilities and solving problems than control. They see rules as means to an end rather than as ends in themselves.

> When we trusted teachers to have more say over their time, whether they wanted to teach on the block or not, whether to team, and how they arranged their time within the block, to take breaks when it made sense to them within their lessons, we noticed that it trickled down and that they began to trust their students more too.
>
> —*Dan, high school principal*

Mediating

Even the most trustworthy of school leaders will have to deal with times of betrayal and conflict in the school environment. But trustworthy principals know how to deal with conflict and repair trust through the process of mediation. For one thing, principals lift up the vision that such repair is possible. In a disposable society known for revolving door relationships, trustworthy school leaders stand for something different. They let all their constituencies know that conflict and even betrayal are not necessarily the last word. They hold out the hope for reconciliation and the repair of trust.

But it's not enough to just lift up a vision; trustworthy leaders must also play the role of mediator when trust breaks down. It is important that the members of the school community, whether students, teachers, or parents, have a trusted resource to turn to when they find themselves in the midst of conflict. Trustworthy school leaders are not only skillful themselves in conflict management strategies, but they also create the structures and provide the training for others to improve in this realm. Cultivating more productive ways of dealing with conflict is an important part of building a school culture of trust. Such skills help in restoring trust that has been broken; moreover, they can prevent the breaking of trust in the first place by supporting disputants with norms and processes that help them negotiate solutions that meet the needs of all parties.

Successful Schools

Trustworthy leaders are at the heart of successful schools. Trustworthy leadership gets everyone on the same team, pulling in the same direction. At Brookside, Brenda's trustworthy leadership was contagious; it resulted in more trusting relationships throughout the school community. The faculty clearly came to care for one another. This caring was not limited to small groups of friends within cliques, but extended to every person on the faculty. On a professional level, this faculty looked out for one another, and especially for new teachers. Teachers freely shared ideas and resources. On a personal level, people were also willing to share about their lives outside of school with the expectation that they would receive a caring response. Teachers respected one another's expertise and enjoyed a strong sense of shared commitment to the mission of the school. There was not a sense of competition to outdo one another or to prove who was a better teacher. Teachers were not defensive about their classroom performance. Teachers welcomed one another into their classrooms, whether informally for a visit or to borrow something, or more formally for a peer observation. Teachers were not worried about being judged harshly or unfairly. They respected each other's integrity and could count on one another to be reliable in their commitments.

Trust was no less important among students and parents. In making trust judgments about children, teachers looked for respect—respect for teachers and other adults, respect for other children, and respect for self. All of the other facets of trust—judgments of honesty, openness, reliability, and competence—seemed to follow from this baseline assessment of respect. Teachers wanted to feel that the parents of their students were as concerned about the children's well-being as they themselves were. They also wanted the parents to believe that teachers had the child's best interests at heart and that they were willing to work together to solve any problems as a team. Teachers also trusted parents who avoided blame but were willing to take responsibility for their own actions. They respected parents who encouraged their children to do the same.

Across the various actors in schools, whether principals, teachers, or students, the same facets were important to the cultivation of trust. At its most basic level, trustworthiness had to do with concern for relationships combined with a concern for the task. At the administrative level, this balance was evident in the high-support, high-challenge principal. Among teachers it was expressed as the high-commitment, high-competence teacher. For students, it was the high-respect, high-motivation student. No matter the level within the school community, earning trust had to do with guarding both qualities of care. Trustworthy leadership shows the way through example and by providing the resources, norms, and structures for others to be trustworthy as well. Trustworthy leaders create a culture of trust in their buildings; this trust is at the heart of successful schools.

Putting It into Action

You can make use of the ideas presented in this book to foster greater trust and reap the benefits of greater efficiency, adaptability, and quality in your school. By interfacing the five facets of trust with the five functions of leadership as you relate to the various stakeholders of your school, you will gain new insight and direction as to what needs to be done. Through increased awareness of how trust works and its importance to productive schools, you will be more successful in your job.

When there is a high level of trust in the interpersonal relationships within the school, you and your teachers can celebrate that fact and take action to strengthen the cycle, thereby fostering even greater levels of trust. When there are problems surrounding trust in your school, the model presented in this book can increase your awareness as to the importance of and strategies for fixing those problems. This model can generate new ideas and possibilities, enabling you and your constituents to interrupt the spiral of distrust and begin the journey back to restored trust.

You will find several instruments on my website (www.MeganTM.com) to assess various aspects of your school, such as the school climate, collective sense of efficacy, and level of organizational citizenship. These instruments can help you map your leadership style as perceived by teachers, as well as the interpersonal interactions among teachers and between teachers and students and the relationship of your school with the community. Once a profile of the school is drawn, you and your teachers can decide whether the trust, climate, and collective efficacy of the school are in need of attention.

These instruments can provide an important window into the perceptions of teachers, students, and parents. Principals are often quite surprised to see that their perceptions of the school are different from those of their teachers. In fact, it is not unusual for principals to describe their schools in more favorable terms than others. The issue then is not who is correct, but to understand the nature of the discrepancy. If teachers perceive the school as low in trust, a place where they have to feel on guard, it is important to know why that is the case and then take appropriate action.

Identifying a lack of trust as a problem is not the same as solving it. There are no quick fixes. The instruments at hand are merely tools for analysis and diagnosis; they cannot solve the problems. But they do provide a basis for examining important features of trust in the school that may be in need of change. Only in conversation with your teachers and other constituents can you solve the problem. Once the diagnosis is made, you will be in a position to engage in a positive strategy of change. The five-facet model of trust presented in this book will generate new commitment, ideas, and strategies for individual coaching, as well as organizational and professional development activities. For example, a problem-solving team can be formed to diagnose the causes of the existing situation, develop an action plan, implement the plan, and assess its success.

Awareness brings with it the responsibility to take constructive action for change. It is the duty of the person with greater power within a hierarchy to accept greater responsibility for the cultivation of trust. Even if you feel wronged and misunderstood, you have the opportunity to work toward renewed trust through being meticulously trustworthy and by announcing these intentions to others. Restoring lost trust is possible, but it is not easy. The effort requires courage, persistence, and forgiveness. The rewards, however, are worth the effort for schools mired in the dysfunctional consequences of a distrustful culture.

Trust is a significant factor in successful schools. Schools that enjoy a culture of trust are likely to benefit from members of the school community willingly working together and going beyond the minimum requirements of their positions. Communication flows more freely when teachers are not afraid of the consequences of candor. A high level of trust helps these schools be wonderful places to learn and grow: a positive, open, and healthy climate pervades the school. The costs of broken trust are great. When distrust pervades a school, constrained communication, poor organizational citizenship, and a proliferation of dysfunctional rules are often the result. Trust matters because it hits schools in their bottom line; it makes a difference in student achievement. It is related to teachers' collective sense that they can make a difference and in dealing constructively with conflict. Although the building of trust in schools requires time, effort, and leadership, the investment will bring lasting returns. Trust pays dividends in helping schools succeed at fulfilling their mission to be productive, professional learning communities.

KEY POINTS ABOUT BECOMING A TRUSTWORTHY LEADER

- Trustworthy leadership applies the five facets of trust to the five functions of leadership. This multidimensional model can assist educational leaders to proactively foster a culture of trust in their schools. It can also assist them to diagnosis and correct problems of trust before they become insurmountable.

- Trustworthy leaders lift up the vision, model the behavior, provide the coaching, manage the environment, and mediate the breakdowns of trust.

- At all times, trustworthy leaders put the culture of trust ahead of their own ego needs. Skillful principals often earn the trust of their faculty by leading quietly.

- Trustworthy principals foster the development of trust in schools by demonstrating flexibility, focusing on problem solving, and involving teachers in important decisions.

- Trustworthy leaders strike the right balance between pushing too hard and pushing too little. They are soft on people and tough on projects. They combine personal humility—exercising restraint and modesty—with tenacity and the professional will to see that the task is accomplished and accomplished well.

- Trust matters to successful leaders and their schools.

QUESTIONS FOR REFLECTION AND DISCUSSION

1. What are some of the costly structures, systems, and practices at your school that could be reduced or eliminated if there was more trust between parents and the school, teachers and administrators, and teachers and students?

2. What is the greatest area in need of attention to trust within your school community? What could you do to improve the level of trust?

REFERENCES

Collins, J. *Good to Great: Why Some Companies Make the Leap . . . and Others Don't.* New York: HarperBusiness, 2002.

Evans, R. *The Human Side of Change: Reform, Resistance, and Real-Life Problems of Innovation.* San Francisco: Jossey-Bass, 1996.

Fox, A. *Beyond Contract: Work, Power and Trust Relations.* London: Farber & Farber, 1974.

Fulk, J., Brief, A. P., and Barr, S. H. "Trust in the Supervisor and Perceived Fairness and Accuracy of Performance Evaluations." *Journal of Business Research,* 1985, *13,* 301–313.

Fullan, M. *Leading in a Culture of Change.* San Francisco: Jossey-Bass, 2001.

Fullan, M. *The Moral Imperative of School Leadership.* Thousand Oaks, CA: Corwin, 2003.

Gallwey, W. T. *The Inner Game of Work.* New York: Random House, 2000.

Govier, T. "Distrust as a Practical Problem." *Journal of Social Philosophy,* 1992, *23,* 52–63.

Hoy, W. K., and Tarter, C. J. *Administrators Solving the Problems of Practice: Decision-Making, Concepts, Cases, and Consequences.* Boston: Allyn & Bacon, 2003.

International Coach Federation. "Coaching Core Competencies." March 30, 1999. Retrieved June 15, 2006, from http://www.coachfederation.org/ICF/For+Current+Members/Credentialing/Why+a+Credential/Competencies/.

Little, J. W. "The Persistence of Privacy: Autonomy and Initiative in Teachers' Professional Relations." *Teachers College Record,* 1990, *91,* 509–536.

Meier, D. *In Schools We Trust: Creating Communities of Learning in an Era of Testing and Standardization.* Boston: Beacon Press, 2002.

Podsakoff, P. M., MacKenzie, S. B., Moorman, R. H., and Fetter, R. "Transformational Leader Behaviors and Their Effects on Followers' Trust in Leader, Satisfaction, and Organizational Citizenship Behaviors." *Leadership Quarterly,* 1990, *1,* 107–142.

Putnam, R. T., and Borko, H. "Teacher Learning: Implications of New Views of Cognition." In B. J. Biddle, T. L. Good, and I. F. Goodson (eds.), *The International Handbook of Teachers and Teaching* (pp. 1223–1296). Dordrecht, The Netherlands: Kluwer, 1997.

Roberts, K. H., and O'Reilly, C. O. "Failure in Upward Communication in Organizations: Three Possible Culprits." *Academy of Management Review,* 1974, *17,* 205–215.

Schein, E. H. *Organizational Culture and Leadership.* (2nd ed.). San Francisco: Jossey-Bass, 1992.

Smylie, M. A., and Hart, A. W. "School Leadership for Teacher Learning and Change: A Human and Social Capital Perspective." In J. Murphy and K. S. Louis (eds.), *Handbook of Research on Educational Administration* (pp. 421–441). San Francisco: Jossey-Bass, 1999.

Tschannen-Moran, M. "Fostering Organizational Citizenship: Transformational Leadership and Trust." In W. K. Hoy and C. G. Miskel, *Studies in Leading and Organizing Schools* (pp. 157–179). Greenwich, Conn.: Information Age Publishing, 2003.

Watson, M. *Learning to Trust: Transforming Difficult Elementary Classrooms Through Developmental Discipline.* San Francisco: Jossey-Bass, 2003.

Whitener, E. M., Brodt, S. E., Korsgaard, M. A., and Werner, J. M. "Managers as Initiators of Trust: An Exchange Relationship Framework for Understanding Managerial Trustworthy Behavior." *Academy of Management Review,* 1998, 23, 513–530.

9

THE MANAGER AS POLITICIAN

Lee G. Bolman
Terrence E. Deal

BILL GATES WAS STANDING in the right place in the early 1980s when IBM's fledgling personal computer business came looking for an operating system. Gates didn't have one, but his partner, Paul Allen, knew someone who did. Gates paid $75,000 for QDOS (Quick and Dirty Operating System) in the deal—or steal—of the twentieth century. Gates changed the name to DOS and resold it to IBM, but he shrewdly retained the right to license it to anyone else. DOS quickly became the primary operating system for most of the world's personal computers. Gates himself was on the road to becoming one of the world's richest men (Manes and Andrews, 1994; Zachary, 1994).

Windows, a graphic interface riding atop DOS, fueled another great leap forward for Gates's Microsoft empire. But by the late 1980s, Gates had a problem. He and everyone else knew that DOS was obsolete, woefully deficient for existing personal computers and even more inadequate for those to come. Millions of PC users were stuck in a high-tech version of *Waiting for Godot.*

The solution was supposed to be OS/2, an operating system developed jointly by Microsoft and IBM. It was a tense partnership. IBMers saw "Microsofties" as undisciplined adolescents. Microsoft folks moaned that "Big Blue" was a hopelessly bureaucratic producer of "poor code, poor design, poor process and other overhead" (Manes and Andrews, 1994,

p. 425). Increasingly pessimistic about the viability of OS/2, Gates decided to hedge his bets by developing a new operating system to be called Windows NT. Gates recruited the brilliant but crotchety Dave Cutler from Digital Equipment to head the effort. Cutler had led the development of the VMS operating system that helped DEC dominate the minicomputer industry for many years. Zachary (1993) described Cutler as a rough-cut combination of Captain Bligh and Captain Ahab. Gates agreed that Cutler was known "more for his code than his charm" (Zachary, 1993, p. A1).

Things started well, but Cutler insisted on keeping his team small and wanted no responsibility beyond the "kernel" of the operating system. He figured someone else could worry about such things as the user interface. Gates began to see a potential disaster looming, but issuing orders to the temperamental Cutler was as promising as telling Picasso to paint differently. Gates then brought in the calm, understated Paul Maritz. Born in South Africa, Maritz had studied mathematics and economics in Cape Town before deciding that software was his destiny. After five years with Intel, Maritz joined Microsoft in 1986 and became the leader of its OS/2 effort. When he was assigned informal oversight of Windows NT, no one told Cutler, who adamantly refused to work for Maritz. Twelve years Cutler's junior, Maritz got a frosty welcome:

> As he began meeting regularly with Cutler on NT matters, Maritz often found himself the victim of slights. Once Maritz innocently suggested to Cutler that "We should—" Cutler interrupted, "We! Who's we? You mean you and the mouse in your pocket?" Maritz brushed off such retorts, even finding humor in Cutler's apparently inexhaustible supply of epithets. He refused to allow Cutler to draw him into a brawl. Instead, he hoped Cutler would "volunteer" for greater responsibility as the shortcomings of the status quo became more apparent. (Zachary, 1994, p. 76)

Maritz enticed Cutler with tempting challenges. In early 1990, he asked Cutler if it would be possible to put together a demonstration of NT in November for COMDEX, the industry's biggest convention. Cutler took the bait. Maritz knew that the effort would expose NT's weaknesses (Zachary, 1994). When Gates subsequently seethed that NT was too late, too big, and too slow, Maritz scrambled to "filter that stuff from Dave" (p. 208). Maritz's patience eventually paid off when he was promoted to head all operating systems development: "The promotion gave Maritz formal and actual authority over Cutler and the entire NT project. Still, he avoided confrontations, preferring to wait until Cutler came to see the benefits of Maritz's views. Increasingly Cutler and his inner circle viewed Maritz as a powerhouse and not an empty suit. 'He's critical to the project,' said [one of Cutler's most loyal lieutenants]. 'He got into it a little bit at a time. Slowly he blended his way in until it was obvious who was running the show. Him?'" (p. 204).

The *Challenger* case teaches a chilling lesson about how political pressures distort momentous decisions. Similarly, the implosion of firms such as Enron and WorldCom shows how the unfettered pursuit of self-interest by powerful executives can bring even a giant corporation to its knees. Many believe that the antidote is to free management from politics. But this is unrealistic so long as the political frame's basic conditions apply. Enduring differences lead to multiple interpretations of what is important, and even what is true. Scarce resources require tough decisions about who gets what. Interdependence means that people cannot ignore one another; they need each other's assistance, support, and resources. Under such conditions, efforts to eliminate politics drive differences under the rug or into the closet. There they fester into counterproductive, unmanageable forms. In our search for more positive images of the manager as constructive politician, Paul Maritz offers an example.

Kotter (1985) contends that too many managers are either naive or cynical. Naive managers view the world through rose-colored glasses, insisting that most people are good, kind, and trustworthy. Cynical managers believe the opposite: everyone is selfish, things are always political, and "get them before they get you" is the best survival tactic. Neither stance is effective: "Organizational excellence . . . demands a sophisticated type of social skill: a leadership skill that can mobilize people and accomplish important objectives despite dozens of obstacles; a skill that can pull people together for meaningful purposes despite the thousands of forces that push us apart; a skill that can keep our corporations and public institutions from descending into a mediocrity characterized by bureaucratic infighting, parochial politics, and vicious power struggles" (p. 11).

Organizations need "benevolent politicians" who steer a course between naivete and cynicism: "Beyond the yellow brick road of naivete and the mugger's lane of cynicism, there is a narrow path, poorly lighted, hard to find, and even harder to stay on once found. People who have the skill and the perseverance to take that path serve us in countless ways. We need more of these people. Many more" (Kotter, 1985, p. xi).

In a world of chronic scarcity, diversity, and conflict, the astute manager has to develop a direction, build a base of support, and learn how to manage relations with both allies and opponents. In this chapter, we start by laying out four basic skills for the manager as politician. Then we tackle ethical issues, the soft underbelly of organizational politics. Is it possible to be political and still do the right thing? We discuss four instrumental values to guide ethical choice: mutuality (is everyone playing by the same rules?); generality (would it be good if everyone did it?); openness (are we open to public scrutiny?), and caring (are we looking out for anyone beyond ourselves?).

Political Skills

The manager as politician exercises four key skills: agenda setting (Kanter, 1983; Kotter, 1988; Pfeffer, 1992; Smith, 1988), mapping the political terrain (Pfeffer, 1992; Pichault, 1993), networking and forming coalitions (Kanter, 1983; Kotter, 1982, 1985, 1988; Pfeffer, 1992; Smith, 1988), and bargaining and negotiating (Bellow and Moulton, 1978; Fisher and Ury, 1981; Lax and Sebenius, 1986).

Agenda Setting

Structurally, an agenda outlines a goal and a scheduled series of activities. Politically, agendas are statements of interests and scenarios. In reflecting on his experience as a university president, Warren Bennis (1989) arrived at a deceptively simple observation: "It struck me that I was most effective when I knew what I wanted" (p. 20). Kanter's study of internal entrepreneurs in American corporations (1983), Kotter's analysis of effective corporate leaders (1988), and Smith's examination of effective U.S. presidents (1988) all reached a similar conclusion: the first step in effective political leadership is setting an agenda.

The effective leader creates an "agenda for change" with two major elements: a *vision* balancing the long-term interests of key parties and a *strategy* for achieving the vision, recognizing competing internal and external forces (Kotter, 1988). The agenda must impart direction while addressing the concerns of major stakeholders. Kanter (1983) and Pfeffer (1992) underscore the close relationship between gathering information and developing a vision. Pfeffer's list of key political attributes includes "sensitivity," knowing how others think and what they care about so that your agenda responds to their concerns: "Many people think of politicians as arm-twisters, and that is, in part, true. But in order to be a successful arm-twister, one needs to know which arm to twist, and how" (Pfeffer, 1992, p. 172).

Kanter (1983) adds: "While gathering information, entrepreneurs can also be 'planting seeds'—leaving the kernel of an idea behind and letting it germinate and blossom so that it begins to float around the system from many sources other than the innovator" (p. 218). This was exactly Paul Maritz's approach. Ignoring Dave Cutler's barbs and insults, he focused on getting information, building relationships, and formulating an agenda. He quickly concluded that the NT project was in disarray and that Cutler had to take on more responsibility. But Maritz's strategy was exquisitely attuned to his quarry: "Maritz protected Cutler from undue criticism and resisted the urge to reform him. [He] kept the peace by exacting from Cutler no ritual expressions of obedience" (Zachary, 1994, pp. 281–282).

A vision without a strategy remains an illusion. A strategy has to recognize major forces working for and against the agenda. Smith (1988, p. 333) makes this point about the American presidency:

> In the grand scheme of American government, the paramount task and power of the president is to articulate the national purpose: to fix the nation's agenda. Of all the big games at the summit of American politics, the agenda game must be won first. The effectiveness of the presidency and the capacity of any president to lead depend on focusing the nation's political attention and its energies on two or three top priorities. From the standpoint of history, the flow of events seems to have immutable logic, but political reality is inherently chaotic: it contains no automatic agenda. Order must be imposed.

Agendas never come neatly packaged. The bigger the job, the more difficult it is to wade through clamoring issues to find order amid chaos. Contrary to Woody Allen's dictum, success requires more than just showing up. High office, even if the incumbent enjoys great personal popularity, is no guarantee. Ronald Reagan was remarkably successful in his first year as president following a classic strategy for winning the agenda game: "First impressions are critical. In the agenda game, a swift beginning is crucial for a new president to establish himself as leader—to show the nation that he will make a difference in people's lives. The first one hundred days are the vital test; in those weeks, the political community and the public measure a new president—to see whether he is active, dominant, sure, purposeful" (Smith, 1988, p. 334).

Reagan began with a vision but without a strategy. He was not gifted as a manager or a strategist, despite extraordinary ability to portray complex issues in broad, symbolic brushstrokes. Reagan's staff painstakingly studied the first hundred days of four predecessors. They concluded that it was essential to move with speed and focus. Pushing competing issues aside, they focused on two: cutting taxes and reducing the federal budget. They also discovered a secret weapon in David Stockman, the only person in the Reagan White House who really understood the federal budget process. Stockman later admitted that he was astounded by the "low level of fiscal literacy" of Reagan and his key advisers (Smith, 1988, p. 354).

According to Smith, "Stockman got a jump on everyone else for two reasons: he had an agenda and a legislative blueprint already prepared, and he understood the real levers of power. Two terms as a Michigan congressman plus a network of key Republican and Democratic connections had taught Stockman how to play the power game" (p. 351). Reagan and his advisers had the vision; Stockman brought strategic direction.

Mapping the Political Terrain

It seems foolhardy to plunge into a minefield without knowing where explosives are buried, yet managers unwittingly do it all the time. They launch a new initiative with little or no effort to scout the political turf. Pichault (1993) suggests four steps for developing a political map:

1. Determine channels of informal communication.
2. Identify principal agents of political influence.
3. Analyze possibilities for both internal and external mobilization.
4. Anticipate strategies that others are likely to employ.

Pichault offers an example of planned change in a large government agency in Belgium. The agency wanted to replace antiquated, manual records with a fully automated, paperless computer network. But proponents of the new system had virtually no understanding of how the status quo actually functioned. Nor did they anticipate the interests and power of key middle managers and front-line bureaucrats. It seemed obvious to the techies that better access to data would dramatically improve efficiency. In reality, front-line bureaucrats made almost no use of the data. They applied standard procedures in 90 percent of the cases they encountered and asked their bosses what to do about the rest. Their queries were partly to get the "right" answer, but even more important they wanted to cover themselves politically. Even if the new technology were installed, front-line bureaucrats were likely to ignore or work around it. After a consultant clarified the political map, a new battle erupted between unrepentant techies, insisting their solution was correct, pitted against senior managers arguing for a less ambitious, more grounded approach. The two sides ultimately compromised.

A simple way to develop a political map for any situation is to create a two-dimensional diagram mapping players (who is in the game), power (how much clout each player is likely to exercise), and interests (what each player wants). Figures 9.1 and 9.2 present two hypothetical versions of the Belgian bureaucracy's political map. Figure 9.1 shows the map as seen

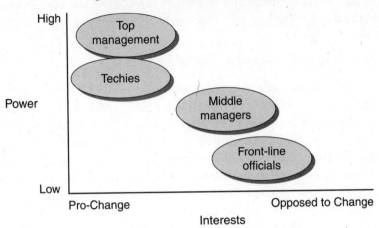

Figure 9.1. The Map the Techies See.

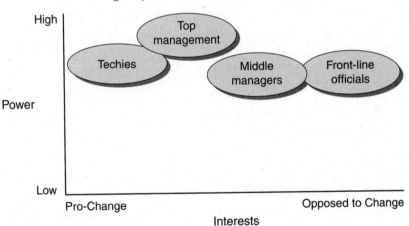

Figure 9.2. The Real Political Map.

by proponents of the new technology (the techies). Their view of the terrain shows little serious opposition to the new system, and they hold all the high cards; their map suggests a quick and easy win. Figure 9.2, the real map (as it might be seen by an objective analyst), paints a very different picture. Resistance is more intense and opponents more powerful. This view of the political terrain forecasts a stormy process imbued with protracted conflict. Though less comforting, the second map has an important message: success requires substantial effort to realign the existing field of political forces. The third and fourth key skills of the manager as politician, discussed in the next two sections, include strategies for doing that.

Networking and Building Coalitions

The *Challenger* disaster occurred despite recognition of the 0-ring problem by engineers at both Morton Thiokol and NASA. For a long time, they tried to get their superiors' attention, mostly through memos. Six months before the accident, Roger Boisjoly, an engineer at Morton Thiokol, wrote: "The result [of an 0-ring failure] would be a catastrophe of the highest order—loss of human life" (Bell and Esch, 1987, p. 45). Two months later, another Thiokol engineer wrote a memo that opened, "HELP! The seal task force is constantly being delayed by every possible means" (p. 45). The memo detailed resistance from other departments in Thiokol. A memo to the boss is sometimes effective, but it is just as often a sign of political innocence. Kotter (1985) suggests four basic steps for exercising political influence:

1. Identify relevant relationships (figure out who needs to be led).
2. Assess who might resist, why, and how strongly (figure out where the leadership challenges will be).
3. Develop, wherever possible, relationships with potential opponents to facilitate communication, education, or negotiation.
4. If step three fails, carefully select and implement either more subtle or more forceful methods.

These steps underscore the importance of developing a sufficient power base. Moving up the ladder confers authority but also incurs increasing dependence, because success depends on the cooperation of many others (Kotter, 1985, 1988). People rarely give their best efforts and fullest cooperation simply because they were ordered to do so. They accept directions when they perceive the people in authority as credible, competent, and sensible.

The first task in building networks and coalitions is to figure out whose help you need. The second is to develop relationships so people will be there when you need them. Middle managers seeking to promote change typically begin by getting their boss on board (Kanter, 1983). They then move to "preselling" or "making cheerleaders": "Peers, managers of related functions, stakeholders in the issue, potential collaborators, and sometimes even customers would be approached individually, in one-on-

one meetings that gave people a chance to influence the project and [gave] the innovator the maximum opportunity to sell it. Seeing them alone and on their territory was important: the rule was to act as if each person were *the* most important one for the project's success" (p. 223).

Once you cultivate cheerleaders, you can move to "horse trading": promising rewards in exchange for resources and support. This builds a resource base that helps in getting the necessary approvals and mandates from higher management (Kanter, 1983). Kanter found that the usual route to success in "securing blessings" is to identify critical senior managers and to develop a polished, formal presentation to sway their support. The best presentations respond to both substantive and political concerns. Senior managers typically care about two questions: Is it a good idea? How will my constituents react? Once innovators obtain higher management's blessing, they can formalize the coalition with their boss and make specific plans for pursuing the project (Kanter, 1983).

The basic point is simple: as a manager, you need friends and allies to get things done. To get their support, you need to cultivate relationships. Hard-core rationalists and incurable romantics sometimes react with horror to such a scenario. Why should you have to play political games to get something accepted if it's the right thing to do? One of the great works in French drama, Moliere's *The Misanthrope,* tells the story of a protagonist whose rigid rejection of all things political is destructive for him and everyone around him. The point that Moliere made four centuries ago still has merit: it is hard to dislike politics without also disliking people. Like it or not, political dynamics are inevitable under conditions most managers face every day: ambiguity, diversity, and scarcity.

Ignoring or misreading those dynamics is costly. Smith (1988) reports a case in point. Thomas Wyman, board chairman of the CBS television network, went to Washington in 1983 to lobby U.S. Attorney General Edwin Meese. A White House emergency forced Meese to miss the meeting, and Wyman was sent to the office of Craig Fuller, one of Meese's top advisers:

> "I know something about this issue," Fuller suggested, "Perhaps you'd like to discuss it with me."
>
> Wyman waved him off, unaware of Fuller's actual role, and evidently regarding him as a mere staff man.
>
> "No, I'd rather wait and talk to Meese," Wyman said.
>
> For nearly an hour, Wyman sat leafing through magazines in Fuller's office, making no effort to talk to Fuller, who kept working at his desk just a few feet away.

Finally, Meese burst into Fuller's office, full of apologies that he simply wouldn't have time for substantive talk. "Did you talk to Fuller?"
he asked.

Wyman shook his head.

"You should have talked to Fuller," Meese said. "He's very important on this issue. He knows it better than any of the rest of us. He's
writing a memo for the president on the pros and cons. You could have
given him your side of the argument." (Smith, 1988, pp. xviii–xix)

Wyman missed an important opportunity because he failed to test his assumptions about who actually had power.

Bargaining and Negotiation

We often associate bargaining with commercial, legal, and labor relations
settings. From a political perspective, though, bargaining is central to all
decision making. The horse trading Kanter describes as part of coalition
building is just one of many examples. Negotiation is needed whenever two
or more parties with some interests in common and others in conflict need
to reach agreement. Labor and management may agree that a firm should
make money and offer good jobs to its employees but disagree on how to
balance pay and profitability. Engineers and top managers at Morton
Thiokol had a common interest in the success of the shuttle program. They
differed sharply on how to balance technical and political trade-offs.

A fundamental dilemma in negotiations is choosing between "creating
value" and "claiming value":

> Value creators tend to believe that, above all, successful negotiators
> must be inventive and cooperative enough to devise an agreement that
> yields considerable gain to each party, relative to no-agreement possi-
> bilities. Some speak about the need for replacing the win-lose image
> of negotiation with win-win negotiation. In addition to information
> sharing and honest communication, the drive to create value can re-
> quire ingenuity and may benefit from a variety of techniques and atti-
> tudes. The parties can treat the negotiation as solving a joint problem;
> they can organize brainstorming sessions to invent creative solutions
> to their problems.
>
> Value claimers, on the other hand, tend to see this drive for joint
> gain as naive and weak-minded. For them, negotiation is hard, tough
> bargaining. The object of negotiation is to convince the other guy that
> he wants what you have to offer much more than you want what he
> has; moreover, you have all the time in the world, while he is up

against pressing deadlines. To "win" at negotiating—and thus make the other fellow "lose"—one must start high, concede slowly, exaggerate the value of concessions, minimize the benefits of the other's concessions, conceal information, argue forcibly on behalf of principles that imply favorable settlements, make commitments to accept only highly favorable agreements, and be willing to out wait the other fellow. (Lax and Sebenius, 1986, pp. 30–32)

One of the best-known win-win approaches to negotiation was developed by Fisher and Ury (1981) in *Getting to Yes*. They argue that people too often engage in "positional bargaining": they stake out positions and then reluctantly make concessions to reach agreement. Fisher and Ury contend that positional bargaining is inefficient and misses opportunities to create an agreement beneficial to both parties. They propose an alternative: "principled bargaining," built around four strategies.

The first strategy is to *separate the people from the problem*. The stress and tension of negotiations can easily escalate into anger and personal attack. The result is that a negotiator sometimes wants to defeat or hurt the other person at almost any cost. Because every negotiation involves both substance and relationship, the wise negotiator will "deal with the people as human beings and with the problem on its merits." Maritz demonstrated this principle in dealing with the prickly Cutler. Even though Cutler continually baited and insulted him, Maritz refused to be distracted and persistently focused on getting the job done.

The second rule of thumb is to *focus on interests, not positions*. If you get locked into a particular position, you might overlook other ways to achieve the goal. An example is the 1978 Camp David treaty, resolving issues between Israel and Egypt. The sides were at an impasse over where to draw the boundary between the two countries. Israel wanted to keep part of the Sinai, while Egypt wanted all of it back. Resolution became possible only when they looked at each other's underlying interests. Israel was concerned about security: no Egyptian tanks on the border. Egypt was concerned about sovereignty: the Sinai had been part of Egypt from the time of the Pharaohs. The parties agreed on a plan that gave all of the Sinai back to Egypt while demilitarizing large parts of it (Fisher and Ury, 1981). That solution led to a durable peace agreement.

Fisher and Ury's third recommendation is to *invent options for mutual gain*, looking for new possibilities that bring advantages to both sides. Parties often lock on to the first alternative that comes to mind and stop searching. Efforts to generate more options increase the chance of a better decision. Maritz recognized this in his dealings with Cutler. Instead of trying to bully Cutler, he asked innocently, "Could you do a demo at November COMDEX?" It was a new option that created gains for both parties.

Fisher and Ury's fourth strategy is to *insist on objective criteria*—standards of fairness for both substance and procedure. When a school board and a teachers' union are at loggerheads over the size of a pay increase, they can look for independent standards, such as the rate of inflation or the terms of settlement used in other districts. A classic example of fair procedure finds two sisters deadlocked over how to divide a pie between them. They agree that one will cut the pie into two pieces and the other will choose the piece that she wants.

Fisher and Ury devote most of their attention to creating value—finding better solutions for both parties. They downplay the question of claiming value. Yet there are many examples in which shrewd value-claimers have done very well. In 1980, Bill Gates offered to license an operating system to IBM about forty-eight hours before he had actually obtained the rights. Meanwhile, Microsoft neglected to mention to QDOS's owner, Tim Paterson of Seattle Computer, that they were buying his operating system to resell it to IBM. Microsoft gave IBM a great price: only $30,000 more than the *$50,000* they'd paid for it. But they were smart enough to retain the rights to license it to anyone else. At the time, IBM was an elephant and Microsoft was a flea. Almost no one except Gates saw the possibility that people would want an IBM computer made by anyone but IBM. But the new PC was so successful, IBM couldn't make enough of them. Within a year, Microsoft had licensed MS-DOS to fifty companies, and the number kept growing (Mendelson and Korin, n.d.). Onlookers who wondered why Microsoft was so aggressive and unyielding in battling the Justice Department's antitrust suit twenty years later might not have known that Gates had been a dogged value claimer for a long time.

A classic treatment of value claiming is Schelling's 1960 essay *The Strategy of Conflict,* which focuses on the problem of how to make a credible threat. Suppose, for example, that I want to buy your house and am willing to pay $250,000. How can I convince you that I'm willing to pay only *$200,000?* Contrary to a common assumption, I'm not always better off if I'm stronger and have more resources. If you believe that I'm very wealthy, you might take my threat less seriously than if I can get you to believe that *$200,000 is* the farthest I can go. Common sense also suggests that I should be better off if I have considerable freedom of action. Yet I may get a better price if I can convince you my hands are tied—for example, I'm negotiating for a very stubborn buyer who won't go above *$200,000,* even if the house is worth more. Such examples suggest that the ideal situation for a bargainer is to have substantial resources and freedom while convincing the other side of the opposite. Value claiming gives us a picture of the bargaining process:

1. Bargaining is a mixed-motive game. Both parties want an agreement but have differing interests and preferences. (IBM and Microsoft both wanted an operating system–deal. But the IBM negotiators probably thought they were stealing candy from babies by buying it royalty-free for a measly $80,000. Meanwhile, Gates was already dreaming about millions of computers running his code.)

2. Bargaining is a process of interdependent decisions. What each party does affects the other. Each player wants to be able to predict what the other will do while limiting the other's ability to reciprocate. (IBM was racing to bring its PC to market; a key challenge was making sure they had an operating system to go with it.)

3. The more player A can control player B's level of uncertainty, the more powerful A is. (Microsoft was an intermediary between Seattle Computer and IBM but kept each in the dark about the other.)

4. Bargaining involves judicious use of *threats* rather than sanctions. Players may threaten to use force, go on strike, or break off negotiations. In most cases, they much prefer not to bear the costs of carrying out the threat.

5. Making a threat credible is crucial. It is effective only if your opponent believes it. A noncredible threat weakens your bargaining position and confuses the process.

6. Calculation of the appropriate level of threat is also critical. If I underthreaten, I may weaken my own position. If I overthreaten, you may not believe me, may break off the negotiations, or may escalate your own threats.

Creating value and claiming value are both intrinsic to the bargaining process. How does a manager decide how to balance the two? At least two questions are important: "How much opportunity is there for a win-win solution?" and "Will I have to work with these people again?" If an agreement can make everyone better off, it makes sense to emphasize creating value. If you expect to work with the same people in the future, it is risky to use value-claiming tactics that leave anger and mistrust in their wake. Managers who get a reputation for being manipulative and self-interested have a hard time building networks and coalitions they need for future success.

Axelrod (1980) found that a strategy of conditional openness works best when negotiators need to work together over time. This strategy starts with open and collaborative behavior and maintains the approach if the other responds in kind. If the other party becomes adversarial, however, the negotiator responds in kind and remains adversarial until the opponent makes a collaborative move. It is, in effect, a friendly and forgiving version of tit for tat—do unto others as they do unto you. Axelrod's research revealed that this conditional openness strategy worked better than even the most fiendishly diabolical adversarial strategy.

A final consideration in balancing collaborative and adversarial tactics is ethics. Bargainers often deliberately misrepresent their positions—even though lying is almost universally condemned as unethical (Bok, 1978). This leads to a profoundly difficult question for the manager as politician: What actions are ethical and just?

Morality and Politics

Block (1987), Burns (1978), and Lax and Sebenius (1986) explore ethical issues in bargaining and organizational politics. Block's view assumes that individuals empower themselves through understanding: "The process of organizational politics as we know it works against people taking responsibility. We empower ourselves by discovering a positive way of being political. The line between positive and negative politics is a tightrope we have to walk" (Block, 1987, p. xii).

Block argues that bureaucratic cycles often leave individuals feeling vulnerable, powerless, and helpless. If we confer too much power to the organization or others, we fear that the power will be used against us. Consequently, we develop manipulative strategies to protect ourselves. To escape the dilemma, managers need to support organizational structures, policies, and procedures that promote empowerment. They must also empower themselves.

Block urges managers to begin by building an "image of greatness"— a vision of what their department can contribute that is meaningful and worthwhile. Then they need to build support for their vision by negotiating agreement and trust. Block suggests dealing differently with friends than with opponents. Adversaries, he says, are simultaneously the most difficult and most interesting people to deal with. It is usually ineffective to pressure them; a better strategy is to "let go of them." He offers four steps for letting go: (1) tell them your vision, (2) state your best understanding of their position, (3) identify your contribution to the problem, and (4) tell them what you plan to do without making demands.

Such a strategy might work for conflict originating in a misunderstanding of one's self-interest. But in a situation of scarce resources and durable differences, bringing politics into the open may backfire. It can make conflict more obvious and overt but offer little hope of resolution. Block argues that "war games in organizations lose their power when brought into the light of day" (1987, p. 148), but the political frame questions that assumption.

Burns's conception of positive politics (1978) draws on examples as diverse and complex as Franklin Roosevelt and Adolph Hitler, Gandhi and Mao, Woodrow Wilson and Joan of Arc. He sees conflict and power as central to leadership. Searching for firm moral footing in a world of cultural and ethical diversity, Burns turned to the motivation theory of Maslow (1954) and the ethical theory of Kohlberg (1973). From Maslow he borrowed the idea of the hierarchy of motives. Moral leaders, he argued, appeal to a higher level on the needs hierarchy.

From Kohlberg he adopted the idea of stages of moral reasoning. At the lowest, "preconventional" level, moral judgment is based primarily on perceived consequences: an action is right if you are rewarded and wrong if you are punished. In the intermediate or "conventional" level, the emphasis is on conforming to authority and established rules. At the highest, "postconventional" level, ethical judgment rests on general principles: the greatest good for the greatest number, or universal and comprehensive moral principles.

Maslow and Kohlberg offered a foundation on which Burns (1978) constructed a positive view of politics:

> If leaders are to be effective in helping to mobilize and elevate their constituencies, leaders must be whole persons, persons with full functioning capacities for thinking and feeling. The problem for them as educators, as leaders, is not to promote narrow, egocentric self-actualization, but to extend awareness of human needs and the means of gratifying them, to improve the larger social situation for which educators or leaders have responsibility and over which they have power. What does all this mean for the teaching of leadership as opposed to manipulation? "Teachers"—in whatever guise—treat students neither coercively nor instrumentally but as joint seekers of truth and of mutual actualization. They help students define moral values not by imposing their own moralities on them but by positing situations that pose moral choices and then encouraging conflict and debate. They seek to help students rise to higher stages of moral reasoning and hence to higher levels of principled judgment. (pp. 448–449)

In Burns's view, positive politics evolve when individuals choose actions appealing to higher motives and higher stages of moral judgment. Lax and Sebenius (1986), regarding ethical issues as inescapable, present a set of questions to help managers decide what is ethical:

1. Are you following rules that are mutually understood and accepted? (In poker, for example, everyone understands that bluffing is part of the game.)

2. Are you comfortable discussing and defending your action? (Would you want your colleagues and friends to be aware of it? Your spouse, children, or parents? Would you be comfortable if it were on the front page of your local newspaper?)

3. Would you want someone to do it to you? To a member of your family?

4. Would you want everyone to act that way? Would the resulting society be desirable? (If you were designing an organization, would you want people to act that way? Would you teach your children to do it?)

5. Are there alternatives that rest on firmer ethical ground?

Although these questions do not yield a comprehensive ethical framework, they embody four important principles of moral judgment. These are instrumental values—guidelines not about the right thing to do but about the right way of doing things. They do not guarantee right action, but they substantially reduce ethical risks. As evidence, we note that these values are regularly ignored wherever we find an organizational scandal.

1. *Mutuality.* Are all parties to a relationship operating under the same understanding about the rules of the game? Enron's Ken Lay was talking up the company's stock to analysts and employees even as he and others were selling shares. In the period when WorldCom illegitimately improved its profits by booking some of its operating expenses as capital investments, it made major competitors look bad and generated considerable puzzlement. Top executives at both AT&T and Sprint felt the heat from analysts and shareholders and wondered, *What are we doing wrong? Why can't we get the results they're getting?*

2. *Generality.* Does a specific action follow a principle of moral conduct applicable to all comparable situations? When WorldCom violated a basic accounting principle to inflate their results, they were secretly breaking the rules, which does not amount to following a broadly applicable rule of conduct.

THE MANAGER AS POLITICIAN 131

3. *Openness.* Are we willing to make our thinking and decisions public and confrontable? It was Justice Oliver Wendell Holmes who observed many years ago that "sunlight is the best disinfectant." Keeping others in the dark was a consistent theme in the corporate ethics scandals of 2001–2002. Enron's books were almost impenetrable, and the company was hostile to anyone who asked questions, such as *Fortune* reporter Bethany McLean. Enron's techniques for manipulating the California energy crisis had to be secret to work. One device involved creating the appearance of congestion in the California power grid, and then getting paid by the state for "moving energy to relieve congestion without actually moving any energy or relieving any congestion" (Oppel, 2002, p. 1).

4. *Caring.* Does this action show care for the legitimate interests of others? Enron's effort to protect its share price by locking in employees so they couldn't sell Enron shares in retirement accounts as the market plunged is only one of many examples of putting the interests of senior executives ahead of everyone else's.

The scandals of the early 2000s were not unprecedented; such a wave is a predictable feature of the trough that follows every business boom. The 1990s, for example, gave us Ivan Boesky and the savings and loan crisis. There was another wave of corporate scandals back in the 1970s, and in the 1930s the president of the New York Stock Exchange literally went to jail in his three-piece suit (Labaton, 2002). There will always be temptation whenever gargantuan egos and large sums of money are at stake. Top managers too rarely think or talk about the moral dimension of management and leadership. Porter (1989) notes the dearth of such conversation: "In a seminar with seventeen executives from nine corporations, we learned how the privatization of moral discourse in our society has created a deep sense of moral loneliness and moral illiteracy; how the absence of a common language prevents people from talking about and reading the moral issues they face. We learned how the isolation of individuals—the taboo against talking about spiritual matters in the public sphere—robs people of courage, of the strength of heart to do what deep down they believe to be right" (p. 2).

If we choose to banish moral discourse and leave managers to face ethical issues alone, we invite dreary and brutish political dynamics. In a pluralistic secular world, an organization cannot impose a narrow ethical framework on employees. But it can and should take a moral stance. It can make its values clear, hold employees accountable, and validate the need for dialogue about ethical choices. Positive politics, absent an ethical framework and a moral dialogue, is no more likely to occur than farming without sunlight or water.

Conclusion

The question is not whether organizations are political but rather what kind of politics they will have. Political dynamics can be sordid and destructive. But politics can also be the vehicle for achieving noble purpose. Organizational change and effectiveness depend on managers' political skills. Constructive politicians recognize and understand political realities. They know how to fashion an agenda, map the political terrain, create a network of support, and negotiate with both allies and adversaries. In the process, they encounter a practical and ethical dilemma: when to adopt an open, collaborative strategy or when to choose a tougher, more adversarial approach. They have to consider the potential for collaboration, the importance of long-term relationships, and most important their own values and ethical principles.

REFERENCES

Axelrod, R. "More Effective Choice in the Prisoner's Dilemma." *Journal of Conflict Resolution*, 1980, 24, 379–403.

Bell, T. E., and Esch, K. "The Fatal Flaw in Flight 51-L." *IEEE Spectrum*, Feb. 1987, pp. 36–51.

Bellow, G., and Moulton, B. *The Lawyering Process: Cases and Materials.* Mineola, N.Y.: Foundation Press, 1978.

Bennis, W. G. *Why Leaders Can't Lead: The Unconscious Conspiracy Continues.* San Francisco: Jossey-Bass, 1989.

Block, P. *The Empowered Manager: Positive Political Skills at Work.* San Francisco: Jossey-Bass, 1987.

Bok, S. *Lying: Moral Choice in Public and Private Life.* New York: Vintage Books, 1978.

Burns, J. M. *Leadership.* New York: HarperCollins, 1978.

Fisher, R., and Ury, W. *Getting to Yes.* Boston: Houghton Mifflin, 1981.

Kanter, R. M. *The Change Masters: Innovations for Productivity in the American Corporation.* New York: Simon & Schuster, 1983.

Kohlberg, L. "The Claim to Moral Adequacy of a Highest Stage of Moral Judgment." *Journal of Philosophy*, 1973, 70, 630–646.

Kotter, J. P. *The General Managers.* New York: Free Press, 1982.

Kotter, J. P. *Power and Influence: Beyond Formal Authority.* New York: Free Press, 1985.

Kotter, J. P. *The Leadership Factor.* New York: Free Press, 1988.

Labaton, S. "Downturn and Shift in the Population Feed Boom in White Collar Crime." *New York Times*, June 2, 2002.

Lax, D. A., and Sebenius, J. K. *The Manager as Negotiator.* New York: Free Press, 1986.

Manes, S., and Andrews, P. *Gates.* New York: Touchstone, 1994.

Maslow, A. H. *Motivation and Personality.* New York: HarperCollins, 1954.

Mendelson, H., and Korin, A. "The Computer Industry: A Brief History." Palo Alto, Calif.: Stanford Business School, n.d.

Oppel, R. A. "How Enron Got California to Buy Power It Didn't Need." *New York Times,* May 8, 2002, p. A1.

Pfeffer, J. *Managing with Power: Politics and Influence in Organizations.* Boston: Harvard Business School Press, 1992.

Pichault, F. *Ressources humaines et changement stratégique: Vers un manage- ment politique* [Human Resources and Strategic Change: Toward a Politi- cal Approach to Management]. Brussels, Belgium: DeBoeck, 1993.

Porter, E. "Notes for the Looking for Leadership Conference." Paper presented at the Looking for Leadership Conference, Graduate School of Education, Harvard University, Dec. 1989.

Schelling, T. *The Strategy of Conflict.* Cambridge, Mass.: Harvard University Press, 1960.

Smith, H. *The Power Game.* New York: Random House, 1988.

Zachary, G. P. "Climbing the Peak: Agony and Ecstasy of 200 Code Writers Beget Windows NT." *Wall Street Journal,* May 26, 1993, pp. A1, A6.

Zachary, G. P. *Showstopper! The Breakneck Race to Create Windows NT and the Next Generation at Microsoft.* New York: Free Press, 1994.

10

THE AUTHENTIC LEADER

Robert Evans

The true force that attracts others is the force of the heart.

—James Kouzes and Barry Posner (1987, p. 125)

TRANSFORMATION BEGINS with trust. Trust is the essential link between leader and led, vital to people's job satisfaction and loyalty, vital to followership. It is doubly important when organizations are seeking rapid improvement, which requires exceptional effort and competence, and doubly again to organizations like schools that offer few extrinsic motivators (money, status, power). And it is as fragile as it is precious; once damaged, it is nearly impossible to repair. When we have come to distrust people, either because they have lied to us or deceived us or let us down too often, we tend to stay suspicious of them, resisting their influence and discounting efforts they may make to reform themselves. In work groups, the more people doubt one another, the more they "ignore, disguise, and distort facts, ideas, conclusions, and feelings that [might] increase their vulnerability to others" (Kouzes and Posner, 1987, p. 147), increasing the likelihood of misunderstanding. Imagine two schools that are virtual clones, identical in faculty, administration, student body, community, budget, and physical plant, identical even in their problems and in the improvements they are undertaking. Now introduce a single difference: the principal in the first school is distrusted by the faculty. An abyss opens. Despite their resemblance, they are disparate institutions, different in climate, morale, energy level, and responsiveness to innovation. The contrast in the scope and complexity of the tasks confronting their two principals is vast.

Clearly, then, school leaders seeking change need to begin by thinking of what will inspire trust among their constituents. The answer is direct: we admire leaders who are honest, fair, competent, and forward-looking. Although these qualities seem so obvious that they are easy to gloss over, they are the basis of trust (Kouzes and Posner, 1987, pp. 16, 21). (Imagine how our national cynicism about politics would change if we found our elected officials to be honest, fair, and competent, not to mention forward-looking.) For "honest" we may read "consistent." Consistency is the lifeblood of trust. People who do what they say they will do—meet their commitments, keep their promises—are trustworthy; those who don't, aren't. Most of us prefer to be led by someone we can count on, even when we disagree with him, than someone we agree with but who frequently shifts his position (Bennis, 1985, p. 21).

Innovation can't live without trust, but it needs more than trust—it needs confidence. We cannot have confidence in those we distrust, but we do not necessarily have confidence in all those we trust. Some people whose sincerity and honesty are beyond reproach lack the capacity to translate their goals into reality. They may have lofty ideals, and even fulfill them in their personal lives, but be unable to communicate clearly to others or be inept at handling daily events. Their heart, as we say, is in the right place, but they lack something that makes us follow them. To transform schools, principals and superintendents must inspire such confidence along with trust.

The key to both is authenticity. Leaders who are followed are authentic; that is, they are distinguished not by their techniques or styles but by their integrity and their savvy. Integrity is a fundamental consistency between personal beliefs, organizational aims, and working behavior. It is increasingly clear that leadership rests on values, that commitment among constituents can only be mobilized by leaders who themselves have strong commitments, who preach what they believe and practice what they preach.[1] But they must also know what they're doing. Savvy is practical competence, a hard-to-quantify cluster of qualities that includes craft knowledge, life experience, native intelligence, common sense, intuition, courage, and the capacity to "handle things." Most of us seek in a leader this combination of genuineness and effectiveness. It makes him authentic, a credible resource who inspires trust and confidence, someone worth following into the uncertainties of change.

This chapter explores the concept of authentic leadership, its roots and its implications for practice. It sketches authenticity's essentials—integrity and savvy—and describes a process for discovering one's own authentic core, a process that highlights the personal, idiosyncratic nature of leadership. From this flow three consequences: that there are many ways to excel as a leader; that we must recast our notions of vision and strategy; and, most important of all, that effective leadership rests on a set of strategic biases that simplify leadership and make transformation possible.

Integrity: Character in Action

Integrity is a fundamental consistency between one's values, goals, and actions. At the simplest level it means standing for something, having a significant commitment and exemplifying this commitment in your behavior. Leaders who have no strong values and no aspirations for their school may provide a dull consistency, but this is not something we would confuse with integrity. Even if they manage daily details adequately, they inspire no special motivation or attachment that enhances performance or makes being part of the school valuable. They are, at best, maintaining, not leading. Followership is not just impossible under their administration, it is irrelevant.

In a different way, leaders who do claim to stand for something but whose goals and actions are not aligned with their stated values also lack integrity. Those who profess aspirations that do not truly matter to them are easily seen through. When a principal dutifully introduces a district priority that she herself does not share, the discrepancy between her announced aims and her underlying beliefs will be apparent to all who know her well, even if she tries to muster up sincerity. Her falseness will ultimately be as evident as if she were adopting a style that is not her own. Similarly, when leaders do not model the values they assert or the goals they proclaim—when a superintendent announces "respect for others" as a district goal but treats staff disrespectfully—they breed cynicism and resistance. The problem of inconsistency is so widespread that it needs little elaboration, except to note that it can occur unconsciously. A leader may be sincere about his goal and unaware that his behavior is contradictory. In such cases, the leader may seem "out of it" and incompetent more than cynical or manipulative, but he will still invite disrespect and resistance instead of followership.

Integrity can take many forms. Let us begin with two examples:

Jane Carroll, principal of Worthington High School, is a strong believer in "challenge." A triathlon competitor and ardent chess player,

she values self-discipline and perseverance. She is overt about rewarding students and faculty who demonstrate these qualities: "Effort
matters far more than talent—for teachers as well as students. Success
comes from striving. As Aristotle said, 'Excellence is not an act, but a
habit.'" Jane leads the school with a firm hand and engages herself in
aspects of curriculum, assessment, and staff development that in many
schools have more teacher involvement and control. Some faculty find
her "cold," others "elitist and controlling," but she enjoys wide support, even among most of these critics, because her commitments are
so clear, because she holds herself to them as firmly as she holds others
to them, and because they have come to embody the school's pursuit
of excellence. "She drives everyone hard," says a teacher, "but she sets
the example, and we all feel the end result is an exceptional school."

Tom Russell, the principal of Jackson Elementary School, believes in
individual development. He reveres Thoreau and sees school as a place
where everyone, child and adult, should grow at their own pace through
rich opportunities and the freedom to explore, not through pressure to
produce. Jackson has comparatively few rules and requirements. Tom
rarely issues an order, he tolerates others disagreeing with him, and he
gives the faculty wide latitude to decide policy, even if this involves
heated arguments. He is unhurried in his style but unwavering in his
focus. Each year he meets with each student and each staff member
(including custodians and secretaries) to talk about their growth, interests, and ideas for the school. Some teachers have found Jackson too
"chaotic" and left; some who have remained find Tom too "unstructured." But most agree with the teacher who says, "This guy lives what
he believes: growth, support, respect. Because of him, Jackson really nurtures people."

Few of the principals I know would want to be Jane or Tom. They might
endorse qualities of each but would find both at least a bit extreme. I cite
Jane and Tom here as exemplars not of the perfect principal but of integrity. For both of them, values, goals, and actions are congruent.

(Before going further, an important note: it is impossible to address the
ethical dimensions of leadership that are a primary focus of this chapter
without using terms that have been poisoned by politics. In the 1990s in
America, *values* and *basic values* are among a constellation of terms that
have been appropriated by various political groups and reduced to code
words for particular viewpoints. But all of us see certain values—fairness,
for example—as "basic," even if we define these values differently. There
is no other way to describe them. I use all such phrases and all such words

as *moral* in this primary, generic way, not to refer to a particular political or religious agenda.)

Values and personal integrity come first. At the deepest level, the values of authentic leaders are characterized by three things: personal ethics, vision, and belief in others (Badaracco and Ellsworth, 1989, p. 100). A firm set of personal ethical standards is a hallmark of most successful leaders. Over and over in the research literature, portraits of exceptional leaders describe people with unusually high standards, commitments they keep with a self-discipline that can seem excessive, even fanatical: "Outstanding leaders have sources of inner direction." They may not be terribly religious, but their beliefs give them a sturdy guide for their long-range planning and their routine problem solving (p. 100). Whatever the specific content of their views, honesty and fairness tend to be among their chief tenets. It is not that authentic leaders necessarily preach honesty and fairness as specific virtues, but they demonstrate them through the sincerity of their commitments. This is the basis of trust and loyalty in any group.

Leaders with strong values translate these into organizational vision. Like Jane and Tom, they typically hold the same standards for their school as for themselves. "Challenge and excellence" might well serve as the motto both for Jane and for Worthington, "Freedom to grow" for Tom and Jackson. Such commitments are important; they are crucial to followership because they provide the larger purpose that gives work direction and meaning. Leaders like Jane and Tom are able to communicate very clearly a definite notion of their school and its potential.

Leaders with values and vision tend to believe that other people have the potential to be motivated by the same commitments, not just by narrow self-interest (financial gain, personal power). Though their beliefs are different, neither Jane nor Tom base their leadership on maneuvering or manipulating people through special incentives, political trade-offs, and the like. They have faith that everyone can respond, can benefit from the opportunity the school provides, can fulfill the vision in their own personal ways. This faith may take many forms—Tom offers a chance to blossom, Jane a challenge to excel—but in one way or another it conveys a confidence in the potential of people.

These same three qualities—ethics, vision, belief in others—that are central in the personal beliefs of authentic leaders are reflected in their organizational goals. By "goals" I mean both the kind of institution the leader seeks to build and the improvements he seeks to implement. Leaders with strong personal ethics who exemplify honesty and fairness generally reflect these in a meritocratic approach to management; they want competence to be rewarded. They expect high ethical standards to prevail throughout and believe that when in doubt about a decision or a problem, everyone should behave in accordance with the school's fundamental values. They acknowledge those who observe and fulfill these values, basing recognition on "what you do, not on who you are or who you know," as Jane says. At the same time, they expect members of the organization to come to share the same basic values and goals, and they are usually unambiguous and unembarrassed about this. Authentic school leaders do not necessarily champion a "my way or the highway" philosophy, but they are unwilling to sacrifice their priorities and goals, and when necessary they will challenge those who can't or won't come along. This can sometimes seem harsh and unfeeling, but for many leaders with integrity this approach is simply axiomatic: "buying in" is ultimately a basic condition of organizational membership. A case in point is this high school principal:

> Last year we pushed our restructuring up a big notch: we converted to a block schedule, four 90-minute periods per day, so we could really start implementing an integrated curriculum and in-depth teaching. We'd spent a full year debating it and most people were on board, but six were still strongly opposed. They were angry and terrified at having to face kids for that long and at having to change the curriculum they'd taught for twenty years and start collaborating with other teachers. I met with each. I made it clear that we needed absolutely everyone to be truly committed, that we had finally reached the rock and the hard place; it was "in or out." They were going to be miserable if they stayed. Thanks to a special agreement with the union, we had the option of transferring people. I offered to find each their first choice of another high school in the city if they wished. No hard feelings, no shame, no blame. Four chose to leave. I worked like a maniac, and I got all of them the schools they wanted. It wasn't all happy, but they are happier, and we've made much more progress.

In a similar way, authentic leaders embrace programs or projects that reflect their values and institutional goals. They concentrate on what matters to them, again without embarrassment. They have definite notions of what is important, and they pay attention to these targets. The principal above is committed to the essential schools philosophy, which to him means "real depth learning," and the conviction that "nothing is more important than making our classrooms places where kids and teachers deeply explore challenging, important ideas. Everything else is subordinate to that."

As this principal's example indicates, integrity requires action, behavior that embodies values. Indeed, it is chiefly through consistent beliefs and goals expressed in consistent actions that we perceive a leader's integrity. The importance of setting the example, of leaders' modeling what they value, is one of the most frequently repeated themes in leadership writing. Authentic leaders translate their beliefs and values into concrete actions at a fundamental level:

> Anthony Cortez became a superintendent reluctantly. After years as a teacher and then principal at Clayville Middle School, he filled in as acting superintendent and was offered the permanent position because he was so universally admired. His hesitation was simple: "I like kids. I like being around them. Everything a school does depends on community, which means that kids know they are known: they're missed when they're absent, they're appreciated for their uniqueness, they're helped when they need it, and they're held accountable to do their part. That can't happen unless the adults like the kids and are with the kids." He delegates large amounts of his "paper and policy work" and usually averages at least three school visits—"a real visit, not a sail-through"—per week (he sometimes reads to children in the elementary schools). When he urges Clayville teachers to "reach out to kids, invest in them, know them," his credibility is absolute; his actions have always spoken for him.

When the late Henry Scattergood retired as headmaster at the Germantown Friends School in Philadelphia, a colleague wrote, "His virtues are as simple and uncomplicated as they are rare. They originate in the quality of creating in others a loyalty and affection, and even sometimes a goodness, by being himself, a man of perfect honesty, integrity, and goodness. He does not merely advise virtue, he creates it in others by offering its example and practice. . . . It is the simple yet exceptional use of character in action" (Nicholson, 1995, citing Sharpless). Whether it is challenging thoroughly resistant staff or staying close to students or spending large amounts of time on the job—or exemplifying virtue—authentic leaders embody character in action: they don't just say, they do.

Savvy

In discussing integrity, I have already been referring to "authentic leaders"; but although integrity is the chief defining characteristic of authenticity, it is not the only one. Authenticity also demands savvy, a practical, problem-solving wisdom that enables leaders to make things happen. Savvy subsumes an array of qualities, ranging from knowledge of one's field to having a good "nose" for institutional problems.[2] It includes intangibles like knowing what constitutes a good solution to a dilemma, knowing "what to do and when to do it" (Sergiovanni, 1992, p. 15). These and related qualities are sometimes called "craft knowledge" and are in good part a product of professional experience, learned skills that come with years of practice. But to me, savvy also includes native strengths, basic aspects of temperament, personality, and intelligence that are reflected in qualities like common sense and empathic sensitivity (being able to "read" people), courage and assertiveness, and resilience. These, coupled with craft knowledge, establish a leader's bona fides. In my experience, educators will rarely follow leaders unless they seem to "know their stuff"— not the tricks of leadership but the realities of school life.

Educators want leaders who know education, who are current and well versed without falling victim to fads, but they especially want leaders who are "one of us," who can still see education from a teacher's point of view and are attuned to the real world of classrooms, students, and parents. And they also want leaders who offer proof or promise of being able to "make things happen," whether this means fixing problems, finding resources, or handling people. These traits build a basic platform without which a leader lacks presence and clout and is not taken seriously:

> Jim Colby became a superintendent after a brief stint as a math teacher and then many years as a district business manager (he was never a principal). A devout convert to Total Quality Management, he failed to make it work in two different districts. In both, principals and teachers felt that his goals were formulaic and empty and his expectations unrealistic, that he didn't really understand teaching itself or the running of a school, and that he couldn't manage people. Principals especially felt that he never grasped the daily dilemmas of school life, the intricacies and politics of translating ideas into action. In the words of one, "Jim was a hard worker, but basically out of it. He just didn't have it, and he just didn't get it. You couldn't respect him."

If Jim had been charismatic, one of his districts might have made a temporary exception for him. There are gifted visionaries who can truly inspire others by the power of their ideas, the force of their eloquence, and the depth of their conviction, even though they have little practical aptitude and little grasp of the nitty-gritty. People will sometimes exempt such a leader from the "savvy requirement" (especially if there is a good second-in-command who handles the details), but they will not do so indefinitely and especially not as innovation proceeds from early optimism to actual implementation, with its inevitable obstacles.

Becoming Authentic

Let us say, then, that authenticity is ideal. How does one achieve it? The question is paradoxical. Just as genuineness can't be artificially manufactured—it simply *is*—neither can authenticity: it can't be generated; it can only be discovered. (A person cannot *act* authentic.) Still, one may fairly ask, "How do I get there?" The answer leads us again, as did our discussion of charisma in the preceding chapter, to the personal nature and roots of leadership.

It also leads first to a blunt truth: not everyone can. Despite the popularity of technical notions of leadership, most of us believe that good leaders must have the "right stuff," the right personal qualities to lead, and that these, like savvy or charisma, are to some extent innate: you either have what it takes or you don't. Most of us react to leaders in this way in our daily experience. But this view is not just folk wisdom—experience and research confirm that leadership requires a definite aptitude (Drucker, 1986, p. 159). For example, a study of identical twins who were raised apart concluded that leadership is a trait "strongly determined by heredity" (Goleman, 1986, pp. C1–C2). A study of leaders who achieved significant change in their organizations highlighted the importance of temperament and predisposition and suggested that the impulse and capacity to lead stem largely from innate talents and early childhood experience (Gibbons, 1986). Other research emphasizes that successful leaders tend to be psychologically hardy (Evans, 1996, ch. 7). They are resourceful and resilient. Compared to less successful peers in equally stressful jobs, they are more resistant to illness and experience both a greater sense of control over events and of positive challenge in their work (Maddi and Kobasa, 1984, p. 31). Unmistakably, they have what it takes.

The right stuff, like charisma, is a concept that might seem to suggest that there is little point in trying to teach leadership (a notion widely deplored by those who see leadership as a matter of technique and therefore teachable). But it leads to three less extreme and very practical implications. The first is that *some* central aspects of leadership are innate and unteachable and that not everyone has all the necessary potential, which means that some people will always lead better than others and that some are simply ill-suited for the task. As ordinary as this seems, it is routinely ignored in discussions of preparing school administrators to lead change. To expect that every leader can become authentic or transformational is foolish. The second is to underscore the importance of hardiness: to be effective, leaders must demonstrate and foster it. We don't follow the timid, the indecisive, and those who avoid problems, and we rarely stay committed to causes that distress us (Kouzes and Posner, 1987, p. 68).

The third and most important implication is that leadership begins at one's center: *authentic leaders build their practice outward from their core commitments rather than inward from a management text.* In addition to their craft knowledge, all administrators have basic philosophies of leading, of school functioning, and of human nature, philosophies that are deeply rooted in their personal history and professional experience. These philosophies guide their behavior, but they usually remain tacit. They are the true source of their integrity. They include basic assumptions about human nature, group behavior, and the roots of excellence. "Like a geological deposit," they accumulate during years of experience in life and work. Although few leaders pause to spell out their philosophies explicitly, "these deep assumptions influence almost everything they do" (Badaracco and Ellsworth, 1989, p. 7). Sergiovanni echoes this view when he speaks of an administrator's "known and unknown theories of practice . . . bundles of beliefs and assumptions about how schools and school systems work, authority, leadership, the purposes of schooling, the role of competition, the nature of human nature, and other issues and concerns." These constitute what he calls "mindscapes," frames of reference that, though rarely thought about, are powerful forces that drive one's practice (1991, pp. 10–12).

A leader's philosophy remains tacit in part because none of us can be fully in touch with the entire range of our knowledge, perception, feeling, and skill. At any given moment, our reservoir of expertise is larger than we can encompass, our wellspring of inspiration deeper than we can fully tap. But it also stays hidden—even unconscious—because it is buried and discouraged by formal leadership theory taught in graduate administration courses and disseminated in leadership books. The received wisdom in the field, which emphasizes techniques and styles, encourages school leaders to overlook their personal philosophies and the "hard-earned insights" of their craft knowledge, with the result that they end up drawing upon a tiny portion of their potential (Bolman and Deal, 1991, p. 37).[3] Uncovering this wisdom is the key to becoming authentic.

The Testimonial: What Do You Stand For?

There may be many routes to accomplishing that uncovering of wisdom. I prefer to begin this way: Imagine that your colleagues and friends have decided to honor you at a testimonial dinner, simply because they respect and love you so much. The meal is over, you have already been "roasted" and toasted, and speakers have lavishly praised your skills. Now, your closest colleague, who knows you best, is to offer the final tribute. This person will move the focus away from your competence to your commitment, summarizing what you stand for: the essential principle or core value, the fundamental belief deep inside you that drives your work as an educator and a leader. What will he or she say? (Note: it cannot be something like "He likes people" or "She has always stood for change," unless just liking people or change for its own sake is truly your highest value, the thing you care about most—in which case it would not have earned you a testimonial! The goal is to find out what lies below these kinds of characteristics.)

The task is simple but not necessarily easy. It usually involves talking about values that are at once ordinary and complex, plain and profound. In taking several thousand educators through this exercise, I have found that many tend to begin at a relatively superficial level, describing skills, attributes, or very general beliefs. But when they are encouraged to persevere and to talk to each other in greater depth, their answers gravitate toward values that are much deeper and often disarmingly simple, what one principal called "apple pie and motherhood" values. "I feel corny and sentimental saying this stuff," he said, "but it's all true."

The kinds of "stuff" superintendents and principals and teachers say can lead in many directions. (At one seminar, a principal whose core belief was "everything you do in life should be fun" was seated next to a colleague whose deepest commitment was to "live in the light of Christ.") But frequently the answers cluster around two broad headings, which I summarize as "equity" and "excellence." Most educators share a heartfelt commitment to students and to the development of their full potential, but they differ in their emphasis. Some, like Tom Russell, stress the importance of opportunity, fairness, diversity, and community. They are likely to believe that "all children can learn," which often means to them a commitment to special outreach and compensatory opportunities for children who are disadvantaged. Others, like Jane Carroll, emphasize goals, challenge, responsibility, and striving. They are more likely to speak of "excellence" and "standards," of bringing out the best in children by measuring them against high benchmarks. Most educators share both values to some degree, although differences of emphasis can lead to significant differences in the kinds of schools they develop.

"What do you stand for?" is an excellent point of departure for exploring one's own philosophy of schooling and school leadership, but there are three other questions that I have also found to be useful:

1. *How do I define my role as a leader?* Am I at heart a mover, some-one who redesigns and reshapes, who tolerates—even enjoys—the fric-tion that change can cause? Or am I a maintainer, someone who prefers to keep things running smoothly, who may occasionally modify or enhance things but who is by nature more inclined to accept things as they are? One's preference will of course be affected by the specific situation—a new principal at a school will see his task differently if he finds its pro-grams and teachers weak than if he finds them strong—but by philosophy and temperament every administrator is more drawn in one direction than the other. As they reflect on their conception of their role, some see them-selves as active promoters of change, others don't (Fullan, 1991, p. 167). It is important to be clear about this.

2. *What inspires the best in staff?* Is performance enhanced when a leader actively shapes the work of staff members, or is it best when they are given wide latitude? Should they be free to work as individual arti-sans, or should they be linked in close collaborative groups? There is a famous distinction in human resource theory between three views of human motivation and performance. Theory X holds that people are basi-cally lazy and unambitious, that they need and want to be led; managers must direct and control their work (as with Taylorism and the "expect and inspect" model of management). Theory Y holds that people can be relied upon to show motivation, self-control, and self-direction, provided that essential human needs for safety, independence, and status are met by the workplace (McGregor, 1960, pp. 35–36). Theory Z places maxi-mum emphasis on human potential, calling for higher levels of trust and for egalitarian work relationships and participatory decision making involving stakeholders at all levels (Ouchi, 1981, p. 110). Here again, though local conditions will influence one's preference, each individual school leader will have a primary predisposition.

3. *What are my strengths?* An excellent way to clarify one's basic phi-losophy is to identify one's particular skills and abilities and the parts of one's role that are most rewarding. A tremendous amount of leadership training and school improvement work concentrates on correcting defects. Indeed, ruminating about problems and trying to overcome them con-sumes vast quantities of educators' time and energy. But a person trying to discover her core beliefs and values does far better to start with her strengths, the parts of herself that she feels best about in the exercise of her profession. It is there that the essence of what matters to her is to be found. Trying to articulate this essence is not only informative, it can be hugely satisfying. I love to see superintendents and principals as they

describe where in their work they feel most competent and alive; their faces light up, their enthusiasm is infectious. "When I think about what I love about my work and what I do best, it's helping kids learn important lessons about life," said one principal. "And I realize that this is actually a commitment: nurturing them into healthy growth. I feel it's sacred, and it's also something I really know I can do."

There is a range of related inquiries that can help a leader flesh out the details of his personal leadership landscape. Among them are, How well do I understand the school and its community? How solid is my relationship with my constituents? Where do I think the school ought to be headed? How should the school be governed? How prepared am I to handle the school's problems? How can I improve my ability to advance the school? If he dares, he can even ask himself, Am I the right one to be leading right now?[4]

Where Does It Come From?

The corollary to these "What do you stand for?" questions is, "Where does it come from?" Whatever the answer to the first question, whether it points to equity or excellence or some other set of beliefs, its origin is almost always personal—deeply personal, both in how strongly it is believed and in how old it is. At heart people's philosophies tend to be "dogmatic," in the original sense of the term, notes Nisbet: "The springs of human action, will, and ambition lie for the most part in beliefs about universe, world, society, and man which defy rational calculations and differ greatly from . . . instincts. These springs lie in what we call dogmas. That word comes from Greek roots with the literal meaning of 'seems-good.'" As Cardinal Newman said, "Men will die for a dogma who will not even stir for a conclusion" (1980, pp. 8–9). I don't ask educators whether they will die for what they stand for, but there is little doubt of the depth of their conviction when they speak of the "seems-goods" that matter most to them.

When I ask about the origins of their philosophy, people invariably point to their experience—their experience as an adult, as an educator, and as a student, and primarily to their early experience growing up. Few think of their courses in graduate school. In fact, the actual behavior of administrators has relatively little to do with their formal training. "They [bring] *themselves* with them to graduate school . . . and they [take] themselves back to their schools . . . knowing some new things, perhaps, but still basically themselves" (Blumberg, 1989, pp. 19–20, emphasis in original). The study of management contributes to what they know (and to their espoused values) but has a modest impact on how they act. Administration, after all, mostly involves not the application of theory and data but the "idiosyncratic use of the self in interactive work situations" (p. 183), and people start learning about using themselves in such situations early on in life. Basic ways of thinking, feeling, and behaving that shape one's approach to problems and one's perspective on the world begin early in childhood in the framework of the family, and they are firmly established long before one becomes an administrator (pp. 191–192). "The philosophy which is so important in each of us," as William James said, "is not a technical matter."

I am used to hearing teachers, principals, and superintendents confirm the nontechnical nature of their philosophy. Their stories are often quite wonderful, providing fascinating glimpses into the personal roots of leadership. One such account was offered by Lawrence Briggs, a high school principal, who explained his philosophy this way:

> I can tell you why equity is so important to me. Up through fourth grade our schools were segregated. In fifth grade we all got to go to what had been the white school. On the first day the teacher asked who wanted to perform for the class on the flutaphone. All the white children raised their hands—they had all had flutaphone lessons and music classes; we hadn't had either. I made up my mind I was going to learn to play. I found a woman to teach me and was $17 in debt to her before my parents even knew I was taking lessons. After Christmas, when the teacher asked again, I raised my hand and kept it up until she finally called on me. I stood up and played my song. Nobody is going to tell me that a kid in my school can't do something.

Lawrence is a man of imposing personal presence: big, outgoing, articulate, witty, confident. He would not, I think, claim to be the least directive, most participatory of leaders. But he enjoyed strong support among his faculty, students, and parents—in good part, I believe, because of his authenticity. Lawrence's unmistakable commitment to students—his belief in their potential and in the importance of giving them the opportunity to succeed—makes what we might call "graduate school sense": it is intellectually sound; it would readily find professional, theoretical, and research support. But its roots are far deeper, far more personal; his commitment is in his bones, and it reaches people at a level that is both immediate and fundamental.

Many Ways to Excel

Lawrence Briggs's example, and those of Jane Carroll and Tom Russell, all illustrate that authentic leadership is highly personal and therefore can take many forms, depending upon the specific commitments of particular school leaders. "Personal" here does not mean arbitrary or whimsical but individual. All leaders whose practice is rooted in deep values and strong beliefs will resemble each other in some important ways, no matter how different their philosophies. But they will also differ according to the content of their beliefs and their preferred ways of operating. Authenticity helps to reveal a wonderful, liberating fact of leadership life: there are many ways to excel.

Most leadership research has been conducted in "low-performing systems"—organizations in trouble. It generally attributes their problems in motivation, morale, communication, trust, and performance to the way a leader is working and assumes that a change in approach or style will correct things (Vaill, 1984, p. 102). But when we look at high-performing systems—successful organizations—we find that leadership style is rarely a determining factor in their performance; in fact, we find a wide range of styles among their leaders: "There are tyrants whose almost maniacal commitment to achieving the system's purposes makes one think that they'd be locked up. . . . There are warm, laid-back parent figures who hardly seem to be doing anything at all, until one looks a little more closely. There are technocrats . . . and dreamers. . . . Some are rah-rah optimists and others are dour critics who express their love for the system by enumerating its imperfections" (p. 102).

I know thriving, vital, high-achieving schools that are led by easygoing, democratic authority delegators and by demanding, strict perfectionists; by creative, roll-with-the-punches improvisers and by obsessive, keep-me-posted worriers; by eloquent, expansive preachers and by quiet, modest doers. Research has shown that principals who were successful change agents all fulfilled four key roles (resource provider, instructional resource, communicator, visible presence) but did so in very different ways. Some were "strong, aggressive, fearless," others "quiet, nurturing, supportive" (Fullan, 1991, p. 158). In stark contrast to situational leaders and practitioners of styles, the most successful leaders "are not human chameleons, but . . . people of distinctive personalities who behave consistently in accordance with that personality" (Badaracco and Ellsworth, 1989, p. 208). Their greatest assets are "their own passions for the organization and its mission and their own common sense when it comes to getting the most out of the people they have. Their unwillingness to turn themselves inside out to conform to some behavioral scientist's theory is remarkable" (Vaill, 1989, p. 19).

The corollary of "many ways to excel" is "every way has its weakness." Authentic leaders have shortcomings; they are usually aware of them, but they tend to emphasize their strengths and to find sufficient nourishment in their sense of themselves. One of the greatest flaws in style-based leadership theories is the assumption that one might somehow acquire and apply only the strengths of each particular style, that one might become a composite of stylistic virtues. In fact, every way of leading, like every way of being, has deficits as well as advantages, and these are inextricably linked. Principals with a genuine commitment to a participatory process can show remarkable patience and sensitivity but be poor at asserting themselves, at setting limits on those who abuse the process, and at taking firm action in a crisis. Superintendents with a take-charge capacity and an ability to tolerate conflict can demonstrate impressive courage and perseverance but ride roughshod over people, make enemies where they don't need to, and be ineffective at compromising when it is necessary. As I have already suggested, authentic leaders tend to be unapologetic about the inevitable downsides of being true to themselves. A superintendent I have known for years sometimes says, with both pride and resignation, "Like Popeye in the old cartoons, 'I am what I am.' I know what I want and what I'm good at. I also know what I'm not so good at, and I try to stick with my strengths." The authentic leader who is aware of her basic inclinations, including her limitations, is already better equipped to compensate for the latter but is unlikely to dwell on them.

Philosophy, Vision, and Strategy: What Do I Want?

To see authenticity as profoundly personal is to recast many of the premises that have come to be taken for granted about leadership and organizations, chief among them vision and strategy. In scarcely more than a decade these concepts have become ubiquitous in leadership theory, practice, and parlance. Like mission, culture, and change, they have become buzzwords. They are widely and correctly trumpeted as vital to leading innovation and are almost as widely misunderstood. Vision is seen as a product of rational planning, as deriving from a careful appraisal of the external environment (a company does a market survey, a school does a needs assessment). In fact, successful change agents rarely operate in this way. Largely overlooked in all the enthusiasm for vision is that it typically derives from "a personal and imaginative creativity that [transcends] analysis" (Badaracco and Ellsworth, 1989, p. 101). In charting an orga-

nizational course, successful leaders rely on processes that are more intuitive and holistic than ordered and intellectual, more qualitative than
quantitative (Mintzberg, 1989, p. 52). Though they are typically adept at
gauging needs and identifying markets, the way they meet needs and
approach markets is their own: they construct their vision out of their
own philosophy and commitment, their own experience and judgment,
their own interests and strengths. In education, such leaders have a mental model of what they want for their school, and they trust their own assessment of the school against that model.

To misunderstand this personal source of vision is to misunderstand
the origins of strategy. When, as it all too often does, strategic planning
begins by identifying external goals and then moves on to analyzing internal strengths, it puts the cart before the horse. To capture its core mission—how it will relate to its environment—a group must first understand
its own strengths (Schein, 1985, p. 55). Over my years of consulting in
schools I have been repeatedly struck by how often successful new programs grow out of the conviction or interest of an individual principal or
a small group of leaders rather than out of a formal planned change
process.

The highly personal nature of vision is central to its success. The value
of a vision is not just to clarify goals and plot a strategy but to inspire followers. To change, people must be "moved." This requires not just an
idea but an advocate. Change begins not just with a goal but with a leader
who communicates it, enlisting the organization's members in the pursuit
of a compelling agenda. The leader's own commitment to the agenda is
crucial to its adoption by followers:

> The greatest inhibitor to enlisting others in a common vision is lack of
> personal conviction. There is absolutely no way that you can, over the
> long term, convince others to share a dream if you are not convinced of
> it yourself. . . . The most inspirational moments are marked by gen-
> uineness. Somehow we all are able to spot a lack of sincerity in others.
> We detect it in their voices, we observe it in their eyes, we notice it in
> their posture. We each have a sixth sense for deceit. . . . So there is a very
> fundamental question that a leader must ask before attempting to enlist
> others: "What do I want?" [Kouzes and Posner, 1987, pp. 124–125].

A fundamental question, indeed. Character in action is always vital to
leadership, but it is especially vital when innovation is under way: the
leader must change first—or at least very early. The leader, that is, must
not just advocate but exemplify the change before asking staff to do so.
Why should anyone take an initiative seriously if the leader doesn't? Yet it

is astonishing how often innovation is imposed on schools without administrators' support and how rarely administrators are accorded—or take—
the time and freedom to think through what they want, to identify their
own commitment or at least develop a commitment in response to an
external priority forced upon them.

This lapse could not be more counterproductive, because although the
need for leaders to commit themselves to change applies universally, it is
critical in schools, where veteran teachers have seen many highly touted
reforms fizzle and have watched many administrators depart before their
priorities reached fruition. These teachers are naturally suspicious, sensitive to signs of hypocrisy, and inclined to hold back, waiting for proof that
for once the administration means what it says and will really persevere.
This proof is most crucially needed from the principal.

Principals are widely seen as indispensable to innovation. No reform
effort, however worthy, survives a principal's indifference or opposition.
He is the leader closest to the action, the operational chief of the unit that
must accomplish the change. His involvement legitimates the effort, giving it an official imprimatur that carries symbolic weight and confirms
that staff should take it seriously. And he is often best suited to secure the
whole array of supports, from the material to the spiritual, that implementation demands. Research on the principal's role generally finds that
schools where innovation succeeds are led by principals who are true
Renaissance people: they do everything well. They demonstrate strong
knowledge of and commitment to the innovation, but they approach faculty in a collaborative spirit, fostering open communication. They demand
high standards, but they offer high levels of emotional support. They hold
staff accountable, but they provide strong assistance. They run good meetings, but they reduce the burden of administrative details. The only problem is that there are apparently so few of them.

This should come as no surprise. Most principals are untrained for
leading change. They have been socialized to be maintainers, not encouraged to be what I call authentic. Risk taking, despite the theoretical vogue
it enjoys among academics who write about school reform, has always
been—and remains—rare in schools. Almost everything one learns as a
principal reinforces the old congressional saw: to get along, go along.
After all, principals face the classic double dilemma of middle managers
everywhere: they are given more responsibility than authority (even without reform initiatives, they are assigned more than they can accomplish),
and their success requires maintaining positive connections not just with
their superiors but also with their staff (they have little to gain from challenging people too sharply). And when they are asked to lead projects they

did not choose or develop and may not fully grasp or endorse, they are likely to be ambivalent, especially when these projects require them to change their own roles and become active in areas, such as pedagogy, where previous improvement schemes have met with little success (Fullan, 1991, p. 152).

All of which underscores the necessity for principals to be able to work through their concerns and doubts, to make change meaningful to themselves, to clarify their own commitments. This means that those above principals—superintendents, school boards, state officials—must remember the importance of allowing time for a district's whole administrative team, especially its principals, to thrash out questions of values and goals as these relate to specific programmatic changes. (It also means that teachers who press for reform on their own must realize the importance of bringing the principal along early and, if this fails, the unlikelihood of achieving schoolwide success.) And what is true for principals is true for other key leaders. All those who have responsibility for an innovation need a chance to get on board before it is adopted, to ask themselves "What do I (or we) want?" and then to stay on board, to revisit their answers periodically during its implementation. These steps take time, to be sure, but to skip them is a false economy that reduces "vision" and "strategy" to empty shells and leaders to deceivers of their constituents.

Authenticity in Action: Strategic Biases for Change

Thus far I have concentrated on leadership's overarching concerns and underlying beliefs. But making change in a school is not just a matter of the high and the deep. What about the daily dilemmas of transition, the issues small and large where policy turns into action and change must actually be accomplished? Authenticity would be little more than a nice ideal if it offered no help with these. Clarifying one's philosophy does not automatically make one savvy any more than it makes one charismatic; it does not create the wisdom that comes from experience, say, or provide the gift of empathic sensitivity. But it does wonderfully enrich one's ability to make decisions and solve problems: it makes one, in the best sense of the word, biased.

Spelling out their basic assumptions and discovering their authentic core helps leaders develop strategic biases for action to guide their work and shape the implementation of change. This notion of bias I take from Badaracco and Ellsworth, who suggest that leaders are far more likely to excel if they approach problems with certain prejudices, that is, "with preconceived biases toward handling them in certain ways" (1989, pp. 3–4).[5]

As used here, *bias* refers to a general way of thinking and acting, a predisposition that guides decision making and problem solving. It is the natural outgrowth of authenticity: a reliance on biases represents not bigotry or small-mindedness but "a quest for integrity, an effort that is at once moral, philosophical, and practical," one that seeks "coherence among a [leader's] daily actions, personal values, and [organizational] aims" (pp. 3–4). Its advantage is that it simplifies leadership, accents its essentials. Instead of long lists of "cookie-cutter approaches devised to fit all situations," which overlook the complexity and disorder of real life (p. 8), the concept of bias leads to a small set of guiding principles that help a school leader direct change according to the larger purposes that motivate his work (and do so in a way that maximizes followership by modeling consistency).

Which guiding principles? Having a philosophy does not by itself guarantee effectiveness. Not all biases are equally apt. We need to know which action orientations on the part of a leader foster change. From the organizational research literature and from my own work with schools that are implementing significant reform, four stand out as essential: clarity and focus, participation without paralysis, recognition, and confrontation. None of them is novel, and none is an arcane orientation accessible only to the gifted. They represent a new look at old truths, a reemphasizing of basics about human nature and school life that we have always known but have too often strayed from. But, as the following chapters will show, when viewed through the lens of authenticity, each of these biases acquires a new and practical emphasis.

NOTES

1. The centrality of integrity to leadership has been explored by a number of writers, notably Kouzes and Posner and, with exceptional clarity, Badaracco and Ellsworth. This chapter draws on both, but especially Badaracco and Ellsworth's excellent book *Leadership and the Quest for Integrity* (1989).

2. Arthur Blumberg (1989, pp. 55–69) offers a good summary of what it means for a school leader to have a good "nose" for the job.

3. For example, many leadership trainers have adopted Argyris's well-known distinction (1976) between "espoused theories," the premises leaders profess to hold and to use as guides for their practice, and "theories-in-use," the real beliefs and assumptions they actually rely on. It is common for the two to be quite discrepant but for people to be unaware of this discrepancy. Argyris proposed that leaders should be taught to modify their theories-in-use to make them more congruent with their espoused values, a proposal

widely accepted in leadership training programs. Recently, strategic theorists, led prominently by Vaill, have begun challenging this view. Vaill argues that there are "many subtle modes and mixes of competency" in leaders' actual practice and that their private, personal theories contain much more wisdom than academics realize (1989, p. 35).

4. These questions are adapted from Kouzes and Posner, 1987, pp. 298–299.

5. Badaracco and Ellsworth use *prejudice* instead of *bias*. Several of the biases I advocate (notably "confrontation") correspond closely to theirs and owe a debt to them, but they also draw upon different sources (including, among others, Bolman and Deal) and focus on schools and innovation, not, as Badaracco and Ellsworth's do, on corporations and general leadership.

REFERENCES

Argyris, C. *Increasing Leadership Effectiveness.* New York: Wiley-Interscience, 1976.

Badaracco, J. L., and Ellsworth, R. *Leadership and the Quest for Integrity.* Boston: Harvard Business School Press, 1989.

Bennis, W., and Nanus, B. *Leaders: The Strategies for Taking Charge.* New York: Harper & Row, 1985.

Blumberg, A. *School Administration as a Craft.* Boston: Allyn & Bacon, 1989.

Bolman, L. G., and Deal, T. E. *Reframing Organizations.* San Francisco: Jossey-Bass, 1991.

Drucker, P. F. *The Practice of Management.* New York: Harper & Row, 1986.

Evans, R. *The Human Side of School Change.* San Francisco: Jossey-Bass, 1996.

Fullan, M., with Stiegelbauer, S. *The New Meaning of Educational Change.* New York: Teachers College Press, 1991.

Gibbons, T. "Revisiting the Question of Born vs. Made: Toward a Theory of Development of Transformational Leaders." Unpublished doctoral dissertation, The Fielding Institute, 1986.

Goleman, D. "Major Personality Study Finds That Traits Are Mostly Inherited." *New York Times,* Dec. 2, 1986, pp. C1–C2.

Kouzes, J. M., and Posner, B. Z. *The Leadership Challenge: How to Keep Getting Extraordinary Things Done in Organizations.* San Francisco: Jossey-Bass, 1987.

Maddi, S. R., and Kobasa, S. *The Hardy Executive.* Chicago: Dow Jones-Irwin, 1984.

McGregor, D. *The Human Side of Enterprise.* New York: McGraw-Hill, 1960.

Mintzberg, H. "Planning on the Left Side, Managing on the Right." In H. Mintzberg, *Mintzberg on Management.* New York: Free Press, 1989.

Nicholson, C. "Henry Scattergood." *Germantown Friends School Alumni Bulletin,* 1995, 36(2), 13.

Nisbet, R. *The History of the Idea of Progress.* New York: Basic Books, 1980.

Ouchi, W. Z. *Theory Z.* Reading, Mass.: Addison-Wesley, 1981.

Schein, E. *Organizational Culture and Leadership.* (1st ed.) San Francisco: Jossey-Bass, 1985.

Sergiovanni, T. J. *The Principalship: A Reflective Practice Perspective.* Boston: Allyn & Bacon, 1991.

Sergiovanni, T. J. *Moral Leadership: Getting to the Heart of School Reform.* San Francisco: Jossey-Bass, 1992.

Vaill, P. B. "The Purposing of High-Performing Systems." In T. J. Sergiovanni and J. E. Cobally (eds.), *Leadership and Organizational Culture.* Urbana: University of Illinois Press, 1984.

Vaill, P. B. *Managing as a Performing Art: New Ideas for a World of Chaotic Change.* San Francisco: Jossey-Bass, 1989.

PART THREE

CULTURE
AND CHANGE

THE KEY TO A SUCCESSFUL SCHOOL is often found in the unique attributes of its organizational culture. School culture is nearly a living thing that needs to be actively recognized, valued, and nurtured. It is the leader's role to act as a sentinel who knows which aspects of culture to shape, which to respect, and which to change. The five readings in this section show how difficult this task can be.

In "Culture in Question," Roland S. Barth discusses how important school culture is. If leaders are to achieve the goal of creating and sustaining lifelong learners, then they must continually ask themselves, "What do you see, hear, and experience in the school?" When leaders stay attuned to the everyday realities of school culture, they are better equipped to ensure alignment with, and progress towards, the collective vision of the school's future.

As Michael Fullan explains in "Understanding Change," leaders must know how and when to implement change and must come to terms with the discomfort, confusion, and fear that will likely ensue. There is no quick fix or step-by-step strategy for leading in a culture of change.

As resources shrink and demands for results increase, Kenneth A. Leithwood makes the case in Chapter Thirteen for an approach to leadership that focuses on the larger goals and values of the school community. Transformational leaders are successful because they are able to connect the personal motivations of their employees to the higher aspirations of their organization.

In "Eight Roles of Symbolic Leaders," Terrence E. Deal and Kent D. Peterson explain how a leader's actions, words, values, and routines are woven into the cultural tapestry of a school community. Every little thing a leader does has symbolic meaning that can help reaffirm, redirect, or damage cultural values and beliefs within an institution.

This section closes with a second reading from Roland S. Barth, entitled "Risk." In this piece Barth explores the benefits of a school culture that encourages leaders to take risks so they may discover new pathways to learning.

CULTURE IN QUESTION

Roland S. Barth

*The illiterate of the twenty-first century will not be
those who cannot read and write, but those
who cannot learn, unlearn, and relearn.*

—Alvin Toffler

PROBABLY THE MOST IMPORTANT—and the most difficult—job of the
school-based reformer is to change the prevailing culture of a school. The
school's culture dictates, in no uncertain terms, "the way we do things
around here." Ultimately, a school's culture has far more influence on life
and learning in the schoolhouse than the state department of education,
the superintendent, the school board, or even the principal can ever have.

The culture of a school is quite apparent to the newcomer. In one
school, a new teacher stands up in a faculty meeting to express her views
to the others on, say, pupil evaluation. Her contribution is received with
mockery, cold stares, and put-downs: "Big deal. I've been doing that for
twenty years." "Who does she think she is?" As the new teacher very
quickly learns, the culture at her school dictates that newcomers must not

speak until they have experienced, for at least two or three years, the toil of the old-timers. "That's the way we do things around here." And she learns that cruel and unusual punishments await those who violate the taboos of the school.

In another school, a high school student is tormented by his peers for studying on the day of the football game. And indeed, the culture in all too many secondary schools dictates that learning is not "cool" on Saturdays—or on any day of the week, for that matter.

In yet another school, a teacher encounters trouble managing a class full of difficult youngsters. Within a few days, every other teacher in the building knows of her problem—and volunteers to help. In the same school, when a student is experiencing difficulty with an assignment or a new concept, several fellow students step in to assist. "That's the way we do things around here."

The school culture is the complex pattern of norms, attitudes, beliefs, behaviors, values, ceremonies, traditions, and myths that are deeply ingrained in the very core of the organization. The culture is the historically transmitted pattern of meaning that wields astonishing power in shaping what people think and how they act.

Every school has a culture. Some are hospitable, others toxic. A school's culture can work for or against improvement and reform. Some schools are populated by teachers and administrators who are reformers, others by sheep, others by educators who are gifted and talented at subverting reform. Some school cultures are indifferent to reform.

And all school cultures are incredibly resistant to change. This is precisely why school improvement—from within or from without—is usually so futile. Yet unless teachers and administrators act to change the culture of a school, all "innovations" will have to fit in and around existing elements of the culture. That is, they will be superficial window dressing, incapable of making much of a difference.

To change the culture requires that we be first aware of the culture, the way things are here. This means crafting and using wide-angle, microscopic, and telescopic lenses, and honing our skills at observing. What do you see, hear, and experience in the school? What don't you see and hear? What are the indicators, the clues that reveal the school's culture? What behaviors get rewards and status here? Which ones are greeted with reprimand? Do the adults model the behavior they expect of youngsters? How do leaders react to critical situations? Who gets to make decisions? Do parents experience welcome, suspicion, or rejection when they enter the school?

Nondiscussables

An important part of awareness is attending to "nondiscussables." Non-discussables are subjects sufficiently important that they get talked about frequently but are so laden with anxiety and taboos that these conversations take place only at the parking lot, the restroom, the playground, the car pool, or the dinner table at home. We are fearful that open discussion of these incendiary issues in polite society—at a faculty meeting, for example—will cause a meltdown. The nondiscussable is the elephant in the living room. Everyone knows this huge pachyderm is there, right between the sofa and the fireplace, and we go on mopping and dusting and vacuuming around it as if it did not exist.

Each school has its own nondiscussables. For one, it is "the leadership of the principal." For another, "the way decisions get made here." For all too many, it is "race" and "the underperforming teacher." Schools are full of these land mines from which trip wires emanate. We walk about carefully from day to day, trying not to detonate them. Yet by giving these nondiscussables this incredible power over us, by avoiding them at all cost, we issue that underperforming teacher a hunting license to continue this year as he did last year, taking a heavy toll on countless students and other teachers. We perpetuate poor leadership on the part of the principal, and we force ourselves to live with all the debilitating tensions that surround race.

The health of a school is inversely proportional to the number of its nondiscussables: the fewer the nondiscussables, the healthier the school; the more the nondiscussables, the more pathology in the school culture. And, of course, to change the culture of the school, its residents must name, openly acknowledge the existence of, and address the nondiscussables—especially the nondiscussables that impede learning.

Changing the Culture

It has been said that a fish would be the last creature on earth to discover water, so totally and continuously immersed in it is he. The same might be said of school people working within their culture. By the time that beginning teacher waits the obligatory three years to speak out in a faculty meeting, she too is likely to be so immersed in the culture that she will no longer be able to see with the clarity of a beginner important aspects of the school's culture, such as patterns of leadership, competition, fearfulness, self-interest, or lack of support.

To change the culture requires that we bring in more desirable qualities to replace the existing unhealthy elements of the culture. This is where possession of clear personal and collective visions is so important. Two educators, Saphier and King, identified a dozen healthy cultural norms: collegiality, experimentation, high expectations, trust and confidence, tangible support, reaching out to the knowledge bases, appreciation and recognition, caring celebration and humor, involvement in decision making, protection of what's important, traditions, and honest, open communications (Saphier and King, 1985). The authors believe that these qualities of a school's culture dramatically affect the capacity of a school to improve.

Thus, to change a school's culture requires the courage and skill not to remain victimized by the toxic elements of the school's culture but rather to address them. As one colleague put it, "How do I find the courage within myself to do what I must?" And, finally, culture building requires the skill to transform elements of the school's culture into forces that support rather than subvert the purposes of the school, even though, all the while, no one may be giving us "permission" to do so. Of course, all these acts of culture changing and culture building violate the very taboos of many school cultures themselves—this is why culture changing is the most important, most difficult, and most perilous job of school-based reformers. School cultures cannot be changed from without; they must be changed from within.

E. B. White, a fellow Maine gardener, once observed, "A person must have something to cling to. Without that we are as a peavine sprawling in search of a trellis." We educators are especially in need of a trellis, to keep us up off the ground in the face of the cold rains and hot winds that buffet the schoolhouse. In this chapter I'd like to consider with you what I believe is the trellis of our profession and the most critical element of any school's culture: an ethos hospitable to the promotion of human learning.

Learning Curves off the Chart

It has been said that running a school is about putting first things first: leadership is determining what are the first things, and management is about putting them first. I would like to suggest that the "first thing," the most important feature of the job description for each of us educators, is to discover and provide the conditions under which people's learning curves go off the chart. Sometimes it's other people's learning curves: those of students, teachers, parents, administrators. But at all times it is our own learning curve.

Schools exist to promote learning in all their inhabitants. Whether we are called teachers, principals, professors, or parents, our primary responsibility is to promote learning in others and in ourselves. That's what it means to be an educator. That's what sets us apart from insurance salesmen, engineers, and doctors. To the extent our activities in school are dedicated to getting learning curves off the chart, I'd say what we do is a calling. To the extent that we spend most of our time doing something else in school, I'd say we are engaged in a job.

It is the ability to learn prodigiously from birth to death that sets human beings apart from other forms of life. The greatest purpose of schools is to unlock, release, and foster this wonderful capability. T. H. White put it this way:

> "The best thing for disturbances of the spirit," replied Merlyn, beginning to puff and blow, "is to learn. That is the only thing that never fails. You may grow old and trembling in your anatomies, you may lie awake at night listening to the disorder in your veins, you may miss your only love and lose your monies to a monster, you may see the world about you devastated by evil lunatics, or know your honor trampled in the sewers of baser minds. There is only one thing for it, then—to learn. Learn why the world wags and what wags it. That is the only thing which the poor mind can never exhaust, never alienate, never be tortured by, never fear or distrust, and never dream of regretting. Learning is the thing for you." [White, 1993, p. 228]

A Community of Learners

"Our school is a Community of Learners!" How many times do we see and hear this assertion, now so common in America's schools? For me it is both an ambitious, welcome vision and an empty promissory note. The vision is, first, that the school will be a community, a place full of adults and youngsters who care about, look after, and root for one another, and who work together for the good of the whole, in times of need as well as times of celebration. Every member of a community holds some responsibility for the welfare of every other and for the welfare of the community as a whole. Schools face tremendous difficulty in fulfilling this definition of a community. More are organizations, institutions, or bureaucracies.

As if community were not ambitious enough, a community of learners is ever so much more. Such a school is a community whose defining, underlying culture is one of learning. The condition for membership in the community is that one learn, continue to learn, and support the learning of others. Everyone. A tall order to fill, and one to which all too few schools aspire and even fewer attain.

As I reflect back on the recent years of school reform, I interpret the meaning of this remarkable period in our nation's educational history as an invitation—nay, a demand—to examine every school policy, practice, and decision and ask of it the question, What, if anything, of importance is anyone learning as a consequence of doing that? Who learns what from ability grouping? Who learns what from letter grades of A, B, C? Who learns what from having twenty-six youngsters in a class? Who learns what from the annual practice of principals' evaluating teachers? God didn't create these and the myriad other school practices that now so clutter schools' cultures. We did—because at some time someone believed that this policy, practice, or procedure was capable of getting someone's learning curve off the chart.

A central responsibility of the school-based reformer is to take fresh inventory of these and other habituated practices so encrusted in our schools' cultures and to categorize them. Some, perhaps the practice of giving individual instruction or giving youngsters immediate feedback on their work, seem undeniably associated with promoting learning. They need to be retained. Others, such as ability grouping or parent nights, we may need to study; we need to become practitioner researchers and examine these practices to determine just what effect, if any, they are having on people's learning. Still other practices, perhaps faculty meetings or intrusive announcements over the loudspeaker, in many schools appear to contribute to no one's learning—may even impede learning—and need to be scrapped. A final category is for those activities that must continue to be carried out by a school, but in a more successful manner. We'll call this category "invent a better way."

Let me offer an example. Kim Marshall, a friend of mine and a principal in the Boston public schools, is a very conscientious staff developer, yet he was having a dreadful time with the time-consuming, anxiety-producing practice of annually evaluating teachers according to the system's protocol. He wrote, "Evaluation had become a polite, if near-meaningless matter between a beleaguered principal and a nervous teacher. . . . I had been trying to do a good job evaluating the thirty-nine teachers at the Mather School, but I had to face the fact that my efforts were a sham. Were my evaluations of teachers having an impact on student learning? Very doubtful. Were they having an impact on teachers' learning? Precious little. My learning? No. Were they wasting everyone's time? You bet."

His attempts to connect teacher evaluations with someone's learning curve soaring revealed an educationally bankrupt practice deeply embedded in the culture of his school—and of his school system. Even so, for many reasons we can't just "scrap" the evaluation of teachers. It's important that all of us be evaluated from time to time, including school teachers (and authors!). Having discussed this nondiscussable and having carefully examined and categorized this sacrosanct school practice in terms of its capacity to promote learning, my friend found the courage to make some changes; he invented a better way. (For further discussion of the limitations of the conventional forms of teacher evaluation by the principal, and for a better, if more demanding, way, one which can promote both learning and community, see Marshall, 1996.)

I believe that residing in all the stakeholders in schools—parents, teachers, students, principals—are wonderfully fresh, imaginative ideas about how to invent a better way. It takes moral outrage at ineffective practices, confidence that there is a better way, and the courage and invention to find it and put it into the place of what needs to be scrapped.

As noted earlier, all of us who work in and around schools now not only have the world's permission to take this inventory and act on the findings; the world is demanding these efforts of us. If this is the meaning of school reform, I'd say it is long overdue and to be welcomed by school practitioners. Whose learning curve goes off the chart by doing that? This is a revolutionary question whose time has finally come.

At-Risk Students

I have observed over the years that unhealthy school cultures tend to beget "at-risk" students. One definition of an at-risk student that has special meaning for me is "any student who leaves school before or after graduation with little possibility of continuing learning."

I remember visiting a high school just after the last spring exams and before graduation. As I approached the school grounds, I saw a group of students standing around a roaring fire, to which they were heartily contributing. I went over and asked, "What's up?"

"We're burning our notes and our books," replied one. "We're outta here!"

On further conversation, I learned that these students were not occupants of the bottom ability group, but rather A and B and C students, many headed for college.

That little incident continues to trouble me. I wonder how many students not so labeled are in fact at risk, with little possibility of continuing learning? How many graduate from our schools and exult in the belief that they have learned all they need or intend to know?

One reason why those youngsters were burning those books, literally, and why so many other youngsters burn their books, figuratively, at the conclusion of our treatment of them in schools is that, lurking beneath the culture of most schools (and universities) is a deadening message. It goes something like this: Learn or we will hurt you. We educators have taken learning, a wonderful, God-given, spontaneous capacity of all human beings, and coupled it with punitive measures. We have developed an arsenal of sanctions and punishments that we inextricably link with learning experiences. "Johnny, if you don't improve your multiplication tables, you're going to have to repeat fourth grade." "Mary, if you don't improve your compositions, I'm not going to write a favorable recommendation for college." "Sam, if you don't pass this next test, I'm calling your parents in." "Tom, if your state-administered standardized test scores don't improve, you don't graduate." And so it goes. What the students burning their books are really saying is, "You can't hurt me any more." But so closely have we coupled learning and punishment that the students throw one into the fire with the other. School cultures in which students submit to learning, and to the threats of punishment for not learning, generate students who want to be finished with learning when they graduate from school. And, of course, this plays out for adults as well: the state tells the teacher or principal, "Unless you complete fifteen hours of continuing education credits this year, we will not renew your certification." Learn or we will hurt you.

A challenge of immense proportion to our profession is to find ways to uncouple learning and punishment. We must change the message from "Learn or we will hurt you" to "Learn or you will hurt yourself."

The Lifelong Learner

Why are these youngsters who literally or figuratively burn their books so much at risk? I read recently an estimate that fifty years ago, high school students graduated knowing perhaps 75 percent of what they would ever need to know to be successful in the workplace, the family, and the community. Today, the estimate is that graduates of our schools leave knowing perhaps 2 percent of what they will need to know in the years ahead—98 percent is yet to come. We all know the figures: knowledge doubles every three years; computer technology changes in eighteen months; the borders of Russia won't hold still. Yet today's graduates leave high school knowing far more than they ever did back in the fifties. The notion that we can acquire once and for all a basic kit of knowledge that will hold us in good stead for the rest of our lives is folly.

Business leaders tell us that the skills and abilities their employees will need in the twenty-first century include the following: teamwork, problem solving, interpersonal skills, oral communication, listening, personal development, creative thinking, leadership, goal setting, writing, organizational effectiveness, computation, and reading. Every one of these skills, of course, requires continual lifelong learning. The students who burn their books and their notes and celebrate the conclusion of their learning will be relegated to the periphery of the twenty-first century. And business leaders will continue to lament that they must spend $25 billion each year trying to teach recent graduates what they didn't learn in school.

Those who will thrive in the years ahead, in contrast, will be those who have, during the school experience, become active, voracious, independent lifelong learners—who will always be moving toward that 98 percent yet to come. The nature of the workplace, the nature of our society, and the nature of learning mean that we are all going to be expected to learn as we go along, or we won't survive.

I believe, therefore, that the most important requirement for graduation—whether from fourth, ninth, or twelfth grade—is some evidence that this youngster is becoming or has become an independent, lifelong learner. The telling questions to evaluate are, What evidence is there of enduring intellectual passion in this student? Is there evidence that this student is imbued with the qualities and capacities of the insatiable, lifelong learner? Is the student capable of posing questions, marshaling resources, and pursuing learning with dedication, independence, imagination, and courage?

So if your school has succeeded in getting 95 percent of its students scoring at the 95th percentile on standardized tests, and, at the same time, students are leaving a teacher, a grade, or the school "burning their books" saying "I'm done with this stuff; I'm outta here!" then you have won a battle and lost the war. The price of the short-term success is long-term failure. Enhancement of performance has led to a curtailment of learning. The school has failed in its most important mission. If the first major purpose of a school is to create and provide a culture hospitable to human learning, the second major purpose of a school is to make it likely that students and educators will become and remain lifelong learners.

These days, we use standardized tests to measure everything about everybody, from proficiency in pronouns to the causes of the Civil War. Yet it is disheartening to me that we have not identified as important nor attempted to measure to what extent our teachers, our classes, and our schools are turning out lifelong learners. When students arrive at school at age five, most carry within them the magical powers of lifelong learning. They are explorers, question-askers, inquirers, and risk-takers, and they are excited about finding answers. To paraphrase Pablo Picasso, every child is a learner. The problem is how to remain a learner once he grows up.

If we want to know how well we are doing with second or eighth graders in creating and sustaining lifelong learners, how do we find out? I doubt that standardized tests have much value in measuring or predicting the lifelong learner. There are better ways. One good way is to observe closely what students choose to do on their own time. After the bell rings at three o'clock—or on weekends, or over the summer—in what activities are youngsters engaged until bedtime? They will tell us. Are they going for walks in the woods, collecting and categorizing leaves and flowers and insects? Are they mapping their city street? Are they reading in the library? Are they campaigning for a local candidate? Are they learning to play a musical instrument? Or are they only watching television and hanging out? If it's true that character is what you do when no one is looking, then learning is what you do when you're not graded for it.

Asked seriously, the question, What do students do on their own time? reveals information that would probably alarm parents, educators, and the general public—as it should. When we come to believe that what our schools should be providing is a school culture that creates and sustains students' learning, that this is the trellis of our profession, then we will organize our schools, classrooms, and learning experiences differently. Show me a school whose inhabitants constantly examine the school's culture and work to transform it into one hospitable to sustained human learning, and I'll show you students who graduate with both the capacity and the heart for lifelong learning.

REFERENCES

Marshall, K. "How I Confronted HSPS (Hyperactive Superficial Principal Syndrome) and Began to Deal with the Heart of the Matter." *Phi Delta Kappan,* Jan. 1996, pp. 336–345.

Saphier, J., and King, M. "Good Seeds Grow in Strong Cultures." *Educational Leadership,* Mar. 1985, pp. 67–74.

White, T. H. *The Sword in the Stone.* New York: Philomel Books, 1993.

12

UNDERSTANDING CHANGE

Michael Fullan

REMEMBER THAT a culture of change consists of great rapidity and non-linearity on the one hand and equally great potential for creative break-throughs on the other. The paradox is that transformation would not be possible without accompanying messiness.

Understanding the change process is less about innovation and more about innovativeness. It is less about strategy and more about strategizing. And it is rocket science, not least because we are inundated with complex, unclear, and often contradictory advice. Micklethwait and Wooldridge (1996) refer to management gurus as witch doctors (although they also acknowledge their value). Argyris (2000) talks about flawed advice. Mintzberg, Ahlstrand, and Lampel (1998) take us on a Strategy Safari. Drucker is reported to have said that people refer to gurus because they don't know how to spell charlatan!

Would you know what to do if you read Kotter's *Leading Change,* in which he proposes an eight-step process for initiating top-down transformation (1996, p. 21)?

1. Establishing a sense of urgency
2. Creating a guiding coalition
3. Developing a vision and strategy
4. Communicating the change vision
5. Empowering broad-based action

6. Generating short-term wins

7. Consolidating gains and producing more change

8. Anchoring new approaches in the culture

Would you still know what to do if you then turned to Beer, Eisenstat, and Spector's observations (1990) about drawing out bottom-up ideas and energies?

1. Mobilize commitment to change through joint diagnosis [with people in the organization] of business problems

2. Develop a shared vision of how to organize and manage for competitiveness

3. Foster concerns for the new vision, competence to enact it, and cohesion to move it along

4. Spread revitalization to all departments without pushing it from the top

5. Institutionalize revitalization through formal policies, systems, and structure

6. Monitor and adjust strategies in response to problems in the re-vitalization process [cited in Mintzberg and others, 1998, p. 338]

What do you think of Hamel's advice (2000) to "lead the revolution" by being your own seer?

Step 1: Build a point of view

Step 2: Write a manifesto

Step 3: Create a coalition

Step 4: Pick your targets and pick your moments

Step 5: Co-opt and neutralize

Step 6: Find a translator

Step 7: Win small, win early, win often

Step 8: Isolate, infiltrate, integrate

And, after all this advice, if you did know what to do, would you be right? Probably not. Some of the advice seems contradictory. (Should we emphasize top-down or bottom-up strategies?) Much of it is general and unclear about what to do—what Argyris (2000) calls "nonactionable advice." This is why many of us have concluded that change cannot be managed. It can be understood and perhaps led, but it cannot be controlled. After taking us through a safari of ten management schools of thought, Mintzberg and others (1998) draw the same conclusion when they reflect that "the best way to 'manage' change is to allow for it to happen" (p. 324), "to be pulled by the concerns out there rather than being pushed by the concepts in here" (p. 373). It is not that management and leadership books don't contain valuable ideas—they do—but rather that there is no "answer" to be found in them. Nevertheless, change can be led, and leadership does make a difference.

So our purpose in this chapter is to understand change in order to lead it better. The list that follows summarizes this chapter's contribution to understanding the change process. The goal is to develop a greater feel for leading complex change, to develop a mind-set and action set that are constantly cultivated and refined. There are no shortcuts.

UNDERSTANDING THE CHANGE PROCESS

- The goal is not to innovate the most.
- It is not enough to have the best ideas.
- Appreciate the implementation dip.
- Redefine resistance.
- Reculturing is the name of the game.
- Never a checklist, always complexity.

Before delving into a discussion of each of the items on this list, let's consider Goleman's findings (2000) about leadership that gets results, because they relate to several elements of the list. Goleman analyzed a database from a random sample of 3,871 executives from the consulting firm Hay/McBer. He examined the relationship between leadership style, organizational climate, and financial performance. Climate was measured by combining six factors of the working environment: flexibility, responsibility, standards, rewards, clarity, and commitment. Financial results included return on sales, revenue growth, efficiency, and profitability.

The following are the six leadership styles Goleman identified (2000, pp. 82–83):

1. Coercive—the leader demands compliance. ("Do what I tell you.")
2. Authoritative—the leader mobilizes people toward a vision. ("Come with me.")
3. Affiliative—the leader creates harmony and builds emotional bonds. ("People come first.")
4. Democratic—the leader forges consensus through participation. ("What do you think?")

5. Pacesetting—the leader sets high standards for performance. ("Do as I do, now.")

6. Coaching—the leader develops people for the future. ("Try this.")

Two of the six styles negatively affected climate and, in turn, performance. These were the coercive style (people resent and resist) and the pacesetting style (people get overwhelmed and burn out). All four of the other styles had a significant positive impact on climate and performance.

With this basic introduction to leadership styles, let us now turn to the list items.

The Goal Is Not to Innovate the Most

The organization or leader who takes on the sheer most number of innovations is not the winner. In education, we call these organizations the "Christmas tree schools" (Bryk, Sebring, Kerbow, Rollow, and Easton, 1998). These schools glitter from a distance—so many innovations, so little time—but they end up superficially adorned with many decorations, lacking depth and coherence.

Relentlessly taking on innovation after innovation is Goleman's pacesetter leader (2000, p. 86):

> The leader sets extremely high performance standards and exemplifies them himself. He is obsessive about doing things better and faster, and he asks the same of everyone around him. He quickly pinpoints poor performers and demands more from them. If they don't rise to the occasion, he replaces them with people who can. You would think such an approach would improve results, but it doesn't. In fact, the pacesetting style destroys climate. Many employees feel overwhelmed by the pacesetter's demands for excellence, and their morale drops—guidelines for working may be clear in the leader's head, but she does not state them clearly; she expects people to know what to do.

The pacesetter often ends up being a "lone ranger," as Superintendent Negroni puts it when he reflects on his experience (and on his eventual change to lead learner). During the first three years of Negroni's superintendency in Springfield, Massachusetts, his overall goal was "to change this inbred system": "Intent on the ends, I operated as Lone Ranger. I didn't try to build relationships with the teachers' union or with the board. Instead, I worked around them. Most of the time, I felt that I was way out in front of them. I would change things on my own" (quoted in Senge and others, 2000, p. 426). For all the changes he pushed through, Negroni says, "these were three brutal years for all of us. . . . I was running so fast and making so many changes that I was getting tired. People around me were even more sick and tired" (pp. 426–427).

Eventually, through reflective practice and feedback, Negroni moved to transforming the district into a learning institution. He explains:

> Our most critical role at the central office is to support learning about learning, especially among principals—who will then do the same among teachers in their schools. At the beginning of the year, three or four central office administrators and I conducted forty-six school visits in forty-six days, with the principals of each school alongside us. Then the administrators and all forty-six principals met together to summarize what we had seen. This is one of a series of walk-throughs that principals do during the course of a school year—with me, with other central office administrators, and with each other. The sequence includes a monthly "grand round," when every principal in the district goes with me and the eight academic directors to spend the day in one school. We break up into subgroups for hour-and-a-half visits, then come back and (still in subgroups) discuss what we saw. Then a representative from each subgroup makes a presentation to all of the principals. [quoted in Senge and others, 2000, p. 431]

These principals are still deeply engaged in innovation, but it is less frenetic, more organically built into the culture. Thus pacesetters must learn the difference between competing in a change marathon and developing the capacity and commitment to solve complex problems.

It Is Not Enough to Have the Best Ideas

It is possible to be "dead right." This is the leader who has some of the best ideas around but can't get anyone to buy into them. In fact, the opposite occurs—she experiences overwhelming opposition. The extreme version of this kind of leader is Goleman's coercive leader (2000, p. 82): "The computer company was in crisis mode—its sales and profits were falling, its stock was losing value precipitously, and its shareholders were in an uproar. The board brought in a CEO with a reputation as a turnaround artist. He set to work chopping jobs, selling off divisions and making the tough decisions that should have been executed years before. The company was saved, at least in the short term." Before long, however, morale plummeted, and the short-term success was followed by another, less recoverable downturn.

Even the more sophisticated versions of "having good ideas" are problematic. Pascale, Millemann, and Gioja (2000) call these leaders social engineers:

> Corporations around the world now write checks for more than $50 billion a year in fees for "change consulting." And that tab represents only a third of the overall change cost if severance costs, write-offs, and information technology purchases are included. Yet, consultants, academic surveys, and reports from "changed" companies themselves indicate that a full 70 percent of those efforts fail. The reason? We call it *social engineering,* a contemporary variant of the machine model's cause-and-effect thinking. *Social* is coupled with *engineering* to denote that most managers today, in contrast to their nineteenth-century counterparts, recognize that people need to be brought on board. But they still go about it in a preordained fashion. Trouble arises because the "soft" stuff is really the hard stuff, and no one can really "engineer" it. [p. 12, emphasis in original]

But surely having good ideas is not a bad thing. And yes, it is an element of effective leadership, as in Goleman's authoritative style. Goleman (2000) talks about Tom, a vice president of marketing at a floundering national restaurant chain that specialized in pizza: "[Tom] made an impassioned plea for his colleagues to think from the customer's perspective. . . . The company was not in the restaurant business, it was in the business of distributing high-quality, convenient-to-get pizza. That notion—and nothing else—should drive what the company did. . . . With his vibrant enthusiasm and clear vision—the hallmarks of the authoritative style—Tom filled a leadership vacuum at the company" (p. 83).

Goleman's data show that the authoritative leader had a positive impact on climate and performance. So do we need leaders with a clear vision who can excite and mobilize people to committing to it, or don't we? Well, the answer is a bit complicated. For some situations, when there is an urgent problem and people are at sea, visionary leaders can be crucial. And at all times, it helps when leaders have good ideas. But it is easy for authoritative leadership to slip into social engineering when initial excitement cannot be sustained because it cannot be converted to internal commitment.

Put another way, the answer is that authoritative leaders need to recognize the weaknesses as well as the strengths in their approach. They need, as Goleman concludes, to use all four of the successful leadership styles: "Leaders who have mastered four or more—especially the authoritative, democratic, affiliative, and coaching styles—have the best climate and business performance" (p. 87).

Appreciate the Implementation Dip

One of our most consistent findings and understandings about the change process in education is that all successful schools experience "implementation dips" as they move forward (Fullan, 2001). The implementation dip is literally a dip in performance and confidence as one encounters an innovation that requires new skills and new understandings. All innovations worth their salt call upon people to question and in some respects to change their behavior and their beliefs—even in cases where innovations are pursued voluntarily. What happens when you find yourself needing new skills and not being proficient when you are used to knowing what you are doing (in your own eyes, as well as in those of others)? How do you feel when you are called upon to do something new and are not clear about what to do and do not understand the knowledge and value base of new belief systems?

This kind of experience is classic change material. People feel anxious, fearful, confused, overwhelmed, deskilled, cautious, and—if they have moral purpose—deeply disturbed. Because we are talking about a culture of pell-mell change, there is no shortage of implementation dips or, shall we say, chasms.

Pacesetters and coercers have no empathy whatsoever for people undergoing implementation dips. They wouldn't know an implementation dip if they fell into it. Effective leaders have the right kinds of sensitivity to implementation. They know that change is a process, not an event. They don't panic when things don't go smoothly during the first year of undertaking a major innovation or new direction. They are empathic to the lot of people immersed in the unnerving and anxiety-ridden work of trying to bring about a new order. They are even, as we shall discuss, appreciative of resistance.

Leaders who understand the implementation dip know that people are experiencing two kinds of problems when they are in the dip—the social-psychological fear of change, and the lack of technical know-how or skills to make the change work. It should be obvious that leaders need affiliative and coaching styles in these situations. The affiliative leader pays attention to people, focuses on building emotional bonds, builds relationships, and heals rifts. The leader as coach helps people develop and invests in their capacity building (Goleman, 2000).

Further, elements of authoritative leadership help. Enthusiasm, self-confidence, optimism, and clarity of vision can all inspire people to keep going. The problems start when you are only authoritative or only affiliative or only a coach. Thus leaders who are sensitive to the implementation dip combine styles: they still have an urgent sense of moral purpose, they still measure success in terms of results, but they do things that are more likely to get the organization going and keep it going.

Redefine Resistance

We are more likely to learn something from people who disagree with us than we are from people who agree. But we tend to hang around with and overlisten to people who agree with us, and we prefer to avoid and underlisten to those who don't. Not a bad strategy for getting through the day, but a lousy one for getting through the implementation dip.

Pacesetters and coercers are terrible listeners. Authoritative leaders are not that good at listening either. Affiliative and democratic leaders listen too much. This is why leadership is complicated. It requires combining elements that do not easily and comfortably go together. Leaders should have good ideas and present them well (the authoritative element) while at the same time seeking and listening to doubters (aspects of democratic leadership). They must try to build good relationships (be affiliative) even with those who may not trust them.

We need to respect resisters for two reasons. First, they sometimes have ideas that we might have missed, especially in situations of diversity or complexity or in the tackling of problems for which the answer is unknown. As Maurer (1996, p. 49) says, "Often those who resist have something important to tell us. We can be influenced by them. People resist for what they view as good reasons. They may see alternatives we never dreamed of. They may understand problems about the minutiae of implementation that we never see from our lofty perch atop Mount Olympus."

Second, resisters are crucial when it comes to the politics of implementation. In democratic organizations, such as universities, being alert to differences of opinion is absolutely vital. Many a strong dean who otherwise did not respect resistance has been unceremoniously run out of town. In all organizations, respecting resistance is essential, because if you ignore it, it is only a matter of time before it takes its toll, perhaps during implementation if not earlier. In even the most tightly controlled and authority-bound organization, it is so easy to sabotage new directions during implementation. Even when things appear to be working, the supposed success may be a function of merely superficial compliance.

For all these reasons, successful organizations don't go with only like-minded innovators; they deliberately build in differences. They don't mind so much when others—not just themselves—disturb the equilibrium. They also trust the learning process they set up—the focus on moral purpose, the attention to the change process, the building of relationships, the sharing and critical scrutiny of knowledge, and traversing the edge of chaos while seeking coherence. Successful organizations and their leaders come to know and trust that these dynamics contain just about all the checks and balances needed to deal with those few hard-core resisters who make a career out of being against everything—who act, in other words, without moral purpose.

Reculturing Is the Name of the Game

It used to be that governments were the only group constantly reorganizing. Now, with reengineering and mergers and acquisitions, everybody is doing it. And they are getting nowhere. Gaius Petronious nailed this problem almost two thousand years ago: "We trained hard . . . but it seemed every time we were beginning to form up into teams we were reorganized. I was to learn later in life that we tend to meet any situation by reorganizing, and what a wonderful method it can be for creating the illusion of progress while producing confusion, inefficiency, and demoralization" (cited in Gaynor, 1977, p. 28).

Structure does make a difference, but it is not the main point in achieving success. Transforming the culture—changing the way we do things around here—is the main point. I call this reculturing. Effective leaders know that the hard work of reculturing is the sine qua non of progress. Furthermore, it is a particular kind of reculturing for which we strive: one that activates and deepens moral purpose through collaborative work cultures that respect differences and constantly build and test knowledge against measurable results—a culture within which one realizes that sometimes being off balance is a learning moment.

Leading in a culture of change means creating a culture (not just a structure) of change. It does not mean adopting innovations, one after another; it does mean producing the capacity to seek, critically assess, and selectively incorporate new ideas and practices—all the time, inside the organization as well as outside it.

Reculturing is a contact sport that involves hard, labor-intensive work. It takes time and indeed never ends. This is why successful leaders need energy, enthusiasm, and hope, and why they need moral purpose along with the other four leadership capacities described in this book. Reculturing is very much a matter of developing relationships, building knowledge, and striving for coherence in a nonlinear world.

Never a Checklist, Always Complexity

It is no doubt clear by now why there can never be a recipe or cookbook for change, nor a step-by-step process. Even seemingly sophisticated plans like Kotter's (1996) eight steps, or Hamel's (2000) eight, discussed earlier in this chapter, are suspect if used as the basis for planning. They may be useful to stir one's thinking, but I have argued that it will be more productive to develop one's own mind-set through the five core components of leadership because one is more likely to internalize what makes for effective leadership in complex times. This makes it difficult for leaders because they will be pushed to provide solutions. In times of urgent problems and confusing circumstances, people demand leaders who can show the way. (Just try leading by explaining to your board of directors that you have based your strategic plan on the properties of nonlinear feedback networks and complex adaptive systems.) In other words, leaders and members of the organization, because they live in a culture of frenetic change, are vulnerable to seeking the comforting clarity of off-the-shelf solutions. Why not take a change pill? And if that doesn't work, there will be another one next year.

Alas, there is no getting around the conclusion that effective leaders must cultivate their knowledge, understanding, and skills of what has to come to be known as complexity science. (For the latest, best discussion of this subject, see Pascale and others, 2000; and Stacey, 2000; see also my *Change Forces* trilogy, 1993, 1999, 2002). Complexity science is a remarkable convergence of independent streams of inquiry. This science, as Pascale and others claim, grapples with the mysteries of life and living; it is producing exciting new insights into life itself and into how we might think about organizations, leadership, and social change: "Living systems [like businesses] cannot be *directed* along a linear path. Unforeseen consequences are inevitable. The challenge is to *disturb* them in a manner that approximates the desired outcomes" (Pascale and others, 2000, p. 6, emphasis in original).

The Complexities of Leadership

Leading in a culture of change is about unlocking the mysteries of living organizations. That is why this book places a premium on understanding and insight rather than on mere action steps. Complexities can be unlocked and even understood but rarely controlled.

There are, as can be seen, dilemmas in leading change. Goleman's analysis helps us because it informs us that elements of different leadership styles must be learned and used in different situations. But knowing what to do in given circumstances is still not for sure. If you are facing an urgent, crisis-ridden situation, a more coercive stance may be necessary at the beginning. Those dealing with failing schools have drawn this very conclusion: the need for external intervention is inversely proportionate to how well the school is progressing. In a case of persistent failure, dramatic, assertive leadership and external intervention appear to be necessary. In the long run, however, effectiveness depends on developing internal commitment in which the ideas and intrinsic motivation of the vast majority of organizational members become activated. Along the way, authoritative ideas, democratic empowerment, affiliative bonds, and coaching will all be needed.

In the preceding paragraph I deliberately said that more coercive actions may be needed "at the beginning" of a crisis. This is where leadership gets complicated. When organizations are in a crisis they have to be rescued from chaos. But a crisis usually means that the organization is out of synch with its environment. In this case, more radical change is required, and this means the organization needs leadership that welcomes differences, communicates the urgency of the challenge, talks about broad possibilities in an inviting way, and creates mechanisms that "motivate people to reach beyond themselves" (Pascale and others, 2000, p. 74; see also Heifetz, 1994).

Most people would agree that the public school system is in a state of crisis. It needs authoritative leadership before it disintegrates, but the system is still out of line with its environment, which calls for accelerated change and learning. There can be a fine line between coercive and authoritative leadership. Certainly the National Literacy and Numeracy Strategy in England has elements of coercive as well as pacesetting leadership. Is this degree of pressure required to get large-scale change under way? We don't really know, but I would venture to say that the strategy that moved the English school system from near-chaos to a modicum of success is not the same strategy that is going to create the transformation needed for the system to thrive in the future. For that you need plenty of internal commitment and ingenuity. School systems all over the world, take heed.

The need to have different strategies for different circumstances explains why we cannot generalize from case studies of success. In 1982, Peters and Waterman's *In Search of Excellence* galvanized the management world to inspiration and action. As it turns out, however, of the forty-three excellent companies (and they were excellent at the time), "half were in trouble" within five years of the book's appearance; "at present all but five have fallen from grace" (Pascale and others, 2000, p. 23).

To recommend employing different leadership strategies that simultaneously and sequentially combine different elements seems like complicated advice, but developing this deeper feel for the change process by accumulating insights and wisdom across situations and time may turn out to be the most practical thing we can do—more practical than the best step-by-step models. For if such models don't really work, or if they work only in some situations, or if they are successful only for short periods of time, they are hardly practical.

We can also see the complexities of leadership in J. B. Martin's comparison of John F. Kennedy and Robert F. Kennedy:

> Jack Kennedy was more the politician, saying things publicly that he privately scoffed at. Robert Kennedy was more himself. Jack gave the impression of decisive leadership, the man with all the answers. Robert seemed more hesitant, less sure he was right, more tentative, more questioning, and completely honest about it. Leadership he showed; but it has a different quality, an off-trail unorthodox quality, to some extent a quality of searching for hard answers to hard questions in company with his bewildered audience, trying to work things out with their help. [quoted in Thomas, 2000, p. 390]

Robert Kennedy had his ruthless and conspiratorial moments, but it is likely that his style of leadership—committed to certain values, but uncertain of the pathways—is more suited to leading in a culture of change. Being sure of yourself when you shouldn't be can be a liability. Decisive leaders can attract many followers, but it is usually more a case of dependency than enlightenment. The relationship between leaders and members of the organization is complicated indeed.

REFERENCES

Argyris, C. *Flawed Advice and the Management Trap.* New York: Oxford University Press, 2000.

Beer, M., Eisenstat, R., and Spector, B. *The Critical Path to Corporate Renewal.* Boston: Harvard Business School Press, 1990.

Bryk, A., Sebring, P., Kerbow, D., Rollow, S., and Easton, J. *Charting Chicago School Reform.* Boulder, CO: Westview Press, 1998.

Fullan, M. *Change Forces: Probing the Depths of Educational Reform.* Bristol, Pa.: Falmer Press, 1993.

Fullan, M. *Change Forces: The Sequel.* Bristol, Pa.: Falmer Press, 1999.

Fullan, M. *The New Meaning of Educational Change.* (3rd ed.) New York: Teachers College Press, 2001.

Fullan, M. *Change Forces with a Vengeance*. New York: Routledge, 2002.

Gaynor, A. "A Study of Change in Educational Organizations." In L. Cunningham (ed.), *Educational Administration* (pp. 28–40). Berkeley, Calif.: McCutcham, 1977.

Goleman, D. "Leadership that Gets Results." *Harvard Business Review,* Mar.–Apr. 2000, 78–90.

Hamel, G. *Leading the Revolution*. Boston: Harvard Business School Press, 2000.

Heifetz, R. *Leadership Without Easy Answers*. Cambridge, Mass.: Harvard University Press, 1994.

Kotter, J. *Leading Change*. Boston: Harvard Business School Press, 1996.

Maurer, R. *Beyond the Wall of Resistance*. Austin, Tex.: Bard Books, 1996.

Micklethwait, J., and Wooldridge, A. *The Witch Doctors: Making Sense of Management Gurus*. New York: Random House, 1996.

Mintzberg, H., Ahlstrand, B., and Lampel, J. *Strategy Safari: A Guided Tour Through the Wilds of Strategic Management*. New York: Free Press, 1998.

Pascale, R., Millemann, M., and Gioja, L. *Surfing the Edge of Chaos*. New York: Crown Business, 2000.

Peters, T., and Waterman, R. *In Search of Excellence*. New York: HarperCollins, 1982.

Senge, P., Cambron-McCabe, N., Lucas, T., Smith, B., Dutton, J., and Kleiner, A. *Schools That Learn*. New York: Doubleday, 2000.

Stacey, R. *Strategic Management and Organizational Dynamics* (3rd ed.). London: Prentice Hall, 2000.

Thomas, E. *Robert Kennedy: His Life*. New York: Simon & Schuster, 2000.

13

TRANSFORMATION SCHOOL LEADERSHIP IN A TRANSACTIONAL POLICY WORLD

Kenneth A. Leithwood

IN THIS CHAPTER I argue that school leaders face a crucial dilemma in their efforts to improve teaching and learning in their schools. The dilemma is that both theory and evidence have begun to coalesce around "transformational" approaches to their leadership as best suited to the challenges they face, while the policy environment in which they work largely endorses the continuation of "transactional" practices. I suggest that the appropriate response to this dilemma is resistance, of various forms, and appeals to evidence about what works best for improving the learning of students.

This argument is developed in five parts. First, I describe the seismic shift that has taken place in the world of private sector organizations and how transformational approaches to leadership have emerged as one of the most powerful responses to that brave new world. Second, I claim that the eventual impact that seismic shift in the private sector had on public education systems was to produce a flood of policies designed to hold schools more publicly accountable for outcomes. I then argue, third, that these policies have created a strong press toward transactional forms of leadership even though transformational approaches would be more successful. Fourth, the results of selected efforts to develop and assess transformational approaches to school leadership capable of addressing the challenges created by an accountability-oriented policy context are described in order to demonstrate that evidence-based forms of successful school leadership are now in hand and available for adoption and use.

Recession, Globalization, and the Emergence of Transformational Approaches to Leadership

The first part of this argument is a story about endings and new beginnings. The endings are long-standing social contracts between large organizations and their employees, as well as academic researchers' long romance with transactional forms of leadership. The beginnings are about new forms of organization and work better suited to a globalized, knowledge-intensive economy, as well as transformational approaches to leadership designed for productive organizations in such an economy.

Triggering these endings and new beginnings most directly was the worldwide recession of the early to mid 1980s. This recession tested the limits of large organizations like IBM, Xerox, and many others which, until that time, had been considered not only industry giants, but paragons of organizational effectiveness as so famously described, for example, by Peters and Waterman in their bestselling *In Search of Excellence* (1982). Many of these organizations had developed, at least implicitly, a social contract with their many employees. In exchange for loyalty and industry on the part of their employees, these organizations offered a lifetime of employment security—almost no threat of job loss, reasonably generous compensation, comfortable and humane working conditions, and a decent pension at the end of their careers.

The recession changed all that. Most of these companies were forced to dramatically downsize. Many just went out of business. For example, just ten years after the research for *In Search of Excellence* was completed, a surprising number of the forty-three exemplary organizations featured in it had gone bankrupt or were badly wounded. Some tried to stave off, or slow down, the harshest of these consequences and, like Kodak, are still paying the price. In January 2004, Kodak announced its intention of laying off another 15,000 employees worldwide. So much for the social contract.

As an employee of one of these severely downsized companies still with a job, you found yourself with no guarantees of employment in the future. You were likely working much harder to make up for the smaller workforce. You suffered through the anguish of being "downsized" with your not-so-fortunate colleagues, and you were now being asked to do far different work than had been the case before this seismic shift. You may have lost your pension plan. At a minimum, the value of the stock you had accumulated over the years in your company's plan, aimed at putting you on the golf course during your "golden years," had dropped like a rock.

These were not happy times! Loyalty to the company became a thing of the past, replaced by loyalty to oneself. Commitment to the organization's goals was shaky, to say the least, beyond what was needed to continue to draw a paycheck, a still strong motivator for many, of course. Beyond the leverage of a paycheck, forms of leadership that depended primarily on the manipulation of extrinsic rewards had completely run out of gas. Leaders had few of those extrinsic rewards to exchange for anything other than agreement to work. In this new downsized, globalized, highly competitive environment, new forms of leadership were needed that could rekindle employees' commitments to the organization, help develop the capacities needed for this brave new world and encourage greater effort on behalf of the organization.

In parallel with these dramatic changes in work environments, academic leadership theorists were becoming increasingly skeptical about the value of their "transactional" approaches. Such approaches were embedded in bureaucratic and hierarchical forms of organization designed to foster rational and transparent decision making under the best of conditions. Such approaches relied heavily on extrinsic forms of motivation, an exchange of extrinsic rewards such as salary, social status, and perks of various sorts for employees' work on behalf of the organization.

In 1978, Burns published a widely heralded book that seemed to provide a new direction for leadership theory and research. Timing is everything. Based on cases of highly regarded public leaders, Burns argued that such exceptional leaders did not, for the most part, base their influence on those exchange relationships central to the influence strategies of transactional leaders. Rather, they appealed to the personal goals and values of their organizational colleagues and worked to both elevate and transform those goals and values in the collective interest.

Bernard Bass, a highly regarded academic leadership theorist then and now, was attracted to this transformational orientation and launched a series of empirical studies of its nature and effects, which were eventually published in his widely read *Leadership and Performance Beyond Expectations* (1985). Other leadership theorists in nonschool contexts quickly adopted what Bryman (1992) called this new approach to leadership and began to empirically explore its nature (for example, Yammarino, Spangler, and Bass, 1993), causes (for example, Druskat, 1994), and consequences (for example, Kahai, Sosik, and Avolio, 2003) at an increasingly rapid rate. This research was carried out in quite varied organizational contexts, for example, private corporations (for example, Tichy and Devanna,

1986), the military (Popper, Mayseless, and Castelnovo, 2000), colleges (Roueche, Baker and Rose, 1989), and families (Zachartos, Barling, and Kelloway, 2000).

Bass's version of transformational leadership, or something close to it, has dominated this research and includes four categories of practices:

Charisma: practices that arouse strong emotions and identification with the leader's personal qualities and sense of mission

Inspirational leadership: communicating an appealing vision and modeling exemplary practices consistent with that vision

Individualized consideration: providing support and encouragement to employees for their efforts, and opportunities to develop further

Intellectual stimulation: practices that increase followers' awareness of problems and encourage them to think about their work in new ways

Bass's model also includes transactional dimensions, some of which are considered to be necessary for successful leadership, but certainly not sufficient. These include contingent reward (clarifying the work to be done and using incentives and rewards to encourage such work), active management-by-exception (monitoring employees' work and taking corrective action as needed), and passive management-by-exception (taking corrective action in response to deviations from desired practices). A survey instrument designed by Bass—the Multifactor Leadership Questionnaire—has been used as the measure of leadership in many of these studies.

Effects on Schools: Higher Expectations, More Accountability, and Less Money

While the recession of the early 1980s affected the private sector much more quickly than the public sector, by the late 1980s and early 1990s schools, as well as other public sector organizations, were beginning to be squeezed in ways they had rarely experienced in the past. This squeeze was certainly financial, but it was also prompted by a loss of public confidence in schools as the instruments for social improvement (for example, *A Nation at Risk,* by the National Commission on Excellence in Education, 1983) that many had historically believed them to be. This squeeze brought with it the same potential for erosion of educators' loyalty and commitment that was experienced in the private sector. But educators are a famously committed group of people (for example, Lortie,

1975) and loss of morale, rather than loss of commitment, was the more obvious outcome.

The confluence of forces pressing on schools during this period resulted in a combination of heightened expectations for improved student performance, highly aggressive state and national policies for holding schools much more publicly accountable for such improvement, and diminished financial resources. Schools were being asked to do more—much more— with less. And "doing more" meant not just raising the overall achievement bar, but also closing the gap in achievement between students who traditionally do well in schools and those who do not. Now no child was to be left behind, even though the knowledge base to accomplish this goal, *under the conditions found in most schools,* was pitifully weak. No one could deny the desirability of the goal. There was just this minor problem of not actually having any "scalable" solutions, something analogous to passing legislation holding medical practitioners accountable for curing all patients of cancer, even though a cure has yet to be developed—and imposing penalties on those who are unsuccessful! As this analogy makes clear, comparable forms of accountability in nonschool sectors would be considered too bizarre for words.

This is an important point on which to pause. There are by now many proposed solutions to both raising the bar and closing the gap. But very few of these proposed solutions—some would say none—have been demonstrably effective on a large scale under the conditions found in most schools. For evidence on this point, one need look no further than summaries of evidence about the effects on student achievement of the many *Comprehensive School Reform* models (Herman, 1999). These are interventions created through relatively enormous investments of talent, money, and time, yet many more focused on only a small proportion of what most school curricula aspire to for students. Several of these models seem promising (such as Robert Slavin and others' "Success for All" [1994] and Stacey York's *Roots and Wings* [2003]), but most don't seem to produce results much beyond the practices they are intended to replace.

Aside from such direct, programmatic, and potentially quite helpful solutions to raising the bar and closing the gap, the accountability movement brought with it a by now quite familiar flood of "tools," very few of which have demonstrated they are up to the challenge. This is the case in spite of their continuing to be favored by policy makers in many political jurisdictions around the world. These tools include, for example:

Creating quasi markets (such as private schools, charter schools, and tuition tax credits) in which schools must compete for students. While advocated by many as a means of increasing equitable access to high quality teaching and learning and improving student achievement (Chubb and Moe, 1990), this tool has more often than not actually exacerbated the problems it was intended to solve (Hughes and others, 1999).

Restructuring schools in order to increase the voice of parents in school decisions, often through the creation of school councils. Intended to bring schools much closer to their clients to significantly increase schools' sensitivities to client needs, the quite large body of empirical evidence now available about this structural solution shows it is a largely impotent means of improving student learning (Leithwood and Menzies, 1999).

Legislating additional or different course completions for secondary students. While intended to increase the proficiency of many more students in these courses, this policy has been insufficient to accomplish this goal (for example, Teitelbaum, 2003).

Setting higher curriculum standards. Intended to increase students' effort to achieve at school, this tool has distinctly different results depending on the existing level of students' academic self-efficacy and performance: those already feeling self-efficacious and performing adequately are likely to rise to the challenge, work harder, and learn more; those already lacking such efficacy are likely to simply give up and drop out. A recent study in the province of Ontario, Canada, provides compelling evidence of these differential effects (King, 2002).

Introducing high-stakes testing programs that may be used as the basis for grade promotion and judging the quality of a school's performance. As in the case of setting higher curriculum standards, this tool anticipates greater motivation and effort as the outcome, but evidence suggests this is often not the effect. Evidence from several sources has shown that such tests limit the flexibility and creativity of both teachers and students, as well as attention to the development of critical-thinking skills. Nonetheless, the evidence of effects of such testing is mixed (for example, Carnoy and Loeb, 2002).

This depressing litany of disappointing outcomes is not intended to suggest that nothing works and that we should give up trying to improve the performance of our schools and children. Far from it. There are some demonstrably effective strategies capable of doing the job on a large scale including, for example, smaller primary classes, smaller school units, increased teacher pedagogical content knowledge, heterogeneous student grouping, aligned curricula, and effective teacher and administrator leadership. For the most part, however, they cost more, not less, money (Molnar, 2002). More of the Comprehensive School Reform models may eventually prove to be useful as well. But no one is likely to suggest that such success will come cheap either.

The need for more, not less, money flew in the face of many of the policy makers who had by now captured political power almost everywhere. They viewed the public sector generally as a colossal monopoly that simply squandered scarce public resources; a good dose of medicine, in the form of the tools described above, was called for in order to dramatically improve both the efficiency and effectiveness of public schools. Almost every major "reform" initiative in the U.S., Australia, Canada, New Zealand, the U.K., and other parts of Central Europe over the past fifteen years has been aimed, at least in part, at increasing the public accountability of schools while spending less money. A major exception to this pattern has been England's National Literacy and Numeracy Strategies. Significant additional resources were invested in schools as part of these strategies, and the strategies have been associated with measurable improvement in student learning (Earl and others, 2003).

The Dilemma: A Press for Transactional Forms of Leadership

The accountability movement and its related policies rest fundamentally on a mechanistic worldview that assumes motivation to be the key to change; it believes extrinsic incentives and rewards are the strongest motivators and uses control strategies, such as detailed job descriptions and direct supervision of employees, to ensure desired employee performance. In contrast, transformative approaches spring from an organic worldview, assume capacity to be a key to change, offer intrinsic incentives and rewards when additional motivation is required, and use commitment strategies (Rowan, 1996) to ensure desirable performance.

The accountability movement also rests on the "new managerialism" approach to organizational improvement, which includes quite explicit and often linear processes for setting organizational goals and determining how they will be achieved. Mechanistic worldviews and new managerialism both assume transactional forms of leadership; they seem unable to imagine an alternative.

This background helps to explain the adoption of "instructional leadership" in education systems as an integral part of the accountability policy toolbox; it seemed to be a natural ally in the war against unfettered autonomy and the fuzzy thinking of educational "progressives." With its modern roots in the effective schools movement of the late 1970s and early 1980s in the U.S. (Brookover and Lezotte, 1977), instructional leadership has been, and continues to be, widely promoted as the most promising leadership response to the higher student achievement standards the public has come to expect and policy makers are attempting to meet. These roots were largely nourished in inner city elementary schools typically serving children faced with a variety of economic and social challenges to their educational success. From this context emerged an image of "strong," hands-on, leadership provided by a single heroic individual unambiguously committed to the welfare of students. This form of leadership employed most of the strategies associated with a control orientation (Rowan, 1996) to change.

Since those early beginnings, however, the term instructional leadership gradually has become less the designation of a sharply defined set of transactional leadership practices and more a slogan chiding administrators to focus their efforts on the "core technology" of their schools and districts (teaching and learning); they should not be unduly preoccupied with just managing their organizations, as many believed was the primary focus of principals and those who trained them. Simply chiding educational administrators to be "instructional leaders" is, of course, no different—and no more helpful—than simply advocating that leaders of any type of organization focus on the goals of their organization and the effectiveness of the processes used to accomplish those goals; it begs the response, "What else did you think we were doing?"

While the term instructional leadership has been mostly used as a slogan to focus administrators on their students' progress, there have been a small number of efforts to give the term a more precise and useful meaning. Book-length descriptions of instructional leadership by Andrews and Soder (1987) and Duke (1987) are among such efforts, for example. But Hallinger and his colleagues (for example, Hallinger, 2000; Hallinger and Murphy, 1985; Heck, Larsen, and Marcoulides, 1990) have provided us with the most fully specified model and by far the most empirical evidence concerning the nature and effects of that model in practice. By one estimate, this evidence now runs to 125 studies reported between 1980 and 2000 (Hallinger, 2000). Three categories of practices are included in the model, each of which encompasses a number of more specific practices, ten in total:

Defining the school's mission includes framing the school's goals and communicating the school's goals

Managing the instructional program includes supervising and evaluating instruction, coordinating the curriculum, and monitoring student progress

Promoting a positive school learning climate encompasses pro-
tecting instructional time, promoting professional development,
maintaining high visibility, providing incentives for teachers, and
providing incentives for learning

Hallinger's recent review of evidence concerning instructional leadership found that mission-building activities (the most "transformational"
of the dimensions) on the part of principals are the most influential set of
leadership practices. In addition, and especially interesting in light of the
sloganistic uses of the instructional leadership term, his review concluded
that "relatively few studies find a relationship between the principal's
hands-on supervision of classroom instruction, teacher effectiveness, and
student achievement. Where effects have been identified, it has generally
been at the elementary school level and could possibly be explained by
school size" (2003, pp. 333–334).

Toward a Transformational Approach to School Leadership

This last result of Hallinger's review serves as an appropriate introduction
to selected efforts to develop a "transformational" approach to leadership especially suited for schools (as with instructional leadership, many
uses of the term are essentially sloganistic in nature). Whereas instructional leadership aims to narrow the focus of leaders to the core technology of their organizations, transformational leadership asks them to adopt
a much broader, more systemic, view of their work. Somewhat paradoxically, most large-scale educational reform efforts argue for systemic
approaches to change (Elmore, 2003), while at the same time advocating
instructional forms of leadership.

Although relatively modest in size, the body of empirical evidence
about transformational leadership attests to its suitability in schools faced
with significant challenges for change and greater accountability (for
example, Day and others, 2000; Leithwood, Jantzi, and Steinbach, 1999);
it supports the contribution of this form of leadership, when exercised by
principals, to a wide array of organizational and student outcomes (for
example, Leithwood, Tomlinson, and Genge, 1996), parallelling claims
made for this approach to leadership in nonschool contexts (Yukl, 1999;
Dickson, Den Hartog, and Mitchelson, 2003).

All transformational approaches to leadership emphasize emotions and
values and share in common the fundamental aim of fostering capacity
development and higher levels of personal commitment to organizational

goals on the part of leaders' colleagues. Increased capacities and commitments are assumed to result in extra effort and greater productivity. Authority and influence associated with this form of leadership are not necessarily allocated to those occupying formal administrative positions, although much of the literature adopts their perspectives. Rather, power is attributed by organizational members to whomever is able to inspire their commitments to collective aspirations, and the desire for personal and collective mastery over the capacities needed to accomplish such aspirations. Recent evidence suggests that practices associated with transformational leadership may be widely distributed throughout the organization (Leithwood and others, 2004). So there is no need to view this as a "heroic" or "great man" orientation to leadership.

To date, my colleagues and I have provided the most fully developed model of transformational school leadership, one that has been the object of several dozen empirical studies (for example, Leithwood and Jantzi, 1990, 1999, 2000). Three broad categories of practices, including a total of nine more specific sets of practice, are encompassed in this model. Included in the category Setting Directions are the dimensions of building school vision, developing specific goals and priorities, and holding high performance expectations. In the category Developing People are the dimensions of providing intellectual stimulation, offering individualized support, and modeling desirable professional practices and values. The third category, Redesigning the Organization, includes the dimensions of developing a collaborative school culture, creating structures to foster participation in school decisions, and creating productive community relationships. Each dimension is made up of multiple, more specific practices that encourage contingent responses on the part of leaders depending on the contexts of their work.

A small number of other researchers have reported evidence about transformational school leadership during this time as well. For example,

Marks and Printy (2003) have examined the relative contribution to classroom instruction of both instructional and transformational approaches to leadership on the part of principals.

Day and his colleagues (2000) have uncovered the important role values play in the exercise of transformational leadership by principals.

Silins and others (2000) have examined the contribution of transformational leadership to organizational learning in schools.

Geijsel and her colleagues (2003) have tested the effects of such leadership on teachers' levels of effort and commitment.

In spite of a small, steady stream of nonempirical critiques of transformational approaches to school leadership (for example, Allix, 2000), this growing corpus of evidence suggests that such approaches are quite productive. Indeed, Hallinger, one of the most important contributors to models of "instructional leadership," has recently argued for the appropriateness of moving from instructional to transformational approaches to school leadership (Hallinger, 2003).

Conclusion

A compelling body of recent evidence tells us that successfully implementing local change of the sort that accountability policies advocate requires transformational forms of leadership—at the least. So those school leaders who are confused when they are urged to improve their transactional leadership capacities have been paying attention; those who don't experience this confusion probably ought to.

What can be done about this dilemma? The best possible advice is put the interests of your students and communities first and base your actions on what the best available evidence tells us will serve those interests; this is definitely the "high ground." It is also exactly the advice contained in most of the current accountability policies. But these policies also go on to prescribe *how* you should accomplish these ambitious outcomes. And it is those prescriptions that often fly in the face of the best evidence about what works.

So, to offer the most productive leadership possible to your school, you either have to (a) persuade those to whom you are accountable that a transformational approach is appropriate to the task, (b) actively resist efforts to foster the exclusive use of transactional practices, or (c) just do it—on the quite likely grounds that many of those to whom you are accountable don't care what you do as long as it is ethical and gets results.

One of the major obligations you assume when you chose to act on the best available evidence—rather than just doing what you are told—is figuring out what that evidence is, how best to use it for your school's improvement purposes, and how to make the case for its use with your staff, parents, and other colleagues. This requires a level of sophistication about the implications of research for practice that is one of the next frontiers for leadership development.

REFERENCES

Allix, N. "Transformational Leadership: Democratic or Despotic?" *Educational Management and Administration,* 2000, 28(1), 7–20.

Andrews, R., and Soder, R. "Principal Instructional Leadership and School Achievement." *Educational Leadership,* 1987, *44,* 9–11.

Bass, B. M. *Leadership and Performance Beyond Expectations.* New York: The Free Press, 1985.

Brookover, W., and Lezotte, L. *Changes in School Characteristics Coincident with Changes in Student Achievement: Executive Summary.* East Lansing: Michigan State University, College of Urban Development, 1977.

Bryman, A. *Charisma and Leadership in Organizations.* London: Sage Publications, 1992.

Burns, J. M. *Leadership.* New York: Harper & Row, 1978.

Carnoy, M., and Loeb, S. "Does External Accountability Affect Student Outcomes?" *Educational Evaluation and Policy Analysis,* 2002, *24*(4), 305–332.

Chubb, J. E., and Moe, T. M. *Politics, Markets, and America's Schools.* Washington: Brookings Institution, 1990.

Day, D., and others. *Leading Schools in Times of Change.* Buckingham, U.K.: Open University Press, 2000.

Dickson, M. W., Den Hartog, D. N., and Mitchelson, J. K. "Research on Leadership in a Cross-Cultural Context: Making Progress and Raising New Questions. *The Leadership Quarterly,* 2003, *14*(6), 729–768.

Druskat, V. U. "Gender and Leadership Style: Transformational and Transactional Leadership in the Roman Catholic Church." *The Leadership Quarterly,* 1994, *5*(2), 99–119.

Duke, D. L. *School Leadership and Instructional Improvement.* New York: Random House, 1987.

Earl, L., and others. *Watching and Learning 3: Final Report of the External Evaluation of England's National Literacy and Numeracy Strategies.* London: Department for Education and Skills, 2003.

Elmore, R. P. "A Plea for Strong Practice." *Educational Leadership,* 2003, *61*(3), 6–10.

Geijsel, F., Sleegers, P., Leithwood, K., and Jantzi, D. "Transformational Leadership Effects on Teacher Commitment and Effort Toward School Reform." *Journal of Educational Administration,* 2003, *37*(4), 309–328.

Hallinger, P. *A Review of Two Decades of Research on the Principalship Using the Principal Instructional Management Rating Scale.* Paper presented at the annual meeting of the American Educational Research Association, Seattle, Washington, 2000.

Hallinger, P. "Leading Educational Change: Reflections on the Practice of Instructional and Transformational Leadership." *Cambridge Journal of Education,* 2003, *33*(3), 329–351.

Hallinger, P., and Murphy, J. "Assessing the Instructional Management Behavior of Principals." *Elementary School Journal,* 1985, *86*(2), 217–247.

Heck, R., Larsen, T., and Marcoulides, G. "Instructional Leadership and School Achievement: Validation of a Causal Model." *Educational Administration Quarterly*, 1990, *26*, 94–125.

Herman, R. *An Educator's Guide to Schoolwide Reform*. Prepared by American Institutes for Research. Arlington, Va.: Educational Research Service, 1999.

Hughes, D., and others. *Trading in Futures: Why Markets in Education Don't Work*. Buckingham, U.K.: Open University Press, 1999.

Kahai, S. S., Sosik, J. J., and Avolio, B. J. "Effects of Leadership Style, Anonymity, and Rewards on Creativity-Relevant Processes and Outcomes in an Electronic Meeting System Context." *The Leadership Quarterly*, 2003, *14*(4–5), 499–524.

King, A.J.C. *Double Cohort Study: Phase 2 Report*. Ontario Ministry of Education, 2002.

Leithwood, K., and others. "Strategic Leadership for Large-Scale Reform: The Case of England's National Literacy and Numeracy Strategy." *School Leadership and Management*, 2004, *24*(1), 57–79.

Leithwood, K., and Jantzi, D. "Transformational Leadership: How Principals Can Help Reform School Cultures." *School Effectiveness and School Improvement*, 1990, *1*(4), 249–280.

Leithwood, K., and Jantzi, D. "Transformational Leadership Effects: A Replication." *School Effectiveness and School Improvement*, 1999, *10*(4), 451–479.

Leithwood, K., and Jantzi, D. "The Effects of Transformational Leadership on Organizational Conditions and Student Engagement with School." *Journal of Educational Administration*, 2000, *38*(2), 112–129.

Leithwood, K., Jantzi, D., and Steinbach, R. *Changing Leadership for Changing Times*. Buckingham: Open University Press, 1999.

Leithwood, K., and Menzies, T. "Forms and Effects of School-Based Management." *Educational Policy*, 1999, *12*(3), 325–346.

Leithwood, K., Tomlinson, D., and Genge, M. "Transformational School Leadership." In K. Leithwood and P. Hallinger (eds.), *International Handbook of Educational Leadership and Administration* (pp. 785–840). Dordrecht, The Netherlands: Kluwer, 1996.

Lortie, D. *School Teachers: A Sociological Study*. Chicago: University of Chicago Press, 1975.

Marks, H. M., and Printy, S. M. "Principal Leadership and School Performance: An Integration of Transformational and Instructional Leadership." *Educational Administration Quarterly*, 2003, *39*(3), 370–397.

Molnar, A. (ed.). *School Reform Proposals: The Research Evidence*. Greenwich, Conn.: Information Age, 2002.

National Commission on Excellence in Education. *A Nation at Risk: The Imperative for Educational Reform.* Washington, D.C.: Department of Education, 1983.

Peters, T., and Waterman, R. *In Search of Excellence.* New York: Random House, 1982.

Popper, M., Mayseless, O., and Castelnovo, O. "Transformational Leadership and Attachment." *The Leadership Quarterly,* 2000, *11*(2), 267–289.

Roueche, J. E., Baker, G. A., and Rose, R. R. *Shared Vision: Transformational Leadership in American Community Colleges.* Washington, D.C.: Community College Press, 1989.

Rowan, B. "Standards as Incentives for Instructional Reform." In S. H. Furhman and J. O'Day (eds.), *Rewards and Reform: Creating Educational Incentives That Work.* San Francisco: Jossey-Bass, 1996.

Silins, H., Mulford, B., Zarins, S., and Bishop, P. "Leadership for Organizational Learning in Australian Secondary Schools." In K. Leithwood (ed.), *Understanding Schools as Intelligent Systems* (pp. 267–292). Stamford, Conn.: JAI Press, 2000.

Slavin, R., and others. "Success for All: A Comprehensive Approach to Prevention and Early Intervention." In R. Slavin, N. Karweit, and B. Wasik (eds.), *Preventing Early School Failure: Research on Effective Strategies.* Boston: Allyn & Bacon, 1994.

Teitelbaum, P. "The Influence of High School Graduation Requirement Policy in Mathematics and Science on Student Course-Taking Patterns and Achievement." *Educational Evaluation and Policy Analysis,* 2003, *25*(1), 31–58.

Tichy, N. M., and Devanna, M. *The Transformational Leader.* New York: Wiley, 1986.

Yammarino, F. J., Spangler, W. D., and Bass, B. M. "Transformational Leadership and Performance: A Longitudinal Investigation." *The Leadership Quarterly,* 1993, *4*(1), 81–102.

York, S. *Roots and Wings: Affirming Culture in Early Childhood Programs* (rev. ed.) Saint Paul, Minn.: Redleaf Press, 2003.

Yukl, G. "An Evaluation of Conceptual Weakness in Transformational and Charismatic Leadership Theories." *The Leadership Quarterly,* 1999, *10*(2), 285–305.

Zachartos, A., Barling, J., and Kelloway, E. K. "Development and Effects of Transformational Leadership in Adolescents." *The Leadership Quarterly,* 2000, *11*(2), 211–226.

EIGHT ROLES
OF SYMBOLIC LEADERS

Terrence E. Deal
Kent D. Peterson

CULTURE ARISES in response to persisting conditions, novel changes, challenging losses, and enduring ambiguous or paradoxical puzzles. People create culture; thereafter it shapes them. However, school leaders can nudge the process along through their actions, conversations, decisions, and public pronouncements.

Effective school leaders are always alert to the deeper issues agitating beneath a seemingly rational veneer of activity. They read between the lines to decipher complex cultural codes and struggle to figure out what's really going on. Once they get a bead on a situation, they ponder over whether and how to try to shape or reshape existing realities. In effect, they are asking three basic questions: (1) What is the culture of the school now—its history, values, traditions, assumptions, and ways? (2) What can I do to strengthen aspects of the culture that already fit my idea of an ideal school? and (3) What can be done to change or reshape the culture, when I see a need for a new direction?

As they labor to meld past, present, and future into a coherent cultural tapestry, school leaders assume several symbolic roles in their work to shape features of the culture.

Reading the Current School Culture

How do school leaders read and shape the cultures of their respective schools? To find that out, we borrow from anthropology and coin our own metaphors for school leaders' roles: historian, anthropological sleuth, visionary, symbol, potter, poet, actor, and healer.

It is important to remember the formidable nature of school leaders' unofficial power to reshape school culture toward an "ethos of excellence" and make quality an authentic part of the daily routine of school life. School leaders must understand their school—its patterns, the purposes they serve, and how they came to be. Changing something that is not well understood is a surefire recipe for stress and ultimate failure. A leader must inquire below the surface of what is happening to formulate a deeper explanation of what is really going on. To be effective, school leaders must read and understand their school and community culture.

Reading culture takes several forms: watching, sensing, listening, interpreting, using all of one's senses, and even employing intuition when necessary.

First, the leader must listen to the echoes of school history. The past exists in the cultural present.

Second, the leader should look at the present. More important, the leader must listen for the deeper dreams and hopes the school community holds for the future. Every school is a repository of unconscious sentiments and expectations that carry the code of the collective dream—the high ground to which they aspire. This represents emerging energy that leaders can tap and a deep belief system to which he or she can appeal when articulating what the school might become.

A school leader can get an initial reading of the current culture by posing several key questions about the current realities and future dreams of the school (Deal and Peterson, 1990):

What does the school's architecture convey? How is space arranged and used? What subcultures exist inside and outside the school? Who are the recognized (and unrecognized) heroes and villains of the school? What do people say (and think) when asked what the school stands for? What events are assigned special importance? How is conflict typically defined? How is it handled? What are the key ceremonies and stories of the school? What do people wish for? Are there patterns to their individual dreams?

Shaping a School Culture: The Roles of School Leaders

When school leaders have reflected and feel they understand a school's culture, they can evaluate the need to shape or reinforce it. Valuable aspects of the school's existing culture can be reinforced, problematic ones revitalized, and toxic ones given strong antidotes.

Everyone should be a leader. The eight major leadership roles to be listed next can be taken on by principals, teachers, staff members, parents, and community leaders. Cultural leaders reinforce the underlying norms, values, and beliefs. They support the central mission and purpose of the school. They create and sustain motivation and commitment through rites and rituals. It is not only the formal leadership of the principal that sustains and continuously reshapes culture but the leadership of everyone. Deep, shared leadership builds strong and cohesive cultures.

School leaders take on eight major symbolic roles:

> *Historian:* seeks to understand the social and normative past of the school
>
> *Anthropological sleuth:* analyzes and probes for the current set of norms, values, and beliefs that define the current culture
>
> *Visionary:* works with other leaders and the community to define a deeply value-focused picture of the future for the school; has a constantly evolving vision
>
> *Symbol:* affirms values through dress, behavior, attention, routines
>
> *Potter:* shapes and is shaped by the school's heroes, rituals, traditions, ceremonies, symbols; brings in staff who share core values
>
> *Poet:* uses language to reinforce values and sustains the school's best image of itself
>
> *Actor:* improvises in the school's inevitable dramas, comedies, and tragedies
>
> *Healer:* oversees transitions and change in the life of the school; heals the wounds of conflict and loss

School Leaders as Historians

Effective school leaders probe deeply into time, work, social, and normative events that have given texture to the culture of a school. They realize that echoes of past crises, challenges, and successes reverberate in the present. Leaders perpetuate an understanding of where the school has been as a key factor in interpreting present practices and ways. Staff and parents take on this role whenever new people arrive or new parents join the community.

One of the best ways of tracking the past is to construct an "organizational timeline" that depicts the flow of events, ideas, and key personages over several decades. This provides a chronological portrait of the events, circumstances, and key leaders who shaped the personality of the school.

School Leaders as Anthropological Sleuths

Anthropological sleuths are just what the name depicts—a cross between Margaret Mead and Columbo—serious students of the culture as well as dogged detectives. Both roles are important, as school leaders listen and look for clues and signs to the school's present rituals and values.

School leaders must unearth the pottery shards and secret ceremonies of daily activity in teachers' lounges, workrooms, and hallway greetings that reflect deeper features of the culture. Nothing is ever as it seems, and one must look for unexpected interpretations of common human activity.

For example, in one innovative school teachers started wearing the drug program badge that states, "Just Say No." They did it not to reinforce drug awareness week but to uphold their desire to slow the pace of curricular change for a little while. Knowing the meaning of the badge was important to understanding the culture.

School Leaders as Visionaries

In addition to their role as historian or anthropologist, school leaders must also be visionaries. Through a careful probe of past and present, they need to identify a clear sense of what the school can become, a picture of a positive future. Visionary leaders continually identify and communicate the hopes and dreams of the school, thus refocusing and refining the school's purpose and mission. To arrive at a shared vision, they listen closely for the cherished dreams that staff and community hold. They probe for the latent sentiments, values, and expectations for the future and bring these to the front for public discussion, consideration, and enactment.

Developing a shared vision for the school can motivate students, staff, and community alike. It is not simply for the leader; it is for the common good. By seeking the more profound hopes of all stakeholders, school leaders can weave independent ideas into a collective vision (Deal and Peterson, 1994).

Visionaries can be found anywhere in a school. For example, in Chicago's Piccolo Elementary School the president of the local school council, who was a parent and community leader, joined with the principal to identify and communicate the hopes and dreams for the school. Together they worked to focus on developing a caring, safe, and academically focused learning environment. Another example: at Hollibrook Elementary, the principal and the teachers jointly shared and protected the vision for the school, even as staff and administration changed. When Suzanne Still, the principal, and some teachers left for other positions, remaining staff leaders helped preserve the dream by pulling the new principal into the collective vision.

School Leaders as Symbols

Everyone watches leaders in a school. Everything they do gets people's attention. Educational philosophy, teaching reputation, demeanor, communication style, and other characteristics are important signals that will be read by members of the culture in a variety of ways. Who school leaders are—what they do, attend to, or seem to appreciate—is constantly watched by students, teachers, parents, and members of the community. Their interests and actions send powerful messages. They signal the values they hold. Above all else, leaders are cultural "teachers" in the best sense of the word.

Actions of leaders communicate meaning, value, and focus. We rarely "see" an action's symbolic value at the time it occurs. More often we realize it later, as it soaks in. For example, the principal's morning "building tour" may be a functional walk to investigate potential trouble spots or building maintenance problems. In some schools, teachers and students see the same walk as a symbolic event, a ritual demonstrating that the principal cares about the learning environment. Similarly, the visit of a teacher-leader to another's class to observe a unique and successful lesson can send the message that instruction is valued.

Schools are filled with many routine tasks that often take on added significance. Routine tasks take on symbolic meaning when leaders show sincere personal concern for core values and purposes while carrying them out. A classroom visit, building tour, or staff meeting may be nothing more than routine activity—or it can become a symbolic expression of the deeper values the leader holds for the school.

Almost all actions of school leaders can have symbolic content when a school community understands the actions' relevance to shared values. Seemingly innocuous actions send signals as to what leaders value. This is done in many ways, but five possibilities are as follows:

Symbolize core values in the way offices and classrooms are arranged. A principal's office, for example, sends strong messages. Its location, accessibility, decoration, and arrangement reflect the principal's values.

One principal works from her couch in an office in the school's entryway; another is hidden in a corner suite behind a watchful and protective secretary. One principal decorates her office walls with students' work; another displays athletic trophies, public service awards, posters of favorite works of art, and photographs of his family. These social artifacts signal to others what the principal sees as important.

The arrangement of classrooms also sends a powerful message. Is student work displayed? Is it current? Is there a wide variety of learning activities, materials, and books readily available? Do teachers have a professional library, awards, or certificates for professional institutes nearby? Physical arrangements reverberate with values.

Model values through the leader's demeanor and actions. What car a leader drives, his or her clothes, posture, gestures, facial expression, sense of humor, and personal idiosyncrasies send signals of formality or informality, approachability or distance, concern or lack of concern. A wink following a reprimand can have as much effect on a child as the verbal reprimand itself. A frown, a smile, a grimace, or a blank stare—each may send a potent message. Do staff interact with students and parents when they cross into school territory? Are energy and joy apparent in the faces of teachers?

Use time, a key scarce resource, to communicate what is important, what should be attended to. How leaders spend their time and where they focus attention sends strong signals about what they value. A community quickly discerns discrepancies between espoused values and true values by what issues receive time and attention. The appointment book and daily routines signal what a principal values. And whether staff attend and engage in discussions with parents during Parent Association Meetings or site-based council gatherings shows what the culture holds most dear.

Realize that what is appreciated, recognized, and honored signals the key values of what is admirable and achievable. School leaders signal appreciation formally through official celebrations and public recognition and rewards. Informally, their daily behavior and demeanor communicate their preference about quality teaching, correct behavior, and desired cultural traditions. Staff and students are particularly attentive to the values displayed and rewarded by various school leaders in moments of social or organizational crisis.

Recognize that official correspondence is a visible measure of values and reinforces the importance of what is being disseminated. The form, emphasis, and volume of memos and newsletters communicate as strongly as what is written. Memos may be a source of inspiration, a celebration of success, or a collection of bureaucratic jargon, rules, and regulations.

Class or departmental newsletters can send a message to parents that communication and connection are important. Even the appearance of written material will be noticed, from the informality of the penciled note to the care evidenced by the new color inkjet printer. Pride, humor, affection, and even fatigue displayed in writing send signals as to what a school's leaders value.

Taken together, all these aspects of a leader's behavior form a public persona that carries symbolic meaning. They come with the territory of being a school leader and play a powerful role in shaping the culture of a school.

School Leaders as Potters

School leaders shape the elements of school culture (its values, ceremonies, and symbols), much the way a potter shapes clay—patiently, with skill, and with an emerging idea of what the pot will eventually look like. As potters, school leaders shape the culture in a variety of ways. Four illustrations of how leaders shape school culture follow:

They infuse shared values and beliefs into every aspect of the culture. It often falls to the principal, formally and informally, to articulate the philosophical principles that embody what the school stands for. A valuable service is rendered if the principal and other leaders can express those values in a form that makes them memorable, easily grasped, and engaging. But teachers are also powerful communicators of values whenever they meet parents in the hallway, run into a school board member in the grocery store, or jog with a local businesswoman. What they say and do sends messages about the school and its values as compellingly as if they were giving a speech.

Values are often condensed into slogans or mottos that help communicate the character of a school. Of course, to ring true they must reflect the school's practices and beliefs. Examples are (1) "Every child a promise," (2) "A commitment to People. We care. A commitment to Excellence. We dare. A commitment to Partnership. We share," and (3) "A Community of Learners" (Deal and Peterson, 1990). In some schools, symbols take the place of slogans but play a similarly expressive role. One middle school's values are embodied in the symbol of a frog. The frog reflects the school's commitment to caring and affection that eventually can turn all children into "princes and princesses."

They celebrate heroes and heroines, anointing and recognizing the best role models in the school. There are important individuals in most schools, past and present, who exemplify shared virtue. Heroes and heroines, living and dead, personify values and serve as role models for others. Students, teachers, parents, and custodians may qualify for special status and recognition through words or deeds that reflect what a school holds most dear. Like stories about Amelia Earhart or Charles Lindbergh, the stories of these local heroes help motivate people and teach cultural ways. When heroes exemplify qualities a school wants to reinforce, leaders can recognize these individuals publicly. Schools can commemorate teachers or administrators in pictures, plaques, or special ceremonies just as businesses, hospitals, or military units do.

They observe rituals as a means of building and maintaining esprit de corps. School leaders shape culture by encouraging rituals that celebrate important values. As noted earlier, everyday tasks take on added significance when they symbolize something special. School activities may become rituals when they express values and bind people in a common experience.

These rituals are stylized, communal behavior that reinforces collective values and beliefs. Here is an example:

> A new superintendent of schools opened his first districtwide convocation by lighting a small lamp, which he labeled the "lamp of learning." After the event, no one mentioned the lamp. The next year, prior to the convocation, several people inquired: "You are going to light the lamp of learning again, aren't you?" The lighting of the lamp had been accepted as a symbolically meaningful ritual.

Rituals take various forms (Deal and Peterson, 1990). Some rituals are social and others center around work. Americans shake hands, Italians hug, and French people kiss both cheeks when greeting or parting. Surgical teams scrub for seven minutes, although germs are destroyed by modern germicides in thirty seconds. Members of the British artillery, when firing a cannon, still feature an individual who holds his hand in a position that once kept the horse from bolting because "that's the way it has always been done."

Meetings, parties, informal lunches, and school openings or closings provide opportunity for rituals. One principal closes meetings by offering an opportunity for anyone to share stories of positive events. In this setting, issues can be aired, accomplishments recognized, disagreements expressed, or exploits retold. These rituals bond people to each other—and connect them with deeper values that are otherwise difficult to express.

They perpetuate meaningful, value-laden traditions and ceremonies. Schoolwide ceremonies allow us to put cultural values on display, to retell important stories, and to recognize the exploits and accomplishments of important individuals. These special events tie past, present, and future together. They intensify everyone's commitment to the organization and revitalize them for challenges that lie ahead.

When an authentic ceremony is convened in a hallowed place, given a special touch, and accorded a special rhythm and flow, it builds momentum and expresses sincere emotions. Planning and staging these events is often done with extreme care. Encouraging and orchestrating such special ceremonies provide still another opportunity for leaders to shape—and to be shaped by—the culture of the school. Here is an example:

> One group of parents—with input from the high school leadership—planned a joyous celebration for the school's teachers. They decorated the cafeteria using white tablecloths and silver candle holders. They went to the superintendent and asked permission to serve wine and cheese and arranged for a piano bar where teachers and parents could sing together. Each teacher was given a corsage or a ribbon. The supper was potluck, supplied by the parents. After dinner the school choir sang. Several speakers called attention to the significance of the event. The finale came as the principal recognized the parents and asked everyone to join her in a standing ovation for the teachers. The event was moving for both the teachers and the parents and has become a part of the school's tradition.

School Leaders as Poets

We should not forget the straightforward and subtle ways that leaders communicate with language—from memos to mottoes to sagas and stories, as well as in informal conversation. Words and images invoked from the heart convey powerful sentiments. "The achievement scores of my school are above the norm" conveys a very different image from "Our school is a special temple of learning."

Acronyms can separate insiders from outsiders to the school community and tighten camaraderie. (They can also exclude people.) PSAT, CTBS, or NAEP may carry different meanings to educators than to their public. Idioms and slogans ("Every child a promise" or "We Care; We Dare; We Share") may condense shared understandings of a school's values. However, hypocrisy in such slogans can alienate those who hear them. Consider the principal in the satirical book *Up the Down Staircase* (Kaufman, 1966) who would say, "Let it be a challenge to you" in the face of problems that were obviously impossible to solve.

Metaphors may provide "picture words" that consolidate complex ideas into a single, understandable whole. Whether students and teachers think of a school as a factory or a family will have powerful implications for day-to-day behavior.

One of the highest forms of culture-shaping communication is the story. A well-chosen story provides a powerful image that addresses a question without compromising its complexity. Stories ground complicated ideas in concrete terms, personifying them in flesh and blood. Stories carry values and connect abstract ideas with sentiment, emotions, and events.

Stories told by or about leaders help followers know what is expected of them. They emphasize what is valued, watched, and rewarded for old-timers and greenhorns alike. For example, the parents of a third-grade student informed the principal that they were planning to move into a new house at Christmas and would therefore be changing schools. He suggested they tell the teacher themselves, since she took a strong personal interest in each of her students. They returned later with the surprising announcement that they were postponing their move. The principal asked why. The mother replied, "When we told Mrs. Onfrey about our decision she told us we couldn't transfer our child from her class. She told us that she wasn't finished with him yet."

By repeating such stories, leaders reinforce values and beliefs and so shape the culture of the school. Sagas—stories of unique accomplishment, rooted in history and held in sentiment—can convey core values to all of a school's constituents. They can define for the outside world an "intense sense of the unique" that captures imagination, engenders loyalty, and secures resources and support from outsiders.

School Leaders as Actors

Cultures are often characterized as theater, that is, the stage on which important events are acted out. If "all the world's a stage," then aspects of the life of a school are fascinating whether they are comedy, tragedy, drama, or action. Technically, they have been called "social dramas"; the various stages of activity in the school cross all forms of theater.

Much of this drama occurs during routine activities of the school. Periodic ceremonies, staged and carefully orchestrated, provide intensified yet predictable drama in any organization. In crises or in critical incidents (like the murder of students in a school yard or the explosion of the space shuttle Challenger) are moments of unforeseen school drama.

A critical incident like a school closing gives leaders a significant opportunity to act in a social drama that can reaffirm or redirect cultural values and beliefs. An example: a principal was concerned about the effect of a school merger on the students and the community. He convened a transition committee made up of teachers and community members to plan, among other things, a ceremony for the last day of school. On that day, the closing school was wrapped in a large red ribbon and filmed from a helicopter. When wreckers had demolished the building, each student, teacher, parent, and observer was given one of the bricks tied with a red ribbon and an aerial photograph of the school tied with a red bow (Deal and Peterson, 1990).

Such drama provides a heightened opportunity to make a historical transition and reaffirm cultural ties within the school community. Rather than inhibiting or stifling such dramas, school leaders may seize them as an opportunity to resolve differences and redirect the school.

Social dramas can be improvisational theater with powerful possibilities to reaffirm or alter values. In a political sense, such events as faculty or student conflicts are arenas—with referees, rounds, rules, spectators, fighters, and seconds. In the arena, conflicts are surfaced and decided rather than left lingering and seething because they have been avoided or ignored. Such avoidance often leads to the development of toxic cultures or subcultures. Critical incidents from this perspective provide school leaders with a significant opportunity to participate in a social drama that can reaffirm or redirect the values and beliefs of the school.

School Leaders as Healers

Most school cultures are stable but not static, and changes do occur. School leaders can play key roles in acknowledging these transitions— healing whatever wounds they create and helping the school adapt to change in terms of its traditions and culture. Leaders serve as healers when

They mark beginnings and endings. Schools celebrate the natural transitions of the year. Every school year has a beginning and an end. Beginnings are marked by convocations to end the summer and outline the vision and hopes for the coming year. Endings are marked by graduations, which usually unite members in a common celebration of the school culture.

They commemorate events and holidays of cultural importance. The observation of national and seasonal holidays, from Cinco de Mayo to Presidents' Day, may make the school an important cultural center for events in the local community and reaffirm the school's ties to the wider culture. One school convenes a schoolwide festival each fall, winter, and spring, at which they demonstrate the way the students' religions honor a particular holiday. Because of the diversity among students, such festivals provide an opportunity for students to learn different customs and foods. Such observances create a schoolwide unity around differences that would otherwise become divisive.

They remember and recognize key transitional events in the occupational lives of staff. The beginning and end of employment are episodic transitions that a principal may use to reaffirm the school's culture and its values. What newcomers must learn about the school is a good definition of what is important in its culture. Even transfers, reductions in force, terminations, and firings-for-cause are transitions that can be marked by cultural events. In one Massachusetts elementary school, primary students named hallways after teachers who had been let go in the wake of a taxpayer rebellion that required tremendous cost reductions in nearly every school in the state (Deal and Peterson, 1990).

They deal directly and openly with critical, difficult, challenging events in the lives of staff and students, always aware of the message they are sending. Unpredictable, calamitous events in the life of the school, like a death or a school closing, will be upsetting to all members of the school community. These transitions require recognition of pain, emotional comfort, and hope. Unless transitions are acknowledged in cultural events, loss and grief will accumulate. For example, at one school following the death of several classmates by two snipers, the school and its community came together at funerals, services, and informal gatherings to remember and eulogize the students. They came together to grieve over the loss of friends, the loss of classmates, the loss of innocence. These events helped the culture cope with their pain and sadness.

School leaders as healers recognize the pain of transitions and arrange events that make the transition a collective experience. Drawing people together to mourn loss and to renew hope is a significant part of a leader's culture-shaping role. Too often, the technical side of leadership eclipses available time and willingness for its much-needed cultural aspects. As a result schools become sterile, incapable of touching the hearts of students and teachers, or securing the trust and confidence of parents and local residents. By expanding their repertoire of symbolic roles, school leaders can make a real difference. Their artistry can help galvanize a diverse group of people into a cohesive community whose members are committed to a beloved institution.

Symbolic leadership is especially needed when schools are new or when they require considerable transformation to serve their students.

REFERENCES

Deal, T. E., and Peterson, K. D. *The Principal's Role in Shaping School Culture.* Washington, D.C.: Office of Educational Research and Improvement, U.S. Department of Education, 1990.

Deal, T. E., and Peterson, K. D. *The Leadership Paradox: Balancing Logic and Artistry in Schools.* San Francisco: Jossey-Bass, 1994.

Kaufman, B. *Up the Down Staircase.* New York: Avon, 1966.

15

RISK

Roland S. Barth

The trouble is, if you don't risk anything, you risk everything.

—Carl Jung

MONDAY MORNING IN SCHOOL can be a dangerous time, for over the weekend, in addition to healing from the events of the previous week, teachers begin to look ahead, to plan, and to dream.

When I was teaching elementary school, a doctoral student at work on her thesis came through the school. She was interested in the little conversation—little dance, really—that takes place when a teacher comes to the principal on Monday morning with a new idea: "I want to take the kids on a field trip, on a boat around the Farallon Islands. This will culminate our study of marine biology, ecology, geology, and the California coast. In addition, I'll relate the trip to my haiku unit and our study of the early explorers. I've never done it before, but I think it will blow the kids' socks off!"

The enterprising researcher was interviewing teachers and principals about similar conversations in which they had participated. And she was observing as many of these little scenes as she could find and join.

A few months later, as agreed, she returned with her findings, which I remember to this day: she discovered that most school principals greet a teacher's expression of a desire to try something new with a very curious, very similar set of responses:

First response: worried look, hunched back, raised eyebrows, defensive posture. This is quite remarkable, when you think about it. Here is a teacher, very excited about trying something new, willing to go to great lengths to devise a more promising way of teaching youngsters, doing precisely what we hope all teachers will do; and the first response of the principal is a body language that connotes disapproval, fear, and defensiveness.

Second response: the principal parades a litany of reasons why this is a bad idea and cannot possibly work. "The last time anyone took a field trip on the water, five kids got seasick—and I'm still hearing from the angry parents and the school board." "If I let you take this trip, how about the other fourth grades?" "But how will this fit into the district's scope and sequence?" "But we haven't got it in the budget." And, of course, "This field trip will deflect precious time and energy away from preparation for the state's standardized tests." You know the list. I know the list. I've heard the list, and as principal, I've recited the list!

If the heroic teacher is not yet deterred by this reception of her weekend's dream, a third predictable response from the principal awaits her: "Well, let me think it over. Get back to me in a couple of weeks." The stall. And the principal crosses his fingers and hopes the problem will go away, and he'll never see this teacher again—at least not on this subject.

But as T. E. Lawrence (1962) observed, "All men dream: but not equally. Those who dream by night in the dusty recesses of their mind wake in the day to find that it was vanity: but the dreamers of the day are dangerous men, for they may act their dream with open eyes, to make it possible."

Two weeks later, undeterred, our daytime dreamer becomes a teacher leader and shows up in the principal's office again. "I've given this a lot of thought, and I'm even more convinced that this will be a super culminating activity for the class this year. It ties all the strands of our curriculum together. I can get parents involved, the other fourth grades want to participate, and we're going to conduct this as carefully as the invasion of Normandy. And I have lots of seasickness pills!"

The final response of the reluctant principal: "OK. You can go on this field trip. But remember—if anything happens, it's your responsibility."

A Culture of Caution

What an extraordinary series of encounters between principal and teacher. The incontrovertible message from one to the other seems to be, "Look at all the work and all the problems that promoting learning for youngsters is going to cause us." But what's even more disheartening is that the response of this principal to the teacher's wish to take the field trip is the response of most administrators to the initiatives of most teachers.

Moreover, this protocol of responses is endemic in our profession. It's what the principal hears when she approaches the superintendent about setting up an innovative program between inner-city and suburban school children at the Museum of Science. Worried look. A parade of the reasons why not. "Get back to me." "OK, but it's your responsibility."

And it's the set of responses that students hear when they approach the teacher with a novel idea: "Instead of writing a report on the explorers, me and Jimmy want to take a video camera out into the woods and explore them, make a film, and come back and show it to the class." Worried look. A parade of the reasons why not. "Get back to me." And so it goes.

This pattern suggests that the culture of our profession is one of pathological caution. In schools, too often we play not to lose. Everyone is behaving so as not to get a reprimand filed in their "folder." Precious few are playing to win. This, despite the fact that we all know what happens when the team in the final quarter plays not to lose. They lose!

One of the Rhode Island teacher leaders put it this way:

> It seems that when the status quo is threatened by anything new, an immediate systemic defense mechanism comes to life. Even when people appear willing to try something new, they eventually revert to the status quo.

The only good question to ask of that teacher who wants to take the field trip around the Farallon Islands (and to ask of the teacher who this May wants to do exactly what she did last May) is, "So what do you think the students will learn from this experience?" If the teacher responds with, "Well, you know, it's the last month of school, and we all need to get out," there is ample cause to question the field trip. If, however, the teacher responds with a litany of her own about the expected learning the carefully planned trip will yield, the response we'd all like to hear from the principal is, "Let's do it! Can I come along? If it doesn't work out, we'll share the responsibility."

In all too many schools and systems, of course, if one does take the risk and it doesn't work out (and frequently if it does), one is hung out to dry, alone at the end of the branch. Maybe we could acquire some courage and inspiration from Earl Warren, former chief justice: "Everything I did in my life that was worthwhile I caught hell for."

How Much Am I Prepared to Risk?

This brings me to one more question I would like to pose—probably the most important of all, for this is the question on which rests the promise of school-based reform: How much are you prepared to risk? How much are you prepared to risk of what is familiar, comfortable, safe, and perhaps working well for you, in the name of better education for others?

This chapter has been about risk taking. Turning the radio dial off of "sit 'n' git" and discovering the experiential model demands that we get out of the bleachers and onto the field. To shift from being a member of the audience to a participant is a risk of major proportions.

The teachers in Rhode Island, by virtue of being teacher leaders, take enormous risks in their schools and systems. By standing up and violating the taboos against both distinguishing themselves and presuming to know what is best for others, they risk the disapprobation of principal and peer alike.

By thinking otherwise about the preparation of school principals, the Aspiring Principals' Program constitutes one huge risk. And by redefining their lives in schools around learning together, each of the aspiring principals and distinguished principals take big risks—together.

School leaders in New Jersey who have become principal learners take risks by identifying themselves not as learned but as learners. By putting on the oxygen mask of learning, they risk disclosing to the world that they don't know how and that they intend to learn how.

I have suggested conditions necessary for getting learning curves off the chart—observation of practice, conversation about practice, reflection and writing about practice, telling stories, sharing craft knowledge, and maximizing differences in order to maximize learning. Each of them invites, even demands, profound levels of risk taking. The ultimate risk is to disclose ourselves.

To learn is to risk; to lead others toward profound levels of learning is to risk; to promote personal and organizational renewal is to risk. To create schools hospitable to human learning is to risk. In short, the career of the lifelong learner and of the school-based reformer is the life of the risk taker.

The possibility that schools can and will reform from within rests squarely on whether and how much teachers and principals are willing to risk in the name of good education for youngsters. We educators will improve schools only when we take risks. It's as simple as that.

If our profession's prevailing response to risk is that of the principal to the teacher wishing to pursue the field trip, there is little hope. If the response is that of the second principal—who wants to know what children will learn, wants to come along, and is willing to share responsibility—there is cause for much hope indeed.

Risk Taking and Learning

Why is a culture of risk taking so crucial to schools of the twenty-first century? Because human learning is most profound, most transformative, and most enduring when two conditions are present: when we take risks and when a safety strap or belaying line supports us when we fall, so that we don't get killed.

Failure is often far less painful and debilitating than the fear of failure. More important for educators, there is growth and learning in failure. There is no growth and no learning in fear of failure. If you take away a person's right to fail, you take away her right to succeed. Schools are about growth, learning—and success. A failure experience becomes an especially good teacher when accompanied by observation, reflection, conversation, and efforts to make sense of the failure: So what happened? What did you learn from the experience? If you had it to do over again, how would you do it differently? How might you get help?

Schools exist to promote and sustain profound levels of human learning. Yet neither of the two conditions perhaps most closely associated with human learning—risk taking and a safety strap for those who risk—is present in schools. These conditions are interdependent and at the very core of a culture hospitable to human learning.

A refreshing few educators see the connection between leading, learning, and risk taking. They are working to build school cultures in which the presence of safety lines encourages risk taking and even the creation of communities of risk takers. For example, the school system of Appleton, Wisconsin, after lengthy conversations, came to a vision. One of its central elements was the importance of risk taking within the system, within each school, and within each classroom. Risk taking became embedded in the culture of the entire school system. Ready to "walk the talk," the educators in Appleton printed off and distributed to central office administrators, principals, teachers, parents, and students hundreds of little cards, on each of which was printed these words: "I blew it. I tried something new and innovative, and it didn't work as well as I wanted. This coupon entitles me to be free of criticism for my efforts. I'll continue to pursue ways to help our district be successful." What a powerful safety strap! And what a wonderful invitation to risk. And to learn.

I remember coming into a middle school in another district and being welcomed by these words, emblazoned on the wall of the front hall: "Anything worth doing is worth doing badly—at first"—another safety strap that gives all members of the school community permission to risk. In the principal's office of yet another school, I saw these words: "Throughout history the most common, debilitating human condition has been cold feet."

It is possible to transform a culture of caution into one that not only tolerates but also expects, rewards, even celebrates risk taking. There is a repertoire of means. In such a culture, the school is always improving, and the youngsters and adults are always learning.

Take a Risk

For the teacher or administrator who would make risk taking a discussable and embed this quality in the life of the community of learners, I offer the little questionnaire in the box that follows to distribute—and to learn from. Teachers give it to students, principals to teachers, teachers and administrators to parents, and superintendents to the school-based educators.

It is a risk, of course, even to hand out this questionnaire, and especially to ask and learn how those around us experience us as risk takers. Yet there is no more important lens through which the educator who would promote human learning and school reform can examine himself. Try it. Versions of this instrument could be developed and administered to different populations with whom we work. And it could be self-administered. Some of the cautious may be perceived as bold, and some who consider themselves courageous risk takers may learn that this is not how the world sees them. The educator who wishes to build a school culture in which risk taking is prominent can exercise no greater influence than by taking risks himself.

Please check the one that applies most.

I see you as

☐ Very timid—not a risk taker.

☐ Cautious, one who occasionally takes calculated risks.

☐ One who frequently takes risks that promote someone's learning.

☐ One who is always ready to take a risk if it might improve the quality of students' or adults' learning or the quality of the school.

Consider one of Aesop's fables. Once upon a time, a number of mice called a meeting to decide the best means of ridding themselves of a cat that had killed a great number of their friends and relations. Various plans were discussed and rejected, until at last a young mouse came forward and proposed that a bell should be hung round the tyrant's neck, that they might, in the future, have warning of her movements and be able to escape.

The suggestion was received joyfully by nearly all, but an old mouse, who had sat silent for some time, got up and said, "While I consider the plan to be a very clever one and feel sure that it would prove to be quite successful if carried out, I would like to know who is going to bell the cat?"

Like belling the cat, reforming schools is not for the fainthearted. Risk-free change is an oxymoron. Change is always accompanied by risk. Indeed, the ideograph from the Chinese language that represents opportunity is the very same symbol as that which represents danger. They go hand in hand. The ancient Chinese believed that when you approached danger, you must not turn back, for an opportunity was clearly nearby. Similarly, when a new opportunity presents itself, it's important to know that dangers abound.

One principal, faced with impending restructuring, perceptively described to me his conflicting feelings about change:

I feel like a bird that has been caged by rules and regulations for a long time. With school reform, the door is now open. I'm standing at the edge. Will I dare to fly out? I am beginning to realize that the bars of the cage that have imprisoned me all these years have been the very same bars that have protected me from the hawks and falcons out there. I'm not sure I'm going to fly.

Schools are cautious and confusing cages where teachers, principals, and students try to create pockets of safety and sanity for themselves, reluctant to leave these safe quarters for parts unknown. Schools are also storehouses of our memories. To radically transform them is not simply risky; doing so can feel like institutional homicide. Can we reform something to which we have been for so long deeply attached? Do we want to? Altering the way we have always done things carries costs of not only risk and failure but also sadness and loss. In order to change and move to the new, we must accept and grieve the loss of the old.

So the toughest question for you who would reform your schools remains: Just how much are you prepared to risk of what is familiar, comfortable, and safe for you in the name of better education for others?

The trouble is, if you don't risk anything, you risk everything.

REFERENCE

Lawrence, T. E. *The Seven Pillars of Wisdom*. New York: Penguin, 1962.

PART FOUR

STANDARDS
AND SYSTEMS

TODAY'S EDUCATION LANDSCAPE presents a new set of challenges for school leaders—more testing, a greater focus on standards, and accountability pressures all weigh heavily on a leader's mind. Exemplary leaders can better support the success of their students and teachers if they understand how to manage and balance the internal and external forces that bear upon schools.

The three pieces in this section address the nature of systems and standards. In "Understanding the Normative System," Phillip C. Schlechty examines the norms that define the rules, roles, and relationships in school. He also explains why challenging this systemic status quo is key to implementing innovations that will last.

In "Power Standards," Douglas B. Reeves acknowledges that some curricular standards are more important than others and that effective leaders understand how to sort the essential from the peripheral. His process for developing "power standards" goes beyond superficial curriculum coverage by focusing on the long-term value of what students are learning.

The final piece, the Interstate School Leaders Licensure Consortium's "Standards for School Leaders," presents six standards to model and measure school leadership expectations. Although a revision of these standards is in the early stages of development, they remain a useful framework for effective leadership practice.

16

UNDERSTANDING THE NORMATIVE SYSTEM

Phillip C. Schlechty

IF PUBLIC SCHOOLS are to meet the needs of American society in the twenty-first century, they will need to transform themselves from organizations in which the core business is producing compliance and attendance to organizations in which the core business is nurturing commitment and attention. (An organization's core business consists of those things on which the organization's attention is fastened and toward which most of the organization's energy is directed.) This transformation will necessarily disrupt the way schools define critical roles, and this in turn will disrupt critical social systems. For example, if engagement becomes a central focus of schooling, teachers will need to view themselves and be viewed by others as leaders and designers of engaging work for students rather than, as is the case for many now, seeing themselves and being seen by others as performers or diagnosticians and clinicians. The role of the principal will need to be recast to support this new definition of the role of the teacher. Teachers' decision-making autonomy will no longer be an option; it will be a mandate. Similarly, the role of the superintendent will need to be recast, as will the relationship between the superintendent and the board of education. (I have discussed these matters in considerable detail in earlier publications; for example, Schlechty, 1990, 2002). In addition, the relationships among students, teachers, and schools will need to be altered in fundamental ways.

Given the emphasis most schools now place on compliance and attendance, this transition will not be easy. The present tendency in schools is to define students as conscripts, as persons whose attendance can be commanded and whose compliance can be demanded. If engagement, rather than simple compliance, is the goal, then students will need to be defined as volunteers. This means many of the teaching strategies now in vogue will need to be changed because they are aimed at compliance rather than commitment, attendance more than attention. Neither commandments nor coercion will gain commitment and attention. Commitment and attention must be earned; they cannot be commanded or even demanded.

The needed transformation will, of course, require considerable change in the means by which schools do the job they are expected to do. In other words, it will require innovations in the technology of schooling, that is, in "the means of doing the job, whatever the means and the job may be" (Schlechty, 1997; Dreeben, 1970, p. 83). Furthermore, the kinds of innovations required will likely exceed the present social systems' capacity to sustain them. These changes will necessarily be disruptive and will require changes in systems as well as changes in the technical skills and understanding of individual men and women.

If schools' existing systems are not altered to accommodate the disruptive innovations required, one of two things will happen:

- The innovations will be expelled or
- The innovations will be domesticated

If the disruptive innovations are expelled, it is likely that new organizations will be created to take advantage of these innovations, and eventually these new organizations will take over the business of the schools. (For a more detailed, relatively stark appraisal of what I think will happen if those who lead public schools cannot muster the skill and moral energy to install the disruptive innovations required to make the schools truly focused on nurturing student engagement, see the epilogue in Schlechty, 2001.) If the innovations are domesticated—transformed into innovations that do not require much in the way of systemic change—it is again likely that new organizations will be created to take advantage of these innovations in their undomesticated forms. In addition, it is likely that the process of domestication will drain energy from the schools and make them even less productive than they were prior to beginning that process (see, for example, Herriot and Gross, 1979, especially Chapter 14).

Perhaps this is why teachers say they have had too much change. Perhaps they would be more accurate if they said they have had too much innovation and too little systemic change. Perhaps it is time to recognize that the reason so many innovative efforts have failed has to do with the way present systems operate and to recognize further that the only way the dramatic innovations needed to truly "break the mold" will succeed is to change the systems that define public education in America. (The phrase "break-the-mold schools" was quite popular in the years immediately following the issuance of the now famous report by the National Commission on Excellence in Education, *A Nation at Risk* [1983]. It is certainly clear by now that many of these efforts scarcely cracked the plaster. They accepted the mold as a given and tried to work within it.)

The Normative Order

The structure and the culture of schools, like those of other organizations, are defined by social norms. These are the norms that prescribe and proscribe behavior. These norms define the rules, roles, and relationships that govern behavior, and they also contain the beliefs, values, myths, lore, patterns of preference, and tradition that make up the culture of the schools. It is through understanding this normative order that leaders can hope to gain power over the systems they are trying to change, and it is only when leaders have such power that they can begin to move these systems in purposeful ways.

Among the most basic things one needs to understand about norms is that norms are not static and unidimensional. Norms vary in many ways (Williams, 1972). For example, some norms are enforced only episodically or on special occasions. This can be seen in the day-to-day life of schools, where it is commonplace for teachers to be more forgiving of boisterous behavior immediately after a pep rally than they are during a schoolwide testing period. Anyone who has observed school life even casually knows that teachers routinely make situational adjustments in their expectations for students' behavior. However, other norms are expected to be regularly and rigidly enforced, no matter what the situation. Indeed, zero tolerance policies are efforts to reduce variance in the enforcement of those norms that school leaders find especially critical. Whether or not a given norm or set of norms will be enforced often has to do not only with the strength of the norm itself but also with the relationship of the norm enforcer to the norm violator and with the personal commitment the enforcer has to the norm. A zero tolerance policy (which itself is a norm) attempts to forestall these personal variations. A rigorously applied norm is less likely to be challenged when the only violators are students whose parents accept the legitimacy of the norm in question and do not challenge its application to their child. When, however, parents question the applicability of this norm to their child, especially if these parents are socially powerful or have access to such power, school leaders will be pressed to make the enforcement of even this strict norm more flexible.

It is essential that those who would lead systemic change understand how norms function and how they vary, for when leaders seek to change systems they are seeking as well to change the norms that define these systems.

Four Types of Norms

An important way in which norms vary has to do with their content. Robin M. Williams Jr. (1972) describes four sets of norms that are distinguished by their content:

- Moral norms
- Aesthetic norms
- Technical norms
- Conventions

Moral norms have to do with a shared understanding of what is right and what is wrong, good and bad, appropriate and inappropriate. Moral norms are sometimes based on religious traditions and sometimes on long-standing customs that have been bestowed with nearly sacred value. Moral norms provide a primary basis for evaluating the merit and worth of other norms in all areas of social life. Sometimes the principles underlying moral norms become so codified that they are enshrined in sacred and semisacred documents and texts. The Ten Commandments are illustrative of such codified moral norms, as are professional codes of ethics.

Aesthetic norms have to do with matters of taste and refinement, with style as well as substance. Aesthetic norms define the beautiful, the ugly, the eloquent, and the crass. Aesthetic norms, like moral norms, provide a base against which new norms are evaluated while they serve as a vital part of the normative structure itself. Matters such as how a teacher should be addressed (Mr., Ms., Mrs., or by given name) are largely aesthetic choices. Such choices clearly affect—as well as reflect—status systems and relationships between and among teachers and students.

Technical norms define the ways the business of a group is to be conducted: for example, they affect how one prepares a lesson plan, uses a computer, and so on. Unlike moral norms and aesthetic norms, which are usually based on or derived from larger systems of thought and tradition, technical norms are generally based on concrete experience and empirical studies. Technical norms are evaluated by their consequences in action.

Moral norms and aesthetic norms are more likely to be evaluated in terms of their consistency with traditions and sacred or semisacred beliefs. Much that is taught in the curriculum of teacher education institutions has to do with technical norms. Research that bears on teaching and learning is illustrative of the type of knowledge base from which technical norms derive. Technical norms have to do primarily with an organization's instrumental functions. Moral and aesthetic norms have to do primarily with its expressive functions.

Finally, some sets of norms describe the "way things are done around here." Such norms make no particular moral claims, no aesthetic claims, and no technical claims. These norms, which Williams refers to as conventions, simply express local preferences and habits. For example, some teachers' workrooms are quiet and somber places; others are filled with a great deal of joking and backstage behavior. The expected and acceptable behaviors are defined by conventions that have simply grown up in the organization. Failure to understand such conventions and comply with them, however, has been known to do major harm to the reputation and potential effectiveness of newcomers, including new principals and superintendents.

As will be shown in this chapter, the nature of norms and the ways norms interact go far to explain why social systems operate as they do and why some systems produce positive and productive relationships whereas other systems become almost pathological in their effects. Furthermore, a detailed understanding of the ways norms interact can provide powerful clues as to the kinds of reforms that are needed and the likelihood of the success of a given innovation in a given situation.

For example, one of the reasons that teacher educators have difficulty in getting what they teach to directly affect practice is that the technical norms they are trying to transmit are sometimes out of harmony with the moral norms, the aesthetic norms, and the conventions of the workplace (see, for example, Larabee, 2003). This observation lends considerable support to the idea that power and authority systems must be modified so that those who officially transmit technical norms and those who transmit and uphold the moral order of schools can coordinate and unify their work.

The Complexity of Norms: Preachments, Practices, and Pretenses

Those who would lead systemic reform must understand that norms vary not only in their content but also in the ways they relate to human action in groups. All groups have cultural norms that contain the preachments regarding the way things are supposed to be; these may also be called the ought norms. (The preachment, practice, pretense framework was first suggested to me by Professor John F. Cuber in a graduate course I took from him many years ago.) For example, it is a commonly held preachment in education that parents should take an active interest in the education of their children and that schools should solicit and encourage that interest.

Other social norms define practices, prescribing how things are "really done around here" and proscribing certain things. Frequently, preachments and practices get out of synchronization. Indeed, it is variance between preachments and practices that gives rise to some school change efforts. So-called gap analysis, which some researchers use to discover areas where change is needed, is nothing more nor less than an effort to reveal discrepancies between the way things are supposed to be (the preachments) and the way they are (the practices). Returning to the example given in the previous paragraph, school leaders typically hold that parent involvement is a moral imperative. Parents ought to be involved in the education of their children, and schools ought to encourage that involvement. Yet a gap analysis would typically reveal that many parents are not actively involved in the education of their children and that many schools tacitly discourage too much "uncontrolled" interaction from parents.

It would seem that the revelation of such discrepancies would be a powerful motivator for change. Sometimes it is. Sometimes it is not. When discrepancies can be addressed with sustaining innovations, introduced through programs and projects, it is likely that the revelation of these gaps between preachment and practice will encourage innovation. However, when the innovations needed are disruptive, when rules, roles, and relationships must be changed and when moral norms, aesthetic norms, and local conventions are threatened, it is likely that another, more hidden normative structure will come into play—that is, the pretense structure.

Pretenses are cultural fictions—shared myths, stories, and interpretations. (The notion of pretenses is similar to the idea of cultural fictions, which was initially developed by Robin M. Williams Jr. [1972] in his book *American Society*.) They serve to explain away discrepancies between preachments and practices and to make otherwise intolerable conditions tolerable. For example, one of the causes of the home schooling movement in America seems to be that at least some parents who are highly committed to being involved in their children's education do not feel that the public schools provide them with avenues to participate at a level they find satisfying. Furthermore, few educators are willing to reject the idea that parents should be involved in the education of their children. Yet many believe that as professionals they are better qualified than most parents to make decisions regarding the way children should be educated. As Willard Waller observed many years ago:

> From the ideal point of view, parents and teachers have much in common in that both supposedly wish things to occur for the best interest of the child; but in fact, parents and teachers usually live in a condition of mutual distrust and enmity. Both wish the child well, but it is such a different kind of well that conflict must inevitably arise over it. The facts seem to be that parents and teachers are natural enemies predestined each for the discomfiture of the other. The chasm is frequently covered over, for neither parents nor teachers wish to admit to themselves the uncomfortable implications of the animosity, but on occasion it can make itself clear enough. [Waller, 1967, p. 68]

The ways such uncomfortable contradictions are "covered over" take on a normative quality as well. These norms include shared understandings about how discrepancies between preachments and practices are to be handled. The fairy tale about the emperor whose new clothes were no clothes is a morality tale that points up this tendency. And as this morality tale shows, individuals can get in just as much difficulty by violating the pretense norms as they can by violating the preachment and practice norms.

All three of these normative systems relating to group actions are involved in bringing about change. Because sustaining innovations does not require systemic changes, those who lead such innovative efforts need to be only marginally concerned with the pretense structure. When the innovation is disruptive, however, it is likely that little change will occur unless the pretense structure is addressed. Otherwise the pretense structure will ensure that the disruptive innovation is expelled or domesticated. To understand why this is so, consider how pretenses are established and maintained.

Maintaining Fictions and Preventing Systemic Change

As indicated earlier, two conditions give rise to the need for systemic changes in schools:

• *The moral values and commitments expressed in the school culture are demonstrably at odds with manifest reality.* For example, nearly every school's vision and mission statements contain an assertion to the effect that all children will be expected to learn at high levels and that there will be no race-based or social class–based discrepancies in student performance. Yet in nearly every school any reasonable examination of the data will demonstrate that this preachment is regularly violated in practice.

• *Fundamental shifts in the larger culture require that schools serve ends or meet expectations not formerly required.* For example, in the not-too-distant past, society in general assumed that one of the proper functions of schools was the selecting and sorting of students based on the students' demonstrated ability to master a rigorous and standardized curriculum. Nowadays it is generally argued that it is not acceptable for students to fail to meet this standard, dropping out of school is not to be tolerated, and success for each student is a requirement. The schools and those who work in them are accountable for ensuring student success, even for those students who in the past would have been destined for failure. Change outside the schools requires change inside the schools if the schools are to survive.

Organizations use a number of strategies to cope with such discrepancies between preachments and practices. The most obvious is to bring about changes that bring reality and aspiration closer together. To assume that this will happen once the facts are clear is, however, naive. Sometimes facts are enough to drive change, but often facts are not enough.

Systems are inherently conservative, and they encourage the use of strategies designed to maintain the status quo. One of the ways the status quo is defended is through strategies that explain the facts away or that make these facts less obvious and bothersome. Among the more critical of these strategies are

- The use of euphemisms
- The suppression of realists
- The indoctrination of the naive
- The denial of manifest reality

Schools are fraught with euphemisms and misleading statements. Who has not gone into a school and found a lounge where teachers go to relax and talk with each other labeled a teacher workroom? The term study hall is another illustration of the use of a euphemism to mask over uncomfortable facts. This term translates an organizational arrangement that is often nothing more than a managerially convenient way of warehousing large numbers of students in order to ease scheduling problems into a culturally accepted form. Study, after all, is a legitimate school activity. Except for a few students, however, about as much studying goes on in most study halls as resting goes on in rest rooms.

The many labels used to describe special education students may at times serve euphemistic functions as well. For example, the most recent diagnostic fad in education concerns the condition called attention deficit hyperactivity disorder (ADHD). I have no doubt that some students suffer from this disorder and need and deserve special treatment. I am also convinced, however, that many students are labeled attention deficit hyperactivity disordered simply because they do not find much in school worth attending to. Some ADHD-labeled students seem to have little difficulty with attention span or with attending when they find something that interests them (by today's standards, Thomas Edison would probably have been considered ADHD in many schools).[1] The suppression of realists takes many forms, the most common of which is the practice of insisting that only insiders are in a position to know what is going on. People who disagree with the insiders' views of things often have their views dismissed as irrelevant because, as outsiders, they have not been there and done that.

School administrators often find their views increasingly suspect in others' eyes as they move further and further from the classroom. This suspicion becomes even greater when the administrator begins to show that he or she is very serious about the need for systemic changes, changes that will dramatically affect a school's social arrangements. Indeed, one of the easiest ways to discount a person who says that existing realities are different from the present cultural fictions is to charge this source of discomfort with not being in touch with reality, when in fact what the person is not in touch with are the pretenses that mask over the discrepancies between preachments and practices.

Suppression of realists occurs in all groups and at all levels. Sometimes, especially in high schools, a teacher becomes known as a person who "tells it like it is," and sometimes what he or she tells makes others (including the principal and some colleagues) very uncomfortable. One way such persons are managed is by defining their position in the group in such a way that their observations become irrelevant to discussions. Recognizing that deviant (that is, nonnormative) responses are going to be offered by a certain person, the group begins to discount these responses through trivialization: commenting, for example, "Well, there goes old Charlie again. Just wait him out. He always has something crazy or critical to say." This strategy is so common and powerful that it probably should be treated as a separate subject, under the heading "institutionalizing deviancy." In effect the group deals with the person who brings discomfort but continues to be valued by creating a specialty norm that defines the person's role in the group as an idiosyncratic one, tolerated in this person but not in others.

It has also been my observation that when persons in authority present data or arguments that reveal discrepancies between preachments and practices, a preferred way of suppressing the person's impact is to label him or her out of touch or unrealistic. When the person bringing the bad news has little authority or when he or she is challenging the official view promulgated by those in authority, words like crank, gadfly, or advocate are more likely to be employed.

Indoctrination of the naïve is another strategy employed to support cultural fictions and bolster the pretense structure. Every organization and every social group has some preferred images and preferred definitions of situations that group members try to maintain, even in light of considerable evidence to the contrary. One of the ways these preferred definitions are maintained is by systematically exposing new members of the group to cultural guides (sometimes in the form of mentors or faculty friends) who convey not only the way things are but also the way things are supposed to be. (It is for this reason that those who develop mentoring programs should be sure that their selection criteria for mentors lead them to choose individuals enlightened by experience, rather than those blinded by experience.)

The official role of induction is to help new members learn what they are to do and how to do it in the context of their new organization. It is also intended that they will learn to talk about what they are doing in a socially approved way. For example, the new teacher may learn that the teacher who is caustic and disrespectful to students, yet beloved by colleagues for past services rendered (such as leading a movement that resulted in the dismissal of a particularly incompetent principal), is "really not caustic and disrespectful." This behavior is simply his or her way, and it is a way students accept and understand—yet another example of institutionalizing deviancy. One means of maintaining such fictions is to make it taboo (unprofessional) for one teacher to inquire into the perceptions students have of the performance of other teachers.

The denial of manifest reality involves shared distortions of fact. The use of euphemisms, suppression of realists and realism, and indoctrination of the naïve invite participants to look past events and data and to interpret reality in terms of preferences rather than facts. Denying reality requires the invention of shared distortions and the transformation of the facts themselves.

I recall, for example, working in a large urban school district that had located its staff development center near the geographical center of the school district. Although the center was widely used by teachers elsewhere in the district, teachers from an affluent set of schools in the northernmost part of the district were seldom in attendance. When asked why this was the case, they most frequently answered that it took too long to get to the center. When asked how long it took, respondents said, on average, about forty-five minutes and sometimes an hour. Having driven to all the schools on numerous occasions, I personally knew that this trip never took more than twenty-five minutes and sometimes could be made in fifteen. When I reported this fact to respondents who estimated forty-five minutes or more, the typical response was, "You just didn't drive at the right time of day," or, "You must drive a lot faster than I do."

The fundamental problem, of course, was that these teachers had other reasons for not wanting to attend functions at the staff development center. The center was located in a place that had a very different ambiance from the ambiance of their quasi-suburban schools. It was not inner city, but it was not suburban either. Housing in the neighborhood was generally integrated and reflected a nonsuburban motif. ChemLawn had few customers in the vicinity of the staff development center. Rather than rolling lawns, one was more likely to see raised porches with several dogs lying beneath them, and barred windows to protect against break-ins.

Teachers accustomed to suburban living, where the diversity of the district's population was less apparent, were made uncomfortable by this urban setting. (This was affirmed in later interviews with these teachers.) Though they believed they should embrace diversity, many of these teachers (though certainly not all) found it convenient to distort manifest reality so that they could uphold the preachment without engaging in practices with which they were uncomfortable.

No Iconoclasts Needed

As a young man I taught an introductory sociology course to college freshmen. Much of my emphasis was on what was then called the normative order and the ways that order is established, maintained, and changed,[2] and one of the frameworks I presented was the preachment, practice, pretense framework. For my students, who like most young people enjoyed the role of iconoclast, thinking about the world by identifying the disparities between aspirations and performances seemed a great deal of fun. What was not so much fun, and what was more difficult to convey to them, was the fact that myths are not always lies and that fictions contain many truths.

To set out to debunk myths and to do away with fictions without first understanding why the myths exist and what functions they serve is to be an iconoclast rather than a leader of change. Aspirations and visions are in many ways nothing more nor less than myths. They are stories and descriptions of how we want to be. Such myths become harmful only when they are taken as descriptions of how things are in spite of evidence to the contrary.

For example, the idea that faculties ought to be united has clear support in the preachments of school reform. Indeed the literature on effective schools almost enshrines the idea of faculty cohesion, seeing it as a basic underpinning of improved school performance. However, faculty cohesion can also do harm to children, as it does, for example, where the maintenance of cohesion imposes on teachers the expectation that teachers should back each other even when the person needing the backing is demonstrably wrong, or the equally pernicious expectation that a good principal always supports the teacher.

Creating and communicating ennobling and inspiring myths is a critical part of what leaders do. Leaders must be careful, however, about the way they frame the myths they want to perpetuate. Some ways of framing myths inspire action whereas other ways support the maintenance of the status quo.

For instance, the principal or teacher who asserts, "In our schools, all children are expected to learn, and when they do not, we try to figure out why this is so and do something about it," is in a very different position from the teacher or principal who asserts only that "all students can learn." In the former case the myth that all children can learn serves as an inspiring guide to action. In the latter the same myth begs for the creation of pretenses designed to explain why what is supposed to be is at odds with what is observed to be.

To tear down the myth structure of schools without replacing it with equally compelling myths is irresponsible. Myths contain hopes and aspirations, as well as descriptions of some realities. Though they can be used to maintain the status quo, they can also serve to inspire action. Abraham Lincoln's Gettysburg Address is a monument to positive myth making. Standing in the midst of a battlefield of the civil war that was tearing this nation asunder, Lincoln developed an idealized (mythical) vision of an America "conceived in liberty" (the only recently emancipated slaves would not have said so) "and dedicated to the proposition that all men are created equal" (many women nowadays would object to this phraseology). Certainly, a case can be made that the ideas of liberty and equality upon which our nation was founded did not, and do not, square with the facts. Yet the fact is that because we think we ought to believe in liberty and equality, women have received the right to vote, the Civil Rights Act of 1964 has been passed, and the public schools are now integrated.

Sometimes powerful myths are more likely to produce change than is too heavy a reliance on reality.

Myths are not all bad. They are not necessarily even lies. Some of the great truths and principles by which our society aspires to live are conveyed in the myths we choose to perpetuate. One of the tasks of leaders is to ensure that myths are used not to conceal reality but to illuminate it.

Normative Coherence

Without careful attention, the norms that define behavior in one area of school life may develop in ways that are inconsistent with the way behavior is defined in another area of school life. For example, if it is decided that a primary function of a principal is to develop leadership capacity in teachers, then the norms that define how principals are recruited and inducted must be attuned to this expectation. Otherwise, principals may be recruited who are more oriented to command-and-control functions than to teacher development.

Similarly, changes in the technical norms that typify school operation may or may not require changes in the moral and aesthetic norms and in the workplace conventions. So long as the changes in technical norms are simply additive—doing more of or doing better what is already being done—there is little or no need for systemic change. Roles can stay essentially the same. For example, Direct Instruction is a highly touted program of instruction that has been shown to produce relatively dramatic gains in student performance in low-performing schools. Although very scripted and didactic, it simply makes it possible for teachers to do more systematically what many teachers already do. It does not alter the role of the teacher.

Other technological innovations may, however, require changes in moral norms, aesthetic norms, and conventions. For example, to properly use the power of distance learning and the Internet, it is essential to redefine the role of teachers and reassess the value of the individual classroom teacher as the prime source of information. Rather than being an information source, the classroom teacher becomes a guide to sources of information and a source of inspiration in the pursuit of information. Indeed, properly used, new information technology would transform the role of teacher from that of answer giver to question asker and from supervisor of tasks to the leader of learners.

Such changes threaten the existing moral order and aesthetic order, and they require the acquisition of new technical skills. Teachers must learn to derive satisfaction from the performances of their students rather than from the quality of their own performances. They must learn to spend more of their time designing experiences for students and less of their time delivering information to those students. They must learn to see the creation of engaging work for students as being at the core of what they do and renounce the idea that their core business is to perform for students or for those who evaluate them in terms of their performance.

For such changes to occur, the way teachers are evaluated must change, and the way teachers are inducted must change as well. And all of these changes will have an impact on what is defined as good and bad, appropriate and inappropriate, tasteful and in bad taste. Such changes are by definition systemic, and systematic change is, as Adam Urbanski, president of the Rochester Teachers' Association has said, "real hard."

The failure to bring about these changes has, among other things, caused many schools and many educators to view distance learning as a less than desirable alternative to having a real teacher in a real classroom working with real students in real time or, worse, has led to the domestication of distance learning in a way that ensures that once a week—at a given time—all students will be able to watch a professor deliver a lecture on a topic in which he or she is expert and even less engaging than was the case in his or her real classroom.

There is, of course, no way to ensure that even the most competent leaders will always be able to bring about the systemic changes needed to accommodate disruptive innovations, but two things are clear:

• Unless educational leaders are prepared to implement—with fidelity—disruptive innovations, our schools will fail to respond to the dramatic shifts that have occurred in our society since the American school system was invented, and these social changes will almost certainly overwhelm that system. When this happens, the public school system will be replaced.

• Disruptive innovations can be introduced only by leaders who have a detailed understanding of the systems they must change and a grasp of the kinds of questions they need to ask about these systems if they are to understand them and give them direction.

I, like many others, believe that a vital public school system is essential to the quality of life in American democracy. Indeed, I believe the public schools are the last, best hope we have for ensuring the continuation of our grand experiment with democracy. I have written this book as an aid to those educators who are committed to the survival of public schooling and who believe as I do that the only way schools can survive is to undergo disruptive changes in the systems that define how schools and those who work in them go about their tasks.

Key Questions

The questions a leader must be prepared to answer about the school or school district (or any other organization) he or she is trying to change include the following questions about norms and related issues:

- What are the preachments of this organization with regard to moral, aesthetic, and technical norms? More specifically, what do those who have status and power in the organization hold up as the great "oughts" and the official proclamations? How, for example, do they define the core business of schools? "Ought" norms describe aspirations. They indicate what the group believes ought to be the case. Such norms shape the way group members envision themselves and the group more generally.

- To what extent are the "ought" norms of the organization upheld in practice, and what happens when deviations occur? The tolerance the group has for behavior that is at odds with the vision suggested by the group's preachments defines the level of commitment to the vision and the degree to which the beliefs on which the vision is based are compelling. The first act of leadership is getting beliefs straight; for without beliefs there is no vision, and without vision there is no direction.

- What are the prevailing fictions and pretenses in the organization? Newcomers are more likely than old-timers to detect fictions and pretenses, simply because they have not yet learned "the way it's supposed to be." Learning to adopt the posture of a naïf is a critical leadership skill.

- Are some types of norms more apt to be routinely violated than are others? For example, are teachers allowed considerable latitude in applying technical norms but narrowly restricted in applying the organization's moral norms, or is the reverse the case? It is one of the peculiarities of schools that although much more official attention is given to the transmission of technical norms than to the transmission of aesthetic norms and moral norms, it is the moral norms and aesthetic norms that are most resistant to change. Indeed, one of the reasons that many desirable technical changes fail in schools is that few school districts have developed the capacity to deal with moral and aesthetic concerns as well as they deal with technical issues, so their new technical norms lack the necessary moral and aesthetic support.

- What differences, if any, do observed differences in the normative order make in terms of what students and teachers do in classrooms and what students learn in school? Seeking explanations for behavior within systems requires one to look beyond individuals and to locate causal mechanisms in the structure of relationships. Such explanations are sought too seldom when educators confront difficult problems. Rather than fixing the problem, the tendency is to fix the blame.

• How coherent is the normative structure? More specifically, are the norms that define operations in one area of school life (such as evaluations) and the norms that define operations in any another area (such as goal setting and establishing direction) based in the same beliefs and values? One of the greatest problems confronting school leaders is ensuring coherence and maintaining structural integrity. This is especially the case when the school is introducing major innovations, which is to say disruptive innovations. Such innovations are almost always introduced as a means of solving a problem in one area of school, but for these innovations to be successful it may be necessary to bring about changes in other, seemingly unrelated areas. For example, asking teachers to behave as leaders and designers will have a major impact not only on the way knowledge is created and transmitted in the school but also on the way teachers are evaluated and the way curriculum materials are evaluated. It will also likely affect the way induction occurs and may even affect the way power and authority are assigned and distributed.

NOTES

1. I know of no empirical studies that directly relate to my assertions about ADHD diagnoses, but I am a trained observer who has for over forty years and in many schools and school districts observed fads in the labeling of children. In the 1950s, labeling children as brain damaged was a common practice, especially in upper-middle-class schools where most students were high performing. The parents of the low-performing student in effect got a "parenting pass" if they could be satisfied that the reason for their child's poor performance was physiological. I always found it curious that brain damage was more likely to be diagnosed among children of the affluent, even though the affluent were more likely than the less well-to-do to receive sound prenatal care. Some of this statistical difference probably reflects affluent parents' greater willingness to seek clinical explanations for their children's behavior. Moreover, some explanations may be more satisfying than others. It would, for example, be interesting to see how the ratio of students labeled behaviorally disordered (BD) has changed since the more socially acceptable ADHD has come into existence.

2. I generally refrain from using terms like normative order because they make what I say sound a bit archaic. However, those who would lead systemic change would learn much if they read some of the classic literature in sociology, such as Durkheim's *Rules of Sociological Method* (1966) or Robert

K. Merton's *Social Theory and Social Structure* (1968). As Dan Lortie has shown in *Schoolteacher: A Sociological Study* (1975), and as I hope I have shown, Willard Waller's *The Sociology of Teaching* (1967) remains in many ways the most cogent analysis of life in schools ever published and should be read by anyone who wants to understand what goes on in schools.

REFERENCES

Dreeben, R. S. *The Nature of Teaching and Schools: Schools and the Work of Teachers.* Glenview, Ill.: Scott, Foresman, 1970.

Durkheim, E. *Rules of Sociological Method.* New York: Free Press, 1966.

Herriot, R. E., and Gross, N. (eds.). *The Dynamics of Planned Educational Change.* Berkeley, Calif.: McCutchan, 1979.

Larabee, D. F. "The Peculiar Problems of Preparing Educational Researchers." *Educational Researcher,* May 2003, pp. 13–21.

Lortie, D. *Schoolteacher: A Sociological Study.* Chicago: University of Chicago Press, 1975.

Merton, R. K. *Social Theory and Social Structure.* New York: Free Press, 1968.

National Commission on Excellence in Education. *A Nation at Risk.* Washington, D.C.: National Commission on Excellence in Education, 1983.

Schlechty, P. C. *Schools for the 21st Century: Leadership Imperatives for Educational Reform.* San Francisco: Jossey-Bass, 1990.

Schlechty, P. C. *Inventing Better Schools: An Action Plan for Educational Reform.* San Francisco: Jossey-Bass, 1997.

Schlechty, P. C. *Shaking Up the Schoolhouse: How to Support and Sustain Educational Innovation.* San Francisco: Jossey-Bass, 2001.

Schlechty, P. C. *Working on the Work: An Action Plan for Teachers, Principals, and Superintendents.* San Francisco: Jossey-Bass, 2002.

Waller, W. *The Sociology of Teaching.* New York: Wiley, 1967. (Originally published 1932.)

Williams, R. M., Jr. *American Society: A Sociological Interpretation.* (3rd ed.) New York: Knopf, 1972.

17

POWER STANDARDS

HOW LEADERS ADD VALUE TO
STATE AND NATIONAL STANDARDS

Douglas B. Reeves

LEADERSHIP KEYS

Add value to your state standards

Apply the criteria for power standards: endurance, leverage, and readiness for the next grade

Unmask the illusion of coverage

The leader does not micromanage the classroom

The leader knows how students perform on power standards

State standards are typically created through a collaborative process. People of goodwill gather together to craft statements representing what students should know and be able to do. As a result of listening to a variety of viewpoints, the group that drafts standards seeks to ensure that the document is balanced and comprehensive. In most cases, the states have achieved those objectives. Unfortunately, the one objective states did not achieve or even consider was brevity. The number of days in the school year has remained fixed, but the quantity of curriculum has expanded.

This leaves school leaders with two choices. The first option is that they can encourage teachers to engage in coverage of curriculum that is increasingly superficial. If teachers must divide a larger quantity of standards and curriculum into a fixed number of school days, then either rapid speech or curricular superficiality becomes a mathematical certainty. The second option is for the leader and educators to add value to state standards through a process of prioritization. The result of this process is a set of power standards, a small subset of state standards that represent the most important elements of the curriculum. By carefully developing and applying power standards, leaders recognize that the question to be asked at the end of every year is not merely what teachers covered, but rather what students learned.

Value-Added Standards: Focus, Discernment, and Prioritization

There is a great deal of talk about the ideal of instructional leadership among school leaders. Typically, however, the ideal soon devolves to the reality of a laundry list imposed on teachers. An effective leader is not simply defined by what he does, but also by what he chooses not to do. By helping teachers identify systematically and carefully those standards that they will abandon and those that require extra emphasis, the leader does more than merely deliver standards from the state capital to the classroom. These decisions require exceptional discernment, the ability to perceive the subtleties of state standards that are not always obvious on the surface, and insight into connections among standards that are not always evident to the groups that create standards.

By leading a process of inquiry marked by discernment, the leader can articulate what every reader knows to be the truth: some standards are more important than others. In fact, some standards are absolutely essential if students are to enter the next grade with success and confidence, while others are little more than a political addition to a laundry list of requirements. I have never heard a fifth grade teacher remark, for example, that the student would have been more successful "if only he had learned a little more about Jamestown and the Articles of Confederation in the fourth grade." But I have heard many fifth grade teachers lament that students would have been more successful had they learned to read and comprehend grade-level material and write coherent paragraphs.

The same is true with respect to high school content area teachers. Few science and social studies educators at the high school level despair over the lack of content in science and social studies in middle school, but a great many high school teachers in those disciplines know that students who leave middle school unable to read high school textbooks have few opportunities for success in the science and social studies classes that await them. The key to narrowing the focus of standards and thereby adding value to them lies in developing power standards.

The Criteria for Power Standards

Establishing power standards is a building and district function. Many school leaders wish that the state would give them standards in prioritized order, but the function of the state in creating academic standards is collaboration and accumulation. Only in the classroom and building can we separate the essential from the peripheral. Some commentators have suggested that this process can be quickly accomplished by a vote. They quickly rank various requirements, publish the results, and voilà: the essential skills. I dissent. Educational leaders have as a primary calling the ability to distinguish between what is popular and what is effective. Listing what everyone wants to teach or what other groups think is most important is a popularity contest, not a means of adding value to curriculum and standards. A better way is careful application of three criteria to every standard: endurance, leverage, and readiness for the next level of instruction.

Endurance

Standards that meet the criterion of endurance give students skills or knowledge that remains with them long after a test is completed. Standards on research skills, reading comprehension, writing, map reading, and hypothesis testing are all examples of enduring knowledge. Teachers can look years into the future of a student now in elementary school and see how each of those standards will be used again and again. By contrast, there are other requirements, particularly those associated with specific events and people, that may be an important part of the cultural literacy of the citizens of a state but are not more important than learning to read. Moreover, there are classroom activities that have become part of the tradition of many a school and that consume many hours of learning time but do not give students enduring knowledge. This criterion, as with the others that lead to power standards, can be applied not only to state documents but to professional and leadership practices at the classroom and building levels as well.

Leverage

The criterion of leverage helps the leader and teachers identify those standards applicable to many academic disciplines. Two examples that one can find in every set of academic standards are nonfiction writing and interpretation of tables, charts, and graphs. The evidence is quite clear that if students engage in more frequent nonfiction writing, their performance in other academic disciplines improves (Reeves, 2000). Therefore, the power standard of nonfiction writing, accompanied by editing, revision, and rewriting, is worth far more than a single line in a state standards document.

In fact, writing deserves a full hour of emphasis every day in elementary schools, in addition to the sixty to ninety minutes typically provided for reading. If devoting 2.5 hours each day to literacy implies reducing time available for clay models of a Roman amphitheater or perfecting a performance that features a handful of students, then the priority is clear: literacy is more important. Creating and interpreting tables, charts, and graphs is another example of a standard with leverage. These requirements are in every state math standards document, but a careful look at the other academic disciplines reveals that the necessity of mastering the creation and interpretation of tables, charts, and graphs is also present in the social studies, science, and language arts standards as well. If standards possess leverage, they give students skills that have broad applicability and build confidence in essential skills throughout the curriculum.

The principle of leverage also helps teachers in curriculum planning, particularly when a team of teachers is working to create integrated thematic units of instruction. Thus creating a pie chart in math displays population distribution in a geography class; a timeline can be applied to a progression of events in a novel in a literature class, to a sequence of events in a history class, and to the change in a chemical substance in a science lab.

Readiness for the Next Level of Learning

The criteria of leverage and endurance would be sufficient if we were readily introspective, examined our own curriculum, removed some elements, and expanded others that are more important. Unfortunately, it is easy for any of us to fall in love with particular instructional practices. A leader does not have the time or expertise to individually dissect and analyze every single classroom practice. She can, however, facilitate a process in which teachers collaborate not only in systematically reflecting on their own classroom curricula but also in working together across grade levels to apply the criterion of readiness for the next level of learning. The best way to apply this criterion is a role-play exercise in which the leader asks teachers to engage in a scenario the leader introduces with these words: "I'm a new teacher in this building, and in fact I'm new to the profession. I need your advice. I'm teaching in the next grade lower than you; if you're teaching fourth grade, I'm teaching third grade, and if you're teaching seventh grade, I'm teaching sixth grade. Here's what I need you to do. For each subject for which you are responsible, write down the knowledge and skills that I must give to my students this year so that they can enter your class next year with success and confidence."

I have done this exercise with several hundred teachers, and their responses are remarkable. Not once has a teacher ever said, "If your students are to enter my class next year with confidence and success, then this year you must cover every single state standard." Rather, the teachers create a list that is balanced and brief. The list is balanced because it includes information in the content area and also requirements for literacy and behavior. For example, an eighth grade social studies teacher may include some content requirements, such as map-reading skills or basic historical knowledge. Then, after listing four or five content-specific standards, the teachers invariably say, "The students must be able to read an eighth grade social studies textbook." After a few moments of reflection, they add the requirement that "The students must be able to keep an assignment notebook, turn work in on time, and cooperate on a team with other students." All requirements together, including content, literacy, and behavior, rarely exceed a dozen in number. This list, balanced and brief, forms the final threshold for power standards.

In one Midwestern district, I observed fourth grade teachers collaborate with their colleagues in the upper elementary and secondary grades. Their initial quandary was the set of more than two hundred requirements for knowledge and skills of fourth grade students in the subjects of language arts, science, math, and social studies. In half a day of work applying these three criteria—endurance, leverage, and readiness for the next grade—they narrowed the list to twenty power standards. In California, I have observed ninth and tenth grade teachers narrow the math and language arts requirements from more than sixty requirements to fewer than fifteen.

Potential Dangers in Power Standards

The inevitable objections come from those who note that a standard that does not appear in the final list of power standards might be on the state test. This is true. Selecting power standards does not imply universal coverage of every conceivable test item. In fact, the use of power standards virtually guarantees that teachers will omit some items that might be on the state test.

The choice the leader and teachers face is not perfection, but rather these two alternatives. Through use of power standards, we can give our students proficiency with those standards that address 80 to 90 percent of the content of the state test, and also give them the reading, writing, and reasoning skills to help them on any state test question. On the other hand, we can reject power standards and embrace coverage, in which case students will be exposed to 100 percent of the potential content of the state test, and they might master 50 percent of those skills. Both choices entail risk, but the risk of power standards is a far wiser risk for an instructional leader or educator to take.

The Illusion of Coverage

The inevitable rejoinder from curriculum directors, teachers, and principals is: "The state standards require that we cover everything. If we fail to do so, we are shortchanging students by failing to give them the information they need for the test." This statement is seductive. Who would want to shortchange children? However, it depends upon a dangerous illusion: the notion that with just the right mix of perfect schedules, the absence of unforeseen events, cooperative students, and rapid speech by the teachers, a teacher of mythical capabilities can cover all the standards. Conversation with teachers at the end of every academic year reveals the fantasy that lies behind this illusion. Teachers invariably talk about the curriculum areas that they didn't get to, how the year went by so quickly, and how next year will be different. The end of each academic year reveals that what we have is not universal coverage but "coverage by default"—curriculum areas addressed on the basis of an accidental confluence of calendar, student readiness, and teacher plans.

A superior alternative to coverage by default is curriculum by design. In this model, teachers and the leader decide at the beginning of each school year and periodically throughout the year the most important standards to address. They know that as the year progresses, their obligation is to have all students proficient in power standards—not to have a few students proficient in everything, or most students proficient in only a fraction of the standards—but all students exposed to as many standards as the teacher can cover. Leaders must acknowledge this truth: perfect curriculum coverage never happens. There are only two choices left: coverage by default or by design. Power standards help the leader make the wise choice.

Practical Implications for the Leader

Employing power standards is not a theoretical enterprise but a practical approach to leadership and learning. The first and most important practical implication is that the leader must make time for teachers to collaborate within and among grade levels to identify the power standards. Perhaps your school already has regularly scheduled collaboration time for teachers. A growing number of schools have forty-five minutes to an hour for teachers every single day for collaborative work. More than half of this time is typically governed by administrative discretion rather than left for unstructured teacher work time. In the vast majority of school systems, however, time for collaboration is limited and planning time in the daily schedule is already used by teachers for parent communication and evaluation of student work. Therefore, leaders must look at the time they can control and consider how to use those hours wisely.

The two sources of time most frequently misused in a school are faculty meetings and professional development. A growing number of schools where I work have committed themselves to a "zero announcement" policy for faculty meetings. Principals print the announcements on paper or distribute them by e-mail, and faculty members entering a meeting sign a document that simply says, "I have received and read the announcements." The entire meeting is therefore focused on student achievement in which the faculty works independently, in small groups, or as a large group to collaboratively evaluate student work, create power standards, or do other work that is essential for improving professional practice and student learning. Similarly, the model of professional development in many schools is changing from a catalogue of courses offered by outside vendors to blocks of time used by teachers and leaders for collaborative work on assessments, curriculum, and standards that have an immediate and positive impact on the teaching and learning in that school.

By using faculty meetings and professional development wisely, the leader defeats the traditional excuse of "I'd like to develop power standards, but we just don't have the time." This is a fundamentally inaccurate statement, as the clocks in every school in the world are based on the same twenty-four-hour day. The truth is that we have the time, but we have historically chosen to employ the hours available in diverse, frequently nonproductive ways. We must ask, "What is the risk of not making announcements in faculty meetings? The risk that someone may not understand the announcement or may not comply with it?"

This is, of course, precisely the same risk that we have when verbal announcements are made in a faculty meeting. Using faculty meetings to focus on student achievement carries no additional risk and significant additional rewards in curriculum and assessment. What is the risk of diverting professional development time to teacher-led collaboration on curriculum and assessment? The risk that the professional development lessons that might have been delivered would not be applied in the classroom?

This risk prevails even if we continue the traditional series of disjointed workshops and seminars that dominate most professional development in schools. As Guskey (2000) and the National Staff Development Council (2001) have argued persuasively, the most effective professional development is not that characterized by grandiloquent speeches or clever seminars; it is application in the classroom in such a way that there is a measurable impact on student achievement.

Leadership Frameworks: An Alternative to Micromanagement

For many teachers and administrators, the term instructional leadership represents a fantasy, dependent on the magical administrator being present in every classroom all the time to observe, coach, and lead instruction. Teachers resent the specter of micromanagement, while leaders endure the crush of longer days in which they are expected to devote themselves to instructional leadership in the classroom while simultaneously being available in the office for parent communication and student discipline, and at the same time being at every important meeting called by the central office at which principal attendance is mandatory.

In fact, no leader in any organization can lead through direct instruction. We know that the most effective teachers do not cast themselves as the sole source of feedback and instruction in the classroom; instead they make their expectations so clear and their standards of performance so transparent that students regularly evaluate their own work, make appropriate corrections, and proceed to the next level of achievement.

In great standards-based classrooms, I have seen students approach the teacher's desk, apparently ready to hand in a completed assignment. Then the student sees the standard, along with the teacher's clear explanation in student-accessible language boldly printed on a large poster near the teacher's desk. The student stops, turns around, and returns to her seat, making the correction before the teacher has begun to read the student's paper. The best leaders emulate this model of teaching. They know that they cannot and should not dictate every move of the classroom teacher. Rather, they collaboratively create a framework that includes the most important standards along with a clearly agreed definition of what proficient work really means. The framework establishes clear boundaries; within that framework, teacher creativity is encouraged and valued. Neither the leader nor the teacher needs to engage in guesswork about expectations or boundaries. During evaluation, the leader does not need a diary of every activity in the classroom but instead can focus on the framework.

This approach saves the leader time and grants respect to teachers. The question at the end of the first quarter is not "Can I see your lesson plans and the documentary evidence that you covered the standards?" but rather "What percentage of your students are proficient or higher in the three power standards that we agreed on for the first quarter?" This brief report, along with two or three examples of student work that is proficient, allows the leader to know what is being assessed and how the students are performing; the leader then considers midcourse corrections to improve professional practice and student learning.

After identifying the power standards, the leader can take the next step toward leading implementation of standards-based performance assessment. Standards-based assessment is the key to effective implementation of standards. This kind of assessment represents the difference between standards as conceived in an abstract document and standards as a vital presence in every classroom.

REFERENCES

Guskey, T. *Evaluating Professional Development.* Thousand Oaks, Calif.: Corwin, 2000.
National Staff Development Council. *Standards for Staff Development.* (Rev. ed.) Oxford, Ohio: National Staff Development Council, 2001.
Reeves, D. B. "Standards Are Not Enough: Essential Transformations for Successful Schools." *NASSP Bulletin,* 2000, *84*(610), 5–19.

18

STANDARDS FOR
SCHOOL LEADERS

Interstate School Leaders Licensure Consortium
Adopted by Full Consortium
November 2, 1996

Dear Colleague:

For the past two years, the Interstate School Leaders Licensure Consortium (ISLLC), a program of the Council of Chief State School Officers, has been at work crafting model standards for school leaders. Forged from research on productive educational leadership and the wisdom of colleagues, the standards were drafted by personnel from 24 state education agencies and representatives from various professional associations. The standards present a common core of knowledge, dispositions, and performances that will help link leadership more forcefully to productive schools and enhanced educational outcomes. Although developed to serve a different purpose, the standards were designed to be compatible with the new National Council for the Accreditation of Teacher Education (NCATE) Curriculum Guidelines for school administration—as well as with the major national reports on reinventing leadership for tomorrow's schools. As such, they represent another part of a concerted effort to enhance the skills of school leaders and to couple leadership with effective educational processes and valued outcomes.

One intent of the document is to stimulate vigorous thought and dialogue about quality educational leadership among stakeholders in the area of school administration. A second intent is to provide raw material that will help stakeholders across the education landscape (e.g., state agencies, professional associations, institutions of higher education) enhance the quality of educational leadership throughout the nation's schools. Our work is offered, therefore, with these two goals in mind.

It is the desire of the Consortium to raise the bar for the practice of school leadership. Thus the standards and indicators reflect the magnitude of both the importance and the responsibility of effective school leaders.

We encourage you to heavily use this document—circulate it widely to members of the public and the profession as well as to the policy-making community. It is through this shared vision of education that school leaders will be successful and that our children will be assured of the education they will need to carry out the responsibilities of the future.

Sincerely,
Neil Shipman, Director, ISLLC
Joseph Murphy, Chair, ISLLC

PREFACE

OVER THE PAST QUARTER-CENTURY, significant changes have been reshaping our nation. At the same time, new viewpoints have redefined the struggle to restructure education for the 21st century. From these two foundations, educators and policy makers have launched many helpful initiatives to redefine the roles of formal school leaders. In this document, you see the results of one of these efforts—the work of the Interstate School Leaders Licensure Consortium (ISLLC) to establish common standards for school leaders. In this report, we describe the portrait of leadership and the understanding of society and education that guided the work of the ISLLC team. We also provide an overview of ISLLC activity, describing the process we used to develop the standards and discussing central issues embedded in that process. Finally, we present the ISLLC standards and indicators.

Redesigning Leadership

The model of leadership standards one develops depends a good deal on how the design issue is framed. The Consortium tackled the design strategy in two ways. First, we relied heavily on the research on the linkages between educational leadership and productive schools, especially in terms of outcomes for children and youth. Second, we sought out significant trends in society and education that hold implications for emerging views of leadership—and subsequently for the standards that give meaning to those new perspectives on leadership.

An Understanding of Effective Leadership

Formal leadership in schools and school districts is a complex, multi-faceted task. The ISLLC standards honor that reality. At the same time, they acknowledge that effective leaders often espouse different patterns of beliefs and act differently from the norm in the profession. Effective school leaders are strong educators, anchoring their work on central issues of learning and teaching and school improvement. They are moral agents and social advocates for the children and the communities they serve. Finally, they make strong connections with other people, valuing and caring for others as individuals and as members of the educational community.

The Changing Nature of Society

Looking to the larger society that envelops schooling, the Consortium identified a handful of powerful dynamics that will likely shape the future of education and, perforce, the types of leadership required for tomorrow's schools. To begin with, our vision of education is influenced by the knowledge that the social fabric of society is changing, often in dramatic ways. On the one hand, the pattern of the fabric is being rewoven. In particular, we are becoming a more diverse society—racially, linguistically, and culturally. On the other hand, the social fabric is unraveling for many children and their families. Poverty is increasing. Indexes of physical, mental, and moral well-being are declining. The stock of social capital is decreasing as well.

The perspective of the Consortium on schooling and leadership is also colored by the knowledge that the economic foundations of society are being recast as well. The shift to a postindustrial society, the advance of the global marketplace, the increasing reliance on technology, and a growing infatuation with market-based solutions to social needs pose significant new challenges for education. We believe that these challenges will require new types of leadership in schools.

An Evolving Model of Schooling

Turning to schooling itself, Consortium members distilled three central changes, all of which augur for a redefined portfolio of leadership skills for school administrators. On one level, we are seeing a renewed struggle to redefine learning and teaching to more successfully challenge and engage all youngsters in the education process. Educators are rethinking long-prevailing views of knowledge, intelligence, assessment, and instruction. On a second level, we are hearing strong rumblings that community-focused and caring-centered conceptions of schooling will increasingly compete for legitimacy with more established notions of school organizations as hierarchies and bureaucracies. Finally, stakeholders external to the school building—parents, interested members of the corporate sector, and leaders in the community—will increasingly play significantly enhanced roles in education.

ISLLC Initiative

The Consortium's initiative builds on research about skillful stewardship by school administrators and emerging perspectives about society and education. At one level, our work is a continuation of a century's quest to develop a deeper and more productive understanding of school leadership. At the same time, however, primarily because of the fundamental nature of the shift from an industrial to an information society, our work represents one of the two or three major transition points in that voyage.

The Consortium is not alone in its attempt to define the current era of transition in society and schooling and to capture its meaning for educational leadership. Since the 1987 publication of the *Leaders for America's Schools* by the National Commission on Excellence in Educational Administration, all the major professional associations, both practitioner and university based, have devoted productive energy to this issue. Indeed, the National Policy Board for Educational Administration (NPBEA) was created largely in response to this need and in an effort to generate better and more coordinated purchase on the task. Thus, the work of ISLLC is part of the long tradition of regularly upgrading the profession and, we believe, is a central pillar in the struggle to forge a vision of educational leadership for tomorrow's schools.

The ISLLC initiative began in August 1994. Fueled by the contributions of the 24 member states, a generous foundational grant from The Pew Charitable Trusts, and assistance from the Danforth Foundation and the

NPBEA, the program operates under the aegis of the Council of Chief State School Officers. The 24 member states are Arkansas, California, Connecticut, Delaware, Georgia, Illinois, Indiana, Kansas, Kentucky, Maryland, Massachusetts, Michigan, Mississippi, Missouri, New Jersey, North Carolina, Ohio, Pennsylvania, Rhode Island, South Carolina, Texas, Virginia, Washington, and Wisconsin. In addition, the following professional associations are affiliated with ISLLC: American Association of Colleges for Teacher Education, American Association of School Administrators, Association for Supervision and Curriculum Development, Association of Teacher Educators, National Association of Elementary School Principals, National Association of Secondary School Principals, National Association of State Boards of Education, National Council of Professors of Educational Administration, National Policy Board of Educational Administration, National School Boards Association, and University Council for Educational Administration.

Representatives of the member states and affiliated organizations have crafted standards and indicators. As noted previously, in the drafting process the Consortium team drew extensively on the research about productive leadership. We also relied heavily on the knowledge of the representatives themselves. Finally, we employed the collective wisdom of colleagues in schools and school districts, institutions of higher education, and various professional associations at both state and national levels to enrich and leaven the work throughout the development process.

Guiding Principles

At the outset of the project, it became clear that our work would be strengthened considerably if we could craft a set of overarching principles to guide our efforts. Over time we saw that these principles actually could serve two functions. First, they have acted as a touchstone to which we regularly returned to test the scope and focus of emerging products. Second, we believe that they help give meaning to the standards and indicators. Here are the seven principles that helped orient all of our work:

> Standards should reflect the centrality of student learning.
>
> Standards should acknowledge the changing role of the school leader.
>
> Standards should recognize the collaborative nature of school leadership.

Standards should be high, upgrading the quality of the profession.

Standards should inform performance-based systems of assessment and evaluation school leaders.

Standards should be integrated and coherent.

Standards should be predicated on the concepts of access, opportunity, and empowerment for all members of the school community.

Comments on the Standards

Many strategies are being used to upgrade the quality of leadership in the educational arena. For example, institutions of higher education have done extensive work on revising preparation programs for prospective school administrators. Many states have also strengthened licensing requirements and revised procedures for approval of university-based preparation programs. The ISLLC team decided at the outset of this project, however, to focus on standards. This strategy made sense for several reasons. First, based on the work on standards in other arenas of educational reform, especially the efforts of the Interstate New Teachers Assessment and Support Consortium (INTASC), we were convinced that standards provided an especially appropriate and particularly powerful leverage point for reform. Second, we found a major void in this area of educational administration—a set of common standards remains conspicuous by its absence. Finally, we believed that the standards approach provided the best avenue to allow diverse stakeholders to drive improvement efforts along a variety of fronts—certification, program approval, and candidate assessment.

Within that framework, we began work on a common set of standards that would apply to nearly all formal leadership positions in education, not just principals. We acknowledge full well that there are differences in leadership that correspond to roles, but ISLLC members were unanimous in their belief that the central aspects of the role are the same for all school leadership positions.

While acknowledging the full range of responsibilities of school leaders, we decided to focus on those topics that formed the heart and soul of effective leadership. This decision led us in two directions. First, because we didn't want to lose the key issues in a forest of standards, we deliberately framed a parsimonious model at the standard level. Thus, we produced only six standards. Second, we continually focused on matters of learning and teaching and the creation of powerful learning environments. Not only do several standards directly highlight learning and teaching, but all the standards take on meaning to the extent that they support a learning environment. Throughout, the success of students is paramount. For example, every standard begins with the words "A school administrator is an educational leader who promotes the success of all students by . . ."

Finally, a word about the framework for the indicators is in order. The design we employed (knowledge, dispositions, and performances) is borrowed from the thoughtful work of our INTASC colleagues. While there was little debate about the importance of knowledge and performances in the framework, the inability to "assess" dispositions caused some of us a good deal of consternation at the outset of the project. As we became more enmeshed in the work, however, we discovered that the dispositions often occupied center stage. That is, because "dispositions are the proclivities that lead us in one direction rather than another within the freedom of action that we have" (Perkins, 1995, p. 275), in many fundamental ways they nourish and give meaning to performance. Over time, we have grown to understand that these elements—knowledge, dispositions, and performances—belong together. We also find ourselves agreeing with Perkins (1995) that "dispositions are the soul of intelligence, without which the understanding and know-how do little good" (p. 278).

Standard 1

A school administrator is an educational leader who promotes the success of all students by *facilitating the development, articulation, implementation, and stewardship of a vision of learning that is shared and supported by the school community.*

Knowledge

The administrator has knowledge and understanding of

- Learning goals in a pluralistic society
- The principles of developing and implementing strategic plans
- Systems theory
- Information sources, data collection, and data analysis strategies
- Effective communication
- Effective consensus-building and negotiation skills

Dispositions

The administrator believes in, values, and is committed to

- The educability of all
- A school vision of high standards of learning
- Continuous school improvement
- The inclusion of all members of the school community
- Ensuring that students have the knowledge, skills, and values needed to become successful adults
- A willingness to continuously examine one's own assumptions, beliefs, and practices
- Doing the work required for high levels of personal and organization performance

Performances

The administrator facilitates processes and engages in activities ensuring that

- The vision and mission of the school are effectively communicated to staff, parents, students, and community members
- The vision and mission are communicated through the use of symbols, ceremonies, stories, and similar activities
- The core beliefs of the school vision are modeled for all stakeholders
- The vision is developed with and among stakeholders
- The contributions of school community members to the realization of the vision are recognized and celebrated
- Progress toward the vision and mission is communicated to all stakeholders
- The school community is involved in school improvement efforts
- The vision shapes the educational programs, plans, and actions
- An implementation plan is developed in which objectives and strategies to achieve the vision and goals are clearly articulated
- Assessment data related to student learning are used to develop the school vision and goals
- Relevant demographic data pertaining to students and their families are used in developing the school mission and goals

- Barriers to achieving the vision are identified, clarified, and addressed
- Needed resources are sought and obtained to support the implementation of the school mission goals
- Existing resources are used in support of the school vision and goals
- The vision, mission, and implementation plans are regularly monitored, evaluated, and revised

Standard 2

A school administrator is an educational leader who promotes the success of all students by *advocating, nurturing, and sustaining a school culture and instructional program conducive to student learning and staff professional growth.*

Knowledge

The administrator has knowledge and understanding of

- Student growth and development
- Applied learning theories
- Applied motivational theories
- Curriculum design, implementation, evaluation, and refinement
- Principles of effective instruction
- Measurement, evaluation, and assessment strategies
- Diversity and its meaning for educational programs
- Adult learning and professional development models
- The change process for systems, organizations, and individuals
- The role of technology in promoting student learning and professional growth
- School cultures

Dispositions

The administrator believes in, values, and is committed to

- Student learning as the fundamental purpose of schooling
- The proposition that all students can learn
- The variety of ways in which students can learn

- Lifelong learning for self and others
- Professional development as an integral part of school improvement
- The benefits that diversity brings to the school community
- A safe and supportive learning environment
- Preparing students to be contributing members of society

Performances

The administrator facilitates processes and engages in activities ensuring that

- All individuals are treated with fairness, dignity, and respect
- Professional development promotes a focus on student learning consistent with the school vision and goals
- Students and staff feel valued and important
- The responsibilities and contributions of each individual are acknowledged
- Barriers to student learning are identified, clarified, and addressed
- Diversity is considered in developing learning experiences
- Lifelong learning is encouraged and modeled
- There is a culture of high expectations for self, student, and staff performance
- Technologies are used in teaching and learning
- Student and staff accomplishments are recognized and celebrated
- Multiple opportunities to learn are available to all students
- The school is organized and aligned for success
- Curricular, co-curricular, and extracurricular programs are designed, implemented, evaluated, and refined
- Curriculum decisions are based on research, expertise of teachers, and the recommendations of learned societies
- The school culture and climate are assessed on a regular basis
- A variety of sources of information is used to make decisions
- Student learning is assessed using a variety of techniques
- Multiple sources of information regarding performance are used by staff and students

- A variety of supervisory and evaluation models is employed
- Pupil personnel programs are developed to meet the needs of students and their families

Standard 3

A school administrator is an educational leader who promotes the success of all students by *ensuring management of the organization, operations, and resources for a safe, efficient, and effective learning environment.*

Knowledge

The administrator has knowledge and understanding of

- Theories and models of organizations and the principles of organizational development
- Operational procedures at the school and district level
- Principles and issues relating to school safety and security
- Human resources management and development
- Principles and issues relating to fiscal operations of school management
- Principles and issues relating to school facilities and use of space
- Legal issues impacting school operations
- Current technologies that support management functions

Dispositions

The administrator believes in, values, and is committed to

- Making management decisions to enhance learning and teaching
- Taking risks to improve schools
- Trusting people and their judgments
- Accepting responsibility
- High-quality standards, expectations, and performances
- Involving stakeholders in management processes
- A safe environment

Performances

The administrator facilitates processes and engages in activities ensuring that

- Knowledge of learning, teaching, and student development is used to inform management decisions
- Operational procedures are designed and managed to maximize opportunities for successful learning
- Emerging trends are recognized, studied, and applied as appropriate
- Operational plans and procedures to achieve the vision and goals of the school are in place
- Collective bargaining and other contractual agreements related to the school are effectively managed
- The school plant, equipment, and support systems operate safely, efficiently, and effectively
- Time is managed to maximize attainment of organizational goals
- Potential problems and opportunities are identified
- Problems are confronted and resolved in a timely manner
- Financial, human, and material resources are aligned to the goals of schools
- The school acts entrepreneurially to support continuous improvement
- Organizational systems are regularly monitored and modified as needed
- Stakeholders are involved in decisions affecting schools
- Responsibility is shared to maximize ownership and accountability
- Effective problem-framing and problem-solving skills are used
- Effective conflict resolution skills are used
- Effective group-process and consensus-building skills are used
- Effective communication skills are used
- A safe, clean, and aesthetically pleasing school environment is created and maintained
- Human resource functions support the attainment of school goals
- Confidentiality and privacy of school records are maintained

Standard 4

A school administrator is an educational leader who promotes the success of all students by *collaborating with families and community members, responding to diverse community interests and needs, and mobilizing community resources.*

Knowledge

The administrator has knowledge and understanding of

- Emerging issues and trends that potentially impact the school community
- The conditions and dynamics of the diverse school community
- Community resources
- Community relations and marketing strategies and processes
- Successful models of school, family, business, community, government, and higher education partnerships

Dispositions

The administrator believes in, values, and is committed to

- Schools operating as an integral part of the larger community
- Collaboration and communication with families
- Involvement of families and other stakeholders in school decision-making processes
- The proposition that diversity enriches the school
- Families as partners in the education of their children
- The proposition that families have the best interests of their children in mind
- Resources of the family and community needing to be brought to bear on the education of students
- An informed public

Performances

The administrator facilitates processes and engages in activities ensuring that

- High visibility, active involvement, and communication with the larger community are a priority
- Relationships with community leaders are identified and nurtured
- Information about family and community concerns, expectations, and needs is used regularly
- There is outreach to different business, religious, political, and service agencies and organizations
- Credence is given to individuals and groups whose values and opinions may conflict
- The school and community serve one another as resources
- Available community resources are secured to help the school solve problems and achieve goals
- Partnerships are established with area businesses, institutions of higher education, and community groups to strengthen programs and support school goals
- Community youth family services are integrated with school programs
- Community stakeholders are treated equitably
- Diversity is recognized and valued
- Effective media relations are developed and maintained
- A comprehensive program of community relations is established
- Public resources and funds are used appropriately and wisely
- Community collaboration is modeled for staff
- Opportunities for staff to develop collaborative skills are provided

Standard 5

A school administrator is an educational leader who promotes the success of all students by *acting with integrity, fairness, and in an ethical manner.*

Knowledge

The administrator has knowledge and understanding of

- The purpose of education and the role of leadership in modern society
- Various ethical frameworks and perspectives on ethics

- The values of the diverse school community
- Professional codes of ethics
- The philosophy and history of education

Dispositions

The administrator believes in, values, and is committed to

- The ideal of the common good
- The principles in the Bill of Rights
- The right of every student to a free, quality education
- Bringing ethical principles to the decision-making process
- Subordinating one's own interest to the good of the school community
- Accepting the consequences for upholding one's principles and actions
- Using the influence of one's office constructively and productively in the service of all students and their families
- Development of a caring school community

Performances

The administrator

- Examines personal and professional values
- Demonstrates a personal and professional code of ethics
- Demonstrates values, beliefs, and attitudes that inspire others to higher levels of performance
- Serves as a role model
- Accepts responsibility for school operations
- Considers the impact of one's administrative practices on others
- Uses the influence of the office to enhance the educational program rather than for personal gain
- Treats people fairly, equitably, and with dignity and respect
- Protects the rights and confidentiality of students and staff
- Demonstrates appreciation for and sensitivity to the diversity in the school community

- Recognizes and respects the legitimate authority of others
- Examines and considers the prevailing values of the diverse school community
- Expects that others in the school community will demonstrate integrity and exercise ethical behavior
- Opens the school to public scrutiny
- Fulfills legal and contractual obligations
- Applies laws and procedures fairly, wisely, and considerately

Standard 6

A school administrator is an educational leader who promotes the success of all students by *understanding, responding to, and influencing the larger political, social, economic, legal, and cultural context.*

Knowledge

The administrator has knowledge and understanding of

- Principles of representative governance that undergird the system of American schools
- The role of public education in developing and renewing a democratic society and an economically productive nation
- The law as related to education and schooling
- The political, social, cultural, and economic systems and processes that impact schools
- Models and strategies of change and conflict resolution as applied to the larger political, social, cultural, and economic contexts of schooling
- Global issues and forces affecting teaching and learning
- The dynamics of policy development and advocacy under our democratic political system
- The importance of diversity and equity in a democratic society

Dispositions

The administrator believes in, values, and is committed to

- Education as a key to opportunity and social mobility
- Recognizing a variety of ideas, values, and cultures

- Importance of a continuing dialogue with other decision makers affecting education
- Actively participating in the political and policy-making context in the service of education
- Using legal systems to protect student rights and improve student opportunities

Performances

The administrator facilitates processes and engages in activities ensuring that

- The environment in which schools operate is influenced on behalf of students and their families
- Communication occurs among the school community concerning trends, issues, and potential changes in the environment in which schools operate
- There is ongoing dialogue with representatives of diverse community groups
- The school community works within the framework of policies, laws, and regulations enacted by local, state, and federal authorities
- Public policy is shaped to provide quality education for students
- Lines of communication are developed with decision makers outside the school community

REFERENCE

Perkins, D. *Outsmarting IQ: The Emerging Science of Learnable Intelligence.* New York: Free Press, 1995.

PART FIVE

DIVERSITY
AND LEADERSHIP

IN EDUCATION, diversity manifests itself in many ways. There are ethnically and culturally diverse populations, diverse student learning needs, gender diversity, religious diversity, and diverse socioeconomic backgrounds. Diversity in schools is now being viewed through a more optimistic lens, as teachers and administrators focus on the opportunities for growth it offers.

The four pieces in this section examine the nature of leadership needed to fully embrace diversity at all its levels. In "Making Differences Matter," David A. Thomas and Robin J. Ely propose a new way of understanding and managing diversity. They show that leaders must use diversity engagingly, so that it is viewed as a lever for effective organizational and individual advancement.

Moving to the classroom, Mel Levine looks at diversity in learning. To support the wide range of learning needs, Levine encourages leaders to expand student assessment, revisit the curriculum, and focus on offering quality professional development.

In her seminal piece, Cherry A. McGee Banks delves into the research on race and gender in educational leadership. These studies provide an overview of the characteristics and experiences of women and people of color, and hold out the promise that more inclusive leadership will change the face of education for the better.

In "Gender and Supervision," Charol Shakeshaft, Irene Nowell, and Andy Perry examine the influence of gender on leadership. In their research, the authors unearth the varying expectations and behaviors based on gender and discuss how this variance plays out in the school.

19

MAKING
DIFFERENCES MATTER

A NEW PARADIGM
FOR MANAGING DIVERSITY

David A. Thomas
Robin J. Ely

WHY SHOULD COMPANIES concern themselves with diversity? Until recently, many managers answered this question with the assertion that discrimination is wrong, both legally and morally. But today managers are voicing a second notion as well. A more diverse workforce, they say, will increase organizational effectiveness. It will lift morale, bring greater access to new segments of the marketplace, and enhance productivity. In short, they claim, diversity will be good for business.

Yet if this is true—and we believe it is—where are the positive impacts of diversity? Numerous and varied initiatives to increase diversity in corporate America have been under way for more than two decades. Rarely, however, have those efforts spurred leaps in organizational effectiveness. Instead, many attempts to increase diversity in the workplace have backfired, sometimes even heightening tensions among employees and hindering a company's performance.

This article offers an explanation for why diversity efforts are not fulfilling their promise and presents a new paradigm for understanding—and leveraging—diversity. It is our belief that there is a distinct way to unleash the powerful benefits of a diverse workforce. Although these benefits include increased profitability, they go beyond financial measures to encompass learning, creativity, flexibility, organizational and individual growth, and the ability of a company to adjust rapidly and successfully to market changes. The desired transformation, however, requires a fundamental change in the attitudes and behaviors of an organization's leadership. And that will come only when senior managers abandon an underlying and flawed assumption about diversity and replace it with a broader understanding.

Most people assume that workplace diversity is about increasing racial, national, gender, or class representation—in other words, recruiting and retaining more people from traditionally underrepresented "identity groups." Taking this commonly held assumption as a starting point, we set out six years ago to investigate its link to organizational effectiveness. We soon found that thinking of diversity simply in terms of identity-group representation inhibited effectiveness.

Organizations usually take one of two paths in managing diversity. In the name of equality and fairness, they encourage (and expect) women and people of color to blend in. Or they set them apart in jobs that relate specifically to their backgrounds, assigning them, for example, to areas that require them to interface with clients or customers of the same identity group. African American M.B.A.'s often find themselves marketing products to inner-city communities; Hispanics frequently market to Hispanics or work for Latin American subsidiaries. In those kinds of cases, companies are operating on the assumption that the main virtue identity groups have to offer is a knowledge of their own people. This assumption is limited—and limiting—and detrimental to diversity efforts.

What we suggest here is that diversity goes beyond increasing the number of different identity-group affiliations on the payroll to recognizing that such an effort is merely the first step in managing a diverse workforce for the organization's utmost benefit. Diversity should be understood as *the varied perspectives and approaches to work* that members of different identity groups bring.

Women, Hispanics, Asian Americans, African Americans, Native Americans—these groups and others outside the mainstream of corporate America don't bring with them just their "insider information." They bring different, important, and competitively relevant knowledge and perspectives about how to actually *do work*—how to design processes, reach goals, frame tasks, create effective teams, communicate ideas, and lead. When allowed to, members of these groups can help companies grow and improve by challenging basic assumptions about an organization's functions, strategies, operations, practices, and procedures. And in doing so, they are able to bring more of their whole selves to the workplace and identify more fully with the work they do, setting in motion a virtuous circle. Certainly, individuals can be expected to contribute to a company their firsthand familiarity with niche markets. But only when companies start thinking about diversity more holistically—as providing fresh and meaningful approaches to work—and stop assuming that diversity relates simply to how a person looks or where he or she comes from will they be able to reap its full rewards.

Two perspectives have guided most diversity initiatives to date: the *discrimination-and-fairness paradigm* and the *access-and-legitimacy paradigm.* But we have identified a new, emerging approach to this complex management issue. This approach, which we call the *learning-and-effectiveness paradigm,* incorporates aspects of the first two paradigms but goes beyond them by concretely connecting diversity to approaches to work. Our goal is to help business leaders see what their own approach to diversity currently is and how it may already have influenced their companies' diversity efforts. Managers can learn to assess whether they need to change their diversity initiatives and, if so, how to accomplish that change.

The following discussion will also cite several examples of how connecting the new definition of diversity to the actual *doing* of work has led some organizations to markedly better performance. The organizations differ in many ways—none are in the same industry, for instance—but they are united by one similarity: Their leaders realize that increasing demographic variation does not in itself increase organizational effectiveness. They realize that it is *how* a company defines diversity—and *what it does* with the experiences of being a diverse organization—that delivers on the promise.

The Discrimination-and-Fairness Paradigm

Using the discrimination-and-fairness paradigm is perhaps thus far the dominant way of understanding diversity. Leaders who look at diversity through this lens usually focus on equal opportunity, fair treatment, recruitment, and compliance with federal Equal Employment Opportunity requirements. The paradigm's underlying logic can be expressed as follows:

> Prejudice has kept members of certain demographic groups out of organizations such as ours. As a matter of fairness and to comply with

federal mandates, we need to work toward restructuring the makeup of our organization to let it more closely reflect that of society. We need managerial processes that ensure that all our employees are treated equally and with respect and that some are not given unfair advantage over others.

Although it resembles the thinking behind traditional affirmative-action efforts, the discrimination-and-fairness paradigm does go beyond a simple concern with numbers. Companies that operate with this philosophical orientation often institute mentoring and career-development programs specifically for the women and people of color in their ranks and train other employees to respect cultural differences. Under this paradigm, nevertheless, progress in diversity is measured by how well the company achieves its recruitment and retention goals rather than by the degree to which conditions in the company allow employees to draw on their personal assets and perspectives to do their work more effectively. The staff, one might say, gets diversified, but the work does not.

What are some of the common characteristics of companies that have used the discrimination-and-fairness paradigm successfully to increase their demographic diversity? Our research indicates that they are usually run by leaders who value due process and equal treatment of all employees and who have the authority to use top-down directives to enforce initiatives based on those attitudes. Such companies are often bureaucratic in structure, with control processes in place for monitoring, measuring, and rewarding individual performance. And finally, they are often organizations with entrenched, easily observable cultures, in which values like fairness are widespread and deeply inculcated and codes of conduct are clear and unambiguous. (Perhaps the most extreme example of an organization in which all these factors are at work is the United States Army.)

Without doubt, there are benefits to this paradigm: it does tend to increase demographic diversity in an organization, and it often succeeds in promoting fair treatment. But it also has significant limitations. The first of these is that its color-blind, gender-blind ideal is to some degree built on the implicit assumption that "we are all the same" or "we aspire to being all the same." Under this paradigm, it is not desirable for diversification of the workforce to influence the organization's work or culture. The company should operate as if every person were of the same race, gender, and nationality. It is unlikely that leaders who manage diversity under this paradigm will explore how people's differences generate a potential diversity of effective ways of working, leading, viewing the market, managing people, and learning.

Not only does the discrimination-and-fairness paradigm insist that everyone is the same, but, with its emphasis on equal treatment, it puts pressure on employees to make sure that important differences among them do not count. Genuine disagreements about work definition, therefore, are sometimes wrongly interpreted through this paradigm's fairness-unfairness lens—especially when honest disagreements are accompanied by tense debate. A female employee who insists, for example, that a company's advertising strategy is not appropriate for all ethnic segments in the marketplace might feel she is violating the code of assimilation upon which the paradigm is built. Moreover, if she were then to defend her opinion by citing, let us say, her personal knowledge of the ethnic group the company wanted to reach, she might risk being perceived as importing inappropriate attitudes into an organization that prides itself on being blind to cultural differences.

Workplace paradigms channel organizational thinking in powerful ways. By limiting the ability of employees to acknowledge openly their work-related but culturally based differences, the paradigm actually undermines the organization's capacity to learn about and improve its own strategies, processes, and practices. And it also keeps people from identifying strongly and personally with their work—a critical source of motivation and self-regulation in any business environment.

As an illustration of the paradigm's weaknesses, consider the case of Iversen Dunham, an international consulting firm that focuses on foreign and domestic economic-development policy. (Like all the examples in this chapter, the company is real, but its name is disguised.) Not long ago, the firm's managers asked us to help them understand why race relations had become a divisive issue precisely at a time when Iversen was receiving accolades for its diversity efforts. Indeed, other organizations had even begun to use the firm to benchmark their own diversity programs.

Iversen's diversity efforts had begun in the early 1970s, when senior managers decided to pursue greater racial and gender diversity in the firm's higher ranks. (The firm's leaders were strongly committed to the cause of social justice.) Women and people of color were hired and charted on career paths toward becoming project leaders. High performers among those who had left the firm were persuaded to return in senior roles. By 1989, about 50 percent of Iversen's project leaders and professionals were women, and 30 percent were people of color. The thirteen-member management committee, once exclusively white and male, included five women and four people of color. Additionally, Iversen had developed a strong contingent of foreign nationals.

It was at about this time, however, that tensions began to surface. Senior managers found it hard to believe that, after all the effort to create a fair and mutually respectful work community, some staff members could still be claiming that Iversen had racial discrimination problems. The management invited us to study the firm and deliver an outsider's assessment of its problem.

We had been inside the firm for only a short time when it became clear that Iversen's leaders viewed the dynamics of diversity through the lens of the discrimination-and-fairness paradigm. But where they saw racial discord, we discerned clashing approaches to the actual work of consulting. Why? Our research showed that tensions were strongest among midlevel project leaders. Surveys and interviews indicated that white project leaders welcomed demographic diversity as a general sign of progress but that they also thought the new employees were somehow changing the company, pulling it away from its original culture and its mission. Common criticisms were that African American and Hispanic staff made problems too complex by linking issues the organization had traditionally regarded as unrelated and that they brought on projects that seemed to require greater cultural sensitivity. White male project leaders also complained that their peers who were women and people of color were undermining one of Iversen's traditional strengths: its hard-core quantitative orientation. For instance, minority project leaders had suggested that Iversen consultants collect information and seek input from others in the client company besides senior managers—that is, from the rank and file and from middle managers. Some had urged Iversen to expand its consulting approach to include the gathering and analysis of qualitative data through interviewing and observation. Indeed, these project leaders had even challenged one of Iversen's long-standing, core assumptions: that the firm's reports were objective. They urged Iversen Dunham to recognize and address the subjective aspect of its analyses; the firm could, for example, include in its reports to clients dissenting Iversen views, if any existed.

For their part, project leaders who were women and people of color felt that they were not accorded the same level of authority to carry out the work as their white male peers. Moreover, they sensed that those peers were skeptical of their opinions, and they resented that doubts were not voiced openly.

Meanwhile, there also was some concern expressed about tension between white managers and nonwhite subordinates, who claimed they were being treated unfairly. But our analysis suggested that the manager-subordinate conflicts were not numerous enough to warrant the attention they were drawing from top management. We believed it was significant that senior managers found it easier to focus on this second type of conflict than on midlevel conflicts about project choice and project definition.

Indeed, Iversen Dunham's focus seemed to be a result of the firm's reliance on its particular diversity paradigm and the emphasis on fairness and equality. It was relatively easy to diagnose problems in light of those concepts and to devise a solution: just get managers to treat their subordinates more fairly.

In contrast, it was difficult to diagnose peer-to-peer tensions in the framework of this model. Such conflicts were about the very nature of Iversen's work, not simply unfair treatment. Yes, they were related to identity-group affiliations, but they were not symptomatic of classic racism. It was Iversen's paradigm that led managers to interpret them as such. Remember, we were asked to assess what was supposed to be a racial discrimination problem. Iversen's discrimination-and-fairness paradigm had created a kind of cognitive blind spot, and as a result, the company's leadership could not frame the problem accurately or solve it effectively. Instead, the company needed a cultural shift—it needed to grasp what to do with its diversity once it had achieved the numbers. If all Iversen Dunham employees were to contribute to the fullest extent, the company would need a paradigm that would encourage open and explicit discussion of what identity-group differences really mean and how they can be used as sources of individual and organizational effectiveness.

Today, mainly because of senior managers' resistance to such a cultural transformation, Iversen continues to struggle with the tensions arising from the diversity of its workforce.

The Access-and-Legitimacy Paradigm

In the competitive climate of the 1980s and 1990s, a new rhetoric and rationale for managing diversity emerged. If the discrimination-and-fairness paradigm can be said to have idealized assimilation and color- and gender-blind conformism, the access-and-legitimacy paradigm was predicated on the acceptance and celebration of differences. The underlying motivation of the access-and-legitimacy paradigm can be expressed this way:

> We are living in an increasingly multicultural country, and new ethnic groups are quickly gaining consumer power. Our company needs a demographically more diverse workforce to help us gain access to these differentiated segments. We need employees with multilingual skills in order to understand and serve our customers better and to gain legitimacy with them. Diversity isn't just fair; it makes business sense.

Where this paradigm has taken hold, organizations have pushed for access to—and legitimacy with—a more diverse clientele by matching the demographics of the organization to those of critical consumer or constituent groups. In some cases, the effort has led to substantial increases in organizational diversity. In investment banks, for example, municipal finance departments have long led corporate finance departments in pursuing demographic diversity because of the typical makeup of the administration of city halls and county boards. Many consumer-products companies that have used market segmentation based on gender, racial, and other demographic differences have also frequently created dedicated marketing positions for each segment. The paradigm has therefore led to new professional and managerial opportunities for women and people of color.

What are the common characteristics of organizations that have successfully used the access-and-legitimacy paradigm to increase their demographic diversity? There is but one: such companies almost always operate in a business environment in which there is increased diversity among customers, clients, or the labor pool—and therefore a clear opportunity or an imminent threat to the company.

Again the paradigm has its strengths. Its market-based motivation and the potential for competitive advantage that it suggests are often qualities an entire company can understand and therefore support. But the paradigm is perhaps more notable for its limitations. In their pursuit of niche markets, access-and-legitimacy organizations tend to emphasize the role of cultural differences in a company without really analyzing those differences to see how they actually affect the work that is done. Whereas discrimination-and-fairness leaders are too quick to subvert differences in the interest of preserving harmony, access-and-legitimacy leaders are too quick to push staff with niche capabilities into differentiated pigeonholes without trying to understand what those capabilities really are and how they could be integrated into the company's mainstream work. To illustrate our point, we present the case of Access Capital.

Access Capital International is a U.S. investment bank that in the early 1980s launched an aggressive plan to expand into Europe. Initially, however, Access encountered serious problems opening offices in international markets; the people from the United States who were installed abroad lacked credibility, were ignorant of local cultural norms and market conditions, and simply couldn't seem to connect with native clients. Access responded by hiring Europeans who had attended North American business schools by assigning them in teams to the foreign offices. This strategy was a marked success. Before long, the leaders of Access could take enormous pride in the fact that their European operations were highly profitable and staffed by a truly international corps of professionals. They took to calling the company "the best investment bank in the world."

Several years passed. Access's foreign offices continued to thrive, but some leaders were beginning to sense that the company was not fully benefiting from its diversity efforts. Indeed, some even suspected that the bank had made itself vulnerable because of how it had chosen to manage diversity. A senior executive from the United States explains:

> If the French team all resigned tomorrow, what would we do? I'm not sure what we *could* do! We've never attempted to learn what these differences and cultural competencies really are, how they change the process of doing business. What is the German country team actually doing? We don't know. We know they're good, but we don't know the subtleties of how they do what they do. We assumed—and I think correctly—that culture makes a difference, but that's about as far as we went. We hired Europeans with American M.B.A.'s because we didn't know why we couldn't do business in Europe—we just assumed there was something cultural about why we couldn't connect. And ten years later, we still don't know what it is. If we knew, then perhaps we could take it and teach it. Which part of the investment banking process is universal and which part of it draws upon particular cultural competencies? What are the commonalities and differences? I may not be German, but maybe I could do better at understanding what it means to be an American doing business in Germany. Our company's biggest failing is that the department heads in London and the directors of the various country teams have never talked about these cultural identity issues openly. We knew enough to *use* people's cultural strengths, as it were, but we never seemed to learn from them.

Access's story makes an important point about the main limitation of the access-and-legitimacy paradigm: under its influence, the motivation for diversity usually emerges from very immediate and often crisis-oriented needs for access and legitimacy—in this case, the need to broker deals in European markets. However, once the organization appears to be achieving its goal, the leaders seldom go on to identify and analyze the culturally based skills, beliefs, and practices that worked so well. Nor do they consider how the organization can incorporate and learn from those skills, beliefs, or practices in order to capitalize on diversity in the long run.

Under the access-and-legitimacy paradigm, it was as if the bank's country teams had become little spin-off companies in their own right, doing their own exotic, slightly mysterious cultural-diversity thing in a niche market of their own, using competencies that for some reason could not become more fully integrated into the larger organization's understanding of itself. Difference was valued within Access Capital—hence the development of country teams in the first place—but not valued enough that the organization would try to integrate it into the very core of its culture and into its business practices.

Finally, the access-and-legitimacy paradigm can leave some employees feeling exploited. Many organizations using this paradigm have diversified only in those areas in which they interact with particular niche-market segments. In time, many individuals recruited for this function have come to feel devalued and used as they begin to sense that opportunities in other parts of the organization are closed to them. Often the larger organization regards the experience of these employees as more limited or specialized, even though many of them in fact started their careers in the mainstream market before moving to special markets where their cultural backgrounds were a recognized asset. Also, many of these people say that when companies have needed to downsize or narrow their marketing focus, it is the special departments that are often the first to go. That situation creates tenuous and ultimately untenable career paths for employees in the special departments.

The Emerging Paradigm:
Connecting Diversity to Work Perspectives

Recently, in the course of our research, we have encountered a small number of organizations that, having relied initially on one of the above paradigms to guide their diversity efforts, have come to believe that they are not making the most of their own pluralism. These organizations, like Access Capital, recognize that employees frequently make decisions and choices at work that draw upon their cultural background—choices made because of their identity-group affiliations. The companies have also developed an outlook on diversity that enables them to *incorporate* employees' perspectives into the main work of the organization and to enhance work by rethinking primary tasks and redefining markets, products, strategies, missions, business practices, and even cultures. Such companies are using the learning-and-effectiveness paradigm for managing diversity and, by doing so, are tapping diversity's true benefits.

A case in point is Dewey & Levin, a small public-interest law firm located in a northeastern U.S. city. Although Dewey & Levin had long been a profitable practice, by the mid-1980s its all-white legal staff had become concerned that the women they represented in employment-related disputes were exclusively white. The firm's attorneys viewed that fact as a deficiency in light of their mandate to advocate on behalf of all women. Using the thinking behind the access-and-legitimacy paradigm, they also saw it as bad for business.

Shortly thereafter, the firm hired a Hispanic female attorney. The partners' hope, simply put, was that she would bring in clients from her own community and also demonstrate the firm's commitment to representing all women. But something even bigger than that happened. The new attorney introduced ideas to Dewey & Levin about what kinds of cases it should take on. Senior managers were open to those ideas and pursued them with great success. More women of color were hired, and they, too, brought fresh perspectives. The firm now pursues cases that its previously all-white legal staffs would not have thought relevant or appropriate because the link between the firm's mission and the employment issues involved in the cases would not have been obvious to them. For example, the firm has pursued precedent-setting litigation that challenges English-only policies—an area that it once would have ignored because such policies did not fall under the purview of traditional affirmative-action work. Yet it now sees a link between English-only policies and employment issues for a large group of women—primarily recent immigrants—whom it had previously failed to serve adequately. As one of the white principals explains, the demographic composition of Dewey & Levin "has affected the work in terms of expanding notions of what are [relevant] issues and taking on issues and framing them in creative ways that would have never been done [with an all-white staff]. It's really changed the substance—and in that sense enhanced the quality—of our work."

Dewey & Levin's increased business success has reinforced its commitment to diversity. In addition, people of color at the firm uniformly report feeling respected, not simply "brought along as window dressing." Many of the new attorneys say their perspectives are heard with a kind of openness and interest they have never experienced before in a work setting. Not surprisingly, the firm has had little difficulty attracting and retaining a competent and diverse professional staff.

If the discrimination-and-fairness paradigm is organized around the theme of assimilation—in which the aim is to achieve a demographically representative workforce whose members treat one another exactly the same—then the access-and-legitimacy paradigm can be regarded as coalescing around an almost opposite concept: differentiation, in which the objective is to place different people where their demographic characteristics match those of important constituents and markets.

The emerging paradigm, in contrast to both, organizes itself around the overarching theme of integration. Assimilation goes too far in pursuing sameness. Differentiation, as we have shown, overshoots in the other direction. The new model for managing diversity transcends both. Like the fairness paradigm, it promotes equal opportunity for all individuals.

And like the access paradigm, it acknowledges cultural differences among people and recognizes the value in those differences. Yet this new model for managing diversity lets the organization internalize differences among employees so that it learns and grows because of them. Indeed, with the model fully in place, members of the organization can say, We are all on the same team, *with* our differences—not *despite* them.

Eight Preconditions for Making the Paradigm Shift

Dewey & Levin may be atypical in its eagerness to open itself up to change and engage in a long-term transformation process. We remain convinced, however, that unless organizations that are currently in the grip of the other two paradigms can revise their view of diversity so as to avoid cognitive blind spots, opportunities will be missed, tensions will most likely be misdiagnosed, and companies will continue to find the potential benefits of diversity elusive.

Hence the question arises: What is it about the law firm of Dewey & Levin and other emerging third-paradigm companies that enables them to make the most of their diversity? Our research suggests that there are eight preconditions that help to position organizations to use identity-group differences in the service of organizational learning, growth, and renewal.

1. *The leadership must understand that a diverse workforce will embody different perspectives and approaches to work, and must truly value variety of opinion and insight.* We know of a financial services company that once assumed that the only successful sales model was one that utilized aggressive, rapid-fire cold calls. (Indeed, its incentive system rewarded salespeople in large part for the number of calls made.) An internal review of the company's diversity initiatives, however, showed that the company's first- and third-most-profitable employees were women who were most likely to use a sales technique based on the slow but sure building of relationships. The company's top management has now made the link between different identity groups and different approaches to how work gets done and has come to see that there is more than one right way to get positive results.

2. *The leadership must recognize both the learning opportunities and the challenges that the expression of different perspectives presents for an organization.* In other words, the second precondition is a leadership that is committed to persevering during the long process of learning and relearning that the new paradigm requires.

3. *The organizational culture must create an expectation of high standards of performance from everyone.* Such a culture isn't one that expects

less from some employees than from others. Some organizations expect women and people of color to underperform—a negative assumption that too often becomes a self-fulfilling prophecy. To move to the third paradigm, a company must believe that all its members can and should contribute fully.

4. *The organizational culture must stimulate personal development.* Such a culture brings out people's full range of useful knowledge and skills—usually through the careful design of jobs that allow people to grow and develop but also through training and education programs.

5. *The organizational culture must encourage openness.* Such a culture instills a high tolerance for debate and supports constructive conflict on work-related matters.

6. *The culture must make workers feel valued.* If this precondition is met, workers feel committed to—and empowered within—the organization and therefore feel comfortable taking the initiative to apply their skills and experiences in new ways to enhance their job performance.

7. *The organization must have a well-articulated and widely understood mission.* Such a mission enables people to be clear about what the company is trying to accomplish. It grounds and guides discussions about work-related changes that staff members might suggest. Being clear about the company's mission helps keep discussions about work differences from degenerating into debates about the validity of people's perspectives. A clear mission provides a focal point that keeps the discussion centered on accomplishment of goals.

8. *The organization must have a relatively egalitarian, nonbureaucratic structure.* It's important to have a structure that promotes the exchange of ideas and welcomes constructive challenges to the usual way of doing things—from any employee with valuable experience. Forward-thinking leaders in bureaucratic organizations must retain the organization's efficiency-promoting control systems and chains of command while finding ways to reshape the change-resisting mind-set of the classic bureaucratic model. They need to separate the enabling elements of bureaucracy (the ability to get things done) from the disabling elements of bureaucracy (those that create resistance to experimentation).

First Interstate Bank: A Paradigm Shift in Progress

All eight preconditions do not have to be in place in order to begin a shift from the first or second diversity orientations toward the learning-and-effectiveness paradigm. But most should be. First Interstate Bank, a midsize bank operating in a Midwestern city, illustrates this point.

First Interstate, admittedly, is not a typical bank. Its client base is a minority community, and its mission is expressly to serve that base through "the development of a highly talented workforce." The bank is unique in other ways: its leadership welcomes constructive criticism; its structure is relatively egalitarian and nonbureaucratic; and its culture is open-minded. Nevertheless, First Interstate had long enforced a policy that loan officers had to hold college degrees. Those without were hired only for support-staff jobs and were never promoted beyond or outside support functions.

Two years ago, however, the support staff began to challenge the policy. Many of them had been with First Interstate for many years and, with the company's active support, had improved their skills through training. Others had expanded their skills on the job, again with the bank's encouragement, learning to run credit checks, prepare presentations for clients, and even calculate the algorithms necessary for many loan decisions. As a result, some people on the support staff were doing many of the same tasks as loan officers. Why, then, they wondered, couldn't they receive commensurate rewards in title and compensation?

This questioning led to a series of contentious meetings between the support staff and the bank's senior managers. It soon became clear that the problem called for managing diversity—diversity based not on race or gender but on class. The support personnel were uniformly from lower socioeconomic communities than were the college-educated loan officers. Regardless, the principle was the same as for race- or gender-based diversity problems. The support staff had different ideas about how the work of the bank should be done. They argued that those among them with the requisite skills should be allowed to rise through the ranks to professional positions, and they believed their ideas were not being heard or accepted.

Their beliefs challenged assumptions that the company's leadership had long held about which employees should have the authority to deal with customers and about how much responsibility administrative employees should ultimately receive. In order to take up this challenge, the bank would have to be open to exploring the requirements that a new perspective would impose on it. It would need to consider the possibility of mapping out an educational and career path for people without degrees— a path that could put such workers on the road to becoming loan officers. In other words, the leadership would have to transform itself willingly and embrace fluidity in policies that in times past had been clearly stated and unquestioningly held.

Today the bank's leadership is undergoing just such a transformation. The going, however, is far from easy. The bank's senior managers now must look beyond the tensions and acrimony sparked by the debate over differing work perspectives and consider the bank's new direction an important learning and growth opportunity.

Shift Complete: Third-Paradigm Companies in Action

First Interstate is a shift in progress, but in addition to Dewey & Levin, there are several organizations we know of for which the shift is complete. In these cases, company leaders have played a critical role as facilitators and tone setters. We have observed in particular that in organizations that have adopted the new perspective, leaders and managers—and, following in their tracks, employees in general—are taking four kinds of action.

They are making the mental connection. First, in organizations that have adopted the new perspective, the leaders are actively seeking opportunities to explore how identity-group differences affect relationships among workers and affect the way work gets done. They are investing considerable time and energy in understanding how identity-group memberships take on social meanings in the organization and how those meanings manifest themselves in the way work is defined, assigned, and accomplished. When there is no proactive search to understand, then learning from diversity, if it happens at all, can occur only reactively—that is, in response to diversity-related crises.

The situation at Iversen Dunham illustrates the missed opportunities resulting from that scenario. Rather than seeing differences in the way project leaders defined and approached their work as an opportunity to gain new insights and develop new approaches to achieving its mission, the firm remained entrenched in its traditional ways, able to arbitrate such differences only by thinking about what was fair and what was racist. With this quite limited view of the role race can play in an organization, discussions about the topic become fraught with fear and defensiveness, and everyone misses out on insights about how race might influence work in positive ways.

A second case, however, illustrates how some leaders using the new paradigm have been able to envision—and make—the connection between cultural diversity and the company's work. A vice president of Mastiff, a large national insurance company, received a complaint from one of the managers in her unit, an African American man. The manager wanted to demote an African American woman he had hired for a leadership position from another Mastiff division just three months before. He told the vice president he was profoundly disappointed with the performance of his new hire.

"I hired her because I was pretty certain she had tremendous leadership skill," he said. "I knew she had a management style that was very open and empowering. I was also sure she'd have a great impact on the rest of the management team. But she hasn't done any of that."

Surprised, the vice president tried to find out from him what he thought the problem was, but she was not getting any answers that she felt really defined or illuminated the root of the problem. Privately, it puzzled her that someone would decide to demote a fifteen-year veteran of the company—and a minority woman at that—so soon after bringing her to his unit.

The vice president probed further. In the course of the conversation, the manager happened to mention that he knew the new employee from church and was familiar with the way she handled leadership there and in other community settings. In those less formal situations, he had seen her perform as an extremely effective, sensitive, and influential leader.

That is when the vice president made an interpretive leap. "If that's what you know about her," the vice president said to the manager, "then the question for us is, why can't she bring those skills to work here?" The vice president decided to arrange a meeting with all three present to ask this very question directly. In the meeting, the African American woman explained, "I didn't think I would last long if I acted that way here. My personal style of leadership—that particular style—works well if you have the permission to do it fully; then you can just do it and not have to look over your shoulder."

Pointing to the manager who had planned to fire her, she added, "He's right. The style of leadership I use outside this company can definitely be effective. But I've been at Mastiff for fifteen years. I know this organization, and I know if I brought that piece of myself—if I became that authentic—I just wouldn't survive here."

What this example illustrates is that the vice president's learning-and-effectiveness paradigm led her to explore and then make the link between cultural diversity and work style. What was occurring, she realized, was a mismatch between the cultural background of the recently promoted woman and the cultural environment of her work setting. It had little to do with private attitudes or feelings, or gender issues, or some inherent lack of leadership ability. The source of the underperformance was that the newly promoted woman had a certain style, and the organization's culture did not support her in expressing it comfortably. The vice president's paradigm led her to ask new questions and to seek out new information, but, more important, it also led her to interpret existing information differently.

The two senior managers began to realize that part of the African American woman's inability to see herself as a leader at work was that she had for so long been undervalued in the organization. And, in a sense, she had become used to splitting herself off from who she was in her own community. In the fifteen years she had been at Mastiff, she had done her job well as an individual contributor, but she had never received any signals that her bosses wanted her to draw on her cultural competencies in order to lead effectively.

They are legitimating open discussion. Leaders and managers who have adopted the new paradigm are taking the initiative to "green light" open discussion about how identity-group memberships inform and influence an employee's experience and the organization's behavior. They are encouraging people to make *explicit* use of background cultural experience and the pools of knowledge gained outside the organization to inform and enhance their work. Individuals often do use their cultural competencies at work, but in a closeted, almost embarrassed, way. The unfortunate result is that the opportunity for collective and organizational learning and improvement is lost.

The case of a Chinese woman who worked as a chemist at Torinno Food Company illustrates this point. Linda was part of a product development group at Torinno when a problem arose with the flavoring of a new soup. After the group had made a number of scientific attempts to correct the problem, Linda came up with the solution by "setting aside my chemistry and drawing on my understanding of Chinese cooking." She did not, however, share with her colleagues—all of them white males—the real source of her inspiration for the solution for fear that it would set her apart or that they might consider her unprofessional. Overlaid on the cultural issue, of course, was a gender issue (women cooking) as well as a work-family issue (women doing *home* cooking in a chemistry lab). All of these themes had erected unspoken boundaries that Linda knew could be career-damaging for her to cross. After solving the problem, she simply went back to the so-called scientific way of doing things.

Senior managers at Torinno Foods in fact had made a substantial commitment to diversifying the workforce through a program designed to teach employees to value the contributions of all its members. Yet Linda's perceptions indicate that, in the actual day-to-day context of work, the program had failed—and in precisely one of those areas where it would have been important for it to have worked. It had failed to affirm someone's identity-group experiences as a legitimate source of insight into her work. It is likely that this organization will miss future opportunities to take full advantage of the talent of employees such as Linda. When people believe that they must suggest and apply their ideas covertly, the organization also misses opportunities to discuss, debate, refine, and build on those ideas fully. In addition, because individuals like Linda will continue to think that they must hide parts of themselves in order to fit in, they will find it difficult to engage fully not only in their work but also in their workplace relationships. That kind of situation can breed resentment and misunderstanding, fueling tensions that can further obstruct productive work relationships.

They actively work against forms of dominance and subordination that inhibit full contribution. Companies in which the third paradigm is emerging have leaders and managers who take responsibility for removing the barriers that block employees from using the full range of their competencies, cultural or otherwise. Racism, homophobia, sexism, and sexual harassment are the most obvious forms of dominance that decrease individual and organizational effectiveness—and third-paradigm leaders have zero tolerance for them. In addition, the leaders are aware that organizations can create their own unique patterns of dominance and subordination based on the presumed superiority and entitlement of some groups over others. It is not uncommon, for instance, to find organizations in which one functional area considers itself better than another. Members of the presumed inferior group frequently describe the organization in the very terms used by those who experience identity-group discrimination. Regardless of the source of the oppression, the result is diminished performance and commitment from employees.

What can leaders do to prevent those kinds of behaviors beyond explicitly forbidding any forms of dominance? They can and should test their own assumptions about the competencies of all members of the workforce because negative assumptions are often unconsciously communicated in powerful—albeit nonverbal—ways. For example, senior managers at Delta Manufacturing had for years allowed productivity and quality at their inner-city plants to lag well behind the levels of other plants. When the company's chief executive officer began to question why the problem was never addressed, he came to realize that, in his heart, he had believed that inner-city workers, most of whom were African American or Hispanic, were not capable of doing better than subpar. In the end, the CEO and his senior management team were able to reverse their reasoning and take responsibility for improving the situation. The result was a sharp increase in the performance of the inner-city plants and a message to the entire organization about the capabilities of its entire workforce.

At Mastiff, the insurance company discussed earlier, the vice president and her manager decided to work with the recently promoted African American woman rather than demote her. They realized that their unit was really a pocket inside the larger organization: they did not have to wait for the rest of the organization to make a paradigm shift in order for their particular unit to change. So they met again to think about how to create conditions within their unit that would move the woman toward seeing her leadership position as encompassing all her skills. They assured her that her authentic style of leadership was precisely what they wanted her to bring to the job. They wanted her to be able to use whatever aspects of herself she thought would make her more effective in her work because the whole purpose was to do the job effectively, not to fit some preset traditional formula of how to behave. They let her know that, as a management team, they would try to adjust and change and support her. And they would deal with whatever consequences resulted from her exercising her decision rights in new ways.

Another example of this line of action—working against forms of dominance and subordination to enable full contribution—is the way the CEO of a major chemical company modified the attendance rules for his company's annual strategy conference. In the past, the conference had been attended only by senior executives, a relatively homogeneous group of white men. The company had been working hard on increasing the representation of women and people of color in its ranks, and the CEO could have left it at that. But he reckoned that, unless steps were taken, it would be ten years before the conferences tapped into the insights and perspectives of his newly diverse workforce. So he took the bold step of opening the conference to people from across all levels of the hierarchy, bringing together a diagonal slice of the organization. He also asked the conference organizers to come up with specific interventions, such as small group meetings before the larger session, to ensure that the new attendees would be comfortable enough to enter discussions. The result was that strategy-conference participants heard a much broader, richer, and livelier discussion about future scenarios for the company.

They are making sure that organizational trust stays intact. Few things are faster at killing a shift to a new way of thinking about diversity than feelings of broken trust. Therefore, managers of organizations that are successfully shifting to the learning-and-effectiveness paradigm take one more step: they make sure their organizations remain "safe" places for employees to be themselves. These managers recognize that tensions naturally arise as an organization begins to make room for diversity, starts to experiment with process and product ideas, and learns to reappraise its mission in light of suggestions from newly empowered constituents in the company. But as people put more of themselves out and open up about new feelings and ideas, the dynamics of the learning-and-effectiveness paradigm can produce temporary vulnerabilities. Managers who have helped their organizations make the change successfully have consistently demonstrated their commitment to the process and to all employees by setting a tone of honest discourse, by acknowledging tensions, and by resolving them sensitively and swiftly.

Our research over the past six years indicates that one cardinal limitation is at the root of companies' inability to attain the expected performance benefits of higher levels of diversity: the leadership's vision of the purpose of a diversified workforce. We have described the two most dominant orientations toward diversity and some of their consequences and limitations, together with a new framework for understanding and managing diversity. The learning-and-effectiveness paradigm we have outlined here is, undoubtedly, still in an emergent phase in those few organizations that embody it. We expect that as more organizations take on the challenge of truly engaging their diversity, new and unforeseen dilemmas will arise. Thus, perhaps more than anything else, a shift toward this paradigm requires a high-level commitment to learning more about the environment, structure, and tasks of one's organization, and giving improvement-generating change greater priority than the security of what is familiar. This is not an easy challenge, but we remain convinced that unless organizations take this step, any diversity initiative will fall short of fulfilling its rich promise.

The Research

This article is based on a three-part research effort that began in 1990. Our subject was diversity, but more specifically we sought to understand three management challenges under that heading. First, how do organizations successfully achieve and sustain racial and gender diversity in their executive and middle-management ranks? Second, what is the impact of diversity on an organization's practices, processes, and performance? And finally, how do leaders influence whether diversity becomes an enhancing or detracting element in the organization?

Over the following six years, we worked particularly closely with three organizations that had attained a high degree of demographic diversity: a small urban law firm, a community bank, and a two-hundred-person consulting firm. In addition, we studied nine other companies in varying stages of diversifying their workforces. The group included two financial-services firms, three Fortune 500 manufacturing companies, two midsize high-technology companies, a private foundation, and a university medical center. In each case, we based our analysis on interviews, surveys, archival data, and observation. It is from this work that the third paradigm for managing diversity emerged and with it our belief that old and limiting assumptions about the meaning of diversity must be abandoned before its true potential can be realized as a powerful way to increase organizational effectiveness.

20

TEACHING
ALL STUDENTS

CELEBRATING DIVERSE MINDS

Mel Levine

A DISTRAUGHT MOTHER recently sent me this e-mail:

> Every morning when I send Michael off to school, I feel as if I'm send-
> ing him to jail. He can't spell, he forgets his math facts even after we
> study them together, his handwriting is hard to decipher, and he is
> hopelessly absent-minded. The other kids see his papers and say that
> he "writes like a mental case." All day, he faces nonstop criticism from
> his teacher. She scolds him in front of his classmates for not trying. And
> you know, his teacher's right. He's not trying—he's scared to try. He's
> decided that if you're going to fail, it's better to fail without trying.
>
> He can fix absolutely anything that's broken and he is brilliant
> when he plays with his Legos. I can't believe the complicated things he
> makes. He is convinced that he is hopelessly dumb, and he worries
> about school all the time. A lot of nights, Michael cries himself to
> sleep. We are losing this darling boy and he is such a beautiful child,
> such a decent kid. Please help us.

Author's note: Mary Dean Barringer, Stacy Parker-Fisher, Chris Osmond, and
Tamara Nimkoff contributed to this article.

We have all heard the success stories of Albert Einstein, Thomas Edison, Steve Jobs, and Charles Schwab—accomplished adults whose minds failed to fit in school. But what becomes of those whom we never hear about—students like Michael, who give up on themselves because they lack the kinds of minds needed to satisfy existing criteria for school success?

For more than thirty years, my work as a pediatrician has been dedicated to such out-of-step children and adolescents. Although some of them have officially acknowledged collisions with word decoding or attention, many contend with more elusive differences in learning. These students may have trouble organizing time and prioritizing activities, communicating effectively, grasping verbal or nonverbal concepts, retrieving data precisely and quickly from long-term memory, recognizing and responding to recurring patterns, or assimilating fine detail.

Such insidious dysfunctions can constitute daunting barriers, especially when they are not recognized and managed. Most important, these break-downs can mislead us into undervaluing, unfairly accusing, and even undereducating students, thereby stifling their chances for success in school and life.

The Challenge of Disappointing School Performance

Many faltering students have specialized minds—brains exquisitely wired to perform certain kinds of tasks masterfully, but decidedly miswired when it comes to meeting other expectations. A student may be brilliant at visualizing, but embarrassingly inept at verbalizing. Her classmate may reveal a remarkable understanding of people, but exhibit no insight about sentence structure.

Within every student contending with learning differences, an area invariably exists in which her or his mind has been amply equipped to thrive. In the e-mail from Michael's mother, the clue to his mind's early specialization practically jumps out at you: "He can fix absolutely anything that's broken." Michael's mechanical brilliance gets eclipsed by our focus on what he can't do.

I love to spend time explaining his strengths and their possibilities to a student like Michael who feels depleted and diminished (and perhaps even demolished) by the experience of school. I talk to him about the different careers in which he could readily succeed given the abilities he already possesses. I feel as if I have stepped inside a shadowy passageway suddenly illuminated, as revealed by a newly radiant facial expression. I can't help but conclude that the real challenge for schools rests more with identifying and fortifying individuals' strengths than with caulking academic crevices.

My long-term experience working at the interface between pediatrics and education has allowed me to synthesize the body of research on neurodevelopmental function and variation (Levine and Reed, 1999) and to construct a framework for understanding the enigma of disappointing school performance. Three factors play major roles:

- The traditional paradigms for understanding learning differences focus on exposing and fixing deficits, often neglecting the latent or blatant talents within struggling learners.

- Instructional practices and curricular choices fail to provide educational opportunities for diverse learners and to prepare them for a successful life.

- Because knowledge about learning emanating from the explosion of insights from brain research is not yet part of teacher preparation and professional development, most educators lack the expertise to understand and support their students' diverse minds.

To stem the tide of needless and wasteful failure facing thousands of kids, we need to take robust action on three fronts: broadened student assessment, curriculum reexamination, and professional development for educators.

Broadened Student Assessment

The methods that schools typically deploy to assess students with learning problems are not up to the task. The discrepancy formulas used to determine eligibility for specialized assistance have been shown repeatedly to have serious flaws (Kavale and Forness, 2000).

Moreover, testing that merely generates a label, such as LD or ADD, accomplishes little. These vague labels do not suggest specific approaches to remediation; instead, they pessimistically imply a relatively permanent pathological condition. What a colossal self-fulfilling prophecy! Most important, diagnosis spawned from a deficit model fails to take into account the most important feature of a student—his strengths.

SMOKESCREEN LABELS. Phillip's parents reported that he seemed to generate about two highly original and unorthodox ideas per minute. His teacher described this irrepressible fourth grader as a brilliant conceptualizer, always coming up with creative analogies. When the class studied terrorism, Phillip compared suicide bombers to strep germs that make you sick and then die in your throat.

But Phillip's day-to-day performance in school was disappointing. When he listened or read, Phillip missed or forgot much of the information he was expected to absorb. He would tune out and become fidgety during extended explanations or directions. His parents sought help from their son's pediatrician, who diagnosed ADD and prescribed a stimulant medication. This treatment helped, but not much.

It turns out that Phillip owned the kind of mind that becomes enthralled with the big picture and rejects fine detail. Consequently, in math he mastered the concepts readily but couldn't be bothered to notice the difference between a plus sign and a minus sign (a mere detail). His writing was creative and amusing but sparse on specific information. In subject after subject, Phillip's overall understanding far exceeded his handling of the details.

Like Phillip, many kids with problems don't ooze easily into categories. Students with his kind of detail intolerance often get diagnosed with ADD or accused of not really trying. In Phillip's case, the label ADD was a smokescreen that obscured people's view of his remarkable strengths and stopped them short of managing his specific weakness in detail assimilation. Phillip improved markedly after his teacher began encouraging him to make detail thinking a separate step in any activity he undertook—scan first, get the big picture, have some great ideas, and then revisit the material to vacuum up the important details.

Incidentally, society desperately needs big-picture people who can collaborate meaningfully with administrators who thrive on detail. So let's take care not to disparage or discourage the flourishing of Phillip's kind of mind.

ASSESSMENT FOR DIVERSE MINDS. In addition to rethinking the assessments used to diagnose learning problems, schools need to design regular tests and quizzes so that different kinds of minds can show what they know in different ways. Teachers should be careful not to tap exclusively rote memory or straight regurgitation of skills and knowledge. They should often allow students to use notes and encourage them to take as much time as they need to respond to questions. It makes more sense to limit space than time—for instance, telling students, "You can't write more than two pages, but you can take as long as you want to do so."

High-stakes testing can pulverize many mismatched students. How commonly does end-of-grade testing discriminate against certain kinds of minds? Frequently. As a clinician, I encounter many students who have difficulty performing on multiple-choice tests or operating under timed conditions. These students' dysfunctions in certain skill areas are more than outweighed by their assets in other domains, but standardized testing never gives them the opportunity to exhibit their strengths.

On entering the medical profession, we take an oath that in our practice we will first of all "do no harm." I offer five suggestions to my professional colleagues in education so that they may strive for testing practices that do no harm to students with different kinds of minds.

"DO NO HARM" TESTING PRACTICES

1. Testing can help elevate education standards, but not if it creates larger numbers of students who are written off as unsuccessful. When a student does poorly, determine which link in the learning chain is uncoupled. Always have constructive, nonpunitive contingency plans for students who perform poorly on a test. Testing should not be an end in itself, but rather a call to action.

2. Not all students can demonstrate their strengths in the same manner. Allow different students to demonstrate their learning differently, using the means of their choice (portfolios, expert papers, oral presentations, and projects, as well as multiple-choice tests).

3. Never use testing as justification for retaining a student in a grade. Retention is ineffective and seriously damaging to students. How can you retain a child while claiming you are not leaving anyone behind?

4. Some students who excel on tests might develop a false sense of security and confidence, failing to realize that adult careers tap many abilities that no test can elicit. Take care to nurture vital capacities that are not testable.

5. Avoid the hazard of teachers teaching to the tests because your work or school is being judged solely on the basis of examination scores. Teachers should never have their students rehearse or explicitly prepare for tests. Testing should be unannounced. Good results on such tests should be the product of the regular, undisturbed curriculum.

We need to advocate for the elimination of testing practices that inflict needless damage and unfair humiliation on so many students.

Curriculum Reexamination

It's ironic that at the same time that neuroscience is telling us so much about differences in learning, we are imposing curriculum standards that offer our students fewer learning alternatives than ever before. If we aspire to meet the challenge of leaving no child behind, we must provide diverse learners with diverging pathways that lead to their success. Such roads should maintain rigorous performance standards, while permitting innovation and creativity in curricular choices and allowing early, highly specialized minds to envision and prepare for productive adulthood.

For example, children like Michael, with his impressive mechanical aptitude, should not be sentenced to wait until adulthood to experience success. We should encourage, not constrain, the development of magnet schools and vocational education opportunities. I look forward to the day when thousands of students pursue a vocationally oriented curriculum that does not put a ceiling on their aspirations.

While studying auto mechanics (and the physics that is a part of it), a teenager should learn the ins and outs of various related careers. She or he should see the possibility of someday climbing the corporate ladder at Ford Motor Company, owning a repair business franchise, designing solar-powered engines, or managing the service department of a dealership. In this way, no one gets written off or limited because of the nature of his passions or the specialized apparatus of her mind.

Many schools have worked against odds to provide educational experiences that involve all students in conducting independent study projects in their area of personal affinity and ability. One school, for example, asked all third grade students to pick a country and become the school's leading expert on that nation. The projects carried over from third through fifth grade, and the students traversed content areas as they studied their country's culture, history, language, animal life, government, and music. They did art projects and wrote reports on their country.

Students learned how it feels to know more about something than anyone around, including their teachers and parents. They became valued consultants on particular countries; when the newspaper reported a current event in their country, they were asked to provide some commentary in class—a great vitamin for intellectual self-esteem!

Another school pursued a similar strategy during students' three years in middle school. Students selected any topic from a list for long-term pursuit across disciplines. They found experts in the community to assist them with their topics. Any student who did not want to claim one of the listed topics could submit one of his or her own choosing.

I look forward to the day when our schools offer every student the opportunity to become a leading expert on a chosen topic—one that harmonizes with his or her kind of mind—and to share that expertise with the community through Web sites, community-based projects, and other venues. Such a practice would give students a powerful experience of suc-

cess, as well as cultivate their appetite for systematic research and focused,
in-depth knowledge.

While advocating ardently for flexibility in achieving the educational
aims of schooling, we can still preserve student accountability. No student
should be permitted to work, study, or produce less than his or her peers.
But we should never insist that everyone put forth identical output.

Professional Development for Educators

In medical practice, highly specific knowledge of the individual needs of
a patient is indispensable when selecting the best treatment. This holds
true in all "helping" professions—especially in education.

Teachers are in an excellent position to observe, interpret, and celebrate
all kinds of minds on a daily basis. Newly acquired knowledge emanating from neuroscientific and education research can empower educators
to observe and understand students' minds. Most of the phenomena that
determine a student's individual strengths, shortcomings, and preferred
ways of learning and producing cannot be found on any test that a clinician gives. Classroom teachers enjoy exclusive screenings—if they pay
attention and know what to look for.

BECKY. Eight-year-old Becky is an accomplished origami creator, a deft
modern dancer, and a gifted mathematician. She thrives on science and
computers. Yet in school, this girl appears shy, passive, and eternally
anguished. Becky has accurate spelling, but she dislikes writing and avoids
it. Becky's teacher, Mrs. Sorenson, having been educated to observe neurodevelopmental phenomena, has noticed that Becky seems to struggle and
falter when called on in class. Recently, the teacher led a discussion on
whether animals have feelings as people do. She called on Becky and the
following dialogue ensued:

BECKY: My puppy feels, uh, things like happy and, um, sad.

MRS. SORENSON: Becky, what makes her happy or sad?

BECKY *(after a long pause)*: Different things.

MRS. SORENSON: Such as?

BECKY: Like a dog, uh, basket.

MRS. SORENSON: Do you mean a dog biscuit?

BECKY: Yeah, like that.

Becky's reading comprehension is more than a year above grade level. Yet she has trouble with word finding, shows pronounced verbal hesitancy, puts forth only simple or incomplete sentences, and fails to use verbal elaboration. The same phenomena are conspicuous in her writing. Becky has strong receptive language but markedly weak expressive language—she understands better than she talks. No wonder she's so shy, self-conscious, and passive! Language output plays a vital role in school success. Verbal communication affects writing, class participation, social success, and the control of emotions and behavior.

Becky could fall through the cracks because we do not have valid tests of language production. For example, the WISC (the commonly used IQ test in her age group) does little to capture expressive language fluency. In fact, by far the best test of expressive language is a classroom teacher who knows what to listen for in gauging the adequacy of a student's verbal output, and who understands the everyday classroom phenomena associated with breakdowns in language production.

BRUCE. Here's another example of the role that teachers can play in detecting learning differences. Bruce was disruptive in most of his seventh grade classes. He fashioned himself as an entertainer and often disengaged from classroom activities. Mr. Jackson, a social studies teacher knowledgeable about early adolescent development and learning, made the astute observation that Bruce often appeared confused about dates and about the sequences of events in the various historical periods that they studied. Mr. Jackson also noted that Bruce often looked distressed when given directions.

On one occasion, Mr. Jackson told the class: "This morning I want you all to open your books to page 47, read the first three paragraphs, and study the diagram at the top of the page. And when you're finished doing that, read and think about the first two questions at the end of the chapter. I'm going to give you ten minutes, and then I'll be calling on you to discuss the questions."

Bruce seemed to hear only something about page 47 (or was it 57?). His teacher suspected rightly that this boy was having problems processing sequences—sequential directions, chains of events in history, and multi-step explanations. His weak temporal-sequential ordering accounted for his problems in social studies and in math. This insight enabled teachers to give Bruce strategies to manage his sequencing problems: taking notes, whispering sequences under his breath, and picturing sequences in his mind. His behavior and demeanor in class improved dramatically.

Although continuing education programs abound to help teachers stay abreast of their content, we have found few comprehensive programs devoted to helping educators deepen their expertise in the science of learning. Our not-for-profit institute, All Kinds of Minds, has developed a professional development and school service model called Schools Attuned to help experienced classroom educators become knowledgeable about neurodevelopmental function and variation (www.allkindsofminds.org). Participating teachers learn to analyze how their own instructional delivery and content taps specific aspects of memory, attention, motor function, language, and other areas of brain function. They are guided to observe everyday classroom phenomena that open windows on relevant learning processes (Levine, 1994).

Equipped with their Schools Attuned training, teachers lead a coalition involving the students, parents, and other adults in the school to unmask the specific learning profile of a struggling student. With help from professionals trained as neurodevelopmental consultants, whom we call profile advisors (usually school psychologists or special educators), teachers become the primary detectors of student strengths, weaknesses, and content affinities. The teachers then infuse their insights into their daily group instructional strategies and lesson designs. Frequently, a strategy that they develop to help a particular struggling student benefits the entire class. It's called excellent pedagogy.

Schools Attuned teachers are also committed to making sure that all of their students learn about learning while they are learning. Through a process called demystification, they help students whose neurodevelopmental profiles do not currently mesh with expectations to learn about their own strengths and weaknesses and acquire the terms for the specific processes that they need to work on. With profile advisors as their consultants, regular classroom teachers take the lead in formulating management plans for these students.

Where We Need to Go

The core theme of K–12 education in this century should be straightforward: high standards with an unwavering commitment to individuality. In proposing that educators reexamine assessment, curriculum, and the role of teachers, I am advocating neurodevelopmental pluralism in our schools—the celebration of all kinds of minds. Such an ethos will be the most effective and humane way of realizing our commitment to leave no child behind.

REFERENCES

Kavale, K. A., and Forness, S. R. "What Definitions of Learning Disability Say and Don't Say: A Critical Analysis." *Journal of Learning Disabilities,* 2000, *33,* 239–256.

Levine, M. *Educational Care.* (2nd ed.) Cambridge, Mass.: Educators Publishing Service, 1994.

Levine, M., and Reed, M. *Developmental Variation and Learning Disorders.* (2nd ed.) Cambridge, Mass.: Educators Publishing Service, 1999.

21

GENDER AND RACE AS FACTORS IN EDUCATIONAL LEADERSHIP AND ADMINISTRATION

Cherry A. McGee Banks

THIS CHAPTER is a review of the status and characteristics of women and people of color in educational leadership and administration. The author's primary intention is to acquaint readers with significant studies and provide a broad overview of the characteristics and experiences of women and people of color who are superintendents and principals. The chapter reflects a dual concern for research and expert opinion. Theories and research are discussed, but the chapter also includes personal insights, interpretations, and recommendations for improving opportunities for women and people of color in educational leadership.

Available research on women and people of color in educational leadership does not support equal coverage of both groups on all of the topics covered in the chapter. Some sections of the chapter are primarily concerned with women; others focus on people of color. A major aim of the chapter is to identify gaps in the research, compare and contrast the experiences of women and people of color, and explore possible linkages between their experiences.

A major theme running throughout the chapter is the relationship of social context to the underrepresentation of women and people of color in educational leadership positions. A primary objective of this chapter is to review what we have learned and are learning about women and people of color in educational leadership and to identify ways in which a multicultural approach can help extend our knowledge by providing new insights and perspectives on leadership.

The Nature of Leadership

Leadership is a relatively new field of study (Yukl, 1981). Scientific research on leadership did not begin until the late twentieth century. Several of the major theories in leadership, such as social exchange theory and situational theories, were not conceptualized until the 1950s and 1960s.

Women and people of color were almost completely absent from the study of leadership until the late 1970s (Bass, 1981). The lack of research on women and people of color was not viewed as problematic because race and gender were not considered differences of consequence (Bass, 1981). Researchers seemed to assume that their findings could be applied without regard for race and gender. Theories used to frame research, such as McGregor's Theory X and Theory Y and Argyris's Model I and II, were silent on issues of race and gender (McGregor, 1960; Argyris and Schön, 1974).

Leadership theory and practice are evolving and the traditional leadership paradigm is being challenged. Scholars are working to broaden the study of leadership to include women and people of color. They are also developing preservice and continuing education programs to prepare leaders to address the changing context of educational leadership and administration (Cunningham, 1990).

Definitions

Leadership is a broad concept with many different meanings (Burns, 1979; Hemphill and Coons, 1957; Stogdill, 1974; Rost, 1991). While there is no universally accepted definition of leadership, most definitions share two assumptions. They assume that leadership is a group phenomenon and that leaders exercise intentional influence over followers (Yukl, 1981; Janda, 1960). Definitions of leadership differ in terms of who exercises influence, the reasons why influence is attempted, and the ways in which influence is exercised (Yukl, 1981; Immegart, 1988).

One widely used definition of leadership states that leadership is "the initiation and maintenance of structure in expectation and interaction" (Stogdill, 1974, p. 411). This definition incorporates two key categories of leadership behavior: *consideration* and *initiating structure* (Fleishman,

1957; Halpin and Winer, 1957; Hemphill and Coons, 1957). Consideration and initiating structure include a number of specific behaviors. Three questionnaires, the forty-item Leader Behavior Description Questionnaire (LBDQ), the Supervisory Behavior Description Questionnaire (SBDQ), and the Leader Behavior Description Questionnaire XII (LBDQ XII), were constructed by Ohio State University researchers to measure leadership behavior (Fleishman, 1953; Stogdill, 1963; Hemphill and Coons, 1957).

The LBDQ, which was normed on male samples, is still used as a research protocol. In a meta-analysis of studies that examined differences in male and female responses to the LBDQ, Shakeshaft (1979, 1985) found that there were no differences between the two sexes. Shakeshaft (1987) notes that perceptual studies using instruments like the LBDQ, as opposed to behavioral studies, may not pick up real differences in the behavior of male and female leaders. Other researchers have criticized the LBDQ for having a halo effect, reporting implicit theories and stereotypes instead of actual leader behavior, and not relating to leaders' self-descriptions of their behavior (Bass, 1981).

Current State of Leadership

There are radically different views on the status of leadership as a discipline. In a comprehensive review of research and theory on managerial leadership, Yukl (1981) concluded that the field is in a state of ferment and confusion. Yukl's concerns center on three issues: (a) the lack of agreement in the field about leadership as a concept; (b) the lack of agreement in the field as to the ability of a leader to exercise substantial influence on performance in an organization; and (c) the conceptual weaknesses of current theories of leadership and their lack of clear empirical support. Immegart (1988, p. 266), however, argues that leadership is not the "barren ground nor the frustrating arena" portrayed by critics like Yukl. In a review of research on leadership and leader behavior, Immegart notes that the knowledge base in leadership is growing, scholars are building on previous research, and the field's understanding of leadership is increasing.

Research on and conducted by women and people of color in educational leadership is growing. Women and people of color are adding an exciting element to the study of leadership. Their work raises new questions (Scott, 1983; Lomotey, 1989), challenges traditional leadership theory (Evers and Lokomski, 1991), redefines old concepts and presents new language to describe leadership (Ortiz and Marshall, 1988; Shakeshaft, 1987), and is helping to create a new vision of leadership (Astin and Leland, 1991). However, there continues to be a dearth of research on both groups. Of the research that is available, there is considerably more on women than on people of color.

Major Research Approaches

Research on leadership can generally be classified into four approaches: the power-influence approach, trait approach, behavioral approach, and situational approach (Yukl, 1981). The power-influence approach regards power as a relationship that involves persuasion, coercion, indoctrination, and other forms of reciprocal influence (Bell, 1975). Leader effectiveness is measured in terms of the amount and source of power available to leaders and the ways in which power is used (French and Raven, 1960).

At the turn of the century and in the early 1900s, and then again in the 1960s and 1970s, trait theories were a topic of considerable interest in leadership. Trait theories assume that leaders can be differentiated from followers by their personality, character, and other qualities. Personal qualities such as intelligence, self-confidence, high energy, and persuasive skill are commonly identified as traits of leaders (House and Baetz, 1979; Jago, 1982; Stogdill, 1974). Trait theories are no longer in vogue. However, the idea that effective leaders have characteristics traditionally associated with men still has currency and continues to influence contemporary views of women leaders.

Behavioral approaches and situational approaches are somewhat related. Researchers use behavioral approaches to examine what leaders do (Pelz, 1952; Bales, 1950). They are particularly concerned with identifying and understanding effective behaviors and activities of leaders. Situational approaches, which are also known as contingency theories, highlight the importance of context in determining effective leadership (Fiedler, 1967; Vroom, 1976; Vroom and Yetton, 1973). For example, a specific behavior, such as praising a subordinate, is not always effective. In some cases praise may result in the desired outcome, while in other cases it may not. Situational theorists argue that effective leaders must be able to contextualize their behavior (Hersey, 1984).

It is interesting that even though situational theories were created in a society in which racism and sexism are salient, they are silent on issues of race and gender. This is especially perplexing since community factors, cultural values, and other commonly studied situational variables frequently involve issues of race and gender. Situational analysis can help increase our understanding of the behaviors of people of color and women in leadership positions as well as the behaviors of others toward them. It can also enhance our understanding of the ways in which race and gender serve as moderator variables in situations that require personal commitment, risk taking, and a quest for justice and equality.

Barbara A. Sizemore, a former superintendent of schools in Washington, D.C., argues that scholarly work on Black superintendents must be interpreted in the larger social reality of Black life and the historical context of the struggle of Blacks for education. The history of African Americans and their struggle to attend public school and gain access to jobs and positions in public schools is necessary for an informed analysis of Black educational leaders (Sizemore, 1986). Sizemore uses Black schools in Pittsburgh to illustrate her point. She states that after the Black-segregated school in Pittsburgh was closed in 1867, no Black teachers were hired until 1933. The first Black principal since 1867 was hired in 1962.

Social and Role Theory

Social and role theory can help explain the status of women and people of color in leadership theory and their underrepresentation in educational leadership positions. Role theory provides a basis for examining role socialization and for explaining the behaviors of people in occupational roles such as principals and superintendents. Role theory is based on the idea that a role defines how individuals are expected to behave, how individuals occupying roles perceive what they are supposed to do, and the actual behavior of individuals (Toren, 1973; Gross, Mason, and McEachern, 1958).

Scholars, practitioners, and gatekeepers (those who control entry into educational leadership) are socialized and participate in a society that makes cultural assumptions about women and people of color. Those cultural assumptions grow out of societal norms and values that marginalize these two groups. Norms and values are products of socialization, and part of the process of role socialization that begins in infancy and continues through adulthood. Decisions about who is the focus of research, who is recruited and hired, and who does or does not get promoted are made within a social context in which women and people of color experience an inferior social status and are often objects of negative stereotypes.

Role socialization is commonly viewed as a two-way process in which both the socializer and the person being socialized may be changed in significant ways (Goslin, 1969). This characteristic of role socialization is particularly important when race and gender are incorporated into the study of educational leaders. On one hand, leaders learn to accept and adopt appropriate values, rules, and policies through their socialization into the profession and participation in professional organizations (Gross and Etzioni, 1985). Weber (1968) refers to this process as legitimation. On the other hand, women and people of color also have the potential to change the institutions in which they work and their colleagues. More research is needed to increase understanding of this dynamic interchange.

Racism and Sexism as Factors in Socialization

Women and people of color both experience prejudice and discrimination. Racism and sexism are unconscious ideologies and integral parts of the American identity (Franklin, 1993; West, 1993; Freeman, 1984). The values and norms that legitimate prejudice and discrimination are internalized and transmitted to new members of U.S. society through socialization. However, while racism and sexism are both forms of discrimination, they are not necessarily evidenced in the same way. From a sociological perspective, the prejudice and discrimination that women and people of color experience have different origins and different consequences. Developing and implementing effective strategies to reduce prejudice and discrimination require that we acknowledge and work to understand the similarities and differences in the social genesis and maintenance of gender and racial prejudice and discrimination.

Unlike people of color, women are not a numerical minority. Women are a majority in the U.S. population. They are considered a minority group because, like people of color, they lack access to power. However, even though White women lack social, political, and economic power, they enjoy a privileged status in U.S. society based on their race (McIntosh, 1988; hooks, 1990). Women of color experience discrimination based on two factors: race and sex (Butler and Walter, 1991; DuBois and Ruiz, 1990).

Women have more social contact with men and boys who are members of their ethnic or racial group than minorities have with Whites. Men and women interact with each other from birth, whereas most minorities and Whites have little voluntary social contact with each other. Children learn about sex roles directly from parents, friends, and other close associates, but most acquire information about different racial and ethnic groups from secondary sources such as books, television, and individuals who are not members of their primary groups.

Race socialization frequently privileges White characteristics and marginalizes characteristics associated with people of color (Sleeter, 1993). It is particularly pernicious because it frequently occurs in an environment where racism is a powerful though often unidentified variable in the socialization process. Racism affects individual as well as institutional responses to people of color (West, 1993; Franklin, 1993; McCarthy and Crichlow, 1993). Selective perception and reinforcement and other such processes are used to deny variability among people of color in areas such as intellect and accomplishment (H. J. Scott, personal communication, 1993). As a result, it is not uncommon for all members of a group to be reduced to one-dimensional representatives of their phenotype. These representations are codified in images that are presented in media, texts, and other communicative elements in society that forefront racism as an important element in race socialization.

On an institutional level, racism results in barriers that restrict people of color from access to power and privilege within the institution. Racism and its impact on race socialization make it impossible for people of color to dream their dreams free from the dire reality that color is the key that opens the door to the full range of opportunities and benefits of American citizenship (H. J. Scott, personal communication, 1993).

For the most part, race and sex socialization have been explored as independent processes. Researchers who are interested in race have basically disregarded gender, and researchers who have examined issues of gender have tended to overlook race (McCarthy and Crichlow, 1993). This tendency ignores women of color as an integrated whole and presents them in fragments (Pinar, 1993; Dugger, 1991). Exploring race and sex as a collectivity offers exciting possibilities for future research.

Persistence of Prejudice and Discrimination

Schools reflect the race and gender stratification that exists in the wider society (Gaertner, 1980). Both women and people of color are underrepresented in educational leadership positions in schools. In 1992, 97.1 percent of superintendents were White and 89.5 percent were male (Saks, 1992). Female administrative aspirants interviewed by Edson (1987) stated that "they had to be far superior to male candidates just to be considered for an administrative position and, even then, school boards still showed a preference for hiring men" (p. 265).

Efforts to combat prejudice and discrimination, such as affirmative action, have been disappointingly ineffective for people of color and only marginally effective for women (McCarthy and Zent, 1981). In 1992 women held 10.5 percent of superintendencies, while people of color held only 2.9 percent. African Americans constituted 1.9 percent of those superintendencies and Hispanics constituted .5 percent (Saks, 1992). Whites also held most school principalships.

Sex Roles

Over the years, researchers have used the concept of sex roles to explain why women are underrepresented in educational leadership (Schmuck, 1980). The concept of sex roles grew out of social theory and Blau's (1976) research on social exchange. Holter (1970) defines sex roles as the roles that are assigned to men because they are men and women because they are women. Sex roles are acquired through socialization in environments where there are different expectations for men and women. Each sex is socialized in ways that are consistent with specific gender expectations (Holter, 1970). Early investigations of sex roles focused on sex-role identity in terms of attitudes, values, beliefs, and behaviors (Millett, [1969] 1980). These investigations were followed by studies that explored the relationship between sex and the experiences of women and men in organizations (Biklen and Brannigan, 1980).

Schmuck (1980) organized research on sex roles into three broad categories, each representing a specific perspective: the individual perspective, the social perspective, and the organizational perspective. Schmuck notes that individual perspectives on sex roles draw heavily on psychological research and focus on individual attitudes and aspirations. According to Schmuck, the individual perspective is limited by its lack of attention to societal norms, folkways, and traditions. The social perspective focuses on men's and women's work. Schmuck argues that our society maximizes the differences between men's and women's work and gives women's work less status, value, and pay. Even though most institutions in the United States have both male and female workers, Schmuck states that men generally hold the more influential positions. From an organizational perspective, competent women are often discriminated against because they are viewed as threatening and are marginalized with terms such as "girls" and "honey" (Hagen and Kahn, 1975).

The women's movement in the 1960s and 1970s increased awareness of and sensitivity to sex roles and the expectations and norms related to them (Friedan, 1963). An increased awareness of sex roles led to questions about the validity of men's investigating and interpreting research on sex roles (Schmuck, 1980). Researchers such as Huber (1973) and Rossi (1970) argue that much of the research on sex-role characteristics reflects male perspectives and is stereotyped. They question research that creates a dichotomy between males and females by suggesting, for example, that males are frank and straightforward in social relations, intellectually rational, and competent, and that females are interested in social amenities, emotional warmth, and affective matters (Huber, 1973; Rossi,

1970). Feminists have also criticized research that uses male models of organizational behavior to evaluate females. They note that even though most women are clerical or service workers, most of the research on women in organizations focuses on the roles and behavior of women in male-dominated professions (Astin, 1969; Bernard, 1964; White, 1967). Research on sex roles in organizations has become more diverse within the last decade. It includes studies that explore gender differences in graffiti styles, portrait posing, and assertive acts of toddlers (Loewenstine, Ponticos, and Pauldi, 1982; Mills, 1984).

Sex-Role Stereotypes

The presence of sex-role stereotypes in our society has been extensively researched and is well documented (Fernberger, 1948; Komarovsky, 1973). Sex-role stereotypes, however, may be changing. Research on sex-role stereotypes conducted in the 1980s suggests that while sex-role stereotypes seem to remain strong, sex-biased attitudes appear to be less polarized (Ruble, 1983). Nevertheless, sex-role stereotypes continue to be pervasive.

The relationship between sex-role stereotypes and leadership is complex and has not been fully defined. However, we know that sex-role stereotypes are integrated into the self-concepts of men and women (Broverman and others, 1972). O'Leary (1974) reported that the career aspirations of women are influenced by societal sex-role stereotypes and attitudes about their competency. As late as the mid-1970s, Bem and Bem (1975) found that one-third of all working women were concentrated in seven jobs: secretary, retail sales clerk, household worker, elementary school teacher, waitress, and nurse.

Many women internalize societal sex-role stereotypes and attitudes. They express these attitudes and stereotypes in role conflict, as fear of failure, and in low self-esteem (Horner, 1987; O'Leary, 1974). In investigating the relationship between sex-role stereotypes and leadership, Petty and Miles (1976) found that both males and females subscribe to sex-role stereotypes for leadership roles. Research on sex-role stereotypes suggests that there is a tendency to attribute a higher social value to behaviors that are considered masculine than to those that are considered feminine (White, 1950). Women as well as men attribute higher social value to male behaviors even when they work in female-dominated cultures, such as elementary schools. Broverman and colleagues (1972) found that, compared with men, women are perceived as less competent, independent, objective, and logical. Men are perceived as lacking interpersonal sensitivity, warmth, and expressiveness (Broverman and others, 1972; Williams, 1982).

Interestingly, sex-role stereotypes cause the same traits to be perceived differently in men and women (Bayes and Newton, 1978). Consequently, sex-role stereotypes can result in a no-win situation for women. Women are expected to exhibit behaviors associated with sex-role stereotypes in order to be viewed as women, and yet those very behaviors are often seen as being antithetical to effective leadership. Women who behave in ways traditionally associated with males may be passed over for promotions. Brown and Klein (1982) found that women were only allowed to advance into administrative positions when they were able to play the roles of peacemaker and nurturer as well as supervisor. Sex-role stereotypes can limit women's access to and effectiveness in leadership positions.

Since the late 1960s much of the research on sex-role stereotypes has been conducted using the Stereotype Questionnaire (Broverman and others, 1970). Researchers using the Stereotype Questionnaire have found that sex-role stereotypes are commonly found in a variety of groups throughout the nation and are deeply ingrained in U.S. society. Research by Millham and Smith (1981), however, indicates that sex-role stereotypes may be different for African Americans than they are for Whites. In their study comparing sex-role differentiation among Black and White Americans, Millham and Smith concluded that "Blacks are generally less concerned with traditional sex-role differentiation as defined by the White majority" (p. 89).

Role Stress and Conflict

Role stress is a construct that describes a feeling of conflict that results from the inconsistent demands of a role (Goode, 1960; Merton, 1957; Parsons, 1951; Popenoe, 1971). Gross, Mason, and McEachern (1958) found that superintendents experience conflict when they try to satisfy the conflicting desires of teachers, parents, and school board members. Conflict also results from the multiple roles minorities and women in educational administration are expected to assume. Role conflict among White males entering their first administrative positions tends to be lower than that of women and minorities entering their first administrative positions (Ortiz, 1982).

Ortiz (1982) examined the socialization processes of 350 school administrators in California. Her work is particularly important in understanding the relationship between career patterns and role conflict of women and minorities in school districts. Ortiz investigated some of the intervening processes between status and role conflict and found that organizational position can increase as well as decrease role conflict. Women and minority administrators may experience role conflict as a result of the "organization's expectations regarding their ascribed roles such as being feminine or ethnic" (p. 138). This form of role conflict is reduced when "minorities and women accentuate the positions' characteristics and when they refuse to be shattered in the face of conflicting expectations" (p. 138). Ortiz also found that role conflict is dependent on the way minorities participate in their organizations. The potential for role conflict is reduced when minorities are highly competent, limit their area of expertise to issues involving ethnicity and social bias, and do not compete with White males.

The reform role that many Black superintendents are expected to fill can also result in role stress and conflict (Sizemore, 1986). Minority administrators are challenged to maintain loyalty simultaneously to bureaucratic, personal, and community ideologies that often involve incompatible expectations, attitudes, and beliefs. Peterson (1985) makes the following comment on the role of superintendents in school reform in his book on the politics of school reform:

> Reform superintendents were neither heroes nor devils, but they had an agenda that placed them at odds with a diversity of opponents that changed according to the issue at stake and the political context in which it was raised. [p. 155]

Educational administrators are frequently expected to take on the roles of educational superperson, technical manager, and democratic leader (Cunningham and Nystrand, 1969). In his book on Black superintendents, Scott (1980) states that "the relationship Black superintendents have with other Blacks and many Whites is a manifestation of contemporary racial attitudes in America" (p. 57). Scott concludes that African American superintendents are charged with tempering Black hostility and distrust while simultaneously providing the leadership necessary to reform urban school districts.

The small number of women and people of color in educational leadership is another potential source of role stress and conflict. Kanter (1977) argues that three dynamics may result when there are small numbers of women in leadership positions: (a) women in those positions may receive more attention; (b) the additional attention may lead to more pressure to perform; and (c) the organization's cultural boundaries may be heightened due to polarization and the exaggeration of differences between males and females. Women may be channeled, through affirmative action, into special roles set aside for them. The smaller the number of individuals from other groups, the more they are seen as representatives of their group rather than as individuals. That perspective, along with the assumption that minority persons are only interested in appointments in areas such as human rights, immigration, and social assistance, limits them from being considered seriously for advancement.

Gender and Race Stratification in Educational Leadership

Even though both women and people of color have experienced long tenure in the field of education, there are important differences in the social contexts and experiences of the two groups. Programs designed to increase the number of people of color and women in educational leadership positions will continue to be ineffective until a better understanding is gained of the ways in which history and social context influence their underrepresentation (Ortiz and Marshall, 1988; Sizemore, 1986). This section identifies some of the key factors in the backgrounds of the two groups and provides some statistics on their past and current representation in educational leadership positions.

Effect of Gender and Race on Opportunities for Leadership

Leadership opportunities for women in school administration began to increase in the 1980s. However, women continue to be underrepresented in higher-level positions in school administration (Saks, 1992). During the 1981–1982 school year, 25 percent of the school administrators in the United States were women. From 1981 to 1984, the percentage of female elementary and high school principals increased from 12 percent to 17 percent (Marshall, 1984). During that same period, the percentage of female assistant superintendents increased from 9 percent to 15 percent. By 1986, 27 percent of principals and assistant principals were women (U.S. Bureau of the Census, 1992). In 1992 women held 12.1 percent of high school principalships, compared to 7.6 percent in 1991 (Saks, 1992). The percentage of female superintendents increased from less than 1 percent in 1971 to 1.8 percent in 1981–1982, 2.7 percent in 1984–1985, 7.5 percent in 1991, and eventually to 10.5 percent in 1992 (Saks, 1992).

The number of minorities in school administration did not change substantially from 1975–1976 to 1984–1985 (Snyder, 1989). During that period, the number of African American male principals declined .12 percent and the number of Black female principals increased 1.85 percent. By 1986 only 8 percent of all school administrators and 13 percent of elementary and secondary principals and assistant principals were Blacks

(U.S. Bureau of the Census, 1992). A national survey of school administrators, conducted in 1985 by the American Association of School
Administrators (AASA), found that African Americans held 1 percent of
the superintendencies and 6.5 percent of the assistant superintendencies;
Hispanics held 1.4 percent of the superintendencies and 1.8 percent of
the assistant superintendencies; American Indians held .5 percent of the
superintendencies; and Asian Pacific Islanders held .1 percent of the
superintendencies (AASA, 1985). By 1991 the number of African American superintendents had increased only to 2.5 percent. The percentage of African American superintendents dropped to 1.9 percent in 1992
(Saks, 1992).

Historical Context of Underrepresentation

Historically, women and people of color have had limited career options.
For many years education was one of the few careers open to them. Education offered an aura of respectability and professionalism, a realistic
career goal, financial independence, and an opportunity to serve the community. Women constituted almost 98 percent of all elementary school
teachers and 61.7 percent of elementary school principals in 1905 (Shakeshaft, 1987). By 1920 education was the seventh-ranked field of work for
African American women (Shakeshaft, 1987).

Virtually all school administrators are initially recruited from the ranks
of teachers (Clement, 1975). Several states require teacher certification as
a prerequisite for administrative certification. For many years minorities
were not hired as teachers in public schools. Even in the rural South,
teaching and administrative positions in segregated schools did not open
for Blacks until the first half of the 20th century (Perkins, 1989; Clifford,
1982). In a study of the early history of Black superintendents, Jones
(1983) found that the first Black superintendents served in all-Black school
districts between 1930 and 1958. Most of those districts were in the
South. Sizemore (1986) notes that the Black superintendency did not
become a reality in mixed school districts until 1954.

Teaching opportunities for African Americans began to decline during
the 1960s and 1970s. Schools were integrated during those years and
Black students were transferred from Black schools to White schools.
African American teachers and administrators who worked in Black
schools were not generally transferred to White schools. Consequently,
many lost their jobs.

During the 1980s scholarships and other forms of financial aid for students entering higher education began to decrease. As a result, the number

of students of color entering college and available to select education as a major decreased as well. As opportunities opened up for employment in other fields, such as business, students of color began to choose majors outside education (Perkins, 1989). In 1977 African Americans were more likely than Whites to major in education; by 1989 Whites were more likely than Blacks to select education as their major (National Center for Educational Statistics, 1991). Between 1985 and 1990, less than 1 percent of American Indians, 1 percent of Asian Americans, 2 percent of Latinos, and 5 percent of African Americans were hired in teaching positions (Feistritzer, 1990).

The underrepresentation of women in educational leadership, like that of minorities, is embedded in a compelling historical context. After World War II the number of women administrators decreased as more men went into education. During that period, school boards tended to limit new hires to heads of households. School boards also frequently replaced retiring female principals with males (Neely and Wilson, 1978). Decision makers tended to view men as having characteristics that were more favorable in educational administration. The percentage of male elementary teachers increased from 12.8 percent in 1957–1958 to 14.6 percent during the 1967–1968 school year. During that period there was an increase of male teachers at the secondary level from 50.5 percent to 52.9 percent. In 1990 males represented approximately 15 percent of elementary school teachers and almost 46 percent of secondary teachers (U.S. Bureau of the Census, 1992).

Determining Underrepresentation

While both women and people of color are underrepresented in educational leadership positions, the determination of their underrepresentation is derived in different ways. Justification for increasing the number of women in educational administration is frequently based on the disproportionate number of women who hold administrative positions. Jones and Montenegro (1990) found that even though most teachers are women, men hold 96 percent of superintendencies, 77 percent of assistant superintendencies, 88 percent of high school principalships, and 71 percent of elementary principalships.

Increasing the number of minorities in educational administration is frequently justified on the basis of the growing number of students of color in the public schools. The majority of students enrolled in public schools in California are students of color. By 2020 almost half of the students attending public school in the United States will be students of color (Spencer, 1986).

Placement of Minorities in Educational Administration

Many minorities enter administration through special projects and work on minority issues. They frequently work in schools with high minority enrollment and occupy the least powerful positions in the administrative hierarchy. In a national study of high school principals, Byrne, Hines, and McCleary (1978) found that most minority principals served in school districts with more than 20 percent minority enrollment. In a national survey of 210 Black school administrators, Holden (1977) found that 58 percent of the Black administrators worked in predominantly Black school districts with fewer than 10,000 students.

Most minority superintendents are hired in school districts that have a high proportion of students of color. The probability of African Americans being hired as superintendents increases as the number of minority students in school districts increases (Moody, 1971; Jones, 1983; Scott, 1983). By the late 1980s most Black superintendents were located in cities (Sizemore, 1986). Scott (1983) predicts that those school districts with high minority populations, critical financial conditions, and educational problems will have unwanted superintendencies, and those superintendencies will be available to Blacks.

In one of the first national studies of Black superintendents, Moody (1971) found that 72.2 percent of the school districts with Black superintendents were predominantly Black. Many of those districts were large urban school districts. Black superintendents have served in Chicago, Detroit, Minneapolis, Rochester, Washington, D.C., Atlanta, Baltimore, Newark, and New Orleans (Scott, 1983). However, it is important to note that most school districts that have a majority of African American students do not have Black superintendents. In 1982, 66 percent of predominantly Black districts in the United States had White superintendents (Scott, 1983).

Role of School Boards in Underrepresentation of Women

School boards reflect the values of their communities and play an important role in the selection of administrators (Peshkin, 1978). In a 1986 survey of superintendents, personnel directors, and school board presidents, Phillips and Voorhees found that attitudes of school board presidents differed from those of superintendents and personnel directors on the ability of women to advance in educational administration. The superintendents and personnel directors believed women had the ability to advance in educational administration. The board presidents, however, believed that women could be placed in elementary administration, but should not be placed in positions such as assistant superintendent or superintendent.

In a survey of Connecticut school board members, Taylor (1971) found that board members were more likely to appoint women to positions in central office administration and as elementary principals than to positions as superintendents or secondary principals. Taylor found that female school board members, like male board members, favored males for administrative positions. However, those attitudes may be changing. In a 1978 study of California school board members, Beck found that the attitudes of male board members toward women administrators were significantly more traditional than the attitudes of female board members.

Working with women administrators seems to moderate negative attitudes toward them. Male board members who have worked with a female administrator had more favorable attitudes toward women administrators than male board members who have not worked with women administrators. Beck (1978) found that there was a positive correlation between the percentage of women hired in administrative positions and more liberal attitudes toward women.

The number of female school board members remains relatively low. In 1987, 39 percent of school board members were women. By 1992 that percentage had increased only to 39.9 percent. Minority representation on school boards is much lower than female representation. In 1987, 3.6 percent of school board members were Black, 1.5 percent were Hispanic, .1 percent were American Indian, and .2 percent were Asian American. By 1992 the percentage of African American school board members had fallen to 3.1 percent. It increased to .8 percent for American Indians. The percentage of Hispanic and Asian American board members remained the same in 1992 as it was in 1987 (Saks, 1992).

Characteristics of Women and Minorities in Educational Leadership

The assumption that leadership requires male characteristics has led to a body of research in which women and people of color are compared to White men. This research results in men being held up as the ideal to which women and people of color are compared. Conceptualizing research on leadership as a mirror in which women and people of color are expected to be a reflection of White men ultimately marginalizes these two groups because they are viewed as having fewer skills and less power. In a review of empirical studies on male and female leaders, Brown (1979) concludes that "one of the popular reasons given for the differential treatment of women in management stems from stereotyping females as ineffective leaders . . . trait studies consistently supported the traditional attitude that women lack adequate leadership characteristics" (p. 595). In addition to marginalizing women and people of color, research comparing male and female leaders diverts attention away from issues like discrimination in the workplace (Fierman, 1990).

Male and Female Leaders Compared

Researchers frequently use survey instruments to gather data on the personal characteristics of male and female educational leaders. The availability of such data enables researchers to create a profile of women and men who reach high levels in school administration. In general, studies that compare male and female leaders do not demonstrate a clear pattern of difference in leadership style between the sexes (Bass, 1981; Banks, 1991). On occasion, however, individual studies have identified differences in leadership style. In a meta-analysis of fifty studies that compared the leadership styles of male and female principals, Eagly, Karau, and Johnson (1992) found that there is some evidence that men and women have different styles. Women tended to display a democratic and participatory style and to be more task oriented than men. However, Eagly and colleagues state that there are men who practice democratic leadership and women who exercise autocratic leadership. Male and female leadership styles overlap and there are considerable intragroup differences in leadership style.

Studies comparing personal characteristics and experiences of male and female leaders have had mixed results. Some studies suggest that there are differences between male and female leaders, while others suggest that there are no significant differences (Adkinson, 1981; Frasher and Frasher, 1979; Shakeshaft, 1987). Age is one variable on which differences have been consistently noted. Researchers have found that women entering school administration are older and have more school experience than men (Johnston, Yeakey, and Moore, 1980; Gross and Trask, 1976). Males generally have taught five to seven years and females have generally taught fifteen years before they enter educational administration (Gross and Trask, 1976).

Studies have also shown that women leaders share many commonalities. Stevens (1988) interviewed ten women who held superintendencies in Washington State school districts. Most of the women came from homes where they were expected to achieve. Nine of the ten female superintendents were the oldest child in their families, and five began their educational careers as teachers in junior high schools. All of the superintendents saw themselves as collaborative leaders.

The following studies illustrate some of the key factors found in research comparing the personal characteristics of male and female educational leaders. Gross and Trask (1976) conducted a major study of men and women elementary school principals. The study was part of the National Principalship Study that was carried out at Harvard University and supported by the U.S. Office of Education. Gross and Trask used a cluster sampling procedure that gave them a representative sample of 189 elementary principals in cities with a population of 50,000 or more. Secondary principals were not included in the study because the number of female junior and senior high school principals was too small. Data were gathered using a personal and school background questionnaire, a role questionnaire, and a three- to five-hour personal interview.

The average age of the women in the study was 54.3 years, with 59 percent of them between 50 and 59 years old. The average age of the men was 49.2 years. The largest group of men (4 percent) was between the ages of 40 and 49. Ninety-six percent of the women and 92 percent of the men were White. With one exception, the remaining individuals in the study were African American.

The Gross and Trask (1976) study revealed a number of important characteristics of school administrators. Over 95 percent of the men in the study were married, but only about one-third of the women were married. Kanter (1977) notes that some high-level positions, such as superintendent of schools, seem to require two individuals: the individual hired for the position and a spouse to handle its social aspects. Traditionally, women have provided an extra hand in support of their husbands' careers. Women who are married as well as women who are not married generally have to handle both the social and professional components of their positions.

Women in the Gross and Trask (1976) study reported higher academic performance than the men. Twenty-three percent of women and 12 percent of the men indicated that their academic work was far above average; 1 percent of the men and none of the women reported that their academic work was below average. The women also stated that they went into teaching because they were influenced or persuaded by someone else. Men indicated that they went into teaching for financial reasons and for upward mobility. The women in the study reportedly had lower aspirations for career advancement than did the men.

Douglas and Simonson (1982) studied the life experiences and leader behaviors of 25 male and 25 female superintendents. They found that male and female superintendents did not exhibit different leader behaviors; however, they did find other differences. Four times as many male superintendents as female superintendents earned $50,000 or more. Female superintendents were less likely to be married than were male superintendents—92 percent of the men were married, compared to 72 percent of the women. All of the married male superintendents had children, but 28 percent of the married female superintendents had no children. The female superintendents had an average of 11.7 years of teaching experience, compared to 3.2 years for men. Fifty-four percent of the men in the study moved into superintendencies within ten years after they started teaching. None of the women moved into superintendencies within ten years after they started teaching. At the other extreme, 36 percent of the women and 4 percent of the men in the study became superintendents 26 or more years after their first teaching experience. Men served an average of 13.2 years in a superintendency, compared to 4.5 years for women.

In a nationwide study of 791 male and 191 female superintendents, Schuster (1987) found that males and females differ on personal and career variables, politics, and job-related costs and satisfactions. Women superintendents were more often firstborn than were male superintendents. They were more likely to be politically liberal and single, and had on average fewer children than did male superintendents. Females also read more professional books and held more doctoral degrees than did male superintendents. Increasingly, a significantly larger number of women than men sat on school boards that hired female superintendents.

In 1990 Banks surveyed 31 superintendents of the largest public school districts in the United States to gather data on their career patterns, personal and educational characteristics, and perceptions of managerial and leadership styles and skills (Banks, 1991). The respondents included 2 female superintendents and 29 male superintendents—15 European Americans, 13 African Americans, and 3 Hispanic Americans. She found that there was no significant relationship between the gender or race of the superintendents and their perceptions of their leadership styles and skills.

Hollander and Yoder (1978) reviewed research on gender and leadership and concluded that there were general areas where men and women differ in their leadership. They found that men focus more on achieving success in tasks while women seek interpersonal successes; women put more energy into creating a positive group effort; men focus on displaying recognizable leader behavior. They concluded that the differences that they noted in male and female leader behavior are related to role expectations, style, and situational characteristics.

Chapman (1975) compared the leadership styles of males and females. He concluded that differences in male and female leader behavior may result from pressures to display behaviors that are consistent with societal and cultural expectations. In a study of supervisor ratings, female supervisors received higher scores than men in the areas of being friendly, expressing appreciation for good work, and agreeing on values. In addition, female supervisors were less likely to be avoided by subordinates than were male supervisors (Munson, 1979). The Chapman and Munson studies suggest that societal expectations of appropriate female and male behavior are implicated in the ways in which leaders are evaluated. Women are expected to be warm, sympathetic, aware of others' feelings, and helpful. Men are viewed as self-assertive and dominant (Ashmore, Del Boca, and Wohlers, 1986; Williams, 1982).

Morsink (1970) measured twelve dimensions of leader behavior. There were no significant differences between male and female secondary principals on two of the dimensions: tolerance of uncertainty and consideration. Male principals in the study were perceived as having a greater tolerance of freedom than did women principals. While the difference was not significant, female principals were viewed as demonstrating a higher level of consideration than male principals. They generally spoke and acted as a representative of their group, maintained cordial relations with their superiors, and tried to influence them. The idea that females focus on consideration is supported by Josefowitz's (1980) finding that female managers were twice as accessible as male managers. Josefowitz noted that female managers, unlike male managers, tended to maintain an open-door rather than a closed-door policy, did not use their secretaries to screen their calls, and encouraged telephone calls to their homes in the evenings and on weekends.

Pitner (1981) observed three women superintendents for one week to determine whether male and female superintendents focus on different work activities. She found that the nature of the work that men and women superintendents performed was essentially the same. There were, however, some differences in the ways that they handled routine paperwork and the ways in which they observed in schools. The female superintendents in the study interacted more frequently with their peers and female counterparts and used a more informal communication style and language than did males. They also spent more of their unscheduled time working on curriculum and instruction and tended to eat lunch alone at their desks instead of in restaurants.

Pratt (1980) used case studies of critical incidents in leaderless task-oriented small groups to examine seven leadership factors, including the leadership style of males and females. She found that there were no differences between males and females on any of the seven factors, including leadership style. Pratt concluded that, in general, there are more similarities than there are differences between male and female leaders.

In the 1980s women began to challenge openly the idea that masculine characteristics are associated with effective leadership. They argued that intuitiveness, caring, and other characteristics that are typically associated with women make for better managers and leaders (Helgesen, 1990; Loden, 1985; Rosener, 1990). While this line of research presents female characteristics in a more positive light, it maintains the dichotomy between males and females and reinforces a monolithic view of women. That limited view of women is related to their underrepresentation in educational leadership positions (Nichols, 1993). If a decision maker accepts the idea that men are self-assertive and women are caring, it is understandable why a man would be selected over a woman for a job that requires an assertive leader.

Studies of the kind reported here have several limitations. They tend not to focus on the variations within groups of males and females even though there is tremendous intragroup variation (Epstein, 1988, 1991; Fierman, 1990). Some males are more similar to females than to males and some females are more similar to males than to other females. Intragroup differences as well as similarities need further exploration. By focusing on differences between males and females we essentially deny the variation that exists within each group.

The lack of attention to variation within groups is further complicated by the methodology employed in many studies. Most use a form of survey research. Surveys rely on self-report data and are limited to the respondents' frame of reference. Research on the actual behavior of male and female managers does not always support the self-report perceptions through which male and female leaders describe themselves (Epstein, 1988, 1991).

Minorities and Educational Leadership

Research on minorities in school administration is almost exclusively on African Americans. The author was able to locate only two dissertations completed between 1964 and 1989 that were on Latino school administrators. None were located that focused primarily on Native Americans or Asians. Data on Asian Americans, Native Americans, and Latinos are limited to a small number of broad-based surveys of school administrators. In general, those studies simply indicate the number of minorities that serve in specified job categories. They do not provide information on the characteristics of Latino, Asian, or Native American administrators (Lovelady-Dawson, 1980).

Compared to women and White males, there are relatively few studies on minorities in educational leadership. Available research, however, suggests that there are significant differences in the experiences of minority, women, and White male leaders. One of the primary differences involves community relations. African American school administrators tend to be very closely tied to the minority community. Johnston, Yeakey, and Holden (1979) found that African American superintendents often reflect the needs and priorities of their client communities, and that those communities are largely Black. African American principals, to a greater extent than their White colleagues, involve parents and members of the community in school activities (Monteiro, 1977). In a study of African American principals, Lomotey (1989) found that one of the characteristics of African American principals in more successful elementary schools was "a deep compassion for, and understanding of, their students and of the communities in which they work" (p. 150).

Characteristics of Minority Female School Administrators

Edson (1987) has conducted several studies that included minority women in school administration. She argues that there may be a connection between the small number of studies on minority women in school administration and the low number of minority women actually in school administration. This intriguing hypothesis ties together two important realities: Minority females are underrepresented in leadership research and in educational administration. The lack of research on minority female school administrators makes identifying their characteristics much more problematic than identifying the characteristics of White administrators. In a national survey of school superintendents, Schuster (1987) found that no single category of minority women held more than 2 percent of any school administrative position. Revere (1985) found that out of 16,000 public school superintendents, only 29 were African American women. Research that highlights the nature of minority female underrepresentation in educational leadership will not only publicize this problem; it can also serve as a departure point for action to rectify it.

Research on minority women is often incorporated into larger studies of women. Edson's (1987) comprehensive study of female administrative aspirants included 36 minority females: 27 of the women were Black, 7 were Hispanic, 1 was Asian, and 1 was American Indian. Both the minority and White women in Edson's study agreed that race and gender significantly affected their career aspirations. They also acknowledged that competition exists between minority and White females. This finding raises an important question about the extent to which White women and women of color will support and cooperate with each other in what could be called a zero sum game. The reality of competition in the workplace may result in the perception that the advancement of one group of females may hinder the advancement of other groups. Edson (1988) concludes her discussion of minority female administrative aspirants by stating, "Until the field of administration welcomes all female candidates, no matter what their color, minority issues will continue to complicate the lives of minority and nonminority women alike" (p. 193).

Minority females embody two status roles—one related to gender and one related to ethnicity. Doughty (1980) argues that those status roles have negative consequences for Black women who want to enter educational administration. She states that African American female administrators have to cope with the popular myth that Black women are superhuman, capable of solving any problem and dealing with any crisis, and stronger than other women and African American men.

In 1980 Doughty surveyed Black administrators in school districts with populations of 100,000 or more. Data were collected from 1,004 Black administrators. Of those administrators, 250 were Black females. Doughty found that Black females tended to be at the bottom of the administrative hierarchy. White men held top positions such as superintendent and Black males were next, followed by White females. Black females were last. Black females in the study held positions such as supervisor, administrative assistant, and elementary principal.

Doughty (1980) also found that Black and White females who enter educational administration share a number of characteristics. Like White women, Black female administrators tend to be older than male administrators. Most of the women in the study were in their middle forties to middle fifties before they became administrators. Also like White females, Black female administrators, as compared to males, have more education and have spent more time teaching before moving into administration. Doughty also found that the Black females she studied had positive perceptions of themselves and their ability to do their jobs. They tended to reject descriptions of themselves as tokens and felt that they were hired and promoted because of their credentials and past performance.

In an article on Black professional women, Epstein (1972) argued that Black women were in great demand in the labor market because they satisfy two affirmative action criteria: sex and race. Doughty (1980) responded to Epstein in an article on Black female administrators. She argued that Department of Labor statistics clearly indicate that the dual status of minority and female results in lower earning power for Black women than for Black men, White women, and White men. Doughty concludes that the perception that Black women get top jobs because they are minority women is a myth. She challenges her readers to carefully look at the positions Black women hold in educational administration. She notes that they are usually assistants to superintendents, supervisors, vice principals, or elementary principals. Doughty's position that African American women may be doubly challenged by the dual barriers of gender and race is supported by Ortiz (1982) and Korah (1990). They also conclude that while women and minorities encounter barriers to leadership positions, minority women confront both gender and racial barriers.

The Effect of Race and Gender on Career Patterns

Data developed by AASA (1960, 1985) suggest that access to high-level administrative positions is limited to individuals who have followed specific career patterns (1960). While career patterns leading to superintendencies vary over time, two patterns are commonly followed. In school districts with 100,000 or more students, the typical career pattern of superintendents is from teacher to principal to central office administrator to superintendent. In smaller school districts, the most common career pattern leading to a superintendency is from teacher to principal to superintendent.

In a survey of seventy-eight Black superintendents and on-site interviews with six of the superintendents, Banks (1988) found that Black superintendents progressed through a career path that included teacher, principal, assistant superintendent, and superintendent. Most of the Blacks in the survey were in their first superintendency and had served in that position for an average of 6.6 years. The superintendents indicated that their career development had been aided by mentors who took a personal interest in their careers.

Keim (1978) compared the career paths and expectations of 470 male and female superintendents in Pennsylvania. She found that there were significant differences between male and female career paths leading to superintendents. Women tended to teach longer before entering administration and had more certificates and doctorates than did the men in the study.

Revere (1985) conducted one of the few studies investigating the career patterns of minority women. Based on data from her interviews, she concluded that there was no single career pattern that described the accession of minority women to the superintendency. The factors that led to their rise to the superintendency were their self-confidence, industriousness, productivity, and ability to work well with people. Most of the women in the study were married and felt that their husbands were an important source of support.

In another study on the career paths of minority women, Bulls (1986) used ethnographic case studies to investigate the behavioral strategies used by nine Black female leaders to attain superintendencies. Attaining access to high-level administrative positions requires that African American females engage in highly purposeful behavior. For example, Bulls concluded that a doctorate was essential for African American females to become superintendents. Securing mentors, balancing feminine and masculine qualities, networking with other Black female superintendents, and obtaining a visible position in the central office were also identified as critical steps for career advancement.

Ortiz (1982) found that White males, unlike women and minorities, were socialized as teachers to enter administration. When they were assigned to vice-principalships, they were able to move away gradually from work with children and instruction and to assume more administrative responsibilities. As work demands increased, men generally had a supportive and compassionate environment in which to assimilate a new understanding of themselves and their work.

Women were more likely to move into positions where they would continue to see children as central to their work (Ortiz, 1982). Role conflict can occur when women are placed in administrative positions if they believe their children and instruction are supposed to be their primary concern. Ortiz concludes that this role conflict is often viewed as incompetency. She states that one serious consequence of this role conflict is that women may try to resolve it by accentuating male behaviors, an adaptive behavior that is often viewed as unfeminine and may result in increased role conflict.

Minorities frequently enter educational administration through special project positions (Ortiz, 1982). In general, their prior administrative work has focused on working with minorities or on minority issues. These kinds of administrative positions do not prepare them to move away from children and instruction as a primary concern and to administer and manage other adults from a wide range of ethnic groups. In similar fashion, most Whites are not given an opportunity to develop the skills and knowledge necessary to work effectively with traditional minorities and to address minority issues.

Key Factors in the Underrepresentation of Minorities and Women Educational Leaders

Educational administration is highly stratified by race and gender (Ortiz, 1982; Ortiz and Marshall, 1988). The high number of female teachers and the low number of female administrators is an example of stratification by gender (Ortiz and Marshall, 1988). A number of explanations have been offered to account for the low numbers of women and minorities in educational administration. One commonly accepted explanation is that women and minorities are not motivated to enter administration. The research, however, does not support that claim. Diaz (1976) studied male and female teachers and found that women are more highly motivated than males to become administrators. Ortiz and Covel (1978) found that women have high career aspirations. After an extensive case study of a female principal, they concluded that "women have the same career ambitions as men, but they do not have the same opportunities" (p. 214). This conclusion is supported by Valverde (1974), who found that women and minorities held high career aspirations.

In a review of research on women in educational administration, Ortiz and Marshall (1988) concluded that women are underrepresented in educational leadership because of the way in which school administration has developed. They state that over the years school administration developed into a field that favors men over women. They identify four themes that dominated the development of educational administration: (a) teaching and administration were increasingly seen as separate but mutually dependent professions, with women in classroom teaching positions and men in administrative positions; (b) the structure of schools changed, making them more hierarchical and professional; (c) open competition decreased as sponsorship became viewed as the way to build a career in educational administration; and (d) the discussion of gender and power issues was discouraged (Ortiz and Marshall, 1988).

Research conducted by Pavan (1982) suggests that the low number of female administrators is not due to women's lack of qualifications. She found that a number of qualified females in the administrative job pool in Pennsylvania did not hold administrative positions. The women were not selected for administrative positions for several reasons, including sex-role stereotyping. Sex-role stereotyping can exist in employee selection, placement, disciplinary decisions, and preferences for supervisory behaviors (Rosen and Jerdee, 1974a, 1974b, 1974c, 1975). The extent of sex-role stereotyping is related to variables such as the percentage of women on the school board (Forlines, 1984) and the extent to which the individuals involved in the selection process have worked with a female administrator (Mack, 1981).

Woo (1985) surveyed 450 top women educational leaders. He found that many of the factors that were identified in earlier research as important variables in increasing or negating success for women were not identified as such by the women he surveyed. For example, the women in Woo's sample did not believe that affirmative action, flexible working hours, fear of success, mentors, and the "Cinderella syndrome" had any effect on their careers. They did, however, believe that factors such as assertiveness training and career guidance had a small effect on their careers. They believed the greatest obstacle to their career advancement was the lack of job opportunities.

In a 1979 nationwide survey of men and women superintendents, Richardson found that both males and females believed gender was a factor in their career development. Males believed their gender helped them attain administrative positions. Females believed their gender was of no help or was a hindrance. Even though both males and females believed that gender was a factor in access to administrative positions, affirmative action programs were not viewed positively by White males. Nasstrom and Butler (1975) found that male educators have a negative attitude toward affirmative action programs for female educators. Their attitudes were based on (a) their belief that women were not prepared to hold a wider role, (b) perceived differences in leadership behavior between males and females, and (c) concern for their job security.

In 1979 Edson (1988) began a longitudinal study of 142 women who were seeking their first principalship. The initial data collection occurred in 1979–1980. A career update was conducted in 1984–1985. Edson's study of these 142 women provides some important information about the goals, attitudes, career progress, and concerns of women pursuing administrative careers. The subjects varied in age, race, and marital status. They lived all over the United States in cities, suburbs, and rural communities located in the South, West, Northwest, Midwest, Southeast, and Northeast. The women gave three reasons for seeking administrative careers: personal growth and challenge, concern about what was happening to children in schools, and their belief that they could do a better job than current administrators.

Edson's (1988) findings contradict earlier studies that concluded that (a) women were not interested in administration, (b) they would not move to further their careers, (c) family responsibilities were a burden and made career advancement difficult for women, and (d) female educators were uncomfortable with decision and policy making and therefore preferred support, not line, positions (Lesser, 1978; Paddock, 1981). The women Edson studied wanted careers in educational administration and the power and authority to change schools. Twenty-seven percent of the women in the study wanted to become superintendents, 13 percent hoped to become assistant superintendents, 14 percent identified secondary principalships as a career goal, and 26 percent named elementary school principalships as their highest career goal.

Unlike women in earlier studies, the women in the Edson (1988) study were not place-bound. Seventy-five percent of the women in the Edson study indicated that they would move out of their districts and 40 percent indicated that they would move out of their state for improved career opportunities. Only 26 percent of the 42 subjects indicated that their family responsibilities were a problem. Edson's findings on family responsibility are supported by McCamey (1976) who, in a study of African American and White female administrators, found that the women administrators did not believe that they had trouble combining family life and marriage with a career.

Epstein (1970) identified several processes by which male-dominated professions limit the participation of women. Those processes include institutionalized channels of recruitment and protégé systems that are not easily available to women. One of the pressures that women confront when they enter a male-dominated occupation is the inability to obtain information through the "good old boy" network (Harragon, 1977). Surveys of female educators often, although not always, identify the lack of mentors as an important reason why more women are not school administrators (Diaz, 1976; Jones and Montenegro, 1982; Schmuck, Charters, and Carlson, 1981). Pavan's (1987) survey of women administrators in Pennsylvania suggested that men and women have about the same number of mentoring experiences. More women than men, however, reported that mentoring functions were helpful.

The importance of sponsorship and mentoring has been documented in several studies (Collins, 1983; Misserian, 1982; Valverde, 1980; Villani, 1983). While the two concepts are frequently used interchangeably, there are subtle differences between them (Villani, 1983). Sponsors help locate their protégés in positions where they receive informal career socialization experiences. These informal experiences include meeting and interacting with members of the administrator group (Valverde, 1980; Villani, 1983). Valverde (1980) interviewed six mentors to gather information on the sponsor-protégé process. He found that mentors provide four basic functions: exposure, advice, protection, and sanction. Misserian's (1982) survey of women managers resulted in a list of fourteen mentoring behaviors. Collins (1983) surveyed 400 women and identified a similar list of fifteen mentoring behaviors. Mentoring can thus be viewed as a more personal, complex process than sponsorship.

The Future Study of Educational Leadership

A review of dissertations completed between 1964 and 1989, conducted by the author, indicates that studies of educational leaders were very limited in their scope. They tend to focus on educational leaders in a region or state. They also tend to focus on one key variable such as gender, ethnicity, leadership style, or career patterns. They do not usually examine several variables or attempt to identify intersections among them. Future research needs to have a broader scope and to reflect the dynamics of race and gender within the changing nature of our society. As a socially constructed phenomenon, leadership must also be examined within the changing meanings of race and gender.

Future research must look more deeply at the potential benefits of diverse leadership. Commenting on the state of research in educational leadership, F. I. Ortiz (personal communication, 1993) notes that research to date has not specified why it is necessary for women and people of color to assume leadership positions in educational organizations; what women and people of color contribute to educational administration, schools, and society as leaders of educational institutions; and how women and people of color are to be integrated within the leadership ranks of the educational enterprise. Ortiz's point is well taken because, while it is clear that educational administration is stratified by race and gender, relatively little is known about the employment experiences of women and people of color within the dynamics of race and gender in schools. Additional information is needed about the socialization of women and people of color in the workplace. We also need to know more about the initiation process that women and minorities experience when they enter administrative positions.

The roles of minorities and women in our society are clearly changing, and those changes may be reflected in the career patterns and in the leadership and managerial styles and skills of educational leaders. A multicultural approach to research on educational leadership invites opportunities for researchers to use a multidisciplinary approach to examine the intersections of race and gender. Important insights can be gained from comparing and contrasting the experiences of women and people of color in educational leadership. A multicultural approach adds a new dimension to the study of leadership and provides a basis for developing more comprehensive and inclusive approaches for theory and practice.

While there continues to be a significant underrepresentation of women and people of color in educational leadership, firm explanations for the underrepresentation continue to elude us. In terms of advanced training, degrees held, number of years in the profession, and total numbers in the pool from which administrators are drawn, there is no justification for the small number of women and minority educational leaders. Research is needed to explicate the ways in which gender and race affect the recruitment, selection, and retention process for school administrators.

In conclusion, the study of women and people of color presents many challenges to researchers. It also holds out the promise that insights gained from such research will lead to more inclusive leadership that represents the diversity in our pluralistic society. As our knowledge about the experiences of women and minorities in educational leadership deepens, we may be better able to select, train, and nurture more effective leaders for schools in the twenty-first century.

REFERENCES

Adkinson, J. A. "Women in School Administration: A Review of the Research." *Review of Educational Research,* 1981, *51,* 311–343.

American Association of School Administrators. *Profile of the School Superintendent.* Washington, D.C.: American Association of School Administrators, 1960.

American Association of School Administrators. *Women and Minorities in School Administration.* Arlington, Va.: American Association of School Administrators, 1985.

Argyris, C., and Schön, D. A. *Theory in Practice: Increasing Professional Effectiveness.* San Francisco: Jossey-Bass, 1974.

Ashmore, R. D., Del Boca, F. K., and Wohlers, A. J. "Gender stereotypes." In R. D. Ashmore and F. K. Del Boca (eds.), *The Social Psychology of Female-Male Relations: A Critical Analysis of Central Concepts* (pp. 69–119). Orlando, Fla.: Academic Press, 1986.

Astin, H. S. *The Woman Doctorate in America: Origins, Career and Family.* New York: Russell Sage Foundation, 1969.

Astin, H. S., and Leland, C. *Women of Influence, Women of Vision.* San Francisco: Jossey-Bass, 1991.

Bales, R. F. "A Set of Categories for the Analysis of Small Group Interaction." *American Sociological Review,* 1950, *15,* 257–263.

Banks, C.A.M. "City School Superintendents: Their Career Patterns, Traits, and Perceptions of Leadership and Managerial Skill and Style." Unpublished doctoral dissertation, Seattle University, 1991.

Banks, C. M. "The Black School Superintendent: A Study in Early Childhood Socialization and Career Development." Unpublished doctoral dissertation, University of Pittsburgh, 1988.

Bass, B. M. *Stogdill's Handbook of Leadership.* New York: Free Press, 1981.

Bayes, M., and Newton, P. M. "Women in Authority: Sociopsychological Analysis." *Journal of Applied Behavioral Science,* 1978, *14,* 7–20.

Beck, H. N. "Attitudes Toward Women Held by California School District Board Members, Superintendents, and Personnel Directors Including a

Review of the Historical, Psychological, and Sociological Foundations." Unpublished doctoral dissertation, University of the Pacific, Stockton, Calif., 1978.

Bell, D. J. *Power, Influence, and Authority.* New York: Oxford University Press, 1975.

Bem, S. L., and Bem, D. J. *Training the Woman to Know Her Place: The Social Antecedents of Women in the World of Work.* 1975. (ERIC Document Reproduction Service No. ED 082 098)

Bernard, J. S. *Academic Women.* University Park: Pennsylvania State University Press, 1964.

Biklen, S. K., and Brannigan, M. B. (eds.). *Women and Educational Leadership.* Lexington, Mass.: D.C. Heath, 1980.

Blau, P. M. *Exchange and Power in Social life.* New York: Wiley, 1976.

Broverman, I. R., Broverman, D. M., Clarkson, F. E., Rosenkrantz, P. S., and Vogel, S. R. "Sex-Role Stereotypes and Clinical Judgments of Mental Health Professionals." *Journal of Consulting and Clinical Psychology,* 1970, *34,* 1–7.

Broverman, I. R., Vogel, S. R., Broverman, D. M., Clarkson, F. E., and Rosenkrantz, P. S. "Sex-Role Stereotypes: A Current Appraisal." *Journal of Social Issues,* 1972, *28*(2), 59–78.

Brown, L. K., and Klein, K. H. "Woman Power in Medical Hierarchy." *Journal of American Medical Women's Association,* 1982, *37,* 155–164.

Brown, S. M. "Male Versus Female Leaders: A Comparison of Empirical Studies." *Sex Roles: A Journal of Research,* 1979, *5*(5), 595–611.

Bulls, G. P. "Career Development of the Black Female Superintendent." Unpublished doctoral dissertation, University of Pennsylvania, 1986.

Burns, J. M. *Leadership.* New York: Harper and Row, 1979.

Butler, J. E., and Walter, J. C. (eds.). *Transforming the Curriculum: Ethnic Studies and Women's Studies.* Albany: State University of New York Press, 1991.

Byrne, D. R., Hines, S. A., and McCleary, L. E. *The Senior High School Principalship.* Reston, Va.: National Association of School Principals, 1978.

Chapman, J. B. "Comparisons of Male and Female Leadership Style." *Academy of Management Journal,* 1975, *18,* 645–650.

Clement, J. P. *Sex Bias in School Leadership.* Evanston, Ill.: Integrated Education Associates, 1975.

Clifford, G. J. "Marry, Stitch, Die, or Do Worse: Educating Women for Work." In H. Kantor and D. B. Tyack (eds.), *Work, Youth, and Schooling: Historical Perspectives on Vocationalism in American Education* (pp. 223–268). Palo Alto, Calif.: Stanford University Press, 1982.

Collins, N. W. *Professional Women and Their Mentors.* Englewood Cliffs, N.J.: Prentice Hall, 1983.

Cunningham, L. L. "Educational Leadership and Administration: Retrospective and Prospective Views." In L. L. Cunningham and B. Mitchell, *Educational Leadership and Changing Contexts in Families, Communities, and Schools* (pp. 1–18). Chicago: National Society for the Study of Education, 1990.

Cunningham, L. L., and Nystrand, R. O. "Toward Greater Relevance in Preparation Programs for Urban School Administrators." *Educational Administration Quarterly*, 1969, *5*(1), 6–23.

Diaz, S. *The Aspiration Levels of Women for Administrative Careers in Education: Predictive Factors and Implications for Effecting Change.* San Francisco: American Educational Research Association, 1976. (ERIC Document Reproduction Service No. ED 119 376)

Doughty, R. "The Black Female Administrator: Women in a Double Bind." In S. X. Biklen and M. B. Brannigan (eds.), *Women and Educational Leadership* (pp. 165–174). Washington, D.C.: Lexington Books, 1980.

Douglas, L. D., and Simonson, S. V. "A Comparison of Life Experiences and Leader Behaviors Between Male and Female Superintendents." Unpublished doctoral dissertation, Seattle University, 1982.

DuBois, C., and Ruiz, V. L. (eds.). *Unequal Sisters: A Multicultural Reader in U.S. Women's History.* New York: Routledge, 1990.

Dugger, K. "Social Location and Gender-Role Attitudes: A Comparison of Black and White Women." In J. Lorber and S. A. Farrell (eds.), *The Social Construction of Gender* (pp. 38–59). Newbury Park, Calif.: Sage, 1991.

Eagly, A. L., Karau, S. J., and Johnson, B. T. "Gender and Leadership Style among School Principals: A Meta-Analysis." *Educational Administration Quarterly*, 1992, *28*, 76–102.

Edson, S. K. "Voices from the Present: Tracking the Female Administrative Aspirant." *Journal of Educational Equity and Leadership*, 1987, *7*, 261–277.

Edson, S. K. *Pushing the Limits: The Female Administrative Aspirant.* Albany: State University of New York Press, 1988.

Epstein, C. F. *Woman's Place: Options and Limits in Professional Careers.* Berkeley: University of California Press, 1970.

Epstein, C. F. "Positive Effects of the Multiple Negative: Explaining the Success of Black Professional Women." *American Journal of Sociology*, 1972, *78*, 912–915.

Epstein, C. F. *Deceptive Distinctions.* New Haven, Conn.: Yale University Press, 1988.

Epstein, C. F. "Ways Men and Women Lead." *Harvard Business Review*, 1991, *69*(1), 150–153.

Evers, C. W., and Lokomski, G. *Knowing Educational Administration: Contemporary Methodological Controversies in Educational Administration Research.* New York: Pergamon Press, 1991.

Feistritzer, C. E. *Profile of Teachers in the U.S.: 1990.* Washington, D.C.: National Center for Education Information, 1990.

Fernberger, S. W. "Persistence of Stereotypes Concerning Sex Differences." *Journal of Abnormal and Social Psychology,* 1948, *43,* 97–101.

Fiedler, F. E. *A Theory of Leadership Effectiveness.* New York: McGraw-Hill, 1967.

Fierman, J. "Do Women Manage Differently?" *Fortune,* Dec. 1990, pp. 115–118.

Fleishman, E. A. "The Description of Supervisory Behavior." *Journal of Applied Psychology,* 1953, *37,* 1–6.

Fleishman, E. A. "A Leader Behavior Description for Industry." In R. M. Stogdill and A. E. Coons (eds.), *Leader Behavior: Its Description and Measurement* (pp. 89–120). Columbus: Bureau of Business Research, Ohio State University, 1957.

Forlines, A. H. "Superintendents' Perceptions of Public Opinions Toward Women Administrators and Superintendents' Opinions Toward Women Administrators." Unpublished doctoral dissertation, George Peabody College for Teachers, Vanderbilt University, 1984.

Franklin, J. H. *The Color Line: Legacy for the Twenty-First Century.* Columbia: University of Missouri Press, 1993.

Frasher, J. M., and Frasher, R. S. "Educational Administration: A Feminine Profession." *Educational Administration Quarterly,* 1979, *2,* 1–13.

Freeman, J. (ed.). *Women: A Feminist Perspective* (3rd ed.). Palo Alto, Calif.: Mayfield, 1984.

French, J.R.P., Jr., and Raven, B. "The Bases of Social Power." In D. Catwright and A. Zander (eds.), *Group Dynamics: Research and Theory* (pp. 607–623). New York: Harper and Row, 1960.

Friedan, B. *The Feminine Mystique.* New York: Dell, 1963.

Gaertner, K. N. "The Structure of Organizational Careers." *Sociology of Education,* 1980, *53,* 7–20.

Goode, W. J. "A Theory of Role Strain." *American Sociological Review,* 1960, *25,* 483–495.

Goslin, D. A. (ed.). *Handbook of Socialization Theory and Research.* Chicago: Rand McNally, 1969.

Gross, E., and Etzioni, A. *Organizations in Society.* Englewood Cliffs, N.J.: Prentice Hall, 1985.

Gross, N., Mason, W. S., and McEachern, A. W. *Explorations in Role Analysis: Studies of the School Superintendency Role.* New York: Wiley, 1958.

Gross, N., and Trask, A. E. *The Sex Factor and the Management of Schools.* New York: Wiley, 1976.

Hagen, R., and Kahn, A. "Discrimination Against Competent Women." *Journal of Applied Social Psychology,* 1975, *41,* 362–376.

Halpin, A. W., and Winer, B. J. "A Factorial Study of the Leader Behavior Descriptions." In R. M. Stogdill and A. E. Coons (eds.), *Leader Behavior: Its Description and Measurement* (pp. 190–235). Columbus: Bureau of Business Research, Ohio State University, 1957.

Harragon, B. L. *Games Mother Never Taught You: Corporate Gamesmanship for Women.* New York: Warner Books, 1977.

Helgesen, S. *The Female Advantage: Women's Ways of Leadership.* Garden City, N.Y.: Doubleday, 1990.

Hemphill, J. K., and Coons, A. E. "Development of the Leader Behavior Description Questionnaire." In R. M. Stogdill and A. E. Coons (eds.), *Leader Behavior: Its Description and Measurement* (pp. 147–163). Columbus: Bureau of Business Research, Ohio State University, 1957.

Hersey, P. *The Situational Leader.* New York: Warner Books, 1984.

Holden, R. L. *The Chicago Schools: A Social and Political History.* Beverly Hills, Calif.: Sage, 1977.

Hollander, E. P., and Yoder, J. *Some Issues in Comparing Women and Men as Leaders.* 1978. (ERIC Document Reproduction Service No. ED 185 883)

Holter, H. *Sex Roles and Social Structure.* Oslo, Norway: Universitetsforlaget, 1970.

hooks, b. *Yearning: Race, Gender, and Cultural Politics.* Boston: South End Press, 1990.

Horner, M. "Toward Understanding of Achievement-Related Conflicts in Women." In M. R. Walsh (ed.), *The Psychology of Women* (pp. 169–184). New Haven, Conn.: Yale University Press, 1987.

House, R. J., and Baetz, M. L. "Leadership: Some Empirical Generalizations and New Research Directions." In B. M. Staw (ed.), *Research in Organizational Behavior* (Vol. 1). Greenwich, Conn.: JAI, 1979.

Huber, J. *Changing Women in a Changing Society.* Chicago: University of Chicago Press, 1973.

Immegart, G. L. "Leadership and Leader Behavior." In N. J. Boyan (ed.), *Handbook of Research on Educational Administration* (pp. 259–278). New York: Longman, 1988.

Jago, A. G. "Leadership: Perspectives in Theory and Research." *Management Science,* 1982, *28*(3), 315–336.

Janda, K. F. "Towards the Explication of the Concept of Leadership in Terms of the Concept of Power." *Human Relations,* 1960, *13,* 345–363.

Johnston, G. S., Yeakey, C. C., and Holden, R. L. "An Analysis of the External Variables Affecting the Role of the Black School Superintendent." *Educational Research Quarterly,* 1979, *4,* 13–24.

Johnston, G. S., Yeakey, C. C., and Moore, S. E. "Analysis of the Employment of Women in Professional Administrative Positions in Public Education." *Planning and Changing,* 1980, *11,* 115–132.

Jones, E. H. *Black School Administrators: A Review of Their Early History, Trends, Problems in Recruitment.* Arlington, Va.: American Association of School Administrators, 1983.

Jones, E. H., and Montenegro, X. P. *Recent Trends in the Representation of Women and Minorities in School Administration and Problems in Documentation.* Arlington, Va.: American Association of School Administrators, 1982.

Jones, E. H., and Montenegro, X. P. *Women and Minorities in School Administration.* 1990. (ERIC Document Reproduction Service No. ED 273 017)

Josefowitz, N. "Management Men and Women: Closed vs. Open Doors." *Harvard Business Review,* 1980, *58,* 56–62.

Kanter, R. M. *Men and Women of the Corporation.* New York: Basic Books, 1977.

Keim, A. S. "Women and the Superintendency: A Comparison of Male and Female Career Paths and Expectations." Unpublished doctoral dissertation, Lehigh University, Bethlehem, Pa., 1978.

Komarovsky, M. "Cultural Contradictions and Sex Role: The Masculine Case." In J. Huber (ed.), *Chicana Women in a Chicana Society* (pp. 111–112). Chicago: University of Chicago Press, 1973.

Korah, S. "Multiculturalism and the Woman of Colour: Can We Bridge the Gap Between Rhetoric and Reality?" *Tiger Lily: Journal by Women of Colour,* 1990, *6,* 5–20.

Lesser, P. *The Participation of Women in Public School Administration.* 1978. (ERIC Document Reproduction Service No. ED 151 958)

Loden, M. *Feminine Leadership, or How to Succeed in Business Without Being One of the Boys.* New York: Times Books, 1985.

Loewenstine, H. V., Ponticos, G. D., and Pauldi, M. A. "Sex Differences in Graffiti as a Communication Style." *Journal of Social Psychology,* 1982, *117,* 307–328.

Lomotey, K. *African-American Principals: School Leadership and Success.* New York: Greenwood, 1989.

Lovelady-Dawson, F. "Women and Minorities in the Principalship: Career Opportunities and Problems." *NASSP Bulletin,* Dec. 1980, *64,* 18–28.

Mack, M. H. "A Study of Attitude Toward Women as School Administrators." Unpublished doctoral dissertation, Auburn University, Ala., 1981.

Marshall, C. "The Crisis in Excellence and Equity." *Educational Horizons,* 1984, *63,* 24–30.

McCamey, D. S. "The Status of Black and White Women in Central Administrative Positions in Michigan Public Schools." Unpublished doctoral dissertation, University of Michigan, Ann Arbor, 1976.

McCarthy, C., and Crichlow, W. (eds.). *Race Identity and Representation in Education.* New York: Routledge, 1993.

McCarthy, M., and Zent, A. "School Administrators: 1980 Profile." *Planning and Changing,* 1981, *12*(3), 144–161.

McGregor, D. *The Human Side of Enterprise.* New York: McGraw-Hill, 1960.

McIntosh, P. *White Privilege and Male Privilege: A Personal Account of Coming to See Correspondence Through Work in Women's Studies.* Wellesley, Mass.: Wellesley College Center for Research on Women, 1988.

Merton, R. K. *Social Theory and Social Structure.* New York: Macmillan, 1957.

Millett, K. *Sexual Politics.* New York: Ballantine, 1980. (Originally published 1969)

Millham, J., and Smith, L. "Sex Role Differentiation Among Black and White Americans: A Comparative Study." *Journal of Black Psychology,* 1981, *7,* 77–99.

Mills, J. "Self-Imposed Behaviors of Females and Males in Photographs." *Sex Roles,* 1984, *10*(7/8), 633–637.

Misserian, A. K. *The Corporate Connection: Why Executive Women Need Mentors to Reach the Top.* Englewood Cliffs, N.J.: Prentice Hall, 1982.

Monteiro, T. "Ethnicity and the Perceptions of Principals." *Integrated Education,* 1977, *15*(3), 15–16.

Moody, C. D. "Black Superintendents in Public School Districts: Trends and Conditions." Unpublished doctoral dissertation, Northwestern University, Evanston, Ill., 1971.

Morsink, H. M. "Leadership Behavior of Men and Women Principals." *NASSP Bulletin,* 1970, *54*(347), 80–87.

Munson, C. E. "Evaluation of Male and Female Supervisors." *Social Work,* Mar. 1979, *24,* 104–110.

Nasstrom, R. R., and Butler, W. E. "The Professionalism of Women Teachers." *Kappa Delta Pi Record,* 1975, *12*(1), 6–8.

National Center for Educational Statistics. *The Condition of Education 1991: Vol. 2. Postsecondary Education.* Washington, D.C.: U.S. Department of Education, 1991.

Neely, M. A., and Wilson, A. E. *A Program to Overcome Sex Bias in Women's Qualifications for Vocational Administration Posts.* 1978. (ERIC Document Reproduction Service No. ED 166 391)

Nichols, N. A. "Whatever Happened to Rosie the Riveter?" *Harvard Business Review,* 1993, 71(4), 54–62.

O'Leary, V. E. "Some Attitudinal Barriers to Occupational Aspirations in Women." *Psychological Bulletin,* 1974, 81, 809–826.

Ortiz, F. I. *Career Patterns in Education: Men, Women and Minorities in Public School Administration.* New York: Praeger, 1982.

Ortiz, F. I., and Covel, J. "Women in School Administration: A Case Analysis." *Urban Education,* 1978, 13, 213–236.

Ortiz, F. I., and Marshall, C. "Women in Educational Administration." In N. J. Boyan (ed.), *Handbook of Research on Educational Administration* (pp. 123–141). New York: Longman, 1988.

Paddock, S. C. "Male and Female Career Paths in School Administration." In P. A. Schmuck, W. W. Charters, Jr., and R. O. Carlson (eds.), *Educational Policy and Management: Sex Differentials* (pp. 35–52). New York: Academic Press, 1981.

Parsons, T. *The Social System.* New York: Free Press, 1951.

Pavan, B. N. *Certified but Not Hired: Women Administrators in Pennsylvania.* 1982. (ERIC Document Reproduction Service No. ED 263 689)

Pavan, B. N. "Mentoring Certified Aspiring and Incumbent Female and Male Public School Administrators." *Journal of Educational Equity and Leadership,* 1987, 7(4), 318–331.

Pelz, D. C. "Influence: A Key to Effective Leadership in the First-Line Supervisor." *Personnel,* 1952, 29, 209–217.

Perkins, L. M. "The History of Blacks in Teaching: Growth and Decline Within the Profession." In D. Warren (ed.), *American Teachers: Histories of a Profession at Work* (pp. 344–369). New York: Macmillan, 1989.

Peshkin, A. *Growing up American.* Chicago: University of Chicago Press, 1978.

Peterson, P. *The Politics of School Reform 1870–1940.* Chicago: University of Chicago Press, 1985.

Petty, M. M., and Miles, R. H. "Leader Sex-Role Stereotyping in a Female-Dominated Work Culture." *Personnel Psychology,* 1976, 29, 393–404.

Phillips, D. L., and Voorhees, S. V. "Attitudes Toward Female School Administrators in the State of Washington." Unpublished doctoral dissertation, Seattle University, 1986.

Pinar, W. F. "Notes on Understanding Curriculum as a Racial Text." In C. McCarthy and W. Crichlow (eds.), *Race Identity and Representation in Education* (pp. 60–70). New York: Routledge, 1993.

Pitner, N. J. "Notes on the Differences in Behavior of Women Superintendents in Suburban Districts." Paper presented at the annual meeting of the American Educational Research Association, Los Angeles, 1981.

Popenoe, D. *Sociology.* New York: Meredith Corporation, 1971.

Pratt, J.M.M. "A Case Study Analysis of Male-Female Leadership Emergence in Small Groups." Unpublished doctoral dissertation, University of Minnesota, Minneapolis, 1980.

Revere, A.L.B. *A Description of the Black Female Superintendent.* Unpublished doctoral dissertation, Miami University, 1985.

Richardson, J.A.M. "Women Superintendents of Public Schools in the United States: Factors Contributing to Obtaining the Position." Unpublished doctoral dissertation, Drake University, Des Moines, Iowa, 1979.

Rosen, B., and Jerdee, T. H. "Influence of Sex Role Stereotypes on Personnel Decisions." *Journal of Applied Psychology,* 1974a, *59,* 9–14.

Rosen, B., and Jerdee, T. H. "Effects of Applicant's Sex and Difficulty of Job Evaluations of Candidates for Managerial Positions." *Journal of Applied Psychology,* 1974b, *59,* 511–512.

Rosen, B., and Jerdee, T. H. "Sex Stereotyping in the Executive Suite." *Harvard Business Review,* 1974c, *52,* 45–58.

Rosen, B., and Jerdee, T. H. "Effects of Employee's Sex and Threatening Versus Pleading Appeals on Managerial Evaluations of Grievances." *Journal of Applied Psychology,* 1975 60(4), 442–445.

Rosener, J. B. "Ways Women Lead." *Harvard Business Review,* 1990, 68(6), 119–125.

Rossi, A. S. "Sex Equality: The Beginning of Ideology." In M. L. Thompson (ed.), *Voices of the New Feminism* (pp. 113–147). New York: McGraw-Hill, 1970.

Rost, J. C. *Leadership for the Twenty-First Century.* Westport, Conn.: Praeger, 1991.

Ruble, T. L. "Sex Stereotypes: Issues and Change in the 1970s." *Sex Roles,* 1983, *9,* 397–402.

Saks, J. B. "Education Vital Signs." *American School Board Journal,* Dec. 1992, pp. 32–45.

Schmuck, P. A. "Changing Women's Representation in School Management: A Systems Perspective." In S. K. Biklen and M. B. Brannigan (eds.), *Women and Educational Leadership* (pp. 242–263). Lexington, Mass.: D. C. Heath, 1980.

Schmuck, P. A., Charters, W. W., Jr., and Carlson, R. O. (eds.). *Educational Policy and Management: Sex Differentials.* New York: Academic Press, 1981.

Schuster, D. J. "Male and Female Superintendents Compared Nationally: Career Implications for Women in Educational Administration." Unpublished doctoral dissertation, Teachers College, Columbia University, New York, 1987.

Scott, H. J. *The Black School Superintendent: Messiah or Scapegoat?* Washington, D.C.: Howard University Press, 1980.

Scott, H. J. "Views of Black School Superintendents on School Desegregation." *Journal of Negro Education,* 1983, 52(4), 378–382.

Shakeshaft, C. S. "Dissertation Research on Women in Educational Administration: A Synthesis of Findings and Paradigm for Future Research." (Doctoral dissertation, Texas A&M University, 1979.) *Dissertation Abstracts International,* 1979, 40, 6455a.

Shakeshaft, C. S. "Strategies for Overcoming the Barriers to Women in Educational Administration." In S. Klein (ed.), *Handbook for Achieving Sex Equity Through Education* (pp. 124–144). Baltimore, Md.: Johns Hopkins University Press, 1985.

Shakeshaft, C. S. *Women in Educational Administration.* Newbury Park, Calif.: Sage, 1987.

Sizemore, B. A. "The Limits of the Black Superintendency: A Review of the Literature." *Journal of Educational Equity and Leadership,* 1986, 6(3), 180–208.

Sleeter, C. E. "How White Teachers Construct Race." In C. McCarthy and W. Crichlow (eds.), *Race Identity and Representation in Education* (pp. 157–171). New York: Routledge, 1993.

Snyder, T. D. *Digest of Educational Statistics.* Washington, D.C.: National Center for Educational Statistics, Government Printing Office, 1989.

Spencer, G. *Projections of the Hispanic Population: 1983–2080* (Current Population Reports, Series P-25, No. 995). Washington, D.C.: U.S. Bureau of the Census, 1986.

Stevens, K. M. *Profiles of Washington State Women School Superintendents.* Unpublished doctoral dissertation, Seattle University, 1988.

Stogdill, R. H. *Manual for the Leader Behavior Description Questionnaire—Form XII.* Columbus: Bureau of Business Research, Ohio State University, 1963.

Stogdill, R. H. *Handbook of Leadership: A Survey of Theory and Research.* New York: Free Press, 1974.

Taylor, S. S. "The Attitudes of Superintendents and Board of Education Members in Connecticut Toward the Employment and Effectiveness of Women as Public School Administrators." Unpublished doctoral dissertation, University of Connecticut, Storrs, 1971.

Toren, N. "The Bus Driver: A Study in Role Analysis." *Human Relations,* 1973, 26(1), 101–112.

U.S. Bureau of the Census. *Statistical Abstract of the United States* (112th ed.). Washington, D.C.: Government Printing Office, 1992.

Valverde, L. A. *Succession Socialization: Its Influence on School Administrative Candidates and Its Implications to the Exclusion of Minorities from Administration.* Austin: University of Texas at Austin, 1974. (ERIC Document Reproduction Service No. 093 052)

Valverde, L. A. "Promotion Socialization: The Informal Process in Large Urban School Districts and Its Adverse Effects on Non-Whites and Women." Paper presented at the meeting of the American Education Research Association, Boston, 1980.

Villani, D. "Mentoring and Sponsoring as Ways for Women to Overcome Internal Barriers to Heightened Career Aspiration and Achievement." Unpublished doctoral dissertation, Northeastern University, Boston, 1983.

Vroom, V. H. "Leadership." In M. Dunnette (ed.), *Handbook of Industrial and Organizational Psychology* (pp. 1527–1552). Chicago: Rand McNally, 1976.

Vroom, V. H., and Yetton, E. W. *Leadership and Decision Making.* Pittsburgh: University of Pittsburgh Press, 1973.

Weber, M. "Economy and Society: An Outline of Interpretive Sociology." In G. Roth and C. Wittich (eds.), *Wirtschaft und Gesellschaft* (E. Fischoff, trans., pp. 28–72). New York: Bedminster Press, 1968.

West, C. *Race Matters.* Boston: Beacon Press, 1993.

White, J. "Women in the Law." *Michigan Law Review,* 1967, 65, 1051.

White, L. T. *Educating our Daughters.* New York: Harper, 1950.

Williams, J. E. "An Overview of Findings from Adult Sex Stereotype Studies in 25 Countries." In R. Rath, H. S. Asthana, D. Sinha, and J. B. Sinha (eds.), *Diversity and Unity in Crosscultural Psychology* (pp. 250–260). Lisse, Netherlands: Swets and Zeitlinger, 1982.

Woo, L. C. "Women Administrators: Profiles of Success." *Phi Delta Kappan,* 1985, 64(4), 285–288.

Yukl, G. A. *Leadership in Organizations* (3rd ed.). Englewood Cliffs, N.J.: Prentice Hall, 1981.

22

GENDER
AND SUPERVISION

Charol Shakeshaft
Irene Nowell
Andy Perry

COMMUNICATION BETWEEN WOMEN AND MEN has long been the basis of both humor and folklore in the human drama of life. From the cry of "What do women want?" to the characterization of men as unable to express emotions, men and women have been stereotyped as people who talk and act differently.

Because these stereotypes have most often been hurtful to women, especially in the workplace, many of us who have struggled to help women achieve equity have resisted the notion of differences between males and females. Nevertheless, in a society that does not treat females and males the same, the impact of gender on behavior is worthy of study.

Based on our experiences as administrators as well as our collective and individual research, we believe that gender affects both supervisory style and outcome. In this article, we examine some of the ways in which gender may influence the supervisory act.

Sex and Gender

Sex is a biological description, one that divides most of humankind into two types of people—females and males. We say most, since even a variable such as sex, which seems to be easily distinguished, has some ambiguity depending upon the evidence used to determine who is male and who is female (Shakeshaft, 1989).

Gender is a cultural term (Shakeshaft, 1989). It describes the characteristics we ascribe to people because of their sex—the ways we believe they behave or the characteristics we believe they possess, based on our cultural expectations of what is male and what is female.

As far as we can determine from our work and the work of others, one's biological identification as male or female has little to do with how people behave and the work they do in schools. However, one's gender identification has a tremendous influence on behavior, perceptions, and effectiveness (Shakeshaft, 1989). In other words, being born female or male does not in itself affect how we will act as workers; however, the way we are *treated* from birth onward, *because* we are either female or male, does help to determine how we both see and navigate the world.

Although the supervision area abounds with theories and scripts, little has been written on the impact of gender on successful supervision. This issue seems particularly salient given the sex structuring of schools, which results in an organization in which males most often supervise females. It takes on added importance if we examine the stereotypic expectations of behavior and status and imagine what implications they might have when the norm is reversed and a female supervises a male.

Communication and Feedback Patterns

Gender and gender expectations may partially determine how supervisors interact with those they supervise. For instance, research suggests that the sex of participants affects what is communicated and how it is communicated (Borisoff and Merrill, 1985). The same words spoken by a male supervisor have different meanings to male and female teachers. Conversely, an interaction between a female principal and a male teacher is not the same as an exchange between a female principal and a female teacher.

Men and women communicate differently and they listen for different information (Borisoff and Merrill, 1985). In a supervisory conference in which a principal is discussing an instructional issue with the teacher, the woman participant may be listening for the feeling and the man for the facts. Given what we know of the values that males and females carry into their jobs in schools, the woman may be focused upon an instructional issue or a matter concerning the child, while the man may choose to discuss an administrative problem.

Further, research supports the notion that there may be discomfort in communicating with a member of the other sex. Male teachers tend to exhibit more hostility in dealing with female administrators than do female teachers, and women administrators have to work harder to get male teachers to "hear" them (Shakeshaft, 1987).

Perceptions of competence may also influence supervisory styles and effectiveness. Women are initially evaluated less favorably than equally competent men (Shakeshaft, 1987). These perceptions may unknowingly affect supervisory interactions, both when the woman is being supervised and when she is the supervisor.

Nowhere does the impact of gender on supervision become more evident than in the area of feedback. Men receive both more and more types than do women. Women are more likely to get nonevaluative feedback, or neutral responses. Men receive more positive and more negative responses (Shakeshaft, 1987).

A 1987 study found that male administrators are less likely to give direct feedback to females than to males (Shakeshaft, 1987). For instance, when a male subordinate makes a mistake or does not live up to the expectations of his boss, his supervisor tends to level with him, "telling it like it is." When a female errs, she often is not even informed. Instead, the mistake is corrected by others without her knowledge. The results of this behavior are two-fold. For the male, learning takes place instantly. He gets criticism and the chance to change his behavior. He learns to deal with negative opinions of his work and has the option to improve.

Females often do not hear anything negative, being given neutral or slightly positive cues, even if their performance is less than ideal. This results in a woman's misconception of her abilities or, at least, the level of her performance. If she is not given direct criticism, she has neither the opportunity to improve nor the opportunity to reassess her abilities.

These differential feedback patterns are not unique to the adult work setting. The work of Sadker and Sadker (1986) describes similar patterns throughout K–12 schooling, where boys receive more feedback and a wider range of feedback than girls. These early differences not only help us understand why we behave as we do when we become adult workers, they also help us understand women's reactions to criticism in the rare instances when they get it first-hand. (Women get criticism; the issue is whether or not they get to hear it.)

In interviews with women administrators (Shakeshaft, 1987), the women were found to take criticism hard. They tended to think it was an assessment of their very essence. The first time they received criticism or the first time they failed, the women administrators interpreted it as a sign that they were inferior and that they never should have tried to become an administrator in the first place. This is not surprising for two reasons. First, females are less valued than males in this society. Consequently, from birth onward through school and into adult life, women receive subtle and not so subtle messages about their worth. These messages are one of the reasons that women have been found to have lower self-esteem than men (Andrews, 1984). Secondly, if, as girls, females received little direct criticism, they had few opportunities to learn not to take critical comments personally.

When male superintendents and principals were asked why they did not confront women with their misgivings and dissatisfactions, one of the major reasons given was the fear of women's tears (Shakeshaft, 1987). Most of the men were uncomfortable with the prospect of tears. When questioned about what they expected from men to whom they gave negative feedback, most anticipated anger. While none of the administrators in this study liked confronting anyone with negative feedback, the prospect of an angry response was easier for them to face than the prospect of tears. Male superintendents and principals said they did not like to deal with angry subordinates, but that they had the skills to do so. They reported being much less comfortable with crying, and, because of this discomfort, most failed to give women important corrective feedback that would have allowed the women to improve their performance as educators.

This information led to an examination of who cries and how often (Shakeshaft, 1989). The results suggested that there is not a great deal of crying in public schools, and that, although women cry in front of supervisors slightly more than men, the difference in frequency is very small. However, women are reported to cry equally often in front of females and males, while males cry only in front of women. Thus, the study suggested that it is the fear of tears—rather than overwhelming evidence of actual crying—that paralyzes male administrators. Also, since both men and women cry, it is not solely a "female" problem. Finally, although crying is not solely a female problem, and although nobody cries very much, the fear of tears (or the gender expectation about what women do) keeps women from getting honest feedback about their performance and impairs the supervisory effectiveness of male administrators.

Thus, gender perceptions are influencing behavior and interfering with effectiveness. The issues are difficult for both men and women. Women must be aware of the feedback loop and try to determine if they are getting helpful evaluative information. Men, on the other hand, often perceive themselves in a "no-win" position. If a man treats a woman as he does a man, he may be accused of being harsh or unfair. If he does not treat a woman as he does a man, he may be accused of not giving her helpful or corrective feedback. We need to examine our expectations about male and female behavior and confront the issue so that both men and women are as effective as they can be in a supervisory relationship.

Influence of Sexuality on Working Relationships

Another factor that may inhibit or interfere with the supervisory act is heterosexuality and our unspoken beliefs about men and women working together. In a study of the hiring practices of male superintendents (Shakeshaft, 1989), they were asked if they would hire a traditionally attractive female. The term "traditionally attractive" was used so that the superintendents could make their own decisions not only about what was attractive, but also about what was attractive within the acceptable range of school administrators. Almost all of the superintendents in the study said they would hire an attractive woman. When asked for what job, almost all suggested an elementary principalship.

In a follow-up question as to whether they would hire this imaginary woman as an assistant superintendent, in a role that worked very closely with the superintendent, very few of the superintendents said they would. The issue for these superintendents was the combination of the intensity of the working relationship and the attractiveness of the woman. Most of them said they felt uncomfortable in a close working relationship with an attractive woman.

One reason given for this lack of comfort was the superintendents' concern that school board members would see something unseemly in the relationship and that this perception would threaten their effectiveness with their boards. Another reason given by the superintendents was their worry that it would cause marital friction, and few wanted "trouble on the home front" added to their already stressful lives. A third reason, and one that may hurt women the most, was an uncertainty on the part of most of the male superintendents about what their own feelings would be toward an attractive female subordinate. If they were sexually attracted to her, it seemed like a no-win situation. If she did not return the feelings, the superintendent ran the risk of being charged with sexual harassment. If the feelings were mutual, the superintendent's first two fears (school board disapproval and marital friction) might become reality. Thus, most of the superintendents concluded that it was not worth the risks to hire an attractive woman (and for many that translated into woman) into a position with which the superintendent worked closely.

Because of the lack of comfort men in school administration have with issues of sexuality, women have been advised to dress and act in ways that suppress or hide their own sexuality. Women's dress for success formulas are more like dress for asexuality than for any criteria associated with success. Men, on the other hand, are advised to wear "power suits," attire that has high sexual appeal among women (Shakeshaft, 1989).

From the woman's perspective, the issue of sexuality is also a problem. Women administrators are often cautious and suspicious of attention from male superordinates, since they are unclear about the underlying message. Whether or not there is a spoken or unspoken sexual message, women process the possibility and think about their responses and actions in light of that possibility (Shakeshaft, 1987).

In addition to the possible negative effects for women of sexual attraction, some positive ones are also possible. Being noticed initially because one is attractive might open professional doors. Just how much attractiveness helps or hurts women in school administration has not been comprehensively explored; however, sexuality issues may be evident in some supervisory interactions and roles. Therefore, women's notions about what is expected of them may get in the way of how they supervise as well as how they respond to supervision.

The discomfort and lack of knowledge in this area is not surprising. The United States is a country not altogether comfortable with sexuality. Sex integration rarely occurs in U.S. school systems. Starting in about the second grade, boys and girls move apart and segregate themselves along sex lines (Best, 1983). Little is done to change this pattern of segregation by sex, and observations of classrooms and playgrounds find ample evidence of boys competing against girls in spelling bees and athletics (Sadker and Sadker, 1986).

When males and females mix again during late adolescence, it is for sexual or romantic reasons. Men and women have little training or practice in working together as people, except as representatives of different sexes. It is not surprising, then, that sexuality (and particularly heterosexuality) gets in the way of easy working relationships between women and men.

This issue of sexuality comes to our attention because it helps to explain some of the reasons why men are reluctant to hire women into jobs that require working together closely. However, further exploration of sexuality highlights the importance of the cultural meanings we give to people because of their sex and the implications these meanings have for administrative behavior. We need to understand how the issue of sexuality overlays the behavior of men and women in organizations and explore how it both helps and hurts the players involved.

Gender Differences in Expectations

Another example of gender differences and the possible effects on supervision is found in a study by Garfinkel (1988). He attempted to determine whether men and women superintendents conceptualize their administrative teams differently and whether these superintendents and their team members value different traits. Garfinkel found that both men and women value competence and trust, but they give each a different priority. For women superintendents, competence is the first thing they look for in a team member; trust is lower on the list. Men superintendents, on the other hand, identify trust as their number one criterion for team membership and view competence as less important.

To complicate matters, especially for team members, men and women define trust differently. According to Garfinkel (1988), men, both superintendents and team members, were more likely to describe trust as the "ability and comfort to say what they wished to say, confident that the persons they were sharing their thoughts or opinions with would not ridicule or repeat these thoughts elsewhere" (p. 311). Women superintendents defined trust as "an expectancy, held by an individual, that the word, promise or written statement of another individual or group can be relied on" (p. 311).

These differing conceptions of trust call for different indicators of proof. For men to see a person as trustworthy, that person must not divulge information or discuss actions or conversations with others. Women did not interpret those actions as untrustworthy. They expected people to discuss conversations, actions, and feelings with others. What women saw as untrustworthy was someone failing to do what they said they would do, when they said they would do it. Men did not identify a person as untrustworthy if he or she did not deliver on time. Rather, men saw that as an issue of time management or competency.

Garfinkel's study indicates that differences do exist in how people evaluate the job performance of those with whom they work and how that evaluation may be related to gender. The results of this study as well as literature that describes women administrators as differing from men led to an investigation by the three of us of differences in the written evaluations of teachers by male and female principals. The work of Shakeshaft (1987) provided a guide for exploring this issue. This earlier research indicated the following:

1. Relationships with others are more central to all actions for female administrators than they are for male administrators.

2. Teaching and learning is more often the major focus for female administrators than for male administrators.

3. Building community is more often an essential part of the woman administrator's style than it is for the man.

In this study, we did a content analysis of the written evaluations of 108 female teachers by 8 principals (5 males and 3 females) to determine whether male and female principals highlighted different things. All of the principals worked in the same school district and had received the same amount of training in the Hunter (1984) technique. The evaluations were coded without knowledge of the sex of the principal; inter-rater reliability was 77 percent.

We did find some differences in the things that women and men focused on. Women were more likely than men to encourage the empowerment of their teachers, establish instructional priorities, attend to the social and emotional development of the students, focus on student relationships, attend to the feelings of teachers, include more "facts" in the evaluation, look for the teachers' effects on the lives of children, emphasize the technical skills of teaching, comment on the content and quality of the educational program, provide information gathered from other sources, involve the teacher in decision making, issue directives for improvement, provide immediate feedback on performance, and emphasize curricular programs. Men, on the other hand, were more likely than women to emphasize organizational structure and to avoid conflict (Shakeshaft, Nowell, and Perry, 1991). Thus, we found that the evaluations of teachers written by female principals focused on more items, and particularly more items concerned with teaching and learning.

These findings support the literature that women may approach the supervisory process by valuing different characteristics and, thus, may concentrate on a different set of criteria than do men. This study suggests that, even when trained in a similar approach to supervisory interaction, males and females may still bring with them expectations and behaviors based upon gender. While this study is in no way definitive, it does provide some additional support for the need to more fully understand gender in all aspects of school administration, especially supervision.

Summary

In our view, gender does make a difference in how administrators behave. Sometimes these behaviors are just different and interesting. At other times, they may signal treatment that is not only different but more favorable to one sex than to another. When the latter is the case, we need to reexamine practice.

To do this, we might first examine ourselves. Having been raised in a sexist society, it is not surprising that we have ideas about what women and men can do and be, how males and females act, and how to treat men and women. We need to acknowledge our backgrounds and training, understanding that we had no control over what we were taught by society, school, and family. We do, however, have control over our actions today.

One way to gauge whether we are applying different expectations and standards to a situation is to imagine a member of the other sex in that situation. For instance, if a woman is working with a man and wonders if she has lowered her expectations, she might pretend he is a woman and consider how that woman would be treated. Another way to gain insight is to transfer knowledge about racism to male-female situations. When characterizing a woman in a particular way, one might consider whether the same characterization would be acceptable when referring to a minority person. Although racism is still strong, Americans have become more cautious about expressing it publicly, and educators have become more able to identify it. The models learned in one area can help us in another.

Addressing these issues with school administrators is crucial if we are to effect change. Research demonstrates that inservice education on these issues has gone a long way toward changing behavior (Grayson, 1988). For a small investment in time and money, districts can reduce the negative effects of gender issues and enhance the positive ones. The result is an environment more supportive of teaching and learning.

REFERENCES

Andrews, P. H. "Performance—Self-Esteem and Perceptions of Leadership Emergence: A Comparative Study of Men and Women." *Western Journal of Speech Communications*, 1984, 48(1), 1–13.

Best, R. *We've All Got Scars*. Bloomington: Indiana University Press, 1983.

Borisoff, D., and Merrill, L. *The Power to Communicate: Gender Differences as Barriers*. Prospect Heights, Ill.: Waveland Press, 1985.

Garfinkel, E. "Ways Men and Women in School Administration Conceptualize the Administrative Team." Unpublished doctoral dissertation, Hofstra University, Hempstead, N.Y., 1988.

Grayson, D. *The Equity Principal*. Earlham, Iowa: Graymill, 1988.

Hunter, M. "Knowing, Teaching, and Supervising." In P. L. Hosford (ed.), *Using What We Know about Teaching* (pp. 169–192). Alexandria, Va.: Association for Supervision and Curriculum Development, 1984.

Sadker, M., and Sadker, D. "Sexism in the Classroom: From Grade School to Graduate School." *Phi Delta Kappan,* 1986, *67,* 512–515.

Shakeshaft, C. *Women in Educational Administration.* Newbury Park, Calif.: Sage, 1987.

Shakeshaft, C. "The Gender Gap in Research in Educational Administration." *Educational Administration Quarterly,* 1989, *25,* 324–337.

Shakeshaft, C., Nowell, I., and Perry, A. Written evaluations of teachers by male and female principals. Unpublished raw data, 1991.

PART SIX

THE FUTURE
OF LEADERSHIP

IN THIS SECTION the reader will find four pieces describing what good leadership looks like now and what we hope it will look like in the future. Each of these diverse pieces offers a fresh and compelling perspective on effective leadership development in today's world of shifting roles and responsibilities.

Carolyn Kelley and Kent D. Peterson, in "The Work of Principals and Their Preparation," delve into preparation programs to uncover what it takes to create a good principal. They walk us through a day in the life of a school and call for renewed attention to quality in leadership preparation and practice.

In "Teacher Leadership," Ann Lieberman, Ellen R. Saxl, and Matthew B. Miles focus their attention on the role of the teacher in building and maintaining a successful school. As teachers gain a less isolated and more collaborative position within their schools, many assume active leadership roles in the school system's processes.

Author Linda Lambert presents findings that point to the importance of building leadership capacity and collaboration within schools. She argues that sustained improvement is possible only when leadership is distributed across all members of the school community.

In the final piece, Andy Hargreaves and Dean Fink use the language of ecosystems and economics to define the concept of sustainable leadership. They vividly describe leadership that focuses on bringing out the best in an organization without depleting its material and human resources. Clearly, when schools perpetually renew and recycle, there is almost no limit to what they can achieve.

23

THE WORK OF PRINCIPALS AND THEIR PREPARATION

ADDRESSING CRITICAL NEEDS FOR THE TWENTY-FIRST CENTURY

Carolyn Kelley
Kent D. Peterson

There are more vacancies for principals and a greater dearth of qualified candidates than I've seen in the last forty years.

—Seymour Fleigel, Center for Educational Innovation (1999)

FLEIGEL'S COMMENT reflects a broad concern about the quality and quantity of candidates for principalships now being echoed across the United States. The concern is critical because of the central role that the principal plays in orchestrating school reform and improvement. Ultimately, realization of the promise of education reform rests on our ability to enhance the professional development of principals through significantly improved preparation programs and carefully linked ongoing professional development.

American schools remain central to the fabric of society and productivity. Every citizen has the right to develop skills and knowledge that will enhance his or her quality of life—this is a core tenet of the social purpose of education. For almost two decades, since the publication of the *Nation at Risk* report (National Commission on Excellence in Education, 1983), policymakers, communities, and educators have been concerned with creating and maintaining the highest-quality schools to serve both individual and social goals.

However, the quality and improvement of American public schools are threatened by a crisis in school leadership. For some time, critics of principal preparation programs have expressed concern about the inadequacies of systems of recruitment, screening, selection, and training of principal candidates. In the next three to five years, a large proportion of today's principals are expected to retire, and the number of quality candidates for those positions appears to be dwindling.

To address this coming shortfall of candidates, the nation needs to examine carefully the systems that support the development of future school leaders. In this chapter, we examine the principalship; the knowledge, skills, and abilities needed by principals; and some recent efforts to enhance the preparation of principals. While many preparation programs do not possess the curricular coherence, pedagogy, and structure to provide the skills, knowledge, and attitudes necessary to lead America's eighty thousand public schools, we examine model programs that have attempted that task, and we examine features of these programs that do provide the building blocks required to enhance the professional preparation and development of future principals.

Current Principal Characteristics

The nation's schools currently have about 105,000 principals, about 80,000 of them working in public schools. A significant proportion is over fifty years of age. In 1993–94, 15 percent of public school principals were fifty-five or older, and another 75 percent of them were between forty and fifty-five. The proportion of public school principals under age forty declined between 1987–88 and 1993–94 from 19 to 10 percent of the total public school principal population (National Center for Education Statistics, 1997). Given the nature of state retirement systems and current norms, it is highly probable that a significant proportion of the current population of school principals will retire in the next several years.

The rising age of principals may be partly related to the hiring of greater numbers of women into the principalship. Female principals tend to enter the principalship later in their careers (Andrews and Basom, 1990; Miklos, 1988). They tend to have more teaching experience prior to becoming administrators, are as likely to have a master's degree in elementary education as in educational administration, and are more likely to have experience as curriculum specialists or coordinators prior to entering the principalship. While virtually all principals have a background in teaching, about a third of female principals also have prior experience as a curriculum specialist or coordinator; a slightly higher percentage of male principals continues to have a background in athletic coaching. Perhaps as a result, female principals tend to spend more of their time in the classroom and on instruction-related activities. Male principals continue to outnumber female principals, but the proportion of women in the role has been rising, due to changes in hiring patterns favoring female candidates. The proportion of female principals increased from 25 percent of the total in 1987–88 to 34 percent in 1993–94 (National Center for Education Statistics, 1997).

Most minority principals continue to be concentrated in central cities (35 percent of public school central-city principals were minority members) and large districts (29 percent of public school principals in districts with more than ten thousand students were minority members). Overall, the ratio of minority principals is rising slowly, up from 13 percent in 1987–88 to 16 percent in 1993–94 (National Center for Education Statistics, 1997).

A recent survey of superintendents supported self-reported evidence that there is a shortage of qualified candidates for the principalship. About half of districts responding indicated that an inadequate number of qualified candidates were applying for positions open in their districts (Educational Research Service, 1998). Shortages may be even greater in specific regions and districts.

The Schools and Staffing Survey data indicate that 39 percent of principals participated in a program for aspiring principals. New principals were more likely than experienced principals to take part (National Center for Education Statistics, 1997); most of these programs appear to be located in urban rather than suburban or rural school districts (Educational Research Service, 1998). Anecdotal evidence suggests that the demand for principals is even greater in specific regions and districts. For example, in Texas, some 34 percent of all elementary principals reported they planned to retire in the next three years and almost two-thirds within eight years (Sandi Borden, Texas Elementary Principals and Supervisors

Association, personal communication, Jan. 2000). In one Maryland district, the numbers are even more daunting, with upwards of 70 percent considering retirement in three years (Albert Bertani, chief officer for professional development, Prince George's County Public Schools, personal communication, Jan. 2000).

Compensation and the nature of the principal role appear to be the major factors that discourage candidates from seeking principal positions (Educational Research Service, 1998). The average salary for public school principals is often similar to that of teachers at the high end of the salary scale. Since most teachers operate on a nine-month contract and most principals on a twelve-month contract, the daily salary rate is often lower for principals than for teachers.

If teachers accept additional compensated roles in the district, they may make the same amount or even more than the principal. In 1993–94, the average public school principal was paid about $55,000; private school principals earned about $32,000 (National Center for Education Statistics, 1997). The average teacher salary was about $35,000 in that year (American Federation of Teachers, 2000). More recent data show similar differences (see American Federation of Teachers, 2000, tabs. II-6 and V-2).

The averages mask the variation across districts. An analysis of teacher and principal salaries in Wisconsin in 1999 showed that in many districts, the salary differential was negligible. In contrast, some districts such as Chicago have made a concerted effort to raise principal salaries relative to teacher salaries in order to attract stronger candidates. Without a significant salary differential, teachers may decide not to become principals because they will not be sufficiently compensated for the longer workdays, greater pressure and stress, and reduced job security.

Studies of the shortage of principals reiterate the effect of these factors on discouraging potential applicants from seeking a principalship. In the 1998 Educational Research Service study, superintendents with a shortage of qualified candidates identified the following as important factors discouraging principal applicants:

- Compensation is insufficient compared to responsibilities (60 percent)
- Job is too stressful (32 percent)
- Too much time is required (27 percent)
- It is difficult to satisfy parents/community (14 percent)
- Societal problems make it difficult to focus on instruction (13 percent)

- Fewer experienced teachers are interested (12 percent)
- Testing/accountability pressures are high (7 percent)
- Job is viewed as less satisfying than previously (6 percent)

Importance of the Role

Schools need more than leadership. They need a carefully conceived curriculum, quality instructional strategies, assessment strategies that guide planning, and school improvement efforts that continuously improve processes. But research and practical knowledge also point to the key importance of strong principal leadership that can effectively manage complex systems and lead instructional improvement.

Over the past decade, research on school principals has reiterated their importance in promoting school effectiveness, restructuring, school improvement, and the implementation of reform (Elmore and Burney, 1997; Ford and Bennett, 1994; Fullan, 1997; Hallinger and Heck, 1996; Kelley, 1998; Levine and Lezotte, 1995; Louis and Marks, 1998; Murphy and Louis, 1994; Newmann and Associates, 1996). Principals are also central players in the implementation of comprehensive reform programs such as Accelerated Schools and the Comer Model (Peterson, 1995; Yale Child Study Center, 2000). Good principals engage their schools in the core processes of establishing, maintaining, evaluating, and improving their structures and cultures. Schools need a principal to keep the organization going effectively and improving continuously. At times, reform groups have thought that schools could be managed and led by committees of empowered teachers; seldom have these approaches worked. In fact, one seldom finds an instructionally effective school without an effective principal.

The importance of principals to school success makes it essential to examine the role more carefully in order to consider ways to improve the preparation and professional development of these leaders.

Educational Leadership

The recent interest in school leadership follows many years of relative inattention. During the 1990s, educational rhetoric and reform efforts focused primarily on empowering teachers and other stakeholders, with particular attention to elevating the role of the teacher and on restructuring schools, especially school governance. Interestingly, there were calls to replace the principalship with administrative committees of dedicated teachers. Policymakers and state reformers paid relatively little attention to school leadership.

Both research on school reform and practical knowledge of what it takes to run a successful school have pointed to the importance of administrators to school success. Research on the role of principals in effective schools, school improvement, restructuring, instructional improvement, and standards-based reform all support a need for well-prepared leaders. Recent research on implementing reforms demonstrates the central role of principals and other leaders to successful change. Principals are key to initiating, implementing, and sustaining high-quality schools.

Research on the Work of School Principals

Critics call for changes in preparation programs to better match the realities of the work of school principals. Muse and Thomas (1991) summarize this view: "Regardless of the year appointed, [principals] have been trained and certified as administrators through programs largely irrelevant to and grossly inadequate for the work responsibilities found in the school principalship" (p. 32). Any effort to redesign and implement more meaningful preparation programs for school principals must be carried out with a clear picture of the nature of a principal's work.

Work Realities

The daily work world of school principals is little understood and yet extremely complex and demanding. The nature of a principal's work suggests the need for schools and districts to consider ways to substantially reframe or restructure it to enable principals to accomplish the tasks expected of them. One approach might restructure the work to enable principals to engage more fully in instructional improvement. In most districts, this role redesign has not been accomplished. The discussion here focuses on worklife realities, many of which are inadequately addressed in most preparation programs. What are these realities?

The daily work of managers in any organization is shaped by the nature of the core technology, the structure of the organization, and the demands from customers, clients, and colleagues, as well as social mores and the culture of the organization (Deal and Peterson, 1994). Thus what schools are and what people expect and desire of them shape the daily work realities of principals.

For principals, like other managers, brevity, variety, and fragmentation characterize their daily work (Mintzberg, 1973; Peterson, 1982, 1989).

About half of the day is spent dealing with problems, demands, or activities that have not been scheduled and are often unique. More than 80 percent of the day is spent in verbal interaction, much of it face to face. Problems, demands, and new requests for decisions or direction flow to the principal continuously, with many of the problems unique and unexpected, occurring in seemingly random patterns. Routine notions of time management developed by corporate trainers often do not apply as irate parents, injured children, intransigent students, safety issues, and mundane breakdowns are pressed into the principal's office for attention. What is this work like?

First, much of a principal's day is spent on interactions lasting less than a minute, with little time for longer reflection on issues. Principals are expected to address problems and questions quickly, often with little time for careful consideration of alternative solutions (Peterson, 1982).

Second, the tasks vary considerably, depending on many features. These include the nature of the persons involved (social variability), the nature of the problem (problem complexity), the thinking or emotional processes involved (cognitive and affective diversity), and the knowledge base needed (expansive nature of expertise). Presented problems often vary as well, making them more difficult to analyze and address. Complex social and legal issues exacerbate many seemingly simple problems.

Third, the day of principals is characterized by extreme fragmentation, interruptions caused by needs, demands, and problems that come to the principal's office for resolution because no other organizational role is assigned to address them. In most schools, principals are the primary managers of issues and concerns that arise from every source—parents and community members, teachers, and students. District reports and paperwork can sometimes be delegated to skilled staff, but often schools are understaffed and so the task of completing paperwork also falls on the principal.

Thus the day is filled with a flood of problems, issues, ideas, and people; the unexpected becomes the norm, and little time remains to reflect, plan, or strategize on deeper systemic or organizational opportunities (Peterson, 1982, 1989).

Principals, in short, are problem solvers, expected and needed to address and buffer the technical core of the organization (the classroom) from the immediate and pressing demands of students, parents, and other short-term sources of perturbation in the system. But principals are also leaders in the school. If the school is to be successful in helping students learn and in addressing problems of teaching and learning, principals must be able to develop a mission focused on student learning, to conduct analyses of student performance, to design and implement new systems and approaches to improve learning, and to reinforce and enhance the professional culture in the school (Deal and Peterson, 1994; Hallinger and Murphy, 1987).

Principals, like other managers of individual units of organizations, are responsible for a wide variety of basic tasks. They must set goals and develop plans; build budgets and hire personnel; lead the organization of work (in this case, curriculum and instruction); select structures and coordinate time use; evaluate staff and assess student learning at the school level; organize improvement efforts and develop processes for working with clients, customers, and community; and understand and reinforce positive organizational cultures. In sum, they must both maintain the routine functioning of the schools and provide vision and motivation; they must both manage and lead (Deal and Peterson, 1994).

New Responsibilities and New Roles

In recent years, new responsibilities have been added to an already complex and demanding position. Some sources include decentralization of decision making to the school site, increased use of collaborative decision making, expanded accountability for principals and schools, the increasingly diverse nature of communities, and greater concern for listening to stakeholders.

With *decentralization,* principals in many districts are taking on budgetary and decision-making responsibilities that were once the domain of central offices or superintendents. In Chicago, for example, principals have local school councils (acting like miniature school boards) who hire and fire them and oversee the budget and school improvement plans. In Seattle, principals act as chief executive officers of their schools, with broad powers over resource allocation and reallocation, staffing, and instructional technology. San Diego operates a high-stakes environment in which principals' tenure depends on their ability to act as effective instructional leaders, developing and improving instructional programs and student outcomes (Kelley, 2000).

Principals in many schools engage in *collaborative planning and decision making* with staff and parents. In Chicago, this is a useful and important democratizing reform, but it increases the political and governing responsibilities and tasks of principals.

The roles of principals in states with *increased accountability* reforms have been changed qualitatively by curriculum standards reforms, more focus on higher-order thinking, high-stakes testing, and accountability for student learning. They are pressed to be more responsible for student learning and its improvement but must also lead planning efforts that involve developing a clear mission and goals for the school, analyzing student performance data, identifying areas that need improvement, developing sustainable programmatic reforms, and facilitating implementation of those reforms. The new high-stakes tests and the detailed reporting of student scores require a more advanced notion of instructional leadership that involves complex analysis of data, application of new instructional technologies, and other responsibilities.

Principals are also expected to work effectively in increasingly *diverse, fragmented, and pluralistic communities with vocal stakeholders*. They must respond positively and democratically to the vocal stakeholders, who have a legitimate and intense personal interest in schools. "Listening to the customer" (Peters and Waterman, 1982) takes on special meaning in schools where everyone—from states to central offices, from booster clubs to property owners, from teachers to parents—wants to be involved in decision making and governance.

No doubt districts and boards need to consider ways to redesign and support the work of principals. But for those going into the position, preparation programs need to address existing realities—by providing skills, knowledge, and experiences that will prepare future principals until changes are made in the role. Leaders of other organizations face many of these conditions as well. But principals face a special set of problems not found in organizations with clearer goals, more routine technologies, and fewer social expectations.

Special Problems for Principals

As managers of educational organizations for young people, principals face some special problems. Principals, unlike leaders in other organizations, work in settings where the following conditions prevail:

- Local constituencies view schools more as symbols of the community than as places of learning, where looking and acting like "school" may be more important than achieving learning outcomes (Meyer and Rowan, 1978).
- Use of traditional, often outdated, techniques (eight-period days; students working alone on projects; paper-and-pencil tests) are often valued by clients more than improving student learning with new, less traditional approaches.

- Staff norms of autonomy are extremely high, and collaboration on schoolwide projects is often uncommon.
- Existing organizational cultures reinforce conceptions of purpose and pedagogy that are reified and outmoded.
- Organizational goals are constantly shifting, depending on educational fashion, fancy, funding, and politics.
- Many important goals, such as citizenship or lifelong learning, are hard to measure and viewed as achievable in some distant future.
- Informal, competing goals (such as having winning sports teams) may absorb time, effort, and problem-solving attention that could be devoted to improving student learning.
- The core technology needed involves motivating captive participants (called students) to work and produce.

These conditions make leadership more challenging in schools than in many other organizations. They make the work of principals more complex, variable, and difficult both to do and to learn how to do.

Skills and Knowledge for Principals

The foregoing description of the roles and responsibilities of the principal suggests that the job is both complex and demanding. Next, we identify key knowledge, skills, and dispositions that seem important for effectiveness in the role. Various authors have put forward different attributes needed for success in the principalship. Keller (1998, p. 2) suggested that a good principal has the following attributes:

- Recognizes teaching and learning as the main business of a school
- Communicates the school's mission clearly and consistently to staff members, parents, and students
- Fosters standards for teaching and learning that are high and attainable
- Provides clear goals and monitors the progress of students toward meeting them
- Spends time in classrooms and listens to teachers
- Promotes an atmosphere of trust and sharing
- Builds good staff and makes professional development a top concern
- Does not tolerate bad teachers

Others have suggested that to be effective, principals must be able to both manage and lead. In other words, they must be strong administrators, attending to the structural features of the organization, and strong leaders, working to shape the school culture and context to promote student learning (Deal and Peterson, 1994).

The complexity of the principal's role and the innumerable decisions that must be made have led some analysts to focus on the importance of strong problem-identification and problem-solving orientations for school leaders (Hallinger, Leithwood, and Murphy, 1993). Effective principals clearly communicate a vision through their work, which means finding ways to make meaning out of the endless stream of activity in a principal's workday. Some have argued that in order to use these problem-solving activities as a vehicle for communicating values and direction, principals require a clear and highly developed values orientation that can focus and drive decision-making processes (Raun and Leithwood, 1993).

Other critical skills include a working knowledge of educational research findings, methods, and approaches; strong communication skills; and human resource management skills (recruitment, selection, evaluation, professional development, motivation, and so on). Research on some of these knowledge and skill areas is extensive. In the next section, we review some of this literature.

Models of Leadership

A number of models of leadership have been proposed over the years. In an analysis of a decade of articles on leadership in schools, Leithwood and Duke (1999) identified and defined six types of leadership: instructional, transformational, moral, participative, managerial, and contingent. These approaches are defined as follows:

- *Instructional leadership* "typically focuses on the behaviors of teachers as they engage in activities directly affecting the growth of students" (p. 47).

- *Transformational leadership* focuses on "the commitments and capacities of organizational members" and frequently refers to "charismatic, visionary, cultural, and empowering concepts of leadership" (p. 48).

- *Moral leadership* focuses on "the values and ethics of the leader" (p. 50). A major concern in this body of research is the ways in which values and ethics are used in decision making and how conflicts in values are resolved.

- *Participative leadership* examines "the decision-making processes of the group" (p. 51), particularly with respect to shared or group decisions.
- *Managerial leadership* "focuses on the functions, tasks, or behaviors of the leader" (p. 52).
- *Contingent leadership* examines the ways in which "leaders respond to the unique organizational circumstances or problems that they face" (p. 54).

In various ways, each of these approaches to leadership is designed to enhance school culture or performance. For example, instructional leadership focuses on student growth and learning outcomes; transformational leadership, on increasing the capacity for high performance; and moral leadership, on enhancing the ethical and moral purposes in schools (Leithwood and Duke, 1999). An extensive research literature has built up around these leadership styles. We focus here on two forms that have been identified as potentially promising for improving student achievement, transformational and instructional leadership.

Transformational leadership is perhaps the model most fully developed in the literature. Leithwood (1994) has identified six major dimensions: articulating a vision, fostering group goals, conveying high-performance expectations, providing intellectual stimulation, offering individualized support, and modeling best practices and values. To date, modest evidence supports the positive effects of transformational leadership on organizational effectiveness (Leithwood, Steinbach, and Raun, 1993).

Instructional leadership, identified in the early 1980s as a central feature by the effective schools research, was developed and specified in several studies and analyses. The Bossert model (Bossert, Dwyer, Rowan, and Lee, 1982) identified two major components to which Hallinger and Murphy (1987) added a third. The three components are defining the school mission, managing the instructional program, and promoting the school climate. Specific leadership practices were delineated under each of these components, and their function in schools was studied. A number of studies have supported the model and showed how these three components and the specific practices contribute to student achievement and other educational outcomes (see Leithwood, Jantzi, and Steinbach, 1999, for a review).

A complementary approach to leadership can be found in the work of Deal and Peterson (1994), which focuses on principals as both managers and leaders. As managers, principals ensure that the basic roles, rules, responsibilities, structures, and processes of the school are functioning effectively. As leaders, they help foster an engaging, meaningful vision and mission for the school, shape the culture, and provide motivation, high expectations, support, and encouragement. Again, good principals must be able to both manage the school and lead it.

To be effective *managers,* principals must know the administrative, legal, and policy rules and procedures and be able to apply them. To be effective *leaders,* principals must know about and have skills to address the tasks and roles of transformational and instructional leadership. They must also have a well-developed moral and ethical core of values that translate into everyday behavior. In both managerial and leadership roles, principals need strong problem-finding and problem-solving skills that they can draw on to address both routine and unique challenges.

Cognitive Issues and Leadership

Another significant knowledge and skill area researchers identified in the 1980s and early 1990s was cognitive aspects of the principalship (Hart and Pounder, 1999). These scholars delved into the nature of problem finding and problem solving among administrators. Professors generated studies of problem solving, suggestions for changes in preparation programs to foster improved skill at it, and several new techniques for increasing problem-solving skills. These included problem-based learning, design studios, and apprenticeships (see, for example, Bridges and Hallinger, 1993; Hart, 1993; Prestine, 1993). Attention to problem solving may be important in the design of preparation programs.

Problem Solving

Like many managers in other industries, principals must be able and willing to solve a wide variety of problems, both those that are brought to them and those they select. Problem identification and problem solving are central features of their work. An important skill of principals is the ability to take care of the many problems and demands of their jobs, at the same time leading their schools, nurturing teacher leadership, and moving the instructional program forward.

Problems are often complex, ambiguous, unsequenced, hard to analyze, and highly emotional, with few routine solutions. As a contrasting example, consider medicine, which also confronts a large range of problems. In medicine, many problems are routine, some problem-solving processes can be fairly routinized, and even complex problems may have a fixed set of solutions from which to draw. In educational administration, the range of problems that present themselves is also large, but procedures for solving them tend to be less routinized, and unique problems present themselves much more frequently. Few routinized solutions exist for a large proportion of many problems (Leithwood, Jantzi, and Șteinbach, 1999).

Standards for Practice

In an attempt to improve the preparation of school leaders, a number of groups have developed standards for practice that define what good principals should know and be able to do. Some have been long and detailed, such as the list of proficiencies published by the National Association of Elementary School Principals (NAESP); others have been short and broadly defined, like the standard of the National Policy Board for Educational Administration (NPBEA) and the Interstate School Leaders Licensure Consortium (ISLLC).

These models provide another look at the knowledge and skills principals need and provide a potential list of knowledge bases, skills, and abilities that a comprehensive model of preparation might address. Although there are similarities across the standards, each takes a slightly different approach to defining what is important. Because they represent an important indication of what the *profession* considers important, we shall summarize them here.

The NPBEA Standards

One of the earliest sets of standards was developed by the National Policy Board for Educational Administration in an attempt to provide more structure and quality for educational administration preparation programs (Hart and Pounder, 1999). They include the following standards:

1. *Strategic leadership*—the knowledge, skills, and attributes needed to identify contexts, develop with others vision and purpose, use information, frame problems, exercise leadership processes to achieve common goals, and act ethically for educational communities.
2. *Instructional leadership*—the knowledge, skills, and attributes needed to design with others appropriate curricula and instructional programs, develop learner-centered school cultures, assess outcomes, provide student personnel services, and plan with faculty professional development activities aimed at improving instruction.
3. *Organizational leadership*—the knowledge, skills, and attributes needed to understand and improve the organization, implement operational plans, manage financial resources, and apply decentralized management processes and procedures.

4. *Political and community leadership*—the knowledge, skills, and attributes needed to act in accordance with legal provisions and statutory requirements, apply regulatory standards, develop and apply appropriate policies, be conscious of ethical implications of policy initiatives and political actions, relate public policy initiatives to student welfare, understand schools as political systems, involve citizens and service agencies, and develop effective staff communications and public relations programs.

5. *Internship*—the process and product that result from application in a workplace environment of the strategic, instructional, organizational, and contextual leadership guidelines. When coupled with integrating experiences through related clinics or cohort seminars, the outcome should be a powerful synthesis of knowledge and skills useful to practicing school leaders.

NAESP Proficiencies for Principals

A second set of standards (termed "proficiencies") was developed in the mid-1980s and refined through the 1990s by the National Association of Elementary School Principals. This set took a bimodal approach and delineated a detailed set of leadership proficiencies and administrative and management proficiencies. The NAESP created a professional development inventory and professional development activities related to the standards so that aspiring, new, or experienced principals could assess their level of competence and create a professional development plan to strengthen their skills.

The NAESP proficiencies are as follows:

1. Leadership proficiencies
   Leadership behavior
   Communication skills
   Group processes
   Curriculum and instruction
   Assessment
2. Administrative and management proficiencies
   Organizational management
   Fiscal management
   Political management

For each area, specific skills are delineated. For example, under leadership behavior, the National Association of Elementary School Principals (1997, pp. 6–7) states:

In the exercise of leadership, the proficient principal

- Demonstrates vision and provides leadership that appropriately involves the school community in the creation of shared beliefs and values
- Demonstrates moral and ethical judgment
- Demonstrates creativity and innovative thinking
- Involves the school community in identifying and accomplishing the school's mission
- Recognizes the individual needs and contributions of all staff and students
- Applies effective interpersonal skills
- Facilitates the leadership of others
- Conducts needs assessments and uses data to make decisions and to plan for school improvement
- Identifies, pursues, and creatively coordinates the use of available human, material, and financial resources to achieve the school's mission and goals
- Explores, assesses, and implements educational concepts that enhance teaching and learning
- Understands the dynamics of change and the change process
- Advances the profession through participation as a member of local, state, and national professional groups
- Initiates and effectively coordinates collaborative endeavors with local and state agencies
- Participates in professional development to enhance personal leadership skills

Basic analysis of the construct validity and reliability of the NAESP Professional Development Inventory has generally supported the use of the instrument (Coleman and Adams, 1999).

The Connecticut Standards

Leithwood and Duke (1997) developed another useful set of standards for the state of Connecticut. It was to be used to develop assessment and evaluation rubrics for principals and to encourage more aligned and structured preparation programs. These standards begin with an integrated view of education, schools, and teachers, using a set of assumptions about what constitutes an "educated person," the nature of the learning process, and the teacher. The Connecticut model then goes on to delineate specific standards for principals based on these assumptions. The standards address the following areas:

1. Purposes and culture of productive schools

   School goals

   School culture

2. Structural and organizational characteristics of productive schools

   Policies and procedures

   Organization and resources

   Teaching faculty

   Programs and instruction

   School-community relations

3. Keys to school order and stability

   Communications and coordination

   Time management

   Budget and resource management

   School governance

   Student discipline

Like the other standards, these included a subset of skills and knowledge for each of the standards.

Council of Chief State School Officers Standards for School Leaders

The most widely used standards for principals were developed by a team of practitioners, academics, and policymakers in 1996. The Interstate School Leadership Licensure Consortium (ISLLC) consists of a number of states interested in pursuing the use of the ISLLC standards for teacher licensure. The Educational Testing Service has developed an assessment tool for states to use or adapt that assesses candidates' knowledge and skills as they relate to the ISLLC standards.

The purpose of the ISLLC standards was to provide a clear, organized set of curriculum content and performance standards that could be used to drive the preparation, professional development, and licensure of principals. The ISLLC core includes the following standards (Council of Chief State School Officers, 1996):

Standard 1: A school administrator is an educational leader who promotes the success of all students by facilitating the development, articulation, implementation, and stewardship of a vision of learning that is shared and supported by the school community.

Standard 2: A school administrator is an educational leader who promotes the success of all students by advocating, nurturing, and sustaining a school culture and instructional program conducive to student learning and staff professional growth.

Standard 3: A school administrator is an educational leader who promotes the success of all students by ensuring management of the organization, operations, and resources for a safe, efficient, and effective learning environment.

Standard 4: A school administrator is an educational leader who promotes the success of all students by collaborating with families and community members, responding to diverse community interests and needs, and mobilizing community resources.

Standard 5: A school administrator is an educational leader who promotes the success of all students by acting with integrity, fairness, and in an ethical manner.

Standard 6: A school administrator is an educational leader who promotes the success of all students by understanding, responding to, and influencing the larger political, social, economic, legal, and cultural context.

In addition to these standards, the National Council for the Accreditation of Teacher Education (NCATE) has developed standards for preparation programs, and the American Association of School Administrators has developed standards for superintendents. These efforts to develop standards of practice are laudable in that they represent an attempt by the key stakeholder groups—policymakers, preparation programs, and professional associations—to identify a knowledge base for the profession. The standards are being used to shape licensure policy as well as the content and scope of preservice and in-service administrator preparation programs.

In examining the standards, several major areas of emphasis stand out: (1) defining the mission of the school, (2) ensuring that the school is well managed, (3) shaping a positive school culture, (4) managing and leading the instructional program, and (5) building positive relations with parents and community. To their credit, these points closely parallel the research on principals' work, instructional leadership, and effective schools.

Perhaps more important than the broad categories are the specific skills and knowledge defined under each one, the relative emphasis placed on each category (how much of each factor), and the ways the skills and knowledge are learned and can be applied in complex, real-life situations. These features are not systematically detailed in the standards model.

The standards should also be recognized for what they are: an attempt to identify a basic level of knowledge for the profession. The ISLLC, for example, developed a set of licensure standards. As a result, the ISLLC standards reflect a basic understanding of the literature on effective schools and a generic approach to administrator knowledge and skills. They differ from the work of the National Board for Professional Teaching Standards in that they are *not* an attempt to identify the "expert" knowledge of highly effective administrators. They are also divorced from any particular model of administrative practice.

Schools vary considerably on many dimensions, and effective leadership is enacted in a particular context. Skills and knowledge should be developed so that principals can lead effectively in their particular context. Specifically, schools differ in their leadership demands, depending on such factors as level (elementary, middle, and high schools); the socioeconomic, racial, and ethnic characteristics of students and community; school size; the professional culture of the school; and the governance model driving the system. Principals at both the preservice and in-service stages should develop leadership that can be enacted effectively in the context of their particular schools. The standards, therefore, would likely prove inadequate as a template for preparation of administrators for highly decentralized, focused, or specialized management systems like the ones in Seattle, San Diego, or Chicago.

Further, while the standards provide a broad overview of the knowledge, skills, and abilities needed by principals, they do not provide a clear model of daily administrative practice, specific guidance on how administrators best obtain these skills, or information on how these skills interact with one another in the practice of leadership. Leadership is not simply engaging in a smorgasbord of actions. Rather, it involves a carefully selected complex system of thoughts, actions, and processes that occur in a temporal order that solves problems, builds culture, nurtures leadership in others, communicates values and purpose, and institutes meaningful changes.

Thus leadership preparation is not simply a matter of developing a set of discrete skills and building isolated bits of knowledge. Instead it means embedding skills and knowledge in a complex, analytical "mental map" that can be applied to complex, varied, and uncertain situations. Leaders facing complex situations need complex mental maps to address those situations. The more complex the work situations, the more complex the mapping needs to be.

Leadership preparation programs therefore need to do much more than simply address lists of skills. They need to provide learning experiences that develop complex mental maps and models for action in specific contexts.

The Nature of Educational Preparation

Criticism of preparation programs, certification, and licensure is not new. In the late 1980s, considerable attention focused on the problems of preparation programs.

Sirotnik and Mueller (1993) provide an excellent example of a prototypical administrator preparation program. It involves part-time students taking courses at night or on weekends, taught by adjunct faculty. Reading and academic work is often atheoretical, textbook-based, and minimal. Sequencing and scheduling of courses is determined by students according to the scheduling demands of a busy professional rather than by issues of curriculum content and educational purpose. Field experiences are short, poorly organized, disconnected from the curriculum, and planned according to the availability of small blocks of time for working teachers. Curriculum, instruction, and assessment are seldom planned, coordinated, or linked in a coherent manner.

For years, preparation of educational administrators has been criticized in ways that are in fact descriptions of typical programs. Here are some of the critiques' findings (Peterson and Finn, 1985; Sirotnik and Mueller, 1993; Bredeson, 1996):

- Little, if any, recruitment to identify potential leaders and increase diversity in those selected

- Eased entry to graduate programs with few significant selection criteria (if any) and usually no interviews

- Admission policies that allow students to begin the program at any time during the year and continue taking courses in whatever sequence fits their work schedules or preferences

- Convenience scheduling of courses around students' full-time work schedules, with classes offered in the evenings or, more recently, on weekends

- Graduate programs that are a patchwork quilt of courses, sometimes taken at different institutions and transferred in for the final application for certification

- Program content and curricular alignment based more on textbook sequencing or faculty interest than on careful curricular design
- Pedagogic techniques that are frequently lectures and, more recently, case- or activity-based
- In-class performance expectations that are unclear, inappropriately low, or nonexistent
- Program structures and learning activities offering little in the way of meaningful experiential or mentoring opportunities, as they are often arranged by the student or occur in their school during off hours, with little reflection on or analysis of the experience
- Few, if any, programmatic links with local districts that would tie students to existing district realities
- Learning sequences and content that are rarely based on career stages or the development of expert knowledge

Efforts by various programs, associations, and foundations did attempt in the 1990s to ameliorate some of these deficiencies through investment in the development of model programs. (In the following case examples, some of the better programs include those developed during this early reform period.) Nonetheless, with the hundreds of certification programs in the country, many have improved little, and many remain weakly structured, inadequately designed, and poorly implemented. Critics of educational administration programs have suggested that the reform discussion of the late 1980s and early 1990s simply led to add-on features (for example, more case discussions) that did not significantly change the quality or efficacy of these programs (Murphy and Forsyth, 1999).

Program Inertia: Why Quality Suffers

Why haven't more programs improved on their own? Several structural and organizational reasons exist, in spite of association and group pressure and interest in change.

First, overall *accountability* for quality remains with state agencies that approve programs for administrator preparation in their states. Often almost any program with a collection of "appropriate" syllabi can gain approval. Some states have taken a more active role in trying to improve preparation programs for principals and other administrators. These actions include closing programs, requiring significant restructuring, or developing performance-based licensure systems (National Association of State Directors of Teacher Education and Certification, 2000). For example, in North Carolina, programs were required to reapply for the right

372 THE JOSSEY-BASS READER ON EDUCATIONAL LEADERSHIP

to offer administrator preparation classes. Some programs were closed. In Ohio, several educational administration doctoral programs were closed and offered the chance to reapply for status. But in most states, educational administration programs have proliferated, with private universities expanding into states where they have no campuses with part-time programs.

The *norms and values* of many universities are focused more on research and grant getting than on instruction. Faculty norms, especially in major research universities, encourage time and attention to scholarship and publication. Incentives and merit are often tied to research and not to teaching or to the development of meaningful connections with the field.

Financial incentives are considerable for universities to support marginal programs with adjunct faculty. These programs have been for many colleges and universities the proverbial "cash cow," with adjunct faculty paid a few thousand dollars to teach twenty to thirty paying students in their own schools. It has always been easy to hire adjunct faculty and build an entire program around low-paid, part-time practicing administrators. Although these people are often superb in bringing real-life experiences to the classroom, they are seldom expected to devote time to current research or to program development, alignment, and refinement.

Improving preparation programs takes *time and money,* two resources in short supply in many programs. Many educational administration programs have huge doctoral advising loads compared to the arts and sciences, taking time away from program improvement. Furthermore, few departments have the budgets necessary to design, develop, or purchase instructional materials, let alone invest in the development of new course materials using current information technologies.

So even though the barriers to enhancing principal preparation programs are significant, the research literature suggests a number of program foci that could better prepare principals for the challenge of leadership. These will be considered in the next section.

Considerations in Program Design

We found several additional features beyond simple lists to be important when considering program design. These include career stages, district and state context, problem finding and problem solving, and the nature of expert leadership.

Career Stages and Leadership Development

The development of effective school leaders cannot occur in any single program or time period. Rather it must be part of a long and complex process that builds and accumulates skills and knowledge over time and in different ways. Leadership development is part of the broader career and personnel process that includes recruitment to the profession, early preparation and licensure, recruitment and selection to a district and placement in a school, ongoing evaluation and supervision and coaching, and continuous careerlong professional development. At each stage of the career, a different set of possibilities exists for leaders to gain knowledge, skills, and values that match the needs of the school and district.

We have insufficient room in this chapter to describe all the points along the career that offer opportunities for states or districts to enhance leadership development, so we will focus here on preservice preparation programs. Considerable attention is being paid to both preservice and in-service arenas in recent years, but little systematic research or evaluation has enlightened the field about these efforts.

District and State Context

Corporate leadership training has regularly viewed local organizational context as a central feature of effective leadership development. This is also the case in education, though it is less frequently addressed. Programs should consider linking leadership development, both in preparation and in in-service settings, to the district and increasingly the state context of curriculum reform and accountability.

Problem Finding and Problem Solving

During the 1980s and early 1990s, a number of programs designed opportunities to develop cognitive skills in problem finding and problem solving (Bredeson, 1996; Hart and Pounder, 1999). Given the continuous problem-finding and problem-solving tasks of principals, especially in the area of instructional improvement, this is a key feature of their work. It should thus be an explicit feature of preparation and in-service programs.

Expert Knowledge

The need to address problem solving in developing leaders is considered by several writers. Most organizations do not expect new hires to be experts. But over time, additional training, experience, and mentoring should work to make neophytes into experts. Such training should be carefully built into ongoing programs.

What does expert behavior look like? Ohde and Murphy (1993, pp. 75–76) suggest that the features of expert behavior integrated into some of the model preparation programs include the following:

1. An expert within a specific domain will have amassed a large yet well-organized knowledge base.

2. This extensive body of knowledge allows experts to classify problems according to principles, laws, or major rules, rather than by surface features.

3. The knowledge base is highly organized, allowing experts to identify patterns and configurations quickly and accurately. This ability reduces cognitive load and permits the expert to attend to other variables within the problem.

4. The problem-solving strategies of experts are proceduralized. Experts can invoke these skills automatically, whereas novices often struggle with the problem-solving process.

5. The acquisition of this complex knowledge base takes a long time. Expertise within a domain is linked to years of practice, experience, or study.

The Landscape of Licensure

The National Commission on Teaching and America's Future (1996) identified licensure, certification, and accreditation as critical foundations on which teacher quality rests. *Licensure* refers to the initial permit to practice and is typically granted by the state. *Certification* refers to recognition by the profession of high levels of professional practice. *Accreditation* refers to the review of an educational unit to acknowledge and ensure that the unit is meeting specific standards of quality (Hart and Pounder, 1999).

The landscape of licensure requirements for principals is evolving slowly. As of 2000, twenty-three states required administrators to take at least one of five different examinations for licensure. The exams include the National Teachers Examination, the California Test of Basic Skills, Program for Licensing Assessments for Colorado Educators, individual state exams, and one or more examinations from the PRAXIS series of the Educational Testing Service. More recently, the ETS assessment linked to the ISLLC standards has been adopted in a large number of states. In 1998, twenty-five states were using or planning to use that assessment in some form (Crawford, 1998).

Appendix A in this chapter presents the licensure requirements for a sample of eight states. Typical requirements include teaching certification and experience, a master's degree, and administrator training in an approved program, with continuing professional development needed to retain the license. The modal requirement is three years of teaching experience for principal licensure; the range is from one to seven years. In most states, the initial license is issued for five or fewer years, with renewal granted for additional coursework or participation in other professional development activities. As of 2000, three states—Louisiana, New Jersey, and Texas—remained the only ones that issue lifetime administrator licenses (Crawford, 1998; National Association of State Directors of Teacher Education and Certification, 2000).

Promising Programs: Case Examples

The following are case examples of particularly promising programs. Though most programs have not conducted rigorous evaluations of their effectiveness, these seem to have developed some successful approaches to preparation. These descriptions of programs and their features are not meant to be exhaustive, but they should provide some insights into the most current thinking about leadership preparation. (A description of the methodology used to collect case data and the interview protocol used can be found in Appendix B in this chapter.)

University of Washington: Danforth Educational Leadership Program

The University of Washington's Danforth Educational Leadership Program is a cohort-based program focusing on the development of moral leadership and organizational change, implementation, and evaluation. The program uses intensive twelve-month internship placements with carefully screened and trained mentors to provide an experiential base for the development of moral and ethical leadership. Classroom instruction is provided by faculty and practicing administrators in modular units of varying length rather than in traditional course-length units. The instructional staff, mentors, and internship supervisors maintain a close collaboration to give students continuity in educational experience. The program also communicates the value and process of evaluation through an intensive formative evaluation from students and other program participants.

As is reflected in its name, the University of Washington program was developed through seed money from the Danforth Foundation. The program itself began in 1988–89 as a small experimental program for administrator training. In 1992, the traditional program was closed, and Danforth became the only administrator preparation program offered by the University of Washington.

Selection. Students are selected through an evaluation of academic credentials and leadership potential. Candidates must submit recommendations focusing on leadership ability that are completed by the candidate's

principal, a teacher of the principal's choice, and a second teacher identified by the candidate. Candidates must also participate in an interview
focusing on their values and clarity in use of those values in leadership
decisions and in a one-hour essay exercise centered on how they would
lead given the current context of today's schools. Participants are required
either to possess a master's degree prior to entry or to obtain one through
additional coursework.

Program Structure, Pedagogy, and Curricular Focus. Each year, from
about forty applicants, a cohort of no more than twenty students is
selected to participate in the yearlong program, which features a summer
institute, internships, and classroom instruction.

An intensive ten-day summer institute uses interaction, reflection, cases,
simulations, and discussions to build the cohort and begin the transition
into leadership. The summer institute provides an opportunity to socialize students to challenge one another in productive ways and to clarify
their values and beliefs about education. The institute also gives program
staff an opportunity to get to know the students' strengths, weaknesses,
and personalities, which facilitates placement in productive internship
experiences.

Internships involve placement of candidates with carefully screened
mentor administrators. Mentors are nominated by district administrators
and must provide peer recommendations and put together a portfolio
describing the school, its program, its staff, and its community situation.
A university team visits the site to develop a miniportrait of the site
dynamics and leadership behaviors of the principal. Selected administrators sign a letter of commitment, including a detailed description of the
nature of their role and the extent of their involvement. Mentors are not
compensated but have an opportunity to interact with faculty and maintain access to current research and faculty participants.

About half the students participate in full-time internships (about fourteen hundred hours); the other half are placed in internships for at least
four half-days per week throughout the academic year (about seven hundred hours). Districts are asked to provide students with half-time leave
from their positions to participate in the program. (The state requires a
320-hour internship for educational administration certification and provides some monetary compensation for districts to defer this cost.) Students are expected to participate in three different internships during the
year; only one of the three can be a placement in the student's own district. At least one of the placements must be at a different level from the
one at which the student intends to administer; and at least one must be
from a different setting (urban or rural, for example).

Field experiences are supervised by faculty and the program coordinator, with the expectation that supervisors will meet with students and mentors in the field at least five times during the year. Faculty are given a course reduction of two quarter-length courses for every four students they supervise.

Classroom instruction is integrated with the internship experience and organized into modules. Students meet every Thursday and on selected weekends (Friday or Saturday) throughout the year for this classroom component. The modules vary in length, depending on content, and are taught with collaborative teams of faculty and practicing administrators selected for their content expertise.

"The most fundamental assumption of [the program] is that human inquiry and action are never value-free, suggesting that explicit treatment of values, beliefs, and human interests should be a routine and rigorous part of organizational life. Also suggested is a position that eschews value-relativism; we argue that one set of values is *not* just as good as any other. . . . The set of values promoted in the Danforth Program is rooted in the ideals of human caring and social justice" (Sirotnik and Mueller, 1993, pp. 62–63).

Program Effects. Evaluation is a core value of the program and is communicated through student and faculty participation in ongoing evaluation and feedback. The evaluations suggest that key factors in producing individual change were the cohort structure, seminar format, significant relationships, integrated theory and internship experiences, involvement in program change, role models provided by faculty and mentor principals, and program intensity. Key individual changes include gaining an understanding of multiple perspectives, strengthening personal values and beliefs, improved ability to discuss substantive issues, and important changes in habits of thought and interaction (Sirotnik and Mueller, 1993).

The evaluation data show that approximately 75 percent of program graduates move directly into administrative positions, compared to only 25 percent in the traditional program (Milstein and Associates, 1993).

Program Cost and Other Challenges. The program requires a significant commitment from the university in that it is significantly more costly than the traditional program structure. Key costs include a program coordinator, faculty release time for internship supervision, and the opportunity cost of choosing not to run an income-generating certification program. The program also requires a willingness on the part of the university to sidestep traditional educational delivery mechanisms (the program is a thirty-six-credit program, which students can take in variable credit units); significant commitment from faculty to maintain the level of collaboration, supervision, and curriculum revision demanded; commitment from districts to provide release time for participating students; and the time and talents of mentors, compensated primarily through intrinsic rewards of participation.

East Tennessee State University

The East Tennessee State University (ETSU) administrative endorsement program was also developed in the 1980s and was one of the original Danforth program sites. Ongoing commitment to the Danforth program is shown by the fact that the former executive director of the Danforth Foundation is a faculty member in the program.

Program Structure. The ETSU administrator training program is designed to accommodate the work schedules of full-time teachers. Students enter the two-year program in January. The cohort group meets once a week from 4:00 to 10:00 p.m. (twice a week during the six-week summer term). Students are expected to participate in five separate placements in a 540-hour internship, which extends for the duration of the program. Placements include elementary, middle, high school, special education, and community services. Internship placements are identified by students, and the internship experience is woven into the curriculum throughout the program. For example, when coursework focuses on school finance and law, students may be asked to participate in the development of school budgets and may become involved in legal issues emerging in the school or district. The internship mentors are not screened, since the purpose is not to provide models of ideal leadership but rather to expose students to issues and examples that can be analyzed and discussed in the classroom context. The internship itself can be carried out in the context of a full-time teaching schedule, since students are largely required to participate in interviews, observations, and projects that can be conducted outside regular teaching hours.

Students complete their program requirements in December and are then available for hire at the peak hiring time of the year, spring semester.

Curriculum. The curriculum is based on the ISLLC standards and matrix, with particular attention given to the ethical and moral dimensions of leadership. The following is a list of required courses:

Interpersonal Relations (6 credits)

Emerging Perspectives Influencing the School (6 credits)

Professional Needs of Individuals and Groups (6 credits)

Developing Learners Through Instructional Leadership (6 credits)

Implementation Strategies (6 credits)

Shaping the Quality and Character of the Institution (6 credits)

No dominant pedagogical approach is used, but field experiences and use of technology are required in eleven courses.

Core and Supplementary Faculty. The faculty all hold doctorates and have experience as educational administrators. Classes are planned and taught by "tag teams." Adjuncts are rarely used, but when they are, they are paired with faculty and are current practitioners. Most adjunct faculty are graduates of the ETSU program and are selected for their familiarity with the innovative teaching strategies used by ETSU.

Recruitment and Selection. Only twenty students are admitted into each cohort; the program currently admits only one new cohort per year. Just over half of applicants are admitted; demand is thought to be related to the program's strong reputation in the region. Students are screened through both written application and an interview; criteria include academics, experience, and leadership potential. The program's commitment to strong moral and ethical leadership is indicated by the fact that it recently turned down a student with an outstanding academic record because she did not appear to share the program's values. In addition, the capstone to the master's degree is a portfolio, which has an ethical component.

Relation to State Policies. The program has recently aligned itself with the ISLLC standards in response to state action to adopt those standards and an ISLLC-based exam for administrator licensure. The state also requires a minimum grade point average and teaching experience. Two forms of certification are available from the state: internship-based and non-internship-based; ETSU requires the internship version for its participants. Administrators are also required to hold a master's degree.

California State University, Fresno

The California State University (CSU)-Fresno's principal preparation program is a third example developed with seed money from the Danforth Foundation. The program began in 1991 and involves a strong collaboration with area superintendents. It uses the Professional Development Inventory (PDI) of the NAESP as part of its initial student assessment. Scores on the PDI help shape the students' initial professional growth plan (similar to an individual educational plan), which is advanced throughout their work. A portfolio is used to build evidence that they have addressed any deficiencies identified in the assessments. Students have exit interviews at the end of each semester with faculty and district supervisors. These evaluations serve as preliminary evaluations for the next semester. At the same time, students are taking coursework linked to their field experiences.

Program Structure. Students enroll in a sequenced set of courses. The program is divided into two tiers of twenty-four credits each, and each tier takes about two years to complete. The first tier provides the training required by the state to become an entry-level administrator; students meet one night a week for two classes. The second tier is for beginning practicing administrators and provides the advanced credential for continuing administrators. Classes meet on weekends, and students take one course per semester.

Pedagogy. The program is experience-based. Students apply knowledge and skills developed through coherent fieldwork coordinated with coursework. Some faculty use case studies or simulations as well. Technology is available for the second-tier program in the form of teleconferencing for students who cannot travel to Fresno.

Curriculum. The program has developed a matrix that conceptualizes knowledge development and identifies course content and sequencing.

The first-tier program is focused on developing strong instructional leaders. Students participate in a 120-hour internship as a master teacher; many work as resource teachers for two to three years. During their first semester, they take two courses, one in advanced educational psychology and the other in administrative theory and management; second-semester coursework includes curriculum management and educational leadership; the third semester focuses on site-based leadership, and students do a simultaneous research project. Graduates typically advance to vice principal positions for three to four years and then to principal.

The second-tier program, designed for beginning administrators, focuses on developing transformational leaders. In addition to an internship, students take practice-based courses, including organizational development, school law, and public relations (first semester) and school finance, personnel, and systems analysis and design (second semester). Courses are scheduled to coincide with principals' responsibilities. Since these are practicing, licensed administrators, they carry out all the functions of their roles. So the program has scheduled the school finance course in early spring, when students are planning their budgets, and the personnel course in late spring, when they are starting the hiring process.

The first summer of the second-tier program is a two-unit induction course in which students take assessments and develop their growth plans. In the fall semester, students take three two-unit courses in transformational leadership, law and policy, and school-community relations. In the spring, students take three two-unit courses: school finance, personnel, and an elective. In addition, students participate in eight units of professional development activities throughout the academic year. Students take eight one-unit seminars from a menu of offerings. In the second summer, they take part in a two-unit assessment seminar in which they produce a portfolio highlighting their knowledge and skills.

Students in both tiers are assessed when they first enter the program and again at the end of each semester. Three measures are used. The first is a test on the content of the sixteen courses that they will take (based in part on state performance indicators). Students are given data on the means and standard deviations of the entire group so that they can compare themselves to others. Second, they go through the PDI, the NAESP performance-based assessment that is designed to assess knowledge and performance in relation to planning, organizing, problem solving, creativity, decisiveness, systems analysis, vision, communications, instructional analysis and supervision, instructional leadership, group leadership and team building, climate development, and moral responsibility. Third, they are required to submit their district's most recent job performance evaluation. These elements all contribute to the professional development plan that each student will complete as part of the advanced credential. The plan is updated on the basis of assessments and evaluations relating to fieldwork or internship.

Core and Supplementary Faculty. For the first-tier program, the courses are all taught by faculty, with the exception of site-based leadership, which is taught by an alumnus Ph.D. and current principal. Three former well-respected superintendents conduct a significant share of the fieldwork supervision. Faculty members supervise other field experiences.

The second-tier program relies largely on adjunct faculty experts to teach the content areas. For example, a school lawyer teaches law, a school finance person teaches finance, and a district human resource director teaches personnel management. A faculty member teaches the organizational development and systems courses.

Recruitment and Selection. The program has a strong working relationship with area districts. A group of local superintendents meets four times a year with program staff to provide feedback on the program. Many of these districts screen and select candidates, although district selection is not a requirement for program participation. Although the two-tier program is demanding in terms of student time and commitment, the two-tier structure is a requirement of California state law. Many students are attracted to the CSU-Fresno program because of the relatively low price (competitors in the area are more expensive private schools). The program also attracts students for its perceived quality and strong placement record. Each of the area districts' high schools has a vice principal who is a graduate of the program. The quality of these graduates is an excellent recruitment tool.

To enter the program, students must have a master's degree. Selection is based on academic credentials and experience. The program typically seeks outstanding teachers who have a knack for providing leadership, although they may not be aware of their leadership skills.

Relation to State Policies. The state of California requires everyone pursuing the principalship to go through a two-stage process. Candidates participate in a provisional training program (twenty-four credits) to work in an administrative capacity; once in an administrative position, they need another twenty-four credits to achieve advanced certification.

The California accountability context provides an interesting backdrop to the administrator preparation environment. The state has enacted regulations requiring school accountability, peer review, and competency exams to graduate from high school and has banned social promotion. As part of the accountability program, low-performing schools have three years to improve performance on the Stanford Nine Achievement test. If schools don't improve, principals face losing their jobs. This has affected the demand for quality preparation programs. Principals and districts are looking carefully at their professional needs, identifying weak areas, and coming to the universities for help in addressing those areas. This has provided another important incentive to educators to focus on professional development plans.

Program Effectiveness. CSU research shows significant growth in the perceived competencies between beginning and ending participants. Student self-assessment scores are consistent with district supervisors' assessments. In addition, Donald Coleman, a member of the faculty, has conducted research on the validity and reliability of the PDI assessment, and on the validity of the ISLLC standards (Coleman and Adams, 1999; Coleman, Copeland, and Adams, 2000). Coleman and his colleagues have found the PDI to be both valid and reliable, and based on a limited sample, they have found that the ISLLC standards need modification to improve their validity.

Program Cost and Other Challenges. The program is funded primarily through state funds. Local districts pay for the PDI assessment ($450 per student) and donate the time for program feedback and some supervision of interns.

University of Louisville: IDEAS

The University of Louisville (UL) now runs two different program models. Officials are conducting an internal evaluation to determine whether to continue with both models or to eliminate the traditional one. The two share some characteristics and overlap in some places but have major differences as well. The first model is traditional in that students take classes to become certified and develop a portfolio to meet the state ISLLC-based requirements for certification.

The second program is called IDEAS (Identifying Educational Administrators for Schools). It was developed in collaboration with the Jefferson County school district and initially involved a cohort of prospective administrators from Jefferson County schools. Now two cohorts run simultaneously: one from Jefferson County and one from the Ohio Valley Education Cooperative, a cooperative of outlying districts.

In addition, Jefferson County and the University of Louisville run a yearlong program called Principals for Tomorrow for administrators who are certified but have not taken administrative positions. Principals for Tomorrow provides additional professional development opportunities to enhance the knowledge and skills of these licensed administrators. This review focuses on the preservice training program.

Program Structure. The entire administrator training program is one-and-a-half years in length (eighteen units). IDEAS is a nine-credit unit with traditional coursework and modules of field experience. The internship is part time; students are recommended and sponsored by a principal with whom they work eight to ten hours per week shadowing or collaborating. IDEAS integrates coursework and internship for nine of the eighteen credits needed for certification. The remaining courses are taken with students in the traditional administrator training program.

IDEAS cohorts begin in late May, using two National Association of Secondary School Principals (NASSP) Individual Professional Development (IDP) programs to shape a professional development path for each student based on needs. The cohorts meet twice a month and have an embedded internship during the school year. They are expected to have a minimum of sixty hours of school-site leadership. The bimonthly meetings of courses are rotated among district sites. When the course is taught at a school site, the principal at that school serves as a guest speaker.

Each participant has a sponsor-mentor who is a principal. Sponsors are responsible for providing access to internship experiences, reviewing the student's portfolio (with two faculty members) for ISLLC standards, and participating in the summer NASSP program as coaches and to provide feedback.

Pedagogy. The program is predominantly field-based, with some lectures but field experiences in all classes. Students have two mentors—one in the school and one out of it. Students intern at their schools. Program leaders are also experimenting with using Web-based technology to enhance classes between face-to-face meetings. For example, to review and discuss University Council for Educational Administration (UCEA) case studies, discussions are on-line. Technology is also used for things like PowerPoint presentations.

Three of the classes are largely traditional in delivery but are somewhat interdisciplinary, taking advantage of school-year variations to teach a variety of issues.

Curriculum. The curriculum is based on the ISLLC standards but has a significant focus on instructional leadership, including best practices, diversity, knowledge of instruction, and evaluation training. Prior to the ISLLC, the UL program used standards developed by the Educational Policy Standards Board (EPSB); some students are still grandfathered into these standards.

Core and Supplementary Faculty. The department is small and recently hired additional people. Five of the six professors are former practitioners; two are higher education professors and former higher education administrators. The off-campus classes are team-taught, and much learning is practice-based; the mentors provide an important additional learning resource.

Recruitment and Selection. Students in the IDEAS program are recommended for participation by the district and the sponsoring principal. If after formal admission procedures at UL there are too many candidates, the executive director for administration and recruitment for the Jefferson County schools chooses among them. The program has a growing number of women and elementary school principals, but it is having trouble attracting middle school and high school principals.

Students are attracted to the IDEAS program in large part because it is an honor to be selected by the district to participate. It suggests that the district is interested in promoting them to administrative positions upon completion of the program. IDEAS is also the only public program in the area, and the district defers a small amount of the cost for many applicants; therefore, some applicants may select it on cost considerations.

The formal educational experience of applicants is declining. Until recently, Kentucky allowed certification only for individuals who already had master's degrees, so applicants tended to have more teaching experience. These students came in with a significant length of service and usually a master's degree in a curricular area. The newer students have much less experience (some are first- and second-year teachers), and most have only a bachelor of science degree. There is no admission requirement for teaching experience, but Kentucky does require three years of teaching experience for certification.

Relation to State Policies. Kentucky state requirements mandate that students take credits at a program certified by the state teacher standards board. Graduates must pass the Kentucky specialty certification test, which is multiple-choice and focuses on school law and the Kentucky Education Reform Act. In addition, students must pass the Student Leadership Licensure Assessment (SLLA), ETS's ISLLC exam.

Program Effects. The University of Louisville surveyed 170 local administrators, 70 percent of whom are program graduates. The respondents indicated that the cohort model is probably better than conventional approaches, but the logistics make it hard for everyone who wants or needs training to use that method. They also indicated the following:

- The internship is highly valued. Respondents wanted more of them, early in their program.
- Women were more positive about the portfolio than men.
- The cohorts were viewed as very valuable for support and networking during the job search.

The Jefferson County school district has also evaluated program effectiveness based on feedback from participants and district evaluation of program graduates' effectiveness (the district has placed eighty to ninety principals). The evidence suggests that the program is very effective.

Program Costs and Other Challenges. Districts pay for many cohort activities, and some districts provide release time for the program. They also donate mentoring services and commit significant time from district leadership for evaluation and feedback. The districts also heavily market the program internally.

Wichita State University

The Wichita State University administrator preparation program was developed following a major revision in the doctoral program. It has a field-based research emphasis that parallels the research emphasis of the doctoral program. Based on feedback from graduates, the most valuable experience of the certification program was field placement. So the program was turned around. Now, rather than have fieldwork supplement coursework, the program is structured around fieldwork and continuous practical research, and coursework supplements the fieldwork.

Program Structure. The cohort-based program is designed not just to accommodate the lives of practicing teachers but also to use their access to schools as a core building block. Classes are held from 5:00 to 6:30 p.m. From 6:30 to 8:00 p.m., students work with their field study teams. In addition, the team has two field days during the semester to collect and analyze data. One professor guides the team on its problem or topic, and members conduct the study as a full participatory team (even the professor participates). At the end of the semester, the teams present their research. Students stay with their teams (of six to eight students) throughout the two-year program.

The internship represents fifteen of the thirty-three hours of required coursework, spread over the two-year period. This equals twelve hours per week of internship experience. Of the twelve hours, students are expected to gain six hours of experience per week during the day, with the remaining six hours conducted before or after school hours. Students are also expected to spend a full week in internship placement before and after the school year, participating in planning activities.

Pedagogy. Students learn content primarily through participation in individual and group research studies. Coursework accounts for half the total credit hours required for the master's degree. The courses themselves are heavily field-based, so that (for example) a law course is made up of twelve to fifteen contact hours rather than forty. The remaining time is dedicated to developing and carrying out a research project related to the coursework.

Curriculum. Coursework is provided in interwoven units: law with personnel; interpersonal communication with supervision; finance with leadership. The integration of curriculum works well with some subjects and less well with others. Students are assessed on research projects and coursework (papers and exams), and individual competencies are reviewed in a leadership performance assessment (Furtwengler and Furtwengler, 1998). Graduation is based on team reports and performance evaluations. Students are also scored on papers, research, and exams. The program includes a comprehensive written exam done in teams of two to four people. If the group meets the required standard, its members all pass; if it does not, they are given further assistance.

Core and Supplementary Faculty. The faculty are all full-time university faculty members. The department carefully selects them to fit with the philosophy of the program, which is heavily based on collaboration. New faculty need to learn to work in a highly collaborative environment, a unique feature of this program. Faculty members team-teach all courses in groups of three, and the courses are integrated on the basis of content.

Recruitment and Selection. The program is in high demand, due to its strong reputation in the region. It has a waiting list from year to year; candidates are typically hired for principalships before completing the program. The standards for admission are high, involving academic criteria, personal statements, and recommendations. Some students have been counseled out of the program for underperforming.

Relation to State Policies. The state is moving toward the ISLLC standards, but they won't be fully implemented until 2004–05. The Wichita program is aligned with the ISLLC standards. When designing the program, originators discussed the features of leadership they felt to be important and found a high correlation between these criteria and the ISLLC standards.

Program Effects. The program is about to undertake an extensive review by external evaluators; they anticipate strong positive results. An informal gauge of success is the growth of study groups in schools where graduates work. On their own initiative, many graduates have established discussion groups on problems or current research.

Program Costs and Other Challenges. With only thirty students admitted each year, the program is costly to run. However, the department has enjoyed support from the university for this small-cohort approach. In 1990, the regents indicated a desire to end the practice of using professional certification programs as cash cows or diploma mills and moved to raise the quality and rigor of their offerings.

A bigger challenge for the program has been the need to fight the university culture of faculty individualization and competition. The faculty had to overcome bureaucratic barriers to collaboration. To obtain approval for team teaching, for example, the department negotiated a deal with the dean that all courses would be divided such that every professor would end up with the same workload. Faculty in other departments sometimes view the program with suspicion.

San Antonio: Region 20 Educational Service Center

The Region 20 Educational Service Center in San Antonio, Texas, provides an alternative certification for principal licensure, as well as an aspiring-leader program and a project for first-year principals. Our review will focus on the alternative certification program.

In Texas, an organization can be a licensing agency at a traditional university or apply through a school district to be an alternative certification program. The Region 20 Service Center currently works with fifty-one school districts in the San Antonio area to provide certification for educational administrators.

Program Structure. The program is structured in cohort groups of twenty to twenty-two participants called a "cohort of leadership associates," or COLA. During the program, candidates take training classes and some take university classes at the university of their choice, and they all participate in an extensive paid internship. After two years, they can take the exit exam (state test), or if they do not feel ready, they can extend one or more years in the program. Applicants need 130 hours of pretraining up front. In the end, they have close to four hundred hours of training over and above the internship. If participants have not taken courses beyond their master's degree, they must take at least two university courses, depending on their districts' priorities. Despite the alternative nature of this program, its philosophy is that good practitioners stay linked to universities.

Pedagogy. The program uses the NASSP selecting and developing assessment as a checkpoint and five-year growth plan for the participants. It also uses the NASSP mentor and coaching model. Early in the process, all participants are assigned mentors from their schools or districts or from outside their districts. Candidates spend the duration of the program (two years) with the same mentors. Each candidate must spend 70 percent of the day in a leadership capacity.

For the classroom portion of the program, trainers use case studies that draw from the Quality School Leaders Strand and use workbooks with in-basket items. They also use role playing and simulations. They do some skill building, such as learning to run effective meetings. They have to apply their training at their sites and return with evidence of how the meeting went. Skill building is taught in each area except law and ethics, which is taught in a more traditional style. Participants also work on media skills by training in front of a camera to react to different scenarios—speeches, news conferences, interviews with aggressive reporters, and so on.

Students are encouraged to subscribe to at least one professional journal to keep up with some of the literature and to follow education news items, which are often incorporated into classes.

Candidates are taught to use the Web for research; they also use the Center for Creative Leadership, as well as on-line training sponsored by the Colorado Education Department on conflict resolution. Candidates are encouraged to research the Web to familiarize themselves with the views of controversial critics of education.

Curriculum. The curriculum is currently under revision. Candidates are required to participate in four hundred hours of noninternship training aligned to the state's seven standards for school leaders, Texas's version of the ISLLC standards. Students have to pass a state exit exam that is aligned with the standards, which focuses on ethics and morality, communication, management, instructional leadership, curriculum, school improvement, and resource development. The program administrator indicated that of these, ethics and communication seem to be the critical knowledge and skill areas. The program has a three-day module on ethical aspects of practice but tries to weave ethics throughout the curriculum.

The primary focus of the program is the internship and its related administrative duties. Districts choose mentors, but the program has final approval of them.

Core and Supplementary Faculty. The Educational Service Center conducts a variety of professional development activities for area districts. This program has five staff members who conduct training. In addition, national speakers are hired to make presentations, and the program gets agreement from them to allow use of their materials for other sessions. Around one hundred people in the area do some guest lecturing. Among the core faculty are district mentors who are trained using the NASSP mentoring and coaching model. They are trained on how to gather data, give feedback, conduct observations, and coach others.

Recruitment and Selection. The program invites applications from people with master's degrees in "just about anything" who are interested in school leadership. Participants must have 130 hours of "pretraining" up front, but they can substitute relevant experience for some of the requirements. A rigorous application process includes an IQ-like test and a personality profile to ensure that candidates have at least some of the attributes of successful principals. Applicants must also have excellent references. Applicants are interviewed, with follow-up questions based on the application materials and assessments. Consistent with state requirements, applicants must have at least a 3.0 GPA, a valid teaching certification, at least two years' teaching experience, and some form of leadership responsibility.

The program markets itself to superintendents and principals. It also runs advertisements on its Web site and in newspapers statewide. It has a good relationship with university programs and gets referrals from them of candidates who are not interested in the traditional university approach.

Among the three cohorts to complete the program to date, the first was highly experienced and all white; the second has two African American females and two Hispanic males; the third is all white. All participants except one have had ten to fifteen years of experience. Students choose this program over traditional ones because of the significant quality of the training they get. Graduates are typically hired as principals by their placement district.

Relation to State Policies. State policy allows for alternative certification programs approved by local districts. It also requires participants to pass an ISLLC-based assessment for licensure. Continued state approval for the program requires that 90 percent of participants pass the assessment.

Program Effects. Only one cohort has completed the program to date; 100 percent of its participants passed the state licensure assessment. Program officials frequently survey participants and districts regarding program features; these are formative rather than summary evaluations and are used to modify the program.

Program Costs and Other Challenges. The program charges $400 per course, comparable in cost to university-based programs in the area. Participating districts hire interns at a relatively low wage; they also agree to allow participants off campus for five days during the year for training in addition to the evening sessions. The mentors receive a $500 stipend from the district; some districts provide compensatory time off. Districts also have the incentive of having an intern on the job who is paid at a lower rate than the assistant principal.

Conclusions

Our analysis of the role of the principal, the knowledge and skill it demands, and this set of promising principal training programs together suggest a number of characteristics that may be useful in developing and improving administrator preparation programs. These characteristics differ from the norm of typical preparation programs. In many cases, evaluation data or anecdotal evidence from program administrators suggest that these characteristics have contributed to program quality. It is worth reiterating that these programs tend to be more demanding of participants than traditional ones, yet the programs are all in demand because of their reputation for producing highly qualified, competent administrators and for placing their graduates in administrative positions.

The programs differ from traditional programs in *selection and screening* as well as in *structure and content.* Administrators who had data on placement rates prior to the development and implementation of their model programs report that placement rates for participants are much higher in the model program than in traditional ones. They attribute these higher rates to enhanced preparation of candidates, which leads graduates to be more open to and interested in taking on challenging princi-palships. It also makes these candidates more attractive, so that those that seek placement actually land the job. The higher placement rates are important because model programs are typically smaller than their tradi-tional predecessors. Although the number of graduates is lower, their rate of placement into actual administrative positions is high.

Important features of these programs include coherence, curriculum focus, sequencing of courses, structured scheduling, collaboration with districts, screening and selection, and membership. Each of these will be discussed in turn.

Unlike the prototypical administrator preparation program, each of these programs was characterized by significant *coherence in curriculum, peda-gogy, structure, and staffing.* Significant collaboration was involved in devel-opment of the program vision, and each element of the program was carefully designed to reflect program goals rather than happenstance or con-venience. In several of the programs, the experiential component was viewed as the core, with classroom-delivered curriculum content designed to support and make meaning of the experiential component. The intern-ships themselves tended to be much longer than in a typical program (usu-ally six hundred hours or more over at least one year), and they were structured to take advantage of cyclical variations in the principal's role. Thus school-based budgeting would be taught to coincide with the budget cycle at the school site.

Program structures were designed to support the core vision and oper-ational goals of the program. The programs were virtually all cohort-based, with typical cohorts of about twenty to twenty-five students. Evaluation, feedback, and purposive program design provided cohorts with an opportunity to engage in more meaningful conversations about administrative practice. The programs provided a forum for making explicit the values and decision-making processes underlying principal leadership and the management decisions observed or experienced in the internship. The cohort structure also provided a significant support sys-tem and professional network for graduates in the early stages of their administrative careers.

Schedules were designed around students' working lives, but several programs required that students obtain significant release time from their districts to participate. Others designed program structures to minimize the inconvenience to students while remaining true to the overall objec-tives of the program.

Program staffing was purposive. Many programs were team-taught, and all had significant faculty discussions about the curriculum, with careful assignment of academic faculty and practitioners as demanded by the subject under study. The programs also typically found ways to work around traditional semester-length course structures, which were viewed as inappropriate for classroom content designed to meet student learning needs and the ebb and flow of administrative cycles. Since primary learning occurred in the field and classroom work was designed to support that, traditional semester-length classes did not fit well with the pedagogical approach.

Each of these programs had a *clear, well-defined curriculum focus*. Each program had a hallmark, a big idea that drove the curriculum design of the program—for example, moral leadership and organizational change at the University of Washington, research-based practice at Wichita State, ethics and communication at San Antonio, instructional leadership and transformational leadership at CSU-Fresno, and standards-based reform in Kentucky and Louisville.

In many of these programs, the *curriculum was sequenced and mapped* against the annual cycle of regular work responsibilities and the random, nonroutine responsibilities of the principal or else against a vision of the knowledge, skills, and abilities needed to be an effective school leader. The curriculum sequence varied among the programs; perhaps the most sophisticated sequencing strategy occurred at CSU-Fresno, where students were expected to become instructional leaders first and then transformational leaders. Coursework and state licensing requirements were aligned to serve those sequential purposes.

As with traditional programs, class meetings were arranged around work schedules, although in some cases students were required to obtain leave or to quit their jobs in order to participate. As mentioned earlier, program structure was typically driven by content rather than by university bureaucracy or tradition.

All of these programs were characterized by *significant collaboration* among the faculty and between the university and the practitioner community in the region. Some programs described overcoming the university culture of autonomy as one of the primary challenges of implementing the program effectively.

Another key feature of these programs was the degree to which applicants were *screened and selected*. In some cases, district leaders had to identify participants in order for them to apply. The University of Washington is an interesting example, using both academic and leadership potential as criteria for admission. Applicants must submit recommendations from their principals, another teacher, and a teacher that the principal selects. They are also interviewed and screened for their potential as moral leaders.

Together, these features affect the quality of the candidate, the quality of the experience, the focus of the program, the reputation and links to current practitioner communities and problems, and ultimately the quality of program graduates. Many of the program structures require more effort than a traditional program, potentially reduced revenues, and more time in planning and collaboration. Most of the model programs receive significant support from universities more interested in enhancing the quality of their offerings than in generating additional revenue.

Another important characteristic of the programs we have studied here relates to the challenges of development, planning, and implementation. Unlike traditional programs, each of these was developed through strong collaboration with local districts. In Louisville, Washington, and San Antonio, districts applied pressure on program administrators to develop the program to better meet their needs. The Jefferson County school district plays such an active role in the program that its officials actually screen and select applicants from their district from among those who apply to the program. They also provide considerable in-kind support for maintenance and program operations. Other catalysts for program development include external support, such as the Danforth Foundation grants (in Washington, CSU-Fresno, and ETSU), and program champions who encourage and lead the change effort. Among the examples here are East Tennessee, which has on its faculty the former director of the Danforth program, and CSU-Fresno, whose program director was formerly affiliated with the NAESP. In addition, extensive preplanning and discussion went into the design of these new programs. Finally, it appears that further discussions and continued planning and redesign occurred during implementation.

This examination of several model programs suggests important directions that could be followed to enhance the quality of administrative preparation across the country. One feature that may be difficult to replicate is the time and effort expended by the faculties and practitioner communities to discuss, plan, and agree on a direction for the programs. It was also necessary to make meaningful changes in program structure and content that required significant increases in faculty workload. Finally, it took the collaborative involvement of local districts with university faculties to make the programs successful. Nonetheless, these programs demonstrate that changes can occur that significantly redefine what preparation programs can accomplish.

REFERENCES

American Federation of Teachers. *Survey and Analysis of Teacher Salary Trends, 1998.* Washington, D.C.: American Federation of Teachers, 2000. [http://www.aft.org/research/survey].

Andrews, R. L., and Basom, M. R. "Instructional Leadership: Are Women Principals Better?" *Principal,* 1990, *70*(2), 38–40.

Block, J. H. "Reflections on Solving the Problem of Training Educational Leaders." *Peabody Journal of Education,* 1997, *72,* 167–178.

Bossert, S. T., Dwyer, D. C., Rowan, B., and Lee, G. V. "The Instructional Management Role of the Principal." *Educational Administration Quarterly,* 1982, *18*(3), 34–64.

Bredeson, P. V. "New Directions in the Preparation of Educational Leaders." In K. Leithwood, J. Chapman, and D. Corson (eds.), *International Handbook of Educational Leadership and Administration.* New York: Kluwer, 1996.

Bridges, E., and Hallinger, P. "Problem-Based Learning in Medical and Managerial Education." In P. Hallinger, K. Leithwood, and J. Murphy (eds.), *Cognitive Perspectives on Educational Leadership.* New York: Teachers College Press, 1993.

Coleman, D. G., and Adams, R. C. "Establishing Construct Validity and Reliability for the NAESP Professional Development Inventory: Simplifying Assessment Center Techniques." *Journal of Personnel Evaluation in Education,* 1999, *13*(1), 27–45.

Coleman, D. G., Copeland, D., and Adams, R. C. "A Report on the Reliability and Validity of the ISLLC Performance Standards." Paper presented at the National Council of Professors of Educational Administration NCPEA/ASSA Conference Within a Conference, San Francisco, Mar. 2000.

Council of Chief State School Officers. *Interstate School Leaders Licensure Consortium Standards for School Leaders.* Washington, D.C.: Council of Chief State School Officers, 1996. [http://www.ccsso.org/isllc.html].

Crawford, J. "Trends in Administrator Preparation Programs." *UCEA Review,* Fall 1998.

Deal, T. E., and Peterson, K. D. *The Leadership Paradox: Balancing Logic and Artistry in Schools.* San Francisco: Jossey-Bass, 1994.

Educational Research Service. *Is There a Shortage of Qualified Candidates for Openings in the Principalship? An Exploratory Study.* Arlington, Va.: Educational Research Service, 1998.

Elmore, R. F., and Burney, D. *Investing in Teacher Learning: Staff Development and Instructional Improvement in Community School District #2, New*

York City. New York: National Commission on Teaching and America's Future, 1997.

Fleigel, S. "Lured Away and Forced Out, Principals Leave New York City Schools at Record Pace." *New York Times,* Sept. 20, 1999, pp. 18, 20.

Ford, D., and Bennett, A. L. "The Changing Principalship in Chicago." *Education and Urban Society,* 1994, *26,* 238–247.

Fullan, M. G. *What's Worth Fighting for in the Principalship.* New York: Teachers College Press, 1997.

Furtwengler, W., and Furtwengler, C. "Performance Assessment in the Preparation of Educational Administrators: A Journey." *Journal of School Leadership,* 1998, *8,* 65–85.

Hallinger, P., and Heck, R. H. "Reassessing the Principal's Role in School Effectiveness: A Review of Empirical Research, 1980–1995." *Educational Administration Quarterly,* 1996, *32*(1), 5–44.

Hallinger, P., Leithwood, K., and Murphy, J. (eds.). *Cognitive Perspectives on Educational Leadership.* New York: Teachers College Press, 1993.

Hallinger, P., and Murphy, J. "Instructional Leadership in the School Context." In W. Greenfield (ed.), *Instructional Leadership: Concepts, Issues, and Controversies.* Boston: Allyn & Bacon, 1987.

Hart, A. W. "A Design Studio for Reflective Practice." In P. Hallinger, K. Leithwood, and J. Murphy (eds.), *Cognitive Perspectives on Educational Leadership.* New York: Teachers College Press, 1993.

Hart, A. W., and Pounder, D. G. "Reinventing Preparation Programs: A Decade of Activity." In J. Murphy and P. B. Forsyth (eds.), *Educational Administration: A Decade of Reform.* Thousand Oaks, Calif.: Corwin Press, 1999.

Keller, B. "Principal Matters." *Education Week on the Web,* Nov. 11, 1998. [http://www.edweek.org/ew/1998/11prin.h18].

Kelley, C. "The Kentucky School-Based Performance Award Program: School-Level Effects." *Educational Policy,* 1998, *12,* 305–324.

Kelley, C. "What Works in Education: Innovative School Management Approaches in the United States." Paper prepared for the Organization for Economic Cooperation and Development, Center for Educational Research and Improvement, Paris, 2000.

Leithwood, K. "Leadership for School Restructuring." *Educational Administration Quarterly,* 1994, *30,* 498–518.

Leithwood, K., and Duke, D. L. *Defining Effective Leadership for Connecticut's Schools.* Hartford: Connecticut Department of Education, 1997.

Leithwood, K., and Duke, D. L. "A Century's Quest to Understand School Leadership." In J. Murphy and K. S. Louis (eds.), *Handbook of Research on Educational Administration.* San Francisco: Jossey-Bass, 1999.

Leithwood, K., Jantzi, D., and Steinbach, R. *Changing Leadership for Changing Times.* Philadelphia: Open University Press, 1999.

Leithwood, K., Steinbach, R., and Raun, T. "Superintendents' Group Problem-Solving Processes." *Educational Administration Quarterly,* 1993, *29,* 364–391.

Levine, D. U., and Lezotte, L. W. "Effective Schools Research." In J. Banks (ed.), *Handbook of Research on Multicultural Education.* Old Tappan, N.J.: Macmillan, 1995.

Louis, K. S., and Marks, H. M. "Does Professional Community Affect the Classroom? Teachers' Work and Student Experiences in Restructuring Schools." *American Journal of Education,* 1998, *106, 532–575.*

McCarthy, M. M. "The Evolution of Educational Leadership Preparation Programs." In J. Murphy and K. S. Louis (eds.), *Handbook of Research on Educational Administration.* San Francisco: Jossey-Bass, 1999.

Meyer, J. W., and Rowan, B. "The Structure of Educational Organizations." In M. W. Meyer and Associates, *Environments and Organizations.* San Francisco: Jossey-Bass, 1978.

Miklos, E. "Administrator Selection, Career Patterns, Succession, and Socialization." In N. J. Boyan (ed.), *Handbook of Research on Educational Administration.* New York: Longman, 1988.

Milstein, M. M., and Associates. *Changing the Way We Prepare Educational Leaders: The Danforth Experience.* Thousand Oaks, Calif.: Corwin Press, 1993.

Mintzberg, H. *The Nature of Managerial Work.* New York: Harper & Row, 1973.

Murphy, J., and Forsyth, P. B. (eds.). *Educational Administration: A Decade of Reform.* Thousand Oaks, Calif.: Corwin Press, 1999.

Murphy, J., and Louis, K. S. (eds.). *Reshaping the Principalship: Insights from Transformational Reform Efforts.* Thousand Oaks, Calif.: Corwin Press, 1994.

Muse, I., and Thomas, G. J. "The Rural Principal: Select the Best." *Journal of Rural and Small Schools,* 1991, *4*(3), 32–37.

National Association of Elementary School Principals. *Elementary and Middle Schools: Proficiencies for Principals.* (3rd ed.) Alexandria, Va.: National Association of Elementary School Principals, 1997.

National Association of State Directors of Teacher Education and Certification. *The NASDTEC Manual on the Preparation and Certification of Educational Personnel.* (5th ed.) Dubuque, Iowa: Kendall/Hunt, 2000.

National Center for Education Statistics. *Public and Private School Principals in the United States: A Statistical Profile, 1987–88 to 1993–94.* Washington, D.C.: National Center for Education Statistics, 1997.

National Commission on Excellence in Education. *A Nation at Risk*. Washington, D.C.: U.S. Government Printing Office, 1983.

National Commission on Teaching and America's Future. *What Matters Most: Teaching for America's Future*. New York: National Commission on Teaching and America's Future, 1996.

Newmann, F., and Associates. *Authentic Achievement*. San Francisco: Jossey-Bass, 1996.

Ohde, K. L., and Murphy, J. "The Development of Expertise: Implications for School Administrators." In P. Hallinger, K. Leithwood, and J. Murphy (eds.), *Cognitive Perspectives on Educational Leadership*. New York: Teachers College Press, 1993.

Peters, T. J., and Waterman, R. H., Jr. *In Search of Excellence: Lessons from America's Best-Run Companies*. New York: Warner Books, 1982.

Peterson, K. D. "Making Sense of Principals' Work." *Australian Administrator*, 1982, 3, 1–4.

Peterson, K. D. *Secondary Principals and Instructional Leadership: Complexities in a Diverse Role*. Madison: National Center on Effective Secondary Schools, University of Wisconsin, 1989.

Peterson, K. D. *The Professional Development of Principals: A Portrait of Programs*. Unpublished manuscript, University of Wisconsin, 1995.

Peterson, K. D., and Finn, C. E. "Principals, Superintendents, and the Administrator's Art." *Public Interest*, 1985, 79, 42–62.

Prestine, N. A. "Apprenticeship in Problem-Solving: Extending the Cognitive Apprenticeship Model." In P. Hallinger, K. Leithwood, and J. Murphy (eds.), *Cognitive Perspectives on Educational Leadership*. New York: Teachers College Press, 1993.

Raun, T., and Leithwood, K. "Pragmatism, Participation, and Duty: Value Themes in Superintendents' Problem-Solving." In P. Hallinger, K. Leithwood, and J. Murphy (eds.), *Cognitive Perspectives on Educational Leadership*. New York: Teachers College Press, 1993.

Sirotnik, K. A., and Mueller, K. "Challenging the Wisdom of Conventional Principal Preparation Programs and Getting Away with It (So Far)." In J. Murphy (ed.), *Preparing Tomorrow's School Leaders: Alternative Designs*. University Park: University Council for Educational Administration, University of Pennsylvania, 1993.

Yale Child Study Center. *Professional Development at SDP: The National Events*. New Haven, Conn.: Yale Child Study Center, Yale University, 2000. [http://info.med.yale.edu/comer/profdev.html].

Appendix A: State Principal Licensure Policies, 2000

California

Preliminary Credential: Valid educator credential; three years of experience; fifth year of study (post-baccalaureate); approved professional preparation program in educational administration; recommendation by an approved college; special education (mainstreaming); and CBEST. Nonrenewable. (Candidates prepared outside of California eligible by verifying completion of a master's degree in educational administration, eligibility for the equivalent credential in originating state, three years' experience, CBEST, and the valid prerequisite credential).

Professional Clear Credential: Preliminary administrative services credential, two years of successful full-time experience in a position while holding the preliminary credential; and a Commission-approved program of advanced study and field experience. Valid five years, renewable with 150 clock hours of professional growth activities and one-half year of appropriate experience.

Connecticut

Initial Educator: Master's degree from an approved institution; completion of 18 semester hours of graduate credit in addition to master's degree; completion of 50 school months of successful teaching service in public or approved nonpublic schools, in positions requiring a Connecticut public school certification, or in a state education agency as a professional or managerial staff member (portions may be waved for applicants who have completed a one-year internship as part of an administrator preparation program); recommendation by an approved administrator preparation program that indicates applicant is personally and professionally qualified to serve as a public school administrator, and has completed an approved program, with not less than 15 graduate credits taken at the recommending institution. Has completed graduate study in each of the following areas: psychology and pedagogical foundations of learning; curriculum development and program monitoring; school administration, personnel evaluation and supervision, and contemporary educational problems and solutions from a policy-making perspective; and has completed a course of study in special education (comprised of not fewer than 36 clock hours). Valid three years.

Provisional Educator: Successful completion of Initial Educator Requirements, plus successful completion of beginning educator support and training, 10 months of successful service under the initial educator certificate, or 30 school months of successful service as an educational administrator within the 10 years prior to application; served a Board of Education in Connecticut successfully under a provisional certificate for the school year immediately preceding application. Valid eight years.

Professional Educator: Successful completion of 30 school months under the provisional educator certificate; and not less than 30 semester hours of graduate credit at an approved institution or institutions in addition to the master's degree. Valid five years, renewable with 90 contact hours of continuing education activities or six graduate credits.

Illinois

Master's degree from a recognized institution; approved program, or comparable certificate from another state, and 25–27 graduate semester hours in instructional leadership management, program development and operation, and policy; and two years of full-time teaching or school service personnel experience. The Illinois Certification Tests must be passed. Valid five years, renewable.

Kansas

Graduate degree and a state-approved building level administrator program; three years of accredited experience in the school setting at the level of the building administrator endorsement; and recommendation from an accredited teacher education institution. Renewable with six hours of recent credit, or comparable in-service points.

Kentucky

Three years of full-time classroom teaching experience; master's degree; approved Level I curriculum for school administration and instructional leadership; passing scores on the School Leaders Licensure Assessment (SLLA) and the Kentucky Specialty Test of Instructional and Administrative Practices. Upon confirmation of employment, an internship certificate issued for the first year of employment. Upon successful completion of the internship, the certificate is extended for four years. First renewal requires approved Level II curriculum. Successive renewals: two years of experience as a school principal, or three semester hours additional graduate credit, or 42 hours of approved training.

Tennessee

Master's degree in Educational Administration from an accredited college or university in a member state; PRAXIS (Principles of Learning and Teaching) and the Specialty Area Test in Educational Leadership: Administration & Supervision, with a minimum score of 530 points.

Texas

Master's degree, two years of teaching experience; complete required assessments; and complete the required program and induction period.

Washington

Initial Certificate: Current teaching certificate from any state; master's degree through a regionally accredited institution; complete a state-approved program of the principalship; and 540 days of full-time classroom teaching. Valid seven years.

Continuing Certificate: Must have completed all the requirements for the initial certificate; 15 quarters or 10 semester hours through an approved college/university or 150 approved clock hours based on specified performance domains. Verification of 540 days (three contracted years) of full-time experience as a principal, vice principal, or assistant principal; a course or coursework in issues of abuse, including the identification of physical, emotional, sexual, and substance abuse, its effects, legal requirements, and methods of teaching abuse prevention. Valid five years; renewable with completion of 150 hours of continuing education every five years.

Source: National Association of State Directors of Teacher Education and Certification, 2000.

Appendix B: Data Collection, Methodology, and Sources

We collected information from a variety of sources in order to gain a broad picture of issues related to the preparation and professional development of principals. These sources included research and interviews with key individuals and association members and with leaders of the preparation and in-service programs.

Initially, with the assistance of Hanna Alix Gallagher and Steve Kimball, we conducted a selective review of literature on leadership, principals' work, characteristics of preparation programs, and other topics related to preparation and in-service training. We looked for research-based knowledge as well as conceptualizations of the role and examples of best practices.

Next, we conducted structured interviews with a selected group of people who were involved in the training and preparation of principals, who had helped develop new certification standards, or who had been critics of such programs. Additional interviews were conducted with officials of the U.S. principals' associations to learn their concerns and initiatives in this area.

We then collected information on existing credentialing policies, as well as data on a variety of new standards for preparation. These policies and standards were compared to the knowledge base on the nature of principals' work and the needs of first-year principals.

We then developed a formal interview protocol to collect data on preparation programs. This provided the tool for gathering data on preparation programs.

We used a "snowball" sampling technique to find programs that were identified as particularly effective or innovative. We were able to identify several programs that were using a variety of different standards or approaches to preparation and that one or more informants viewed as successful.

The team conducted interviews with a select group of program leaders from every region in the country, spotlighting programs that approached preparation in nontraditional ways. The interviews lasted from one hour to several hours. Interview data were collected and organized around our core rubrics for describing and comparing programs. In addition, written materials, curricula, and schedules were requested from the programs. These materials were reviewed with attention to the core issues under investigation. Case descriptions were prepared and sent to respondents for a member check of accuracy of the information.

24

TEACHER LEADERSHIP: IDEOLOGY AND PRACTICE

Ann Lieberman
Ellen R. Saxl
Matthew B. Miles

THE "SECOND WAVE" of school reform has been characterized by much talk of restructuring schools and professionalizing teaching. Commission reports from business, education, and statewide policy groups are calling for major changes in the ways schools go about their work and the ways teachers are involved in their decision-making structure (Darling-Hammond, 1987). There is clearly an attempt to change the organizational culture of schools from one that fosters privatism and adversarial relationships between and among teachers and principals to one that encourages collegiality and commitment (Lieberman and Miller, 1984; Little, 1986; Lortie, 1975; Rosenholtz, 1989). On the political level, some states and school districts are creating new roles and new structures in an attempt to change the social relations of the people who do the work at the school level. The leap from report to reality, however, is a difficult one, for there are few precedents, few models, and no guidelines. We are literally learning by doing. What is needed, then, is a beginning description of this work and some understanding of the people involved—what they know and do, what the dynamics of their interactions look like—as these new forms come into being. What are these new structures? What can we learn about the meaning of these new roles for teachers? What is teacher leadership? What actually happens when teacher-leaders help other teach-ers? Our purpose here is to understand some of these new roles and begin to answer some of the questions now being raised as we look at a partic-ular group of successful teacher-leaders in a major metropolitan area. We consciously use the term *teacher-leaders* to suggest that there is not only a set of skills that are teacherlike, but a way of thinking and acting that is sensitive to teachers, to teaching, and to the school culture.

The Skills of Teacher-Leaders

From 1983 to 1985 we had a unique opportunity to study seventeen for-mer teachers who played leadership roles in a variety of schools in a large eastern city (see Miles, Saxl, and Lieberman, 1988). (We have continued to work with some of them for an additional two years.) Within that time, we were able to collect a great deal of information about who these peo-ple were, what they had learned in their new roles, what they did in the context of their school, and even, in their own words, their view of being teacher-leaders. The seventeen teacher-leaders worked in three different programs, and all were considered successful in the work they did within their schools. The criteria for success varied, depending on the context, all the way from creating a healthy climate, to making organizational change, to raising achievement scores.

The programs represented three different approaches to working with school people. The first was based on the "effective schools research," the second had as its major strategy the formation of a large school site com-mittee with a broad constituent group, and the third utilized an organic approach to working with teachers on a one-to-one as well as a group basis—providing support and expanded leadership roles for teachers. Despite the differences in strategy, we looked to see if there was a core of skills that was common to these people in their roles as teacher-leaders. (Skills to us meant knowing how to do something rather than knowing that something was appropriate to do. Our focus was on the *capabilities* of these people to activate strategies for change.) We reasoned that, as leaders, these people had to have or develop both process and content skills and that they had to be able to adapt to different contexts and dif-ferent situations. It is important to note that although these people were very experienced, they learned from both their new role and the context of their particular program.

First, it was necessary to separate out what these teacher-leaders knew when they came to the job from what they had learned while on the job. This gave us not only a sense of the possible criteria that were used in choosing these leaders, but what their new learnings had been as they worked to create these new roles and structures. Ultimately, we were looking for what skills would be teachable to new teacher-leaders in the future.

We found that these leaders had a broad range of skills, abilities, and experience, which included teaching children at several grade levels as well as adults. They were truly "master teachers." In addition, many had been involved in *curriculum development* in the past, as well as having held positions that enabled them to teach new curriculum to others. Their enthusiasm for learning was made manifest by an impressive array of *academic pursuits* and accomplishments. They held many academic degrees, as well as having attended a broad spectrum of courses, conferences, and workshops on topics as diverse as conflict resolution, teacher effectiveness, and adult development. They came to their work knowledgeable about schools, the change process, and how to work with adults. Most had held positions in which they had gained experience in *administrative and organizational skills* and had learned something about the complexity of school cultures. They were knowledgeable about community concerns as well as schools, some having served as school board members, community organizers, and in a variety of support positions in schools.

These leaders were risk-takers, willing to promote new ideas that might seem difficult or threatening to their colleagues. Their *interpersonal skills*—they knew how to be strong, yet caring and compassionate—helped them legitimate their positions in their schools amidst often hostile and resistant staffs.

On-the-Job Learning

In spite of this impressive array of skills and abilities, it was significant that these leaders had so much to learn to cope with their new positions. Where before, working in a variety of roles, they had been sensitive to individual personalities and perspectives, now they had to be aware of the interests of teachers, principals, and the community as a whole. These new conditions made it necessary for them to seek new ways of working, which, in turn, led them to find new sets of learnings. They found that what had worked in more narrowly defined positions would not work in the pursuit of a larger, common vision.

LEARNING ABOUT THE SCHOOL CULTURE. Without exception, these leaders learned about the school culture as if it were a new experience for them. They saw how isolated teachers were in their classrooms and what this isolation did to them. They realized how hard it would be to create a structure to involve them, to build trust within the staff, and to cut through the dailiness of their work lives. They were confronted with the egalitarian ethic held by most teachers—the belief that teachers are all alike, differing only in length of service, age, grade level, or subject matter, rather than function, skill, advanced knowledge, role, or responsibility (Lortie, 1975). They saw that while some principals understood the need for teacher involvement in their own growth and for allocating time during the school day for reflection and adult interaction, other principals pressed for "outcomes"—with or without a structure or process for teachers to learn being in place. In some schools, they saw literally no one supporting anyone. It came as no surprise then that some of these leaders said that the school climate and the administrator's style were the two most critical components of the school culture.

NEW SKILLS AND ABILITIES. All of these leaders learned a variety of techniques for gaining acceptance by teachers and principals. They learned to break into the everyday activities and provide hands-on experiences to get teachers interested. They provided new environments and activities in which people could communicate with one another and learned how to facilitate both group and individual learning and involvement. They learned to be part of the system, but not get co-opted by it—a difficult but essential ability. They struggled with the collegial/expert dichotomy, one that clearly contradicts the egalitarian ethic that was being disrupted. In working with adults, they tried hard to listen more and suggest less and to resist jumping in with too many solutions. In spite of a high self-regard, several reported that they had not realized how much they did not know (Goodwin and Lieberman, 1986).

These new leadership roles tend to expose the powerful infantalizing effects on teachers of the existing structure of most schools. It is not that no one is in charge, or that people are inherently distrustful, but that the structure itself makes it difficult for adults to behave as adults. Rather than work collectively on their problems, everyone must struggle alone. This ubiquitous isolation dramatizes what "restructuring schools" means. New organizational forms enabling people to work together are certainly necessary, but in order for them to be established, the teachers must be organized, mobilized, led, and nurtured, with the principal's support, participation, and concern and the support and concern of all who share in the life of the school.

SELF-LEARNING. In addition to the techniques, skills, abilities, and new understandings that these leaders learned in their schools, they strongly expressed the feeling that they had learned a great deal about themselves as well. Many spoke of a new confidence that they felt in their own abilities. Some thought that they had acquired a more complex view of how to work with people. One said, "I can't believe I have learned to motivate, to lead, to inspire, to encourage, to support, and yes, even to manipulate." Assuming leadership in schools, then, may provide the means for greatly expanding one's own repertoire. Providing and facilitating for other people in the school offers opportunities for learning how to work with others, how to channel one's time, how to develop one's own abilities—to stretch both intellectually and personally.

It is paradoxical that, although teachers spend most of their time facilitating for student learning, they themselves have few people facilitating for them and understanding their needs to be recognized, encouraged, helped, supported, and engaged in professional learning. Perhaps this is what we mean by "professionalizing" teaching and "restructuring the work environment" of teachers. Maybe the opportunities for participating in the leadership of schools, and the structures created as a result, are the means to break the isolation of teachers and engage them in collective efforts to deal with what surely are large and complex problems.

Building Colleagueship: A Complicated Process

Researchers have found the building of collegiality to be essential to the creation of a more professional culture in schools (Little, 1986; Rosenholtz, 1989). They have also documented that norms of collaboration are built through the interactions created by the principal's facilitation of collegial work. In Little's now-classic study, she describes how these norms were built as daily routines of isolation were replaced by talking, critiquing, and working together. In Rosenholtz's study, schools were differentiated as being of two kinds—"collaborative" or "isolated." In "collaborative settings" teachers perceived the principal to be supportive, concerned with treating any problems as collective schoolwide opportunities for learning; in "isolated settings" teachers and principals were alienated, with teachers feeling that any requests they made threatened the principal's feelings of self-esteem.

Since our study focused on the introduction of a new role that expanded the structure of leadership in a school, we were looking for the kinds of skills, abilities, and approaches that these leaders utilized in building collegiality in schools. In our search to understand how these teacher-leaders worked, we created sets of clusters, each cluster representing different skills, abilities, and approaches to building collegiality among the faculty. Although their contexts and styles were different, the similarity of the ways these leaders worked has added to our understanding of the complexities involved in changing a school culture when the leadership team is expanded beyond the principal.

The clusters were drawn from eighteen different skills that were manifested by these leaders (Saxl, Miles, and Lieberman, 1990). They include:

Building trust and rapport

Organizational diagnosis

Dealing with the process

Using resources

Managing the work

Building skill and confidence in others

Building Trust and Rapport

A very important cluster, this set of skills appears early in the development of the work of all teacher-leaders. We found that these leaders did a variety of things to gain the trust of the people in their buildings and that, even when the person was previously known to all the teachers, the same kind of work was still necessary. Because these leaders, in every case, did not have a teaching load, they were immediately suspect: "How come this person doesn't have a class load like me? What are they supposed to be doing anyhow?" Thus the first problem to be faced was how to clarify the expectations of their role for the teachers in the school.

To begin with, the leaders had to figure out for themselves what they could realistically do in the school. Then, they tried to explain to the teachers what they were going to do, describing in a broad way why they were there and what might be the effects of their work. In some ways, perhaps, it is like the beginning of school, where the students want to know what kind of teacher this is, what will be expected of them, and what will go on in the classroom. The relationship here is similar, in that these expectations are negotiated over time, but different, in that the adult culture in schools is not kind to newcomers, especially those of their own rank. The image and the reality of a new role (a teacher without a class) is not the norm, and it is often easier to use a new person as the source of one's frustrations rather than to accept her or him as a helper, go-between, or leader of a different kind.

Just as in the teacher-class relationship, the leader must come to be seen by the teachers as legitimate and credible. They try to accomplish this by finding various ways to demonstrate their expertise and value to the teachers. For some, it is giving a make-or-break workshop—one that they know will either give them immediate credibility if it is successful or set them back for months if it fails. For others, it means becoming a "gofer" and providing resources: going to the library, bringing new materials, keeping the coffee pot going and the cookie jar filled. Somehow they have to do enough to show the staff that they are "good"—experts and helpers, important enough to belong in "their" school. It is at this point that these leaders must learn to deal with *addressing resistance,* for they are coming into a social system with well-developed formal and informal ties. Sometimes this resistance is based on old disappointments and unfulfilled promises from past years. Other times a newcomer takes the brunt of all kinds of existing tensions in a school, caused by everything from lack of adequate communication to complaints about space, resources, time, and so forth.

Engaging in open supportive communication is part of building trust. These leaders found ways of working with teachers and proving to them that they were capable of being open without betraying trust—that they were there for the staff in a helping nonevaluative way. As they worked with the teachers, they began to *build a support group,* people who came to see that they could work together, struggle collectively, and feel comfortable working as a group rather than alone. For many leaders this meant finding teachers who could be experts in their own right, teachers who could teach other teachers things that they had learned. In the process of facilitating for others, the leaders began to *develop shared influence* and shared leadership. The idea that there are problems common to teachers and problems in a school that can be addressed collectively began to take hold, and teacher-leaders began to build a set of *productive working relationships.*

The abilities mentioned above appear to be necessary to the building of trust and rapport, which are the foundation for building collegiality in school. Regardless of the size or complexity of the school, the age or experience of the staff, or the differences in the programmatic thrust, the same kinds of skills were used to legitimate the leadership role.

Organizational Diagnosis

This set of skills—an understanding of the school culture and the ability to diagnose it—is crucial if a leader is to have the basis for knowing how and where to intervene to mobilize people to take action and begin to work together. Leaders did this in very different ways. Some people had an intuitive awareness of the formal and informal relationships in a school, while others consciously worked out strategies to help them collect data to help them better understand the school social system.

Depending on the specifics of the program, the methods of collection ranged from a formal needs assessment that asked teachers what they would find useful, to an informal collection of information about the principal, curriculum, resources, and so on. However it was accomplished, some initial *data collection* gave teacher-leaders a beginning awareness of the school environment. All were involved in picking up cues from staff, bulletin boards, teachers rooms, principals, parents—anyone who could provide information.

> In the beginning . . . I had to overcome my own personality—the tendency to move too quickly and speak out.

> When you are a teacher, you only know your classroom problems. Now I look at the whole system. . . . When I was in the classroom, I controlled it; the higher you go, the less control you have.

As we can see, collecting information while being conscious of one's self within the larger system was a strategic part of the teacher-leaders' way of working. Either as an insider or as one who came to a school with a leadership role, these people came to form some kind of a *conceptual scheme* in their minds—a map of what the school looked like, who one might work with, where the trouble spots were, who was open to thinking about working on schoolwide problems. As they collected information about the school by being there, hanging around, talking to people, and so on, they began to get enough information to *make a diagnosis*.

If action and change were what their diagnosis called for, these leaders had to find ways to engage key school people with their observations, to *share the diagnosis* with them to see if it was theirs as well. This series of steps, not always consciously thought out, formed the basis for action plans for the school. We begin to see a process: understanding the school, collecting information about the people and how they work, constructing a valid picture of the organization, sharing the picture with others, and planning a strategy for action.

Dealing with the Process

Critical to the work of teacher-leaders was their understanding of and skill in managing the change process. Since this meant, among other things, promoting *collaborative relationships* in schools where people had little experience in working together, it involved the use of *conflict mediation* and *confrontation skills*. They soon learned from the realities of their work that when one tries to get people to work together where they have previously worked alone, conflicts arise, and that their job was to find the means to deal with them. As they worked in their schools, building and modeling collaborative work, they were called upon to weave their way through the strands of the school culture. This involved many types of interactions with teachers, staff members, and administrators.

The relations with the principal varied according to the style of the principal and the structures for collaboration that were being created. When the structure called for working as a team and the principal had been used to working alone, the teacher-leader had to show the principal the benefits to the school of shared decision making. Where a teacher center had been created, the principal had to learn to give support for teachers to work independently without feeling that the existence of this room threatened her or his perceived role as "instructional leader." The tact, skill, and understanding of the teacher-leader was crucial to the involvement of the principal in supporting these new modes of collaboration.

Sometimes the school was in conflict from the start: "The first mission was to bring teachers together to talk to each other. There was a general distrust of the administration by the teachers." Sometimes the job entailed helping the faculty work through conflicts. "At committee meetings, many conflicts come up. He helps us talk them out. . . . We ventilate and direct our energy in a specific way."

Collaboration does not come as a natural consequence of working in a school. It must be taught, learned, nurtured, and supported until it replaces working privately. There were times when these teacher-leaders were the ones who had to confront negative information and give feedback where it was appropriate. Where conflicts appeared as a result of personal incompatibilities or differing interests, their job was not merely to smooth them over, as had often been the case in the past, but to find areas of agreement based on a larger view of the school and its problems.

They worked hard to *solve these problems* by making decisions collaboratively. This was a key skill: Who will do what, how will we do it, when will we make it happen, and how will we come to agree? They found that it took more than a vote to build consensus. It was always necessary to be alert to discontent and to practice and work on being open, communicating together, and finding ways to bring people, as individuals, to think of themselves as part of the group with group concerns.

Using Resources

The fourth cluster of skills involved the use of resources. This refers to people, ideas, materials, and equipment—all part of the school, but often not utilized in the pursuit of collective goals. The teacher-leaders found themselves engaged in providing material things for teachers that helped to link them to the outside world.

> I'm a reader. I need follow-up materials from the literature to find out about good ideas.
>
> They needed a lot of resources.
>
> I would attend conventions, day and weekend seminars, and collect handouts.
>
> I keep on top of things. What texts are good?

They did workshops for teachers, demonstrated techniques, and provided follow-up. They also looked inside the school to plug people in to what was already there and, where appropriate, to link people together.

In the process of finding resources and using existing staff to help, these teacher-leaders also began to build a *resource network,* which included developing active linkages between teachers and other members of the school community. It was not just knowing where or who to go to for help, but choosing the right person or right thing at the right time. Matching local needs and capabilities became the key skill.

Finally, it was necessary to help people make good use of the resources. Just getting the "stuff" there was not enough. The leaders had to perform a brokerage function and then follow up to see that the resources were being used. As we observed, this cluster of skills is part of a complicated process: from finding people and materials, both inside and outside the school, to building networks with these resources, to seeing that whoever, whatever, and wherever they were, they were available and utilized.

Managing the Work

The teacher-leaders worked hard to maintain a balance between the process of getting people to work on collective problems and providing the content or substance around which they worked. Managing this work required a subtle blend of skills, including managing time, setting priorities for work, delegating tasks and authority, taking initiative, monitoring progress, and coordinating the many strands of work taking place in their schools. (It should be noted that these leaders differed in the amount of time they spent in a school. Some spent four days a week in one school, while others spent one day a week in four schools.)

Administrative/organizational skills, although part of their qualifications, were far more complex in these roles than the teacher-leaders had faced before. Time was a persistent problem. How much time does one spend with people having difficulties, or getting resources, or making arrangements for workshops, or demonstrating, or troubleshooting? This proved to be a formidable task, with the successful teacher-leaders we studied gaining great skill in allocating their time as they became experienced in their role.

Managing and controlling skills were needed to organize and manage the work. The teacher-leaders had to learn to move from thought to action. Some used charts to keep track of their activities; some did not. But all of them had to learn how to mobilize the staff and coordinate the many activities, while walking the fine line between exerting influence and "overmanaging" the process of change.

Although contexts differed, these leaders shared the skill of being proactive, that is, having a bias for action. This included modeling specific new techniques as well as promoting a general vision of more productive ways of working. Maintaining momentum in their work without usurping the authority or the prerogatives of other leadership in the school required them to take initiative while negotiating their way through the delicate yet tough relationships between and among teachers and principal.

Building Skill and Confidence in Others

The last cluster of skills involved the continuous monitoring and *individual diagnosis* of teachers' communication needs and concerns, while attending to the general organizational health of the school. Working for several years in the same schools, these leaders tried to make normative the notions that it was both legitimate to have technical assistance and necessary to have in place some structure for problem solving. They were attempting to socialize a whole staff to have individual teachers look at themselves critically and take action on their own behalf while continuing to build supportive structures to better carry out the work as a whole.

They tried to involve as many people as possible in leadership roles by institutionalizing a process or mechanism for dealing with improvement goals, at the same time trying to make sure that constructive changes occurred that would be visible to the whole school. They were concerned with building a support network for the school community based on commitment and involvement that was sensitive to individual teachers and

other members of the community and, at the same time, promoted organizational change. This required constant vigilance: building networks for
support, continuously recognizing and rewarding positive individual
efforts that improved the school, helping to create short-term goals, and
always working to institutionalize individual and collective efforts at
improvement so that they would become "built into the walls."

Teacher-Leaders in the Context of Their Schools

The skill clusters we have been describing are based on interview and
observational data from the seventeen teacher-leaders we studied from
1983 to 1985. We can get another view, perhaps more integrated and
dynamic, by being there, by seeing these people in their own contexts. We
did several case studies of these teacher-leaders in 1985 and 1986. The
following summary of two of them will help round out the picture we
have drawn thus far (Miles, Saxl, James, and Lieberman, 1986).

Urban High School

Urban High is a large comprehensive high school that also serves as the
special education center for the entire area. It is in a blighted area in a
large urban city. There are 3,500 students in the school, 62 percent Hispanic and 30 percent black. Achievement is low overall. The majority of
the students (2,000) are enrolled in general education. Reading, math, and
writing scores are low. The principal is young, energetic, and extremely
receptive to innovative ideas and any means to improve the school. He is
very concerned with raising the level of instruction and increasing the professionalism of teachers through staff development and increased teacher
control of the curriculum.

In March 1985, a teacher center opened in the school. Brenda C., a
former English teacher at Urban, became the teacher-specialist—a full-
time teacher-leader hired to run the teacher center and work with the staff.
Because the school was in the process of reorganizing from departments
to clusters, experienced teachers were becoming the coordinators or heads
of special projects, causing them to leave teaching and move to these new
positions. (Given the harsh conditions of the school context—crime, purse
snatchings, noise, pitted chalkboards, lack of necessary supplies, prison-
like rooms, and other difficult teaching conditions—it is not hard to see
why teachers would want these positions.) When they left, new teachers
replaced them.

Brenda wanted to do three things during her first year: improve morale, facilitate communication between the various groups in the school, and encourage the staff to utilize the center for professional growth. Subtle resistance plagued her efforts in the beginning. There was the natural resistance to being "improved," as well as the notion that being a high school teacher—a subject-matter specialist—somehow made one already expert.

She began, during her first month, by just offering free coffee and refreshments to the teachers. (The principal had supplied a large room and the coffee.) She spent a great deal of time and money (her own) buying materials that would be of interest to the teachers. She tried hard to get materials that would engender self-help as much as possible, attempting to be sensitive to the sensibilities of her peers. She spoke at department meetings to advertise the availability of these materials to the teachers.

Little by little the teachers began to come to the center. At first they came only for coffee. Brenda wrote personal notes to people to encourage them to come back and to participate in other activities. To enhance communication, she formed a site committee made up of representatives from the various cluster groups. (Finding a common meeting time for everyone was impossible, so staggered meetings went on during the day.)

With encouragement from the director of the teacher center consortium, Brenda helped create a workshop, given after school was over in June, to teach teachers about the latest research on classroom management, mastery learning, and learning styles. The workshop was planned in such a way that the teachers had an obligation to attempt one or more of the ideas in their classrooms in the fall. In this way, Brenda hoped to begin to build a core group of teachers, encourage professional development in the center, and work on greater communication among the teachers.

The impact of these efforts, and others, has been to draw more and more teachers to the center. They read the bulletin boards, look at materials, use the machines, plan lessons, talk together, and work with Brenda. Informally, teachers come for afterschool courses from other schools, which indicates that the center is reaching out to a larger network in the district.

Teachers from the site committee have been instrumental in disseminating information about the center to other teachers. New teachers have talked about being offered nonjudgmental assistance by Brenda in the center. Experienced teachers have spoken about the amenities that make their life easier: a quiet place to work, copy machines, and new materials and supplies. All of this has greatly increased the morale of the staff. (An indication of the center's growing popularity was the success of a party for the staff that was given at the end of June. Almost all the teachers came—a highly unusual occurrence.)

Brenda, who has been a teacher at Urban High for twenty-three years and knows the social system of her school as an insider, has been using this knowledge to create an "oasis in the desert." We see the special role that a teacher in a leadership position can play—encouraged and supported by a sensitive principal—as she gently and cautiously plans for and takes on the function of building morale and professionalism among the staff. She helps alleviate the tensions of a large, experienced staff trying to deal with the tremendous problems that exist in a school in a depressed community. She builds trust among the faculty, recognizing not only the classical resistance to new ideas, but also the special nature of high school teachers (subject-matter specialists with advanced degrees who have their own special reasons to resist being "improved"). Although just a beginning, Brenda's leadership has begun to fill in the tremendous gap between a professional environment and the bare level of subsistence in a complex, difficult high school.

Parkridge Elementary School

At Parkridge Elementary School, Andrea G., a teacher-leader who came from another part of the city, also runs a teacher center. She has been at her school for four years. Her school has always been known as the showcase school of the district. It is a school with 1,500 children. The ethnic mix of the neighborhood has changed over time from Jewish and Italian to Hispanic and black, with a small percentage of Caucasian children.

The school has many fine teachers, many of whom have been there since the 1960s, when additional resources were given to particular schools, including this one, to help with their special problems. These teachers were attracted to the school because of the supply of specialists and the support they would be given. They came because they felt it would be a good place to teach. To this day, the school is still quite special for the area, but it is manifesting problems that are eroding the quality of the program. (Because of the positive reputation of the school, many parents want to send their children there; as a result, the school is suffering from serious overcrowding.) The principal is known to be a real "professional." He is very hardworking and the school is remarkably stable. The principal has been there for fifteen years, which is almost unheard of in this area.

Andrea, unlike Brenda, came from the outside to work at Parkridge, but, like Brenda, she, too, had the problem of legitimating her presence to the teaching staff. Because the staff was large, and because many had been there for a long time, there were numerous cliques among the teachers. There was also a group of eight new teachers who had taken over classrooms with little preparation for the job. (There was a massive teacher shortage in this city at the time.) An all-day kindergarten program had just been implemented, and the district had called for the school to involve the parents in working with their children at home.

In looking over this situation and figuring out her goals for the year, Andrea decided that the new teachers would be a focus for her work. She also decided to take on the responsibility for working with the parents of the kindergarten children to facilitate better understanding of what the school was doing and what the parents could do to reinforce student learning. In addition, she continued to maintain the teacher center—although it was a small, crowded room, teachers would know that at least there was a place to come where they could give and get help, put their feet up, and share some hot soup from the corner deli.

Everyone speaks of Andrea as the "glue" of the school: "She has made the school a family. Everyone feels a sense of gratitude and loyalty to her." Because she is a very giving person, her mere presence and her way of working fill a great void in this large, three-story building. Her first words are always, "How can I help you?" An hour and a half with her illustrates the point.

> On this day Andrea arrives at the center at 8:15 a.m. She is immediately involved in a "major" problem. One of the teachers, who has a refrigerator in his room, is complaining that because people leave food in it his room smells, thus disturbing him and the students. Andrea gets into the conversation to try to sort out who is responsible for cleaning the refrigerator and what needs to be done to get it cleaned. (This may seem like an insignificant problem, but no problem is insignificant. The message to the teachers is that all problems can be worked on in the center.)
>
> Andrea goes downstairs to the auditorium. She is due to hold a meeting there to teach parents how to provide reading-readiness activities for their children. When she gets there she finds someone else is rehearsing a play.
>
> Instead of complaining that the auditorium was reserved for her, she quickly negotiates with the teacher to use his room and runs to the front door to alert the parent sitting there to tell the parents what room to go to. Stopping off at the photocopy room to see that the materials are being run off for the parents, she finds a paraprofessional

having trouble with the photocopy machine and also with someone in the office. Andrea helps her fix the machine and then intervenes to ease the problem with the staff person. She then makes her way to the new room, where several parents are waiting, and quickly makes arrangements for one of the parents to translate for one who does not understand English.

In this one-hour period, Andrea has already made four interventions that do not go unnoticed. She has helped a teacher (with the smelly refrigerator), changed her room (by negotiating with the teacher in the auditorium), helped the paraprofessional with the photocopy machine (and a small problem with an office person), and provided for a translator (so that her work with the parents could go on in two languages). Such sensitivity does not go unnoticed, even in a faculty of this size. As a matter of fact, it turns out to be a mode of leadership that is felt by everyone. The principal is extremely respectful of Andrea's good work with the faculty. The supervisors find her presence welcome, since she helps them with their work without overstepping her authority. The specialists know that Andrea and the teacher center can support their work and also help them deliver services. And the new teachers come to the center because they know they can get help and support from both Andrea and other teachers who serve as a support group for them.

The Teacher-Leader as Learner

From this initial look at teacher-leaders, we see that they are not only making learning possible for others but, in important ways, are learning a great deal themselves. Stepping out of the confines of the classroom forces these teacher-leaders to forge a new identity in the school, think differently about their colleagues, change their style of work in a school, and find new ways to organize staff participation. As we have documented, it is an extremely complicated process, one that is intellectually challenging and exciting as well as stressful and problematic. Changing the nature of an occupation turns out to have the possibilities for both "high gain and high strain" (Little, 1988). The gain is mostly in the personal and professional learnings of the leaders themselves: the technical learnings about teachers, instruction, and curriculum; the social learnings about schools as social systems, including how to build collegiality and manipulate the system to help teachers do a better job; the personal learnings about their own professional competence as they learn new skills and abilities and find new approaches to being a leader among their peers; and even, in some cases, the satisfaction of learning how to create structures that alter the culture of the school.

But the strain is there, too. Building trust among teachers, who have long felt that they have little or no voice in choosing what is best for their students or themselves, is not easy. Initial hostility and resistance is always there, and it is hard not to take some of it personally. (What works with students does not necessarily work with adults.) Dilemmas of being a colleague and also being an "expert" are not easily negotiated. Being nonjudgmental and helping are often in conflict with making value judgments that affect the priorities for one's work. Listening to teachers—rather than giving advice—and working with them *on their terms* is sometimes in conflict with personal style. Learning to negotiate from a position of leadership—in a school where there is little precedent for teacher leadership—without threatening those in existing administrative positions takes skill, courage, and nerve. Teacher-leaders have to learn that these tensions and dilemmas are an inevitable part of the drive to professionalize schools and of the change process itself.

The Teacher-Leader as Professional Model

Part of the ideology developed in these new roles is the belief that there are different ways to structure schools and different means to work with teachers and other members of the school community. This involves such characteristic themes as

Placing a nonjudgmental value on providing assistance

Modeling collegiality as a mode of work

Enhancing teachers' self-esteem

Using different approaches to assistance

Building networks of human and material resources for the school community

Creating support groups for school members

Making provisions for continuous learning and support for teachers at the school site

Encouraging others to take leadership with their peers

We are only beginning to understand the nature and impact of these new roles in schools and the subtleties of fashioning new ways of working with the school community. From studying these teacher-leaders, we see that some sort of team, teacher center, or site committee—a structural change—appears necessary to the creation of collegial norms in a school. More cooperative work, increased interaction across department lines, and support groups for new teachers require new modes of collaboration to replace the existing isolated conditions prevailing in most schools.

What we have, then, is a new leadership role that can help in the creation of new collaborative structures. It appears that a combination of these new roles and structures is necessary to professionalize the school culture and to bring a measure of recognition and respect to teachers—who may be, in the final analysis, the best teachers of teachers as well as children.

REFERENCES

Darling-Hammond, L. "Schools for Tomorrow's Teachers." *Teachers College Record*, 1987, *88*(3), 354–358.

Goodwin, A., and Lieberman, A. "Effective Assistance Personal Behavior: What They Brought and What They Learned." Paper presented at the annual meeting of the American Educational Research Association, San Francisco, April 1986.

Lieberman, A., and Miller, L. *Teachers: Their World and Their Work*. Alexandria, Va.: Association for Supervision and Curriculum Development, 1984.

Little, J. W. "Seductive Images and Organizational Realities in Professional Development." In A. Lieberman (ed.), *Rethinking School Improvement: Research, Craft, and Concept* (pp. 26–44). New York: Teachers College Press, 1986.

Little, J. W. "Assessing the Prospects for Teacher Leadership." In A. Lieberman (ed.), *Building a Professional Culture in Schools*. New York: Teachers College Press, 1988.

Lortie, D. *School Teacher*. Chicago: University of Chicago Press, 1975.

Miles, M., Saxl, E., James, J., and Lieberman, A. "New York City Teacher Center Consortium Evaluation Report." Unpublished technical report, 1986.

Miles, M., Saxl, E., and Lieberman, A. "What Skills Do Educational 'Change Agents' Need? An Empirical View." *Curriculum Inquiry*, 1988, *18*(2), 157-193 .

Rosenholtz, S. J. *Teacher's Workplace: The Social Organization of Schools*. New York: Longman, 1989.

Saxl, E. R., Miles, M. B., and Lieberman, A. *Assisting Change in Education*. Alexandria, Va.: Association for Supervision and Curriculum Development, 1990.

25

LASTING LEADERSHIP

A STUDY OF HIGH
LEADERSHIP CAPACITY SCHOOLS

Linda Lambert

IN THE PURSUIT of a deeper understanding of leadership capacity we discovered a few startling insights about leadership itself. Together, these understandings constitute major findings toward the establishment of sustainable improvement in schools. The discoveries began with the stories of fifteen schools—schools at all levels and in different states and Canada—schools that were serious about getting better. We begin with a few observations.

The mascot at Vantage Elementary School was a trout. Even though the nearby creek had hosted an occasional trout long ago, this mascot lent little pride to California's lowest performing school. Symbols, however worthy, could not mask the despair felt by this school community. Today, Vantage Elementary School boasts significantly higher student performance, pride, and teacher professionalism.

In 1994, Kelly Elementary School in urban Ohio was the lowest performing school in this bustling city. Teachers did not want to be there—neither did the children and their families. Yet from 1998 to the present, Kelly has been the recipient of multiple awards for school improvement.

Caravell High School, in California, was identified as a low-performing school—a label that brought great consternation to the staff and community in this affluent suburb south of San Francisco. The seasoned staff confronted their worst professional nightmare: publicly declared low performance and humiliation. This startling information provoked collective action toward improving student achievement for all students.

Cavalier Elementary School is known as a school on the rise. In 1999, only 17 percent of their students were at or above grade level. Today, more than 58 percent of the children in this poor, urban school are meeting that standard, and performance is continuing to grow.

The majority of fifteen schools in this study are schools that have pulled themselves out of the status of low performance through shared leadership and a professional culture. Some of these schools, such as those mentioned above, virtually hit bottom with nowhere to go but up. They found strength and hope in their own conversations, and with district and networking assistance began the climb to student and adult performance of which they could be proud. This is a study of their journey toward high leadership capacity as well as a story of those schools that had already possessed and sustained high student performance and leadership capacity. The study magnifies our understandings of principal and teacher leadership, while raising critical questions about the future of leadership in schools that sustain success.

Leadership Capacity Study Design

This study did not necessarily begin as a study of formerly low-performing schools and their journeys toward respectability. It is a study of high leadership capacity schools and those that are moving in that direction. Specific criteria framed the invitation to participate. "leadership capacity" herein means "broad-based, skillful participation in the work of leadership" (Lambert, 1998, 2003) and was designed as a means to understand sustainable school improvement. The concept derives its meaning from the substantive literature regarding school improvement and professional learning communities and the correlation of these adult learning factors to student achievement. Leadership is understood as reciprocal, purposeful learning in community (Lambert and others, 1995, 1997, 2002). The features of leadership capacity frame four school types that can be described by the intersection of participation and skillfulness and can be seen in Figure 25.1. Each feature is evidenced in its desired form—that is, the forms described by identified research studies in school improvement. In Quadrant 4, for instance, the role of the principal and others in leadership (involvement in collaboration, problem solving, decision making, professional learning, conversations), vision/purpose and coherence, information and inquiry, relationships, and student performance (Glickman,

Figure 25.1. Leadership Capacity Matrix.

Depth of Leadership Skills and Understandings

Level of Participation

Quadrant 1 (Low participation / Low depth)
- Principal as autocratic manager
- Limited (one-way) flow of information; no shared vision
- Co-dependent, paternal/maternal relationships; rigidly defined roles
- Norms of compliance, blame; program coherence technical and superficial
- Lack of innovation in teaching and learning
- Student achievement is poor, or showing short-term improvements on standardized measures

Quadrant 2 (High participation / Low depth)
- Principal as "laissez faire" manager; many teachers developing unrelated programs
- Fragmentation and lack of coherence of information and programs' lack of shared purpose
- Norms of individualism, lack of collective responsibility
- Undefined roles and responsibilities
- "Spotty" innovation with both excellent and poor classrooms
- Student achievement appears static over-all (unless data are disaggregated)

Quadrant 3 (Low participation / High depth)
- Principal and key teachers as purposeful leadership team
- Limited uses of schoolwide data, information flow within designated leadership groups
- Polarized staff, pockets of strong resistance
- Designated leaders act efficiently; others serve in traditional roles
- Strong reflection, innovation and teaching excellence among selected teachers; program coherence still weak
- Student achievement static, or showing slight improvement

Quadrant 4 (High participation / High depth)
- Principal, teachers, as well as parents and students, as skillful leaders
- Shared vision results in program coherence
- Inquiry-based use of information to inform decisions and practice
- Roles and actions reflect broad involvement, collaboration, and collective responsibility
- Reflective practice consistently leads to innovation
- Student achievement is high or improving steadily

Depth of Leadership Skills and Understandings

Source: L. Lambert, January 2002.

1993; Fullan, 1993; Heifetz, 1995; Lambert, 1998, 2003; Newmann and Wehlage, 1995; Schmoker, 1996; Newmann, King, and Youngs, 1999; Garmston and Wellman, 1999). The presence, configuration, intensity, and quality of these features conspire to form the leadership capacity of schools and are a direct function of participation and skillfulness. Quadrants 1 through 3 are inferred from Quadrant 4 based on school interviews, observations, and case studies.[1]

The findings in this study are organized to tell a story of schools in progress toward high leadership capacity. The sections include (1) student performance and voice—whatever it takes, (2) school improvement conceptual frameworks, (3) the evolving phases toward lasting improvement, and (4) inferences and implications.

These schools stop at nothing to improve student learning. Beginning with an understanding of student strengths and needs, the conversations were efficacious and creative. Unlike conversations that emphasize statements of limitations, boundaries, and hopelessness, these educators and parents accepted no (or few) limitations in their planning for children.

Three performance patterns on standardized measures emerged:

1. In six of the lower performing schools there was a steady arc of improvement, with the greatest improvement occurring the first year. This arc held constant for all groups, although the margin of difference among subgroups continued, narrowing slightly each year.

2. In two of the lower performing schools there was a sharp increase in scores, followed by a limited decline and more gradual continued rise. In these same two schools, a concentrated focus on one ethnic group resulted in a marked improvement for that group and a slight decline in the performance of at least one other subgroup (African-American, Hispanic, Asian, LES; gender differences were not noted).

3. In the seven higher performing schools, student performance grew in a continuous and steady, yet less accelerated, arc.

Approaches for addressing student performance needs exceeded expectations, both in conception (performance viewed as beyond test scores) and in proactivity (they didn't wait for problems to occur, but acted in anticipation of student changes). Cavalier Elementary began a preschool program with a preliteracy emphasis and secured a 21st Century Learning Community grant to hire ten extra reading teachers. Harrison Elementary, refusing to be corralled by the Texas emphasis on tests, used rubrics, portfolios, self-assessments, and running records to secure a deep understanding of student performance. K–5 portfolios show the growth in writing abilities of Harrison students. Eden Gardens Elementary in North Carolina declined the temptation of complacency with good performance and developed "beyond our fours" thinking—beyond the top rung of the four-point rubric. In anticipation of the changing demographics in the school, Eden Gardens staff studied Payne's *A Framework for Understanding Poverty* (2001) as a means of preparing for the new challenges.

Sarason Elementary School, with already high scores (California API ranking from 792 to 852 in the last two years) and continuing to climb, used *Mosaic of Thought* (Keene, 1997) study groups and a strong emphasis on writing to seek a value-added dimension to student learning. Reading and research across the curriculum characterized the secondary schools.

In high leadership capacity schools, student leadership is considered a vital aspect of student performance. At Caravell and Lincoln High Schools, Harrison and Garson Elementary students are involved in action research with faculty. At Garnett Elementary, issues of attendance and suspension were addressed through student leadership of conflict resolution, consultation with students, and culturally responsive leadership (consciously involving children from all subgroups).

At Johnson Junior High in Missouri, student cadres invite feedback from students, which is contributed to the school's steering committee for assistance in planning. Students are also directly involved in developing and monitoring the school vision. The Garnett Gator Guardians is a strategic group of students who participate in school governance and implementation of school vision. At Garson Elementary, the voices of "focal students" (traditionally underserved) are sought out so that the school can keep on course with continuous school improvement for all students.

At Lincoln High, students are assessed by student exhibitions, rubrics (including leadership rubrics), portfolios, and performance assessments within courses and across the four schoolwide outcomes: personal responsibility, social responsibility, critical thinking, and communication. Teachers explicitly teach and model leadership understandings and skills, and governance structures provide extensive opportunities for participation.

At Kelly Elementary School, students helped develop the school vision and norms as well as taking on the responsibility to translate the purpose of the school to the community. Because the school is known as an Accelerated School, the purpose includes building on strengths, a unity of purpose, and strong collaboration among all stakeholders. The students also plan school celebrations and community events.

Each school boasts significantly improved and sustained student performance. This pattern had been sustained for four to ten years at the time of the study. However, each school struggles every day with continuing gaps among subgroups in spite of a sharp focus on their more vulnerable children. Several schools, most notably Garnett, Vantage, Cavalier and Lincoln High, have adopted and adapted an "equity pedagogy" (such as scaffolding, student discourse, reciprocal teaching, and cultural competency) designed to support higher achievement among historically underserved students. No school rested on its laurels or suggested that the journey toward the improvement of student performance was complete.

Conceptual Frameworks for School Improvement

Each school possessed a clear and clearly shared conceptual framework (or schema) for school improvement. Strategic approaches were not accidental or stumbled onto idiosyncratically. Each conceptual framework included the elements of school improvement described by the concept of leadership capacity. The welcome convergence of today's knowledge about school improvement means that several initiatives support and complement each other. For instance, three of these schools are members of the Accelerated Schools network that includes leadership capacity as one of its goals and further emphasizes unity of purpose, building on strengths, and the belief that everyone is a part of the process. Two California initiatives, SB1274 (a state restructuring initiative ending in 1998) and the privately funded Bay Area School Reform Collaborative (BASRC), promote approximately the same approach to school improvement described here. The state IIUSP process (Immediate Intervention of Underperforming Schools Program) in California takes a "let's make a plan to fix the school" approach, although this varies with the level of understanding of school improvement of the external evaluators. The Child Development Project promotes beliefs about children and adults that underlie strong school improvement. "First Things First" emphasizes sustainable relationships through vertical learning communities and "looping" (the use of student achievement evidence) and a professional culture. Further, many conceptions of school improvement were self-initiated at the school or district level and drew understandings from research literature, graduate programs, and school coaches.

These congruent concepts of school improvement involve design structures such as teams, communities, or cadres that organize staff, parents, and students into patterns that enhance relationships, participation, and skillfulness. Everyone is on a team, such as leadership team, vertical grade team, horizontal grade team, vision team, action research team, literacy team, data focus team, book study team, CARE team, or Dreamkeepers.

Everyone participates within a range of intensity. These teams engage in conversations about student performance and problem-solve questions of practice. Vision, beliefs, and values foci guide the development and implementation of initiatives that are congruent with the overall mission of the school (for example, the Vision Team at Carson shepherds the vision; the Dreamkeepers at Garnett monitor equity issues; and the teams at Lincoln High and Riverside Elementary have guiding principles).

Within these teams, as a whole staff, and in one-on-one coaching connections, everyone participates in skillful and focused conversations or dialogue. (Everyone participates in different ways—some still at a minimal level. No one is sabotaging the efforts.) These conversations are usually constructivist in nature: surfacing assumptions and beliefs, inquiring into practice, making sense of what they have found, and framing new or improved action. At Garson Elementary School, these constructivist conversations are referred to as PEP (peer enquiry process). At Johnson Junior High, these conversations take place in interconnected and articulated teams—leadership team, steering committee, cadres, and professional learning communities that are embedded in departments. In multiple other schools, the constructivist process is referred to as action research. The heart of success appears to lie in the shared beliefs and the conversation.

Approaches to problem solving reveal a strong sense of collective responsibility. For instance, when the vice-principal position was eliminated at Toledo Elementary in Canada, and Garson Elementary School, the staff decided how to redistribute the tasks among themselves.

In most of the schools, a high number of staff are involved in outside networks, graduate programs, or the national teacher certification process. The special initiatives or networks included (or had included) an external coach or consultant who worked closely with the school. For instance, this individual might be a coach and guide connected to Accelerated Schools (often the director of the program). The individual in this role at Johnson Junior High and at Kelly and Harrison Elementary served as a coach, trainer, friend, mentor, broker of services and visits, as well as coordinator of the network. Within Midwest City's First Things First program, a School Improvement Facilitator is assigned to each school.

These external coaches became trusted confidantes to whom both the principal and teachers turned for support, advice, and information. The external coach became an important "fluctuation" in the school, meaning a force that moved energy and dissonance through the system much like a small boat disrupts the tranquility of a lake. Such "tranquility" can grow into complacency or acceptance of the mean if an internal or external perturbance doesn't exist. Internally, such a fluctuation was often caused by a strong and insistent staff member (often the principal), a crisis, or student data revealing low performance. Externally, this fluctuation was often a function of an external coach or network. The role of the principal and teachers and their mutual influences can be described in evolving or developmental phases.

Evolving Phases Toward Lasting School Improvement

Principals' characteristics and understandings in schools that have high leadership capacity or are moving actively in that direction are strikingly similar. These individuals may be characterized by (1) clarity of self (that evolves during the process) and values, (2) strong beliefs in democratization, (3) strategic thought about the evolution of school improvement, (4) a deliberate and vulnerable persona, (5) knowledge of the work of teaching and learning, and, ultimately, (6) a capability for developing capacity in others and in the organization. In a high leadership capacity school, teachers evidence similar dispositions and behaviors. Figure 25.2 describes principal behaviors at each phase of development.

In thirteen of the fifteen schools, the six characterizations described above distributed themselves among three major stages of development that may be referred to as instructive, transitional, and high capacity. It should be noted that these phases apply when the principal enters a low or moderately low leadership capacity school. On the occasion of entering a moderately high or high leadership capacity school, the principal's approach was quite different. Those differences are described below.

"Instructive" refers to a period of organization, focusing, and establishing or initiating previously nonexistent collaborative structures and processes (such as teams, vision, examining data as a norm, shared expectations, and processes for working together). It is also a period of "holding on" (Kegan, 1982)—providing early protection and support so that relationships and identities can begin the process of shifting into new patterns. Teacher behaviors varied greatly, but were often remembered as dependent or resistant during the early stages of school improvement.

"Transitional" is the process of letting go—releasing authority and control—while providing continuing support and coaching. This is central to a strategic thought process—that is, knowing where the culture is going and when to pull back as teachers are emerging into leadership. As teachers emerged into leadership, this occurred at varying rates: many were more than ready to think differently about their work and enlarge their identities to include teacher leadership, while others moved more cautiously and deliberately.

Figure 25.2. Phases of Principal Development.

Instructive	Transitional	High Capacity
Principal as teacher, sponsor, director	*Principal as guide, coach*	*Principal as colleague, critical friend, mentor*
Personal attributes and behaviors	*Personal attributes and behaviors*	*Personal attributes and behaviors*
Learns continually Thinks strategically Is value and vision driven Sets norms with staff Supervises and ensures staff accountability Convenes conversations Honors history Sponsors staff growth Accepts responsibility Breaks dependencies Clarifies roles Articulates strategies Involves others in decision-making Creates safe, "holding" environment	Learns—attends to epiphanies Thinks strategically Translates values into vision language "Lets go," provides support—sticks around Scaffolds with ideas and questions Mediates roles Develops structures that build reciprocal relationships Coaches for instructional improvement	Learns continually Thinks strategically Is value and vision driven Continues and expands behaviors initiated in earlier phases *Participates* with other members of the community to: • think strategically • share concerns and issues • share decisions • monitor and implement shared vision • engage in reflective practices (reflection/inquiry/dialogue/action) • monitor norms and take self-corrective action • build a culture of inter-dependency • self-organize • diversify and blend roles • establish criteria for self-accountability • share authority and responsibility (dependent on expertise and interest, rather than role) • plan for enculturation of new staff and succession
Instructs staff in (or arranges for such instruction): • collaboration, group processes, and teaming • conversation and dialogue • inquiry/data use • trust building • best instructional practices • communication skills • facilitation • conflict resolution • accountability	*Guides* staff to: • develop shared vision • establish process • observe norms • participate in leadership • use inquiry • question assumptions • conduct constructivist conversations • problem find and solve • surface and mediate conflict • find resources (time, professional development, monies) • plan	
Uses formal authority to convene and maintain the conversations, challenge complacency or incompetence, make certain decisions.	Uses formal authority to sustain the conversations, insist on a professional development and inquiry agenda, mediate the demands of the district and state, set reform pace.	Uses formal authority to implement community decisions, mediate political pressures, work with less-than-competent staff, work with legal and reform challenges.

"High capacity" refers to developing capacity in the organization and in individuals in ways that encourage the teachers to play out more dominant roles. The role of the principal becomes one of a lower profile, leading from the center or side with an emphasis on facilitating and coparticipation rather than dominance. Teacher influence and actions began to converge with principals as they both became more reciprocal in their behaviors and conversations. This convergence permits a reintegration of new behaviors and relationships.

The Instructive Phase

In the Instructive Phase, the principal and other formal leaders may insist on attention to results, convening conversations, solving miasmic problems, challenging assumptions, confronting incompetence, focusing work, establishing structures and processes that engage others, teaching new practices, and articulating beliefs that may find their way into the fabric of thinking of the school. For most principals, such displays of "strength" were strategies; that is, they understood where they were going in building capacity and felt that they needed to jump-start the process in order to move out of low performing leadership capacity school status.

One such deliberate strategy could be called "pacing and leading" the community. Pacing and leading mean walking alongside of and being empathic so that others know they are being understood before asking a question or taking an action to lead in a new direction. Julie at Vantage described incidences in which she consciously matched cultural experiences and behaviors (in tone, language, and emotional affect), listened, and led community members into a place of participation in solving the deep problems that had besieged the school.

There is little data about teachers during this phase other than reported memories by principals of resistance, disengagement, and dependence. One principal still struggled with subtle and not-so-subtle aspects of dependence from a high school staff: "You just tell us your vision for the school and we'll act on it." These characteristics of teachers in a low leadership capacity school are consistent with my experience with schools throughout the United States and Canada.

Two principals remained strong past the time for letting go. They did the "right thing in the wrong way." Right things mean such actions as setting boundaries, encouraging participation, expecting accountability, and teacher decision making; "wrong way" means taking such actions in an instructive way yet maintaining tight control of the outcomes after the need to let go. Principals at Cavalier and Eden Gardens both lead in this manner. In spite of this instructive approach by the principal at Eden Gardens School in North Carolina, the teachers have created lateral, nested professional communities. The teachers are mature, involved in graduate programs, helpful to young teachers, and work earnestly at peer coaching and collaboration. In both schools, the staff is ready for a different kind of principal, meaning a principal that recognizes their capacities for self-governance. The principals—although not the teachers—in these two schools are situated in this first phase and were included in the study in order to understand more fully the evolution of the teacher culture in spite of the principal.

The second such school, Cavalier Elementary in California, may be seen as an Instructive Phase school that is setting the scene for transition. The principal believes that it is the principal's role and responsibility to set the vision and focus for the school, while teachers are members of a collaborative team that realizes the vision. Principal Laura suggested, "Leadership and vision flow into the community (from the principal) and the community members become part of making the vision happen. . . . Every job description at Cavalier School involves taking part in leadership." Teachers teach each other, develop curriculum, and observe and conference with each other. Student achievement has improved significantly (from 381 to 591 on the California API). Teacher behaviors suggest that they are ready to assume more responsibility for the larger arena of visioning and goal-setting. In order to move into and through the Transitional Phase, the principal will need to let go of some of the reins of power.

The Transitional Phase

A principal may find the transitional phase the most challenging, since the range of teacher development is at its widest. Some teachers may still expect and want an instructive principal (revealing dependent behaviors), others are awakening as more independent professionals, while still others are at a high leadership capacity stage and display self-organizing behaviors. Self-organization and its role in teacher development will be described more fully below.

The Transitional Phase is a time of epiphanies and turning points for both principals and teachers. For instance, Teresa, principal of Caravell High School, noted that her great "strength"—her strength—may have been getting in the way of the growth of others. As a result of this insight, she pulled back into stronger collaboration and peer conversations in order to diminish the reliance on formal authority. A turning point for Caravell was dramatically encountered when the school was identified as a low-performing school by the California State Department of Education. Teresa made this announcement at a faculty meeting by laying out the harsh reality of the low-performing status and declaring: "I don't know what to do. We'll have to figure this out together." They did.

During the third year of her tenure at Caravell, Teresa's husband died of cancer. Teachers filled in—not missing a beat. As Teresa reflected upon that time and her own transformation, she described herself as more aware of her assumptive thinking (her beliefs and truths), an acceptance of impermanence, and an empowering belief in the mission to help others discover who they are.

Julie at Vantage recognized her need to let go of authority and power when her teachers told her, "It is time to let go." Jason at Carson Elementary realized that he needed to rally the energies and diminishing self-respect of the teachers in order to pull out of the crisis of confidence and move forward. He deliberately used longitudinal student data to pronounce: "Look at the progress we have made! We must be doing a number of things well. Now where do we go from here?"

Encouragement during this phase was experienced as both direct and subtle approaches by the principal. At Garson School, Betty framed the need to address the achievement gap more aggressively: "Just remember that a change in practice or instruction will always come from the outside if you don't allow it to come from your own action research." Declaring such a consequence was encouraging and clarifying for Garson teachers.

Dolly, principal of Toledo Elementary in Canada, described both her strategic thought processes and her vulnerability:

> Being a principal in a school is a work in progress. The work of learning to be will never be completed because this is a dynamic role—a role based on human relationships. These relationships are constantly being created and negotiated. During my first year, I was intentional in engaging the individuals with whom I work. I worked on creating a climate of trust. The accomplishments of teams of people on staff were recognized by myself, and eventually by others. My leadership in this area shifted from me to reside within others.

Dolly learned to live with dissonance and tension while growing into her own confidence in the future.

Jason at Carson Elementary described the transition in this way:

> And here just recently I believe we've turned the corner. The last three staff developments have been conducted primarily by Vision Team members. Questions in our staff development have been deep and

meaningful. People are not afraid to take risks. People are staying late to meet with colleagues over professional growth without me prompting the meeting. My role has changed significantly. *People don't line up to ask me questions. They ask each other.* This type of growth means as much to me, if not more, as the quantitative scores. Actually, this type of growth was probably harder. It's like grabbing fog.

"It's like grabbing fog." The willingness of the principal to be vulnerable—to be open to the impermanence of his own role—was a crucial perspective during the transitional phase and served to evoke teacher participation. That is, when teachers became aware that the principal didn't have all of the answers, they actively moved toward more participation.

At a fall staff meeting, Julie declared to the staff: "I am a racist. I need your support to work through this." She was vulnerable. She was authentic. The staff responded well and began a four-year journey into a deeper understanding of their beliefs and assumptions about race, ethnicity, and poverty. The Dreamkeepers, a voluntary group of teachers, now monitors the school's progress toward their core value of equity.

One of the most challenging aspects of the transitional phase is the need to break through dependencies. Dependencies are often occasioned by a culture in which teachers need to ask permission of the principal for most actions—and they come to expect the principal to make the decisions and "take care of them." When a principal is aware of the danger of dependencies and strategic about the process of development, several deliberate strategies can be used to address the issue. In lower-performing schools (where dependencies are most apt to be found), principals turned decisions and problem solving back to the teachers, coached and led for teacher efficacy, while refusing to hold tight to authority and power.

The role of the principal, if there is a principal in the school, varied greatly. The splitting of the principal role into two roles early in its existence (the school has been open for six years) at Easton and Lincoln High Schools became "messy." Power and personality issues added confusion to the redefinition of roles and the development of the leadership team. At Lincoln High, the restructuring of roles into leadership and management or administrative functions has borne fruit: more focus on teaching and learning and continuing to develop the skills and identity of the leadership team. Power dynamics were avoided at Garson and Toledo Elementary schools when the loss of an assistant principal at each site prompted teachers to voluntarily redistribute those tasks. Teacher leaders at these two schools understood the essential nature of administrative roles such as those carried out by the assistant principal. Further, these teachers accepted shared responsibility for the work of the school. Those two factors naturally led them to redistribute tasks. At Riverside, the same factors seemed to lead to a major overhaul of roles when a decision was made to do without a principal.

The Transitional Phase was supported by a continuance of the "holding environment," and an easing out, or letting go, of that condition as teachers gained ascendancy in initiation and responsibility. This holding environment had meant sustained support and tenacity during a period of early change and development. During this time, there is a temptation to give up or abandon the effort—it seems too hard, too difficult to achieve. Support involves continuing conversations, staying in the process (rather than giving way to quick fixes), coaching, and problem solving within an atmosphere of trust and safety. Those leading the effort displayed confidence in the future. For the most part, principals were able to remain in the schools for the reintegration of the new program or goals and teacher identity in the next phase, rather than being pulled out by the district during this critical period.

The external coach had a significant role to play during the transitional phases: observing, coaching, and advising. At Kelly Elementary, when teachers felt that they were losing momentum under the guidance of a new principal, they independently approached the external coach to intervene and bring life back to their school improvement process. She did so in two ways: by working closely with the new principal and by meeting and planning with teachers.

The transitional phase gave way to the high leadership capacity phase when reintegration and self-organization became more nearly achieved. That is not to suggest that phases end and begin with "clean borders." On the contrary, behaviors emerge, dissolve and sometimes reappear in the struggle for capacity.

The High Leadership Capacity Phase

Principals in the high leadership capacity phase displayed many of the qualities and skills that helped them succeed in the previous two phases: caring and collaboration; a capacity for introspection and personal learning; beliefs in the capabilities of others (children and adults) for learning, strategic thinking, and self-governance; and a commitment to social justice. However, behaviors were somewhat different in this phase. The principal evidenced a lower profile than ever before; she or he relinquished and shared critical roles and responsibilities; and teachers as well as principals initiated new actions and posed critical questions.

Strikingly, principals and teachers became more alike than different. As teachers self-organized, initiating and self-responsible behaviors emerged. A leveling or balancing of relationships occurred as reciprocity developed between the principal and teachers. With reciprocity, teachers found their voices, grew confident in their beliefs, and became more open to feedback. The principals no longer had to convene or facilitate the conversations, frame the problems, or challenge assumptions alone. Principals and teachers began to share the same concerns and work together toward their resolution.

The principals at Lincoln High, Easton High, and Sarason Elementary began their tenure in moderate to high leadership capacity schools. As a new charter school, Lincoln High struggled to establish the structures and roles that would define it as one with high leadership capacity. Easton High and Sarason Elementary principals followed highly effective principals. These current principals were carefully selected so that they could carry forth the spirit and behaviors that had brought the schools to this point. Rita at Easton High School explains it this way:

> I view myself as simply one small part of the wheel that turns—at times I am the hub, at times one of the spokes, and at times the rim that meets the road. . . . I believe in the intrinsic good of people and look at my job as helping them to see that within themselves.

Greg, principal at Lincoln High, observed:

> I'm trying to lead for *whenever I may not be here any longer*—by building both systems (through school design choices) and people's capacity for leadership; both of these focused on holding and progressing toward the vision. We have to strengthen both the vision and people's capacity to lead toward that vision.

Riverside Elementary in California has been a high leadership capacity school without a principal for seven years. However, Riverside was brought to this state of self-governance by a principal who set about to develop a self-governing school and did so with the support of the California state SB 1274 restructuring program and the district.

Kelly School in Ohio is an example of the three phases of growth. During the first three years that Principal Margaret was there, she tore down the boundaries among personal and professional roles in order to build trusting relationships. They held retreats on a houseboat. Tough decisions and actions toward less-than-competent teachers (reassignment, dismissal, encouraged retirement) could be carried out without losing trust among others. She sought to hire new teachers so that they could be inducted into the new environment; mentoring was her main approach. Margaret took a strong lead at first and then backed into strong collaboration. Kelly was the lowest performing school in the city and was under threat of closure. She and the staff rallied around a sharp focus on student learning. Two staff overcame their own initial resistance and began to participate when they were convinced that student achievement was improving. High test scores were not enough for Kelly—they measured student achievement by a number of measures: state test scores, attendance, demonstrated performance, fewer discipline referrals, and parent involvement. As described above, four years later and under a new principal, the teachers became concerned that they were losing momentum and asked their external coach for assistance. Today, with a new half-time principal, the school is a high leadership capacity school.

The above comments and statements lead us inevitably to revisit the shifting role of the principal as teacher leadership evolves and the principal takes on a lower profile. Is it possible—even desirable—to "live without a principal"? If so, when is a school ready to operate without a principal? An intriguing criterion of a high leadership capacity school may be that it should be able to exist and thrive without a principal, whether or not this is the chosen action.

Kelly Elementary School has a half-time principal and, the district believes, could probably do without a principal. Riverside Elementary has been without a principal for seven years. Eden Gardens teachers have created a nested professional community in spite of the influence of the principal.

There are many reasons for having a principal. One person can more readily take responsibility for convening and facilitating the conversation, securing focus, monitoring and working through difficulties that have personnel or legal implications. Leadership skills are important, and one person who brings such skills can be the conduit for teaching and modeling them for others. District personnel are often more comfortable with a principal as the main contact with the school, contract manager, and legal representative. This last point has become true in the district where Riverside resides.

However, principals are often mobile, transferred, or reassigned before the transitional phase is complete. The new principal may possess a style or vision incongruent with lasting school improvement. In spite of the problems that may arise from placing so much responsibility on one person, the role of the principal continues to represent the most crucial factor in school improvement, perhaps because teacher behavior is most often a function of principal behavior (unless the school possessed high leadership capacity before the principal arrived). Even when an effective principal sticks around, his goal should be to achieve that which was suggested by Gary P.: "I'm trying to lead for *whenever I may not be here any longer*—by building both systems (through school design choices) and people's capacity for leadership."

When principals lead for "whenever they will no longer be around," teachers can enter a state of self-organization. Within a state of self-organization, staff can outlast, endure, and perhaps energize a marginal principal and often sustain school improvement. "Self-organization" can be observed to occur when the organization of a system spontaneously increases and becomes more complex, new roles and structures (such as webbed or nested communities, or teaming) are formed by the participants. Initiating and self-responsible behaviors emerge that are not dependent on external direction. This emergence brings forth sustainable and higher level properties (such as when a teacher leader or mentor becomes a better teacher). When self-organization occurs on the part of teachers, it is a time that the principal can leave without regrets.

When principals have the forethought to lead toward teacher self-organization, they set about to create multiple interlocking groups, teams, or communities in which the conversations stimulate critical thought. For instance, schools with leadership teams, reading groups, vertical teams, and learning communities evoke disparate ideas and dissonance that challenge assumptions and project new possibilities. Within two years of such a richly textured professional life, teachers will begin to self-organize.

Teachers in a self-organizing state find leadership in each other, assigning both credibility and authority to their peers. They leverage mutual authority by expecting others to initiate and bring problems to the group. Within nested communities, teachers drew learnings, energy and authority from each other. In almost every school, the staffs rejected the idea of waiting a few years to engage new teachers in leadership. At Harrison Elementary, the principal noted that they gave new teachers leadership responsibilities immediately (with a 400 percent increase in student enrollment, this meant that the vast majority of the staff was made up of new teachers).

With or without a principal, teachers performing at a high level of personal and professional capacity tended to also become involved in external opportunities, networks, and graduate programs. Often they moved on to other positions, but their absence doesn't seem to adversely affect the momentum of school improvement. Toledo School closed at the end of 2003 (as a result of an extensive district process that involved the teachers), yet teachers were persuaded that their professional contributions would continue in their new settings.

The notion that schools could aim to do without a principal may prove to be a major conception of lasting school improvement.

Inferences and Implications

At the onset we suggested that this study invited a few startling discoveries, among those the shift to teacher leadership that takes place as leadership capacity grows. Teachers experienced a personal and collective journey from dependency to high levels of self-organization and a readiness to lead a school without a principal. This study further suggests that schools moving toward high leadership capacity reveal a striking internal cohesion or coherence. These interdependent features consist of a comprehensive conceptual framework, improved and sustained student performance, broadly distributed and skilled leadership, vision- and value-driven work, and a professional culture (collaboration, reflection, inquiry, and dialogue). However, these features evolved strategically through three phases of development, noted here as Instructive, Transitional, and High Capacity. These phase titles suggest role, relationship, and cultural evolution: the roles of each group (administrators, teachers, parents, and students) changed, as did the relationships within and among these individuals as well as the culture of the organization. Schools evolved into a projected condition of sustainability for lasting improvement. Sustainability is considered to be a process rather than a state and to hold promise for continued improvement in spite of vital personnel changes.

In addition to the phases of development, multiple additional lessons were learned, detailed, or suggested:

- As noted, a key factor in the evolutionary phases concerned the identity and roles of teachers. As social organization became more complex, teachers transitioned into greater collective responsibility, self-identification as teacher leaders, and self-organization. When stages of self-organization were reached, teachers were able to lead schools without a principal.
- Teacher shifts in identity that constituted reintegration required sustained internal and external support. This finding suggests that it is important for the principal to stick around until reintegration takes place—a significant understanding for districts as they consider their succession practices and policies. School coaches provided important forms of support.
- Reintegration occurred on the organizational level as well. These schools—viewed as a collective of personnel, students, and parents—became increasingly strategic, bold, clearly focused, efficacious, and often insubordinate.

- Conceptual frameworks grew thick with cumulative knowledge and skillfulness, snowballing as people worked together in new ways. For instance, reflective practice may have begun with an examination of quantitative and standardized data and became increasingly complex. Constructivist conversations, examining student work, action research, and peer coaching filled out a framework's inquiry requirement. Shared leadership was joined by distributed leadership (shared leadership is seen as the collective task; distributed leadership is understood here as the dispersion of tasks throughout the organization). Vision statements found life through frequent visits and connectedness to community values.

- While the fifteen schools ranged from urban schools with high poverty and ethnic and language diversity to a few more affluent, suburban schools, the unfolding of lasting improvement did not differ markedly. The primary differences were two-fold: (1) conversations about race and ethnicity were more directly confronted in urban schools, and (2) low performance on state assessments forced public and district attention on the schools. This attention provoked radical action toward change.

- Roles evolved from sharply separate to become blended. "Blended" suggests that viewpoints, skills, and actions become more alike than different. Tasks that were traditionally performed by the principal could be performed by any number of people within the school. Parents and administrators performed teacher tasks. Many roles and tasks were fulfilled collectively. Such diversification of roles is an important dimension of the fabric of sustainability.

- Contextual issues included size, location, and grade levels. Location identifies urban, suburban, and rural and, therefore, location is an influence on resources, accountability press, diversity, and parent concerns. Grade levels were most directly related to the complexity of structures (number and type of teams, particularly) and parent leadership. It might be anticipated that student leadership would be stronger in the high schools than in the elementary schools, but this was not the case. Size was probably the most important variable. Small size allowed for an intimacy and organization that could not be acquired otherwise. The most pertinent example here is Riverside Elementary, a small rural school without a principal. It is strongly recommended that size should be the variable, not a determinant, of school success. We should be able to say, "Let us create small schools because they are directly linked to student success," rather than, "Our school is large so there are certain factors related to school success that we cannot establish."

- Resources (monies and expertise) for professional development were forthcoming from the district and professional organizations such as those described in the section on conceptual frameworks (for example, Accelerated Schools, First Things First, SB 1274, and Annenberg). The districts either provided or supported conceptual frameworks for school improvement. This guidance entailed coaching, training, meetings, and encouragement for networking. In many cases, time was made available to schools for professional development and collaborative work in the form of shortened or full days. In two cases, administrative resources were retrieved when assistant principalship positions were eliminated. Administration resources (the previous principal's salary) at Riverside were partially redistributed to teachers as stipends for performing the instructional tasks of the principal. The district leadership actions that involved guidance, expertise, time, and other resources appear to be a significant factor in the success of these schools.

• Each of the school staffs was involved in networking opportunities beyond the school. Sometimes these networks were formally sought out through sponsored regional conferences, seminars, meetings, and coaching. In other cases, "networking" occurred as part of participation by staff members in district committees or graduate cohorts. The flow of ideas and new relationships coming from these exchanges served to energize the fluctuations as a function of external coaches.

• University professional preparation programs can discover important organizational and curricular ideas in this study. If principals can be prepared to hold fast to values while letting go of power and authority, schools are more likely to attain lasting school improvement. And companion understandings for teacher education would suggest that teachers be prepared to function as full participants and leaders in the school community, attend to the learning of both children and adults, and enter into collegial relationships with principals.

Sustainability, although receiving a great deal of attention in recent years, continues to be the most confounding problem in human organizations. Education is no exception. If anything, the complexity of the "product" (student learning) and bureaucratic limitations places education more at risk. These risk factors include episodic and random improvements subject to rapid diminution with personnel changes.

The work in leadership capacity as described in this study considers leadership as reciprocal, purposeful learning in communities. Therefore, Lasting Leadership embodies the intention that leadership is not only reciprocal and purposeful, but that the learning is a lasting, continuing facet of sustainability. Learning occurs as social interactions and groupings connect in new and complex ways, thereby inspiring critical thought and energizing self-organization. When learning is continuous, and participation in that learning is broad-based and skillful—High Leadership Capacity—we find the potential and the reality of sustainable, lasting school improvement. This study provides greater depth to these understandings and greater hope for its realization.

LEADERSHIP CAPACITY STUDY COINVESTIGATORS

Julie Biddle, director, Ohio Accelerated Schools Network, Dayton

Kaye Burnside, regional superintendent, West Contra Costa School District, California

Dale Clark, principal, Maple Ridge School, Calgary, Canada

Connie Finley, principal, Haslet School, Haslet, Texas

Mary Gardner, former superintendent, Saratoga Union School District, California

Tom Gilchrist, teacher facilitator, Creekside School, Black Oak Mine School District, California

Rhonda Hardie, principal, Eastside High School, Washington

Priscilla Hopkins, principal in residence, California State University, Hayward

Jan Huls, principal, Garfield School, San Leandro, California

Tess Lauffer, principal, Capuchino High School, San Mateo, California

Jose Lopez, associate professor, California State University, Hayward

Belen Majors, principal, Graham School, Newark, California

Margaret McCreary, consultant, San Leandro, California

Gayle Mollar, associate professor, Western Carolina University, North Carolina

Martha Morgan, coordinator, Center for Educational Improvement, Heart of Missouri Regional Professional Development Center, University of Missouri, Columbia

Lynn Shimada, principal, Sedgwick School, Cupertino Union School District, California

Jayson Strickland, principal, Caruthers School, Kansas City, Kansas

Barbara Storms, chair, Department of Educational Leadership, California State University, Hayward

Maggie Szabo, associate professor, California State University, Hayward

Janice Thompson, principal, Verde School, West Contra Costa School District, California

NOTE

1. Study nominations were sought from among schools with which I had worked personally and from colleagues working with initiatives that emphasize the characteristics of high leadership capacity schools. The principal investigators included the principals of the schools themselves working with their staffs to respond to study questions, directors of initiatives and external coaches (such as Accelerated Schools, an external coach acting as an state facilitator, a university), and myself. From the many schools that were nominated, fifteen were chosen. These fifteen schools include eleven elementary schools, one junior high school, and three high schools (one a charter school). Of these, eight are urban, previously low-performing schools; four are suburban, racially and ethnically diverse; one is suburban, not diverse; and two are rural with high poverty communities.

A set of open-ended questions invited participants to describe the leadership capacity of their schools, including obstacles and sustainability. Two all-day conversations were held with principal investigators and with critical friends (those familiar with leadership capacity yet not directly involved in the study). During these conversations, the investigators "presented" their school by describing the context, accomplishments, and struggles. In the second conversation, investigators responded to a rough draft of the study, noting patterns, making inferences, and suggesting conclusions.

REFERENCES

Fullan, M. G. *Change Forces: Probing the Depths of Educational Reform.* Philadelphia: Palmer Press, 1993.

Garmston, R., and Wellman, B. *The Adaptive School: Developing and Facilitating Collaborative Groups.* Norwood, Mass.: Christopher-Gordon, 1999.

Glickman, C. *Renewing American's Schools: A Guide to School-Based Action.* San Francisco: Jossey-Bass, 1993.

Heifetz, R. A. *Leadership Without Easy Answers.* Cambridge, Mass.: Belknap Press, 1995.

Keene, E. O., and Zimmerman. S. *Mosaic of Thought: Teaching Comprehension in a Reader's Workshop.* New York: Heinemann, 1997.

Kegan, R. *The Evolving Self.* Cambridge, Mass.: Harvard University Press, 1982.

Lambert, L. *Building Leadership Capacity in Schools.* Alexandria, Va.: Association for Supervision and Curriculum Development, 1998.

Lambert, L. *Leadership Capacity for Lasting School Improvement.* Alexandria, Va.: Association for Supervision and Curriculum Development, 2003.

Lambert, L., Kent, K., Richert, A., Collay, M., and Dietz, M. *Who Will Save Our Schools? Teachers as Constructivist Leaders.* Thousand Oaks, Calif.: Corwin Press, 1997.

Lambert, L., Walker, D., Zimmerman, D., Cooper, D., Lambert, M., Gardner, M., and Ford-Slack, P. *The Constructivist Leader.* New York: Teachers College Press, 1995.

Lambert, L., Walker, D., Zimmerman, D., Cooper, D., Lambert, M., Gardner, M., and Szabo, M. *The Constructivist Leader.* (2nd ed.) New York: Teachers College Press, 2002.

Newmann, F. M., King, M. B., and Youngs, P. "Professional Development That Addresses School Capacity: Lessons from Urban Elementary Schools." Paper presented at the annual meeting of the American Educational Research Association, New Orleans, April 1999.

Newmann, F. M., and Wehlage, G. *Successful School Restructuring: A Report to the Public and Educators.* Madison: Wisconsin Center for Educational Research, 1995.

Payne, R. K. *A Framework for Understanding Poverty.* Highlands, Tex.: Aha Process, 2001.

Schmoker, M. *Results: The Key to Continuous School Improvement.* Alexandria, Va.: Association for Supervision and Curriculum Development, 1996.

26

RESOURCEFULNESS

RESTRAINT AND RENEWAL

Andy Hargreaves
Dean Fink

*We cannot solve the problems that we have created
with the same thinking that created them.*

—Albert Einstein

SUSTAINABLE LEADERSHIP develops and does not deplete material and human resources. It renews people's energy. Sustainable leadership is prudent and resourceful leadership that wastes neither its money nor its people.

Improvement and Energy

Improvement needs energy. Sustainable improvement needs sustainable energy that can be converted into human and material resources. But what resources? And how do we sustain these resources? There are two prevailing views on this issue. The first concentrates on the finite nature of planetary resources: fossil fuels are disappearing, greenhouse gases are intensifying, and we are running out of time and space. We have to stop producing and consuming more and more because within a century or less, more prosperous countries and their people will have reached the limits to growth. If we want to protect and preserve nature's legacy, along with our own survival within it, the people of more prosperous countries will have to restrain their appetites and start to come to terms with the meaning of enough (McKibben, 2003). The second position accepts the fact that our earth is fragile and imperiled but claims that it is still possible to meet the basic material needs and develop the human potential of everyone without damaging the surrounding environment, if we approach the problem with care and ingenuity (Meadows, Meadows, Randers, and Behren, 1972). The first position is that of sustainability; the second, that of sustainable development. Resourcefulness, we want to argue, entails being willing to recognize and respond to both visions of our relationship with the planet, its people, and their development.

Closed and Open Systems

The finite view of energy draws on an ironclad principle of physics: the second law of thermodynamics. This states that once energy is transformed, it is no longer a resource available for work in the future. The two laws of thermodynamics were first stated in 1865 by a German professor of mathematical physics Rudolf Clausius. They are succinct (Goodstein, 2004, p. 95).

1. The energy of the universe is constant.
2. The entropy of the universe tends to a maximum.

Clausius invented the concept of entropy. Entropy measures the temperature of energy. As energy moves from high to low temperatures, it is not as capable of doing useful work. The energy spreads out; it is not as useful (even though it is still conserved); and so it tends toward disorder or increasing entropy (Goodstein, 2004).

Entropy is nature's penalty for energy transformation (Rifkin, 1981). Human and natural systems are in a perpetual state of dissipation until they reach equilibrium, at which point all the energy has been transformed and ultimately expended, resulting in death. A look in the mirror as we age gives evidence of entropy, as do air pollution and toxic waste. We can only slow down entropy, not stop it. So we exercise, recycle, donate money to poverty groups, and so on. For example, while recycling is an important way to slow down entropy, it also requires the expenditure of other energy sources. When we recycle newspapers, bottles, or cans, placing them in a plastic box provided by our municipality, a truck takes away the contents.

But manufacturing the boxes, fueling the trucks, and running the recycling plant also require energy. Even then, the remnants and residues of the products and the machines that recycle them still end up in landfill sites. We might guzzle gas in large vehicles or conserve fuel in small ones; we might clothe ourselves in ever-changing fashions or prudently wear family hand-me-downs; we might write on brand new paper or rely on recycled products instead, but everything ends up as waste at the end of the line. This is the process of entropy and of design, production, and consumption processes that have a cradle-to-grave life cycle, just as we do.

The ecological implications of entropy for our optimal lifestyle and habits are clear and widely understood: slow down the damage, conserve fuel, reuse and recycle, be prudent and self-sacrificing, limit your appetites, do fewer bad things.

Nobel Prize–winning physicist Ilya Prigogine found this perspective somewhat depressing, and he also observed that living systems evolve in an opposite way from entropy: from simple to complex, from disorder to order. He suggested that some parts of the universe are closed systems, which behave in mechanical ways and are subject to the law of entropy. But most social and biological systems are open, exchanging energy, matter, and information with their environment. Open systems in nature include brains, immune systems, cells, and ant colonies.

In open systems, energy need not be dissipated but can be exchanged, replenished, and renewed, as it is among the practitioners of natural capitalism, who try to convert the waste of one enterprise into a resource for a partner, reducing levels of waste (or entropy) almost to zero (Hawken, Lovins, and Lovins, 1999).

In an even more creative vein, ecological and industrial designers William McDonough and Michael Braungart (2002) demonstrate that the manufacturing process can be designed as an open living system that transforms disorder into order. In the case of shampoo production, for example, instead of asking how we can limit the negative impact of chemical discharge from the production process, we should ask how the shampoo's by-products might actually improve the quality of the river. Indeed, the authors designed a product that not only worked as an effective shampoo but increased the quality of the waste leaving the factory compared with when it entered. Rather than cradle-to-grave design, McDonough and Braungart therefore propose an energy exchange model of cradle-to-cradle design, inspired by the natural processes of living systems as well as by technological ingenuity placed at their service. In this cradle-to-cradle approach, resources are never lost but are renewed and replenished in a way that promotes regeneration and improvement.

So there are two ways to understand and approach environmental, organizational, and educational resourcefulness: restraint and renewal. Restraint urges us to do fewer bad things and avoid or limit actions that will wear out people or things. Renewal inspires us to do more good things and find ways to reenergize people or exchange energy more efficiently within the system. The problems in our work and our world arise when narratives of progress and change deny both of these ways to slow down entropy and renew or exchange energy.

Mechanical Waste

The dominant narrative of progress in the Western world and the scientific era has been the narrative of the machine. This narrative organizes the world as if it obeys universal physical laws of predictable order and as if nature can be controlled through technological mastery. It denies or diminishes the importance of entropy, operating on the assumption that resources of nature, as well as human labor and energy, can be used and exploited without limit, as if their availability were endless. In this mechanical narrative, progress is a ravenous machine of creative destruction, eating up everything in its path in order to create a better world ahead, oblivious to the natural and human waste it leaves strewn in its wake.

In the seventeenth and eighteenth centuries, the scientific method of Francis Bacon and the mathematical arguments of René Descartes and later of Isaac Newton laid the groundwork for this mechanical view of the universe by rejecting all other ways of knowing, such as intuition, ethics, and faith. These thinkers helped create a world that was viewed as rational, linear, and understandable through thought and reason.

The idea of a predictable, knowable universe based on unchanging laws impressed philosopher John Locke, who sought to discover the natural laws in humankind's social and economic activities. Locke rejected the church's teaching that the purpose of life was to prepare for the Last Judgment and asserted that the actual purpose of life was for people to look after their self-interest in the here and now. The job of governments and other institutions was to clear the path for people to achieve what they wanted in life, and if nature had to be exploited to enhance the well-being of people, so be it. There are clear echoes of John Locke among contemporary advocates of the ownership society. Even Frank Sinatra's motto, "He who dies with all the toys wins," has Locke's stamp.

In summary, in the mechanical narrative,

- There is a precise mathematical order to the universe and also to social and economic life.

- People must intervene to change nature's disorder into human order.
- People's self-interest depends on continual growth and development.
- Science and technology are the tools to achieve unlimited progress and growth.

These four principles have dominated our lives for over four centuries and still underpin economic development, political strategy, and top-down educational reform.

Together, these elements have unleashed the power of creative destruction that has produced capitalism, industrialization, modern city living, and globalized economic activity and lifestyles. The mechanical narrative has also created environmental degradation, provoked wars over resources, and wasted millions of human lives (Bauman, 2004). In practice, the mechanical narrative has denied and disregarded Clausius's theory of thermodynamics—the law of entropy, the price of progress. Inability to confront the law of entropy in standardized educational reform practice has also created waste in terms of human stress and burnout (Evans, 1996), as well as loss of deep and broad learning, as the price of short-term targets and results (Hargreaves, Earl, Moore, and Manning, 2001).

Janice Burnley was in her second year as principal at Lord Byron High School when she and her school had to confront the formidable challenges of implementing the government's far-reaching reform agenda in a context of dramatically reduced resources. Changes in the Ontario government's funding formula had cut the number of Lord Byron department heads from nine positions to just four. Each of the four leaders now had to attend to multiple areas of study—for example, one person had responsibility for physical education, art, music, drama, and technical education. The principal described this depletion of the school's middle-level leadership as "devastating." Burnley and her assistant principal had to assume many of the responsibilities previously performed by department heads, such as mentoring the eleven new teachers, teacher supervision, and community and district liaison. The assistant principal explained, "My typical day starts at 7:15 in the morning, phoning in for supply teachers [substitutes], covering classes, making sure that's in place. Seeing a bunch of kids as much as possible in between—I am not as visible as I would like. I feel bad, because I like to be in classes. My night finished last night at 10:30."

With only one full-time guidance counselor now remaining in the school, the administrators were "doing more guidance work than anything else." Some teachers had refused to contribute to extracurricular activities because of their workload, so Burnley sponsored a volleyball team, just to keep the program alive. Burnley felt "responsible for the world." "Every year I say I cannot work any harder, and every year I have to work harder. The support systems to make things happen are just not there anymore."

Burnley and her assistant tried to involve staff in decision making, but pressures of time and multiple, accelerating reform demands obliged her to be more directive and less collegial than she preferred. For example, the district required all schools to implement the Ministry of Education's new reporting system immediately. Although the technology was flawed, Burnley had to mandate in-service sessions for all staff. As a relatively new leader, she was not in a position to say no to her superiors, and she admitted to feeling "pretty isolated." She felt more and more like a manager for the government rather than a leader of her school. "The opportunities as an administrator to initiate changes, or even to get out in the hallways and into classes and network with kids and teachers are certainly restricted," she complained.

The denuded leadership structure forced staff to fend for themselves. The requirement to spend more time in class, the limitations on time outside class, and the overall intensification of work eroded the school's informal leadership. The government's determination to eliminate so-called waste in school district bureaucracies meant that the art teacher had to depend for subject assistance on the good will of colleagues in other schools and that the neophyte music teacher had to rely on a teacher from a neighboring school and a kind-hearted instrument repairman from a private firm.

Concern for the quality of their work and the welfare of their students permeated every conversation with teachers. There was a growing sense of powerlessness. With less resources of time and money, teachers constantly complained about outdated texts, computers that crashed, and the elimination of field trips and sports activities. "We are driven by computers and by the deadlines that somebody else sets," one teacher observed. As budget resources declined, human resources became depleted along with them. Within less than two years, the district's escalating resource crisis resulted in Lord Byron High School being merged with a nearby special education school.

Lord Byron's teachers and leaders were not alone. Teachers we surveyed in Ontario secondary schools felt "tired of being bashed," "beaten down," "browbeaten," "vilified," and "constantly criticized" by repetitive change and imposed reforms. Sixty-seven percent of them stated that since the reforms, they worked less collaboratively with their colleagues; 80 percent reported that their working relationships with school administrators had not improved; 43 percent pointed to reduced contacts with parents; and most tellingly of all, 88 percent indicated that they would be less likely to advise their own children to go into teaching (Hargreaves, 2003).

Caught between teachers' feelings of anger and distress and their own legal obligations to implement multiple reforms in a hurry, principals and assistant principals began to doubt themselves. "My whole life changed in a short time. Why am I feeling overwhelmed by the political shift?" said one. "I'm implementing government policy I do not agree with," another remarked. One captured the feelings of most of his colleagues when he said, "The system is clearly making you into managers but you have memories of how to be leaders. You are now feeling and acting like your teachers. You have tried to pick up the slack of teachers' lack of involvement, but you're beginning to behave as persons who are devalued and disempowered."

Within five years, the government of Ontario had removed resources from the public education system, returned millions of dollars to the taxpayers, imposed a demanding curriculum on students, introduced a range of standardized tests, required teachers to teach more students, and implemented an unwieldy computerized report card. It did all this with alarming alacrity, reinforcing the fast school philosophy of repetitive change. The complexity and speed of its changes and the depletion of financial resources produced monumental waste of emotional energy, confidence, commitment, and trust among principals and teachers. The rage in the government's machine had ravaged the educational environment on which its rational model of progress had been inflicted.

Ecological Restraint and Renewal

There is a better narrative to guide our use of material and human resources: a narrative of restraint and renewal. On one hand, the quest and pressure to continually raise performance standards in tested achievement at any price need not be so all-consuming. On the other, ecosystems are also open systems that exchange energy, matter, and information with their environment. They can renew, restore, and rejuvenate. Losers can become winners, failures can become successes, and the weak can become strong.

In ecosystems, everything is connected to everything else. In *The Power of Full Engagement*, Jim Loehr and Tony Schwartz argue that "the corporate body is a living, breathing entity comprising individual cells of dynamic energy" (2003, p. 23). Fritjof Capra provides the same insight: sustainability "is not an individual property but a property of an entire web of relationships: it involves a whole community" (2002, p. 214). John Locke was wrong. So was Frank Sinatra. The purpose of life is not to amass all the toys for ourselves, but to restrain our appetites where we can and to grow and develop with others so that we can improve our environment along with the public good that benefits us all.

Restraint

Bill McKibben is one of the world's leading environmentalists. He issued some of the earliest warnings about global warming (McKibben, 1989). With great passion and a wealth of evidence, he has argued that the earth is already so despoiled that it will become a wasteland for all species, including humans, unless we change our patterns of production, consumption, and disposal. Many of McKibben's predictions, which were initially seen as extreme and alarmist, are now widely accepted scientific wisdom. In 2005, for example, over a thousand researchers from ninety-five nations, working with the World Resources Institute, undertook a worldwide ecosystem assessment, which concluded that human activity now seriously threatens the earth's ability to sustain future generations because of negative impact on the planet's basic circulation systems of air, water, and nutrients and on the fundamental diversity of life (Reid and others, 2005).

Some energy resources are finite. Even with new discoveries and improved technologies of extraction, the worldwide supply of oil, like any mineral resource, rises from zero to a peak, and when consumption exceeds the possible rate of extraction, it then declines forever. In *Out of Gas*, David Goodstein prophesies that in just a few years, we will be at a point where "increasing demand will meet decreasing supply, possibly with disastrous results" (2004, p. 17). We are reaching the end of the age of oil, and if we are not careful, we will also be reaching the end of clean water, coral reefs, and fresh air. Out of time, out of options, out of gas—this is the future of energy and modern life, unless we can open up alternatives like hydrogen and wind power and severely restrain our consuming appetites and environmentally destructive behavior in the meantime.

The same issues apply in educational leadership and change. Loehr and Schwartz (2003) argue that there are four domains in which we need to conserve and renew energy: physical, emotional, mental, and spiritual energy. Our energy and long-term effectiveness become depleted when we

- Have no time to sleep, relax, or exercise properly
- Feel constantly overwrought or emotionally disengaged from those around us in a world in which we have no time for proper relationships
- Are always having to think too quickly or superficially

- Are disconnected from and unable to pursue or fulfill our own morally compelling purposes

Attending to these energy deficits is partly within our control, Loehr and Schwartz argue. But they also acknowledge that some organizational and work environments are seriously and perhaps toxically energy-depleting. This type of environment has been abundantly evident in educational settings throughout our book, which has described fast school nations that are obsessed with

- A hurried and narrowing curriculum that allows no space for depth and breadth of learning or teaching
- Externally imposed and inescapable short-term achievement targets that turn teaching and learning into not a steady marathon nor a set of spurts and sprints but an enforced and everlasting hurdle race
- An accountability agenda of endless improvement that leaves schools more made over than Michael Jackson
- Subjecting schools to the repetitive change syndrome of bureaucratic overwork and innovation overload that produces exhaustion, insecurity, and lack of opportunity for reflection, replenishment, and renewal
- Shaming and blaming schools that are labeled as underperforming, leaving their teachers with diminished confidence and depleted commitment

These excesses of mechanically driven reform in an overly pressurized environment have led to epidemics of stress, loss of confidence, and emotional withdrawal on the part of teachers in many parts of the world (Dinham and Scott, 1997; Troman and Woods, 2000; Helsby, 1999; Hargreaves, 2003). The wasted contributions of teachers are reflected in the wasted lives of principals. A statewide survey of principals in Victoria, Australia, found that eight in ten principals experienced high levels of stress from the "unnecessary paperwork" and managerial nature of their jobs (Gronn and Rawlings-Sanaei, 2003). In the schools that we researched, only a few years after the onset of standardized reform, Eric West ended up in the hospital three days after his transfer to a new school following his stint at Stewart Heights; North Ridge's Diane Grant transferred to an elite girls' private school after taking her first full principalship in the public system; exemplary teacher leader Greg Allan took early retirement; Janice Burnley moved to another school; and after becoming exhausted by her efforts to turn around two schools in succession in a context of escalating reform requirements, Charmaine Watson opted for early retirement and the life of a graduate student.

In the age of standardization and in the push to meet short-term achievement targets, teachers and leaders have been treated by governments as if they were bottomless pits of energy. They are not. When a few educators fail to relax, regroup, and renew their energy, this is probably due to poor judgment and lack of balance among the individuals concerned. When entire systems experience heightened stress and depleted energy, it is a consequence of their exploitative attitudes toward essential human resources. Under these conditions, it is time for people and their governments to say "enough" (as the voters of Ontario did in 2003, when they elected a new government due to dissatisfaction with the educational and environmental record of the existing one) and to follow the example of system leaders who slow down the entropic process of depletion and waste by

- Infusing additional resources and extra energy into the system— as the governments of Ontario, British Columbia, and the United Kingdom did—for better buildings, smaller class sizes, increased numbers of support staff, and additional in-school time to prepare and plan (Teachernet, 2005)
- Replacing externally imposed targets with internally agreed-on targets for improvement
- Reducing the speed and scope of reform implementation and also the relentless and insatiable pace of expected improvement, accepting that there are human limits to the rate of progress (including how quickly educational standards can be raised)
- Replacing the emotionally depleting strategies of shaming and blaming underperforming schools and their teachers and leaders with supportive strategies that rebuild confidence, competence, and pride among the educators who will be responsible for arresting the decline in performance and for securing improvement

There are more than a few promising examples of school system leadership being willing to rethink its approaches to school improvement and the use of resources.

- The British government has invested over £37 million in its Workplace Remodeling initiative, which recognizes the importance of teachers in raising educational standards by providing schools with the funds to hire, train, and deploy support staff to relieve teachers of administrative tasks, increase teachers' job satisfaction, and improve the status of the profession (Teachernet, 2005).

- A new government in Manitoba, Canada, has reversed eleven years of top-down, mandated changes that left the province's school boards and educators feeling unappreciated and victimized (Levin and Wiens, 2003). It adopted a "better way," focusing on investing in teaching and learning, respecting all partners, building school capacity for improvement, developing classroom-based assessment expertise, and grounding its approach in the best available evidence and research (Levin and Wiens, 2003).

- The Bill and Melinda Gates Foundation is supporting reform efforts to reduce school size in communities across the United States. The foundation is seeking to harness students' and teachers' energy productively by giving teachers time to collaborate and strengthen their skills and by integrating technology into teaching and learning environments (Bill and Melinda Gates Foundation, 2005).

- Despite its questionable commitment to imposing short-term targets, the Liberal government of Ontario has not only infused additional dollars into public education but also agreed to a settlement for peace and stability with key teachers' unions that restores much of the salary and planning time for working with colleagues that teachers lost under the previous government.

Thus, ecological renewal begins with the exercise of restraint—being less ruthlessly exploitative of teachers' and leaders' energy reserves and more prepared to conserve and replace some of their energy by injecting additional human and fiscal resources into the system.

Renewal

John Goodlad is one of the strongest proponents of school renewal. Now in his eighties, Goodlad is a cofounder and director of the Center for Educational Renewal at the University of Washington. The center strives "to advance the simultaneous renewal of K–12 schools and the education of educators within the larger context of education in a democracy" (Goodlad, 1997).

Goodlad distinguishes renewal from reform. Reform originates outside schools, "beyond time and space" (Goodlad, 1997), and it doesn't "accommodate the nature and circumstances of schools" (Goodlad, 1994, p. 218). Goodlad contends that traditional large-scale reform efforts assume that something is wrong and that systemwide restructuring must take place to create standardized "McSchools." Renewal, however, is ecologically grounded in the lives of schools and the people who work within them: "Schools are cultures seeking to maintain a state of equilibrium that allows them to function in the face of perturbations from without. They are ecosystems within larger ecosystems" (Goodlad, 1994, p. 218).

Renewal, Goodlad argues, is a "cottage industry." It is about specific people and places that are linked to other cottage industries through common purposes and cultural ties. Each school becomes an ecosystem within a district ecosystem, and renewal occurs through networked interaction in which schools and districts work cooperatively towards common goals (Goodlad, 1994, p. 217). In a good school these interactions are healthy, enabling the school both to conduct its daily business effectively and to cope with exigencies. In a poor school, these interactions are unhealthy, making the conduct of business difficult. Bad schools are in a constant state of crisis or near crisis (Goodlad, 1994, p. 219).

The ability to maintain equilibrium while dealing with dissonance is essential to school renewal. Goodlad explains, "The language of school renewal is multidimensional, relatively free of good guys and bad guys and of ends, means, and outcomes linearity. The language and the ethos are of the people around and especially in schools acquiring the efficacy and developing the collaborative mechanisms necessary to [produce] better schools" (Goodlad, 1997).

Since 1912, Eastside Technical School has provided vocational programs for generations of students in one of Ontario's most conservative cities. It quickly gained a reputation as a pioneer in vocational education and has remained on the leading edge throughout its history. One example was the development of the Television Arts Department in 1970, when radio and television broadcasting and programming became part of the curriculum. The first FM studio opened in November 1977, and students worked in Educational Television (ETV) studios and shops, running the *Good Morning Eastside Show* every morning. Students were fully involved in production of school television and radio programs and also worked at a local radio station. Business and visual arts programs as well as specific courses for nursing assistants and other careers drew a wide-ranging clientele.

Despite its exemplary record of preparing students for the workplace and its excellent reputation among provincial educators, Eastside's community thought the school was for students who couldn't succeed in a "real" school. Principals of the regular academic schools often used it as a dumping ground "for students who didn't fit." A former Eastside teacher recalled how many people had characterized the school with stigmatizing terms: "In the fifties, it was 'greasers,' in the seventies and early eighties, it was 'druggies' who attended Eastside." When a local newspaper named Eastside "Dope City," a number of teachers challenged it and forced a retraction.

In the 1980s and 1990s, stiff competition from other vocational schools as well as community colleges, along with district pressure to conform to conventional school structures pushed Eastside's principal and his staff to improve their competitive standing in another way by developing creative policies and programs in music and entrepreneurship that ran counter to more conventional district directions. In the midst of all this, Eastside's staff continued to counter the negative "reputation it has not earned."

During the resource cutbacks of the mid- to late 1990s, Eastside was also able to compete with the expanding Catholic school system, which threatened to take its best students, by embarking on an ambitious reconstruction project to "rebuild, renew, and revitalize" the school. This renovation was a turning point in the school's fight to enhance its reputation. The nationally known art program is up and running again in new surroundings, and the technological labs and classrooms are filled with state-of-the-art resources. By the end of the 1990s, Eastside's staff was led by a core of aging but loyal teachers who had devoted their careers to addressing the educational needs of the kinds of students who came to the school. Despite the energy-depleting reform-based indignities of longer hours and increased workloads, they were able to take advantage of the government's relative indifference to vocational programs and focus on renewal and improvement of the school's image.

Teachers still fight against the negative stereotypes traditionally associated with Eastside Tech, but they have now adopted these labels proudly and are beginning to revel in the difference and in the freedom they afford to be more creative and more adaptive to the needs of the special and diverse student population they serve. Indeed, since the renovated school re-opened, there have been only positive articles in hitherto unsupportive public media about accomplishments by students at the school. Over a century, therefore, Eastside has managed to preserve its always imperiled identity through continual renewal of its purposes and programs.

Like Eastside, Blue Mountain School was never a "McSchool." This distinctive professional learning community faced the same kinds of resource reductions and external reform mandates as most schools around it, but with different results. Through multiple successions of leaders, turnover of staff, and corrosive reductions in time and personnel, Blue Mountain's professional learning community remained resilient enough to bounce back when the reform and resource environment eased after the election of a new government in 2003. One of the school's former department heads put it like this:

> Throughout the past six years, the formal and informal leaders who have remained at the school have succeeded in salvaging much of the student-centered nature of the school's program.
>
> There is no question that a lot of storms were happening. For a brief period of time, I believe that a specific faction of the old guard lost faith in the school's leadership. As an outsider to the school now, I can see a renaissance of support and energy, with the staff working more enthusiastically and progressively with the new administration team, working within system directions and initiatives that are building capacity for distributed leadership on many levels; in school-based projects as well as system work teams.

Durant Alternative School is another innovative institution with a distinctive identity that has had to endure endless assaults from an unsympathetic reform environment, but its response has also been resilient, for it has always been ready to reshape and renew itself in response to outside disturbances. In the late 1990s, when the school lost control of its own budget, for example, and of staff and resources as well, the students, teachers, and parents banded together to raise funds to compensate as best they could for this loss of district support. When the state required the school to conform to standardized state testing, the Durant community protested publicly in straitjackets and networked creatively with similar schools across the state to get a special dispensation for more innovative approaches to curriculum and assessment.

All three schools—Eastside, Blue Mountain, and Durant—undertook repeated renewal even in the face of a physically and emotionally depleting resource-poor environment resulting from standardized reform. While teachers in other schools became locked into downward spirals of disillusionment and demoralization in the 1990s, these schools preserved their innovative identities by actively resisting the excesses of standardization, networking with others who could support them, and creating new opportunities through program innovations that renewed teachers' energy and purposes.

These compelling cases point to seven fundamental principles of school renewal that cohere with the seven principles of sustainability:

- The schools re-created deep and broad learning experiences for their students and staff by constantly renewing the unique purpose and mission that distinguished them from other schools in their area. Blue Mountain was a deliberately designed learning organization; Eastside had a century-old commitment to marginalized students; and Durant had built its entire school around flexible student programs linked to individualized learning needs and connections with the community. Schools that stay focused on the integrity of their purpose and products, instead of simply implementing other people's purposes, are more able to renew their spiritual energy.
- The schools secured endurance over time by attending to successions of senior leaders and by retaining and rejuvenating a critical mass of teacher leaders through good times and bad. Schools that maintain some continuity of leadership from year to year and from one teacher generation to the next conserve the collective emotional energy that is otherwise expended on adjusting to constant changes of circumstances and personnel.
- The schools encouraged breadth by deliberately distributing leadership across their staff, even as principals came and went. Schools that distribute leadership widely spread the burdens, the learning, and the rewards that support staff emotionally and make them more resourceful intellectually.
- The schools promoted social justice by defending the distinctive needs of their disadvantaged students; by offering creative and challenging curriculum to ensure that more advantaged students who provided role models for their peers were not enticed away by school competitors; and by not actively undermining neighboring schools as they sought to renew themselves. Eastside and Durant had to struggle hard to preserve their existence and identities against the expansion of the Catholic system in Ontario and of magnet schools in New York state. Blue Mountain established its own learning community without impinging disproportionately on any one institution or age group or teachers around it. Schools that fight for a broad mix of students provide the best support for their most disadvantaged students and avoid creating wasted lives. And schools that work with their neighbors rather than against them save energy that is otherwise expended in time-consuming and emotionally draining competitiveness.
- The schools honored their diversity. Eastside drew its students from across the city and opened its doors to anyone who would benefit from a vocational and technical education. Durant's mandate was to provide educational opportunities for students who found it difficult to succeed in a regular school structure, and Blue Mountain was a fully composite school

that accepted all students in its increasingly multicultural community. Schools that honor their diversity ensure that their most marginal students are not cast on the waste heap; they preserve the student mix that maintains a diverse and productive community of learning, and they promote professional diversity that capitalizes on the school's existing intellectual resources.

• The schools benefited from physical and financial resources. The physical environment is an important resource for renewal. All three schools operated in relatively new or significantly upgraded facilities. Blue Mountain was bright, airy, and new, designed to promote student and teacher interactions in appealing public spaces as well as conventional classrooms and to integrate and promote modern communications technology. Eastside's overdue renovation in the mid-1990s helped to alter its forbidding image and attracted some high-achieving students. Durant's move to a better facility uplifted teachers and students in their quest to adapt their programs to changing conditions in the state. By contrast, schools like Sheldon, Stewart Heights, and Lord Byron that were trapped in downward spirals of demoralization and decline operated in old or overcrowded buildings with serious deficiencies. Schools need financial and physical resources (like decent facilities) as well as human ones in order to meet their learning obligations for all students. This is why initiatives like the United Kingdom's secondary school rebuilding program in economically impoverished communities is central to resourcefulness and renewal. Schools cannot starve their way to improvement.

• The schools attended to the conservation of their historical roots, traditions, and purposes. Each school had a rich and long-lasting sense of what and who it stood for as well as where it was going. School renewal requires passion and purpose that build on pride in the past: one of the most vital emotional and spiritual resources of all.

Enhancing resourcefulness is partly a matter of slowing down entropy, conserving energy, and in the drive for ever-escalating standards, sometimes being prepared to say "enough." Slowing the pace of change, improving the emotional tone of reform, injecting financial and building resources into the system, and generally exercising restraint in how far we go in exploiting people's reserves of energy—these are essential elements of resourcefulness. So too is the commitment to replenishment and renewal among school and system leaders—renewal of purpose, learning, commitment, and emotional capacity through personal and professional development and sheer physical regeneration.

Renewal and restraint are not either-or choices in our challenge to develop resourceful, sustainable leadership. Renewal and restraint, exchanging energy and slowing down entropy, action by individuals and change in the system—all these both-and combinations are needed in our efforts to rethink sustainable leadership and improvement.

Three Sources of Renewal

The power of renewal can be observed by examining three sources of human resourcefulness in educational change: trust, confidence, and emotion.

Trust

If truth is the first casualty of war, then trust is the first fatality of imposed reform. Centuries ago, Confucius said that a government needs three things: weapons, food, and trust. If any of these have to be sacrificed, he said, the last of them should be trust (Confucius, 1998). Trust is an indispensable resource for improvement.

Effective organizations depend and thrive on trust. In relationships and organizations, trust amounts to people being able to rely on each other, so that their world and relationships have coherence and continuity. When we trust, we believe others will act in a reasonably predictable way, according to agreed-on or assumed expectations, in a context of shared understanding and assumptions of good faith—even and especially when we or they are absent.

In *Trust and Betrayal in the Workplace,* Reina and Reina (1999) describe three forms of trust:

- Contractual trust is expressed through impersonal, objective, and often written agreements—in shared performance standards, agreed-on targets, clear job descriptions, homework contracts, and the like. Contractual trust requires us to meet obligations, complete contracts, and keep promises.

- Competence trust involves the willingness to trust oneself and other people to be competent and the willingness to provide sufficient support and learning opportunities for people to become competent. Delegating effectively and providing professional growth and development for others are strong indicators of competence trust.

- Communication trust is evident in human interactions that communicate shared understanding and good intentions. Clear, high-quality, open, and frequent communication is the hallmark of communication trust. So too are sharing information, telling the truth, keeping confidences, and being willing to admit mistakes.

The opposite of trust is betrayal. Betrayal occurs when trust is absent or broken. Some acts of betrayal—unfaithfulness to one's partner or theft of a colleague's ideas, for example—are spectacular. But most betrayals are small, accumulated acts of inconsiderate behavior or mere thoughtlessness. In a study of trust and betrayal in teaching (Hargreaves, 2002), we found that teachers felt they had been betrayed by colleagues when they didn't pull their weight, always taught the same thing, or complained about the union without going to its meetings (contract betrayal); when they were constantly dissatisfied with colleagues, couldn't delegate to them, and tried to script or micromanage everything they did (competence betrayal); or when they gossiped about colleagues and criticized or shamed them in front of others (communication betrayal).

Trust is a resource. It creates and consolidates energy, commitment, and relationships. When trust is broken, people lessen their commitment and withdraw from relationships, and entropy abounds.

In their large-scale study of school reform in Chicago elementary schools, Tony Bryk and Barbara Schneider determined that "trust matters as a resource for school improvement" (2004, p. 121). In *Trust in Schools*, they state that the presence of what they call relational trust (similar to Reina and Reina's communication trust) has positive organizational consequences in terms of "more effective decision-making, enhanced social support for innovation, more efficient social control of adults' work and an expanded moral authority to 'go the extra mile for children'" (p. 22).

When adults in a school work well together, with reciprocal and relational trust, it increases energy for improvement that then benefits students and their achievement. Drawing on year-by-year achievement data across the Chicago public school system from the early to mid-1990s, Bryk and Schneider were able to identify the top and bottom one hundred improving and non-improving schools in terms of year-by-year improvement. The relationships they discovered between adult trust levels and improvements in achievement are consistent and compelling:

> By 1994, much higher levels of trust, on average, were reported in schools that eventually would be categorized as academically improving than for those eventually categorized in the non-improving group. These differences persist through 1997, with almost three-quarters of

the non-improving schools in both reading and mathematics offering negative indicators on the composite indicators of trust. . . . Schools reporting strong positive trust levels in 1994 were three times more likely to be categorized eventually as improving in reading and mathematics than those with very weak trust reports. By 1997, schools with very strong trust reports had a one in two chance of being in the improving group. In contrast, the likelihood of improving for schools with very weak trust reports was only one in seven. Perhaps most tellingly of all, schools with weak trust reports in both 1994 and 1997 had virtually no chance of showing improvement in either reading or mathematics. [Bryk and Schneider, 2004, pp. 110–111]

Trust in schools is essential. Yet we behave less and less like trusting societies. Improvement secured through cultures of shared understanding, joint commitment, and mutual responsibility is being replaced by compliance enforced by impersonal performance standards and abstract accountability. Onora O'Neill, presenter of Britain's annual Reith lectures on public radio, argues that in a world bereft of trust and awash with accountability, "professionals have to work to ever more exacting . . . standards of good practice and due process, to meet relentless demands to record and report, and they are subject to regular ranking and restructuring . . . [in ways that] damage their real work" (O'Neill, 2002, p. 49). By moving from cultures of trust to contracts of performance, she says, we are "distorting the proper aims of professional practice" (p. 50)—effective interaction with those we serve. Each profession, she argues, has its proper aim, and this "is not reducible to meeting set targets following prescribed procedures and requirements" (p. 49). Indeed, she notes, change by contract not only diminishes trust but creates active suspicion, cynicism, and low morale.

Principal and author Deborah Meier (2003) amplifies this argument, pointing to government's pervasive distrust of teachers and schools: "We don't trust teachers' judgment so we constrain their choices. . . . We don't trust the public school system as a whole so we allow those furthest removed from the schoolhouse to dictate policy that fundamentally changes the daily interactions that take place within schools. . . . Social distrust plays itself out in education in the form of draconian attempts to 'restore accountability' through standardized schooling and increasing bureaucratization."

Trust works. It improves organizations, increases achievement, and boosts energy and morale. Trust isn't easy. It is not blind faith; nor is it indifference. In Debbie Meier's words, trust is "hard won"; it is the essence of demanding professional commitment. Years of standardized reform have decimated political trust in teachers and the profession's trust of their governments in turn. In the words of one of the teachers we interviewed, "It is as though someone wishes to demonstrate how broken the system is by not providing the time or development to be successful."

Learning is poorly served by a low-trust environment. The bitterness of lost trust lingers like a stain. The legacy of teachers' distrust of their governments, for example, is seen in adversarial contract talks with political successors. In Ontario, the new minister of education acknowledges that teacher unrest "is simply the leftover of before," and that it will take the profession some time to heal from a "bruising experience." He speaks for many, perhaps, when he urges us "to leave that era behind us," and forge a better path ("Kennedy Blames Tories," 2003).

Confidence

A second source of energy is confidence. Harvard business professor Rosabeth Moss Kanter (2004) explains that confidence "consists of positive expectation for favorable outcomes. Confidence influences the willingness to invest—to commit money, time, reputation, emotional energy, or other resources—or to withhold or hedge investment." Kanter conducted extensive studies of four types of businesses and sports teams—those that had long histories of either success or failure and those that had gone from rags to riches or vice versa. The key ingredient in successful businesses and winning teams, she found, is confidence—in oneself, in team members or colleagues, in the structures and policies of the organization, and in the external environment that provides resources.

Once lost, confidence is difficult to regain. A loss of confidence showed in the panicked response of Lord Byron teachers to the demands of a flawed reporting system, in the withdrawal from change of Talisman Park's cynical coffee circle, in Stewart Heights' teachers' lost belief in their students to improve their own behavior, and in the downward spiral of union-administrator conflict at Sheldon. In the confidence-sapping conditions of standardized reform, all these schools descended into what Kanter calls a doom loop, in which things got progressively worse.

"Decline is not a state, it is a trajectory," Kanter observes (2004, p. 95). "Winning streaks are characterized by continuity and continued investment, losing streaks by disruption, churn, lurching, and lack of investment" (p. 139). Kanter explains, "On the way up, success creates positive momentum. People who believe they are likely to win are also likely to put in the extra effort at difficult moments to ensure that victory. On the way down, failure feeds on itself. . . . The momentum can be hard to stop" (p. 139).

Gill Helsby's study of the effects of large-scale reform on British teachers concluded that while teacher confidence is to some extent always a function of individual attitudes and local cultures, in general, "it is more difficult to retain a sense of professional confidence when responsibility for what teachers perceive as core areas of their work is reduced in favor of external prescription, when resources are lacking and when compliance is required rather than creativity" (Helsby, 1999, p. 173).

Confidence, Kanter explains, is the "sweet spot" between despair and overconfidence (2004, p. 8). Overconfidence is "a person's certainty that his or her predictions are correct, exceeding the accuracy of those predictions" (p. 72). Overconfidence is overpromising. It springs from excessive optimism. Some view it as arrogance. And arrogance is not the prerogative of the gifted, but the self-indulgent conceit of the vain and foolhardy.

Kanter describes how overconfidence among chief executives pushed and pressured employees of Gillette into having to meet increasingly unrealistic quarterly targets, with financially disastrous results. Overconfidence prompts government leaders to wage war in the false and tragic belief that the war will be quick and losses will be small. The Spanish Armada, the fall of Troy, and the debacle of Vietnam are all testimony to the overconfidence of "wooden-headed" leaders who were blind to the evidence, deaf to good counsel, and oblivious to their own folly (Tuchman, 1984). In *Overconfidence and War,* Dominic Johnson (2004) shows how governments are easily susceptible to "positive illusions"—exaggerated ideas of their own virtue and of their ability to control events and the future. In education, overconfident governments extend the scope of their influence, shorten the time lines for improvement, and expect more to be produced with less. Yet all they create are teachers who eventually lose their confidence and spiral into doom loops of performance decline. The result is entropy and waste.

You cannot give people confidence; you can only gain it within yourself. Rebuilding the confidence of teachers in their leaders is a paramount priority. But more important still is the necessity of creating more optimistic conditions in which teachers can regain confidence in themselves, setting them off on the winning streaks of improvement that their students so desperately deserve. In the words of Helen Keller (1990), "Optimism is the faith that leads to achievement. Nothing can be done without hope and confidence."

Emotion

Emotion is an indispensable source of human energy. Positive emotion creates energy; negative emotion saps it. There are many ways of understanding the role of emotions in organizations (Hargreaves, 1998). The best-known and most popular perspective is that of emotional intelligence. This view emphasizes the trainable skills and capacities of individuals in organizations to understand, articulate, and manage their own emotions as well as empathize with the emotions of others around them (Goleman, 1995). Here, we turn instead to a way of understanding emotion and its effects that connects the individual more closely to the organization.

More than two decades ago, sociologist Arlie Hochschild undertook a classic study of flight attendants. The resulting book, *The Managed Heart,* introduced a new concept: emotional labor. In the growing service economy, she said, more and more people were engaged not in manual or even intellectual labor but in emotional labor, in which they had to manufacture or mask their own feelings in order to create the feelings that the organization required in others. Emotional labor, Hochschild argued (1983), "requires one to induce or suppress feelings in order to sustain the outward countenance that produces the proper state of mind in others." For Hochschild, emotional labor requires people to trade part of their selves to motivate clients or subordinates in exchange for financial reward or job security. Selling, consultancy, nursing, the work of flight attendants, and teaching are among the many occupations that involve this kind of labor.

Hochschild describes how the caring work of being a flight attendant—smiling, reassuring, being attentive—becomes increasingly difficult when profit-driven airlines downsize the staff and standardize the work operations so that flight attendants feel they no longer have the time or opportunity to interact with their passengers in the ways they would wish. As their work demands accelerate, some of them leave because the job loses its meaning and purpose for them; some of them burn out as they try to take on the new tasks while still retaining good relationships with passengers; and some of them become cynical, persuading themselves that passengers aren't worth caring for anymore.

Teaching and educational leadership also involve the extensive emotional labor of being responsible for motivating others and managing their moods and feelings. In Australia, Jill Blackmore discovered that women principals found themselves turning into emotional middle managers of unwanted and imposed educational reforms, motivating their staffs to implement the impractical and unpalatable policies of the government and losing something of themselves and their health in the process (Blackmore, 1996; Beatty, 2002).

Among the principals in our study, Charmaine Watson wanted to be inclusive of her teachers, but when reform demands took away their time, she found herself reduced to simply "modeling optimism." Eric West, with his counseling background, wanted to wait and understand the culture of his new school, but pressing reform demands undermined his humanistic approach, and his leadership ended in a hospital bed. Janice Burnley and Linda White found themselves becoming far more directive with their teachers than they wanted to be and transferred on when the opportunity arose. In a support meeting of fellow principals that we convened, North Ridge's new assistant principal, another former counselor, openly wept when he recalled how in the midst of a teachers' work-to-rule action, he had come in early every day to get the school and photocopying machines ready for teachers' strictly timed arrivals, only to be besieged with a pile of written grievances from all of his staff, on the instructions of the union.

Yet these are not the inevitable consequences of emotional labor. Studies conducted after publication of Hochschild's landmark text show that emotional labor can be and often is positive, uplifting, and energizing when people identify with the kind of emotional work the job requires of them and when their working conditions enable them to perform their emotional work properly (Ashforth and Humphrey, 1993). Detectives, for example, find the emotional labor of interrogating suspects fulfilling, but experience the emotional labor of placating upset victims draining (Stenross and Kleinman, 1989). The same is true in education. In positive and supportive working conditions, emotional labor is a labor of love (Fineman, 2000). It creates energy.

The Alberta government and the province's teachers' union were at a standoff regarding the government's proposal to raise student performance. A new minister, along with a teacher's union executive who had always taken a forward-looking stand on improvement through professional development, decided to approach the problem another way.

In 1999, they jointly launched the Alberta Initiative for School Improvement (AISI). The program addressed issues of diversity and flexibility by "fostering initiatives that reflect the unique needs and circumstances of each school authority" (Alberta Learning, 2004, p. 8). An injection of $68 million (Canadian) of resources annually was targeted for local improvement projects.

School improvement projects vary greatly and focus on areas as diverse as improving literacy skills, developing teachers' capacity to use differentiated strategies of instruction in their classrooms, building professional learning communities, improving home-school communication in Aboriginal communities, developing computer technology skills, increasing competency in particular subject environments, and enhancing the quality of school relationships. Cycles of improvement stretch over three years, and 90 percent of Alberta schools are now involved.

The initiative does not operate in a climate of imposed and accelerated government targets. Instead, schools establish their own targets, in terms of impact on student learning and satisfaction levels. Impressively, in this culture of shared targets, 90 percent of schools exceeded their baseline on the majority of measures every year. Over just three years, almost half the project schools improved student learning, and 57 percent improved levels of student, teacher, and parent satisfaction. And this is only the start.

The firm focus on student learning—the first principle of sustainability—is undoubtedly an asset to the initiative. The injection of needed resources into coordinating local support in networks of improvement rather than command-and-control systems of mechanical accountability also certainly helps. But it is the spirit of belief in, trust of, and support for schools and teachers to improve themselves that infuses human as well as financial energy and resources into the system. According to the project's first major report, "Brain research has shown that emotion drives attention, learning, memory and behavior. The emotional investment demonstrated by staff involved with AISI projects has resulted in renewed energy and excitement for school improvement. AISI promotes a culture of shared responsibility for continuous improvement in schools and jurisdictions that clearly align school improvement goals and classroom practices. Schools operating as learning communities actively engage both teachers and students in learning" (Alberta Learning, 2004, p. 5).

AISI has a focus on learning and on building strong professional learning communities in ways that respond to and connect the diverse paths to improvement across the province. It takes a long-term, trusting view of improvement by valuing proximal as well as final measures that indicate progress toward greater student achievement. AISI slows down entropy by injecting additional resources into the system in a way that creates energy exchange and renewal, engaging the hearts, minds, and wills of all teachers in raising standards through shared targets that address authentic improvement in learning and not merely superficial gains in test scores. Imposed and impatient targets in a climate of resource reduction are energy-depleting. Shared targets in an environment in which resources are redirected to the schools that need them most, within a clear model of sustainable improvement, are energy-renewing. In the uncompromising oil territory of Alberta, shared targets and energy renewal are not flights of fancy but hard-nosed practical realities that make a real difference to students and schools.

The ingenuity of Alberta's Ministry of Education, the inspiring leadership of Blue Mountain's founding principal, the energetically resilient leadership of the principals at Durant, and the emotional satisfactions enjoyed by many of our leaders before the onset of standardized reform all exemplify the power of emotional labor as a positive and energizing leadership resource when work conditions and policy environments support it. It is time to end the collusion with cultures of fear and shame and the connivance with mechanical models of top-down implementation that deplete teachers' energy and to embrace instead the hope and optimism in people and professionals that are the lifeblood of educational change and renewal.

Conclusion

Five hours' flight time west of Chile, far out in the Pacific, is an island more than one thousand miles from any other landmass. "Discovered" by the Dutch on Easter Day, 1722, the tiny speck of Easter Island is scattered with huge stone monuments, some of which are seventy feet tall. The mystery of how such gigantic stone statues could have been moved and raised on an otherwise almost barren island lacking timber and rope was addressed by subsequent archeological discoveries.

The current burden of evidence and argument is that Easter Island was once a populous territory, thickly covered by forest and first inhabited by Polynesians. Rich in seafood, the island's ecology gave rise to a population of growing prosperity who cleared the best land for farming. Dividing into separate clans, the people began erecting monuments to their ancestors, each clan's carvings more grand and impressive than its neighbors'.

Over generations, this process of competitive status envy demanded that more trees be felled to make way for the statues to be dragged across the island and to provide the fiber and rope with which to pull them. By the fifteenth century, the last trees had been eliminated. In the grim decades and centuries that followed, the boats that gave the islanders access to fish and other seafood could not be repaired or replenished for want of wood. Sophisticated shelter could no longer be provided, so the diminishing population took refuge in caves and under stones. Captain James Cook described the remnant population he encountered as "small, lean, timid and miserable" (quoted in Wright, 2004, p. 61; see also Tainter, 1998; Diamond, 2005). Famine, war, and possibly cannibalism were the end points of a society that had been complacent in prosperity, neglectful of sustainability, and driven apart by competitive envy.

The educational competition between modern societies for higher and higher performance standards, greater than any international competitors, at any cost to the value of what is actually being learned and at any cost to the teachers and leaders who are the substance and soul of the educational ecosystem, risks turning modern educational systems into Easter Islands of educational change, heedless of sustainability in the ruthless, short-term pursuit of competitive status.

An ecosystem is not a machine. Ecosystems value community interests over self-interests, diversity over sameness, and connectedness over individualism. They consist of interconnections and interrelationships.

Jeremy Rifkin tells us that the word *whole* is derived from the Old English word *hal*, which is also the root word in health, hale, and heal (Rifkin, 1981). Sustainable leadership is healthy leadership. It is hale, and it heals. (*Hale* means "vigorous and healthy," as in *hale and hearty*.) Healthy organizations renew and recycle their resources; unhealthy ones exhaust and abuse them. Healthy organizations promote development and growth that respect the finite aspects of the earth's and our own ability to sustain life; unhealthy organizations are greedy organizations that exploit natural and human resources for the self-interest of a few. Dead leaders don't improve much. But when leaders feel energized and alive, there is almost no limit to what they can achieve. Resourcefulness gives them that chance. It is essential to sustainability.

REFERENCES

Alberta Learning. "Improving Student Learning: Alberta Initiative for School Improvement." Edmonton, Canada: Alberta Learning, 2004.

Ashforth, B. E., and Humphrey, R. H. "Emotional Labour in Service Roles: The Influence of Identity." *Academy of Management Journal*, 1993, *18*(1), 88–115.

Bauman, Z. *Wasted Lives: Modernity and Its Outcasts*. Cambridge, U.K.: Polity Press, 2004.

Beatty, B. "Emotional Matters in Educational Leadership: Examining the Unexamined." Unpublished doctoral dissertation, University of Toronto, 2002.

Bill and Melinda Gates Foundation. *Making the Case for Small Schools*. 2005. Retrieved from www.gatesfoundation.org.

Blackmore, J. "Doing 'Emotional Labour' in the Education Marketplace: Stories from the Field of Women in Management." *Discourse: Studies in the Cultural Politics of Education*, 1996, *17*(3), 337–349.

Bryk, A., and Schneider, B. *Trust in Schools: A Core Resource for Improvement*. New York: Russell Sage Foundation, 2004.

Capra, F. *The Hidden Connections: A Science for Sustainable Living*. New York: HarperCollins, 2002.

Confucius. *Confucius: The Analects*. London: Penguin Books, 1998.

Diamond, J. *Collapse*. New York: Penguin Books, 2005.

Dinham, S., and Scott, C. *The Teacher 2000 project: A Study of Teacher Motivation and Health*. Perth, Aust.: University of Western Sydney, Nepean, 1997.

Evans, R. *The Human Side of School Change: Reform, Resistance, and the Real-Life Problems of Innovation*. San Francisco: Jossey-Bass, 1996.

Fineman, S. (ed.) *Emotion in Organizations*. London: Sage, 2000.

Goleman, D. *Emotional Intelligence*. New York: Bantam Books, 1995.

Goodlad, J. *Beyond McSchool: A Challenge to Educational Leadership*. 1997. Retrieved July 11, 2006, from www.nationalacademies.org/sputnik/goodlad.htm.

Goodlad, J. *Educational Renewal: Better Teachers, Better Schools*. San Francisco: Jossey-Bass, 1994.

Goodstein, D. *Out of Gas: The End of the Age of Oil*. New York: Norton, 2004.

Gronn, P., and Rawlings-Sanaei, F. "Principal Recruitment in a Climate of Leadership Disengagement. "*Australian Journal of Education*, 2003, *47*(2), 172–185.

Hargreaves, A. "The Emotions of Teaching and Educational Change." In A. Hargreaves, A. Lieberman, M. Fullan, and D. Hopkins (eds.), *The International Handbook of Educational Change*. Dordrecht, The Netherlands: Kluwer, 1998.

Hargreaves, A. "Teaching and Betrayal." *Teachers and Teaching: Theory and Practice*, 2002, *13*(4), 393–407.

Hargreaves, A. *Teaching in the Knowledge Society: Education in the Age of Insecurity*. New York: Teachers College Press, 2003.

Hargreaves, A., Earl, L., Moore, S., and Manning, S. *Learning to Change: Teaching Beyond Subjects and Standards*. San Francisco: Jossey-Bass, 2001.

Hawken, P., Lovins, A., and Lovins, L. H. *Natural Capitalism: Creating the Next Industrial Revolution*. New York: Little, Brown, 1999.

Helsby, G. *Changing Teachers' Work: The Reform of Secondary Schooling*. Milton Keynes, U.K.: Open University Press, 1999.

Hochschild, R. *The Managed Heart: The Commercialization of Human Feeling*. Berkeley: University of California Press, 1983.

Johnson, D. *Overconfidence and War*. Cambridge, Mass.: Harvard University Press, 2004.

Kanter, R. M. *Confidence: How Winning Streaks and Losing Streaks Begin and End*. New York: Crown Business, 2004.

Keller, H. *The Story of My Life.* (reissue ed.) New York: Bantam Classics, 1990.

"Kennedy Blames Tories for Teacher Work-to-Rule." *Toronto Star,* Mar. 2, 2003. www.torstarreports.com.

Levin, B., and Wiens, J. "There Is Another Way: A Different Approach to Educational Reform." *Phi Delta Kappan,* 2003, *84*(9), 660.

Loehr, J., and Schwartz, T. *The Power of Full Engagement: Managing Energy, Not Time Is the Key to High Performance and Personal Renewal.* New York: Free Press, 2003.

McDonough, W., and Braungart, M. *Cradle to Cradle: Remaking the Way We Make Things.* New York: North Point Press, 2002.

McKibben, B. *The End of Nature.* New York: Random House, 1989.

McKibben, B. *Enough: Staying Human in an Engineered Age.* New York: Times Books, 2003.

Meadows, D. L., Meadows, D. H., Randers, J., and Behren, W. *The Limits to Growth.* London: Earth Island, 1972.

Meier, D. *In Schools We Trust: Creating Communities of Learning in an Era of Testing and Standardization.* Boston: Beacon Press, 2003.

O'Neill, O. *A Question of Trust: The BBC Reith Lectures 2002.* Cambridge, U.K.: Cambridge University Press, 2002.

Reid, W. V., and others. *Ecosystems and Human Well-Being.* Washington, D.C.: Island Press, 2005.

Reina, D., and Reina, M. *Trust and Betrayal in the Workplace.* San Francisco: Berrett-Koehler, 1999.

Rifkin, J. *Entropy: A New World View.* New York: Bantam Books, 1981.

Stenross, B., and Kleinman, S. "The Highs and Lows of Emotional Labour: Detectives' Encounters with Criminals and Victims." *Journal of Contemporary Ethnography,* 1989, *17*(4), 435–452.

Tainter, J. *The Collapse of Complex Societies.* Cambridge, U.K.: Cambridge University Press, 1988.

Teachernet. "School Workforce Remodelling." 2005. Retrieved from www.teachernet.gov.uk/wholeschool/remodelling.

Troman, G., and Woods, P. "Careers under Stress: Teacher Adaptations at a Time of Intensive Reform." *Journal of Educational Change,* 2000, *1*(3), 253–275.

Tuchman, B. *The March of Folly: From Troy to Vietnam.* New York: Knopf, 1984.

Wright, R. *A Short History of Progress.* New York: Carroll and Graf, 2004.